NONNO, TELL US A STORY

The Story of an Italian Family, from the Old World to the New

PIETRANTONIO LOMBARDI

Nonno, Tell Us A Story

Library of Congress Cataloging-in-Publication Data
Nonno tell us a story
The story of an Italian family from the old world to the new
Lombardi Pietrantonio
Golden, Colorado, USA
LLCN 201790977

Front cover image: *Casa Paternale*, Pietrantonio's birthhouse and also his siblings, father, grandfather, uncles, aunts, and many cousins.

Back cover image: Morning of departure for America, Pietrantonio wiping away tears as family and friends wish him and his parents a tearful goodbye. May 14, 1966.

Brief book description written by Pamela Marcantonio, retired senior Professor of Italian, Department of French and Italian, University of Colorado at Boulder.

Cover and book layout/design by Mark Tweed

> *nonno*: grandfather
> *nonna*: grandmother
> *nonni*: plural for grandparents
> *bisnonno*: great-grandfather
> *bisnonna*: great-grandmother

When we (*Italo-Americani*, Italians, Italian-Americans, American-Italians) hear the words *nonno*, *nonnino*, *nonna*, and *nonnina*, multiple sentiments swim gently in our minds. For me the feelings are numerous. For most of us, these family members are connected to emotions that bring smiles and tears to our eyes. Without a doubt these feelings include images of serenity, sanctuary, haven, honor, freedom, celebrations, meals, snacks, treats, joy, bliss, affection, tenderness, warm embraces, soft kisses, simplicity, humor, humility, compassion, forgiveness, courage, pride, the sweetest smells, and a temporary respite from the disciplinarian parents. There are countless spoils and countless stories.

The word *nonno* probably comes from the late-Latin word *nonnus*, meaning 'monk, tutor, or old person.' It most likely came from children's speeches. In other languages, words close to *nonno* have a religious connotation. In German and French, *nonne* means nun. In Italian, *nonne* is the feminine plural for grandmas. Nun in Italian is *suora, monaca*.

Italian uses similar words, *ninna nanna*, as a children's bedtime lullaby. Other derivations come from *nonno*, especially in America where people use many different variations of the word. This depends on the area of Italy from which their ancestors originated. Many of the slang versions are combinations of what I like to call "Italamericano." *Nona, nana, nanna, nanno, nonni, noni, nonie, nannie, nonnina, nonnino, nonnarella, granni, grandnani, grandpapi, papi, papie, papa, poppi,* and *pops* are just some of the names that we call our grandparents and great-grandparents. These are all terms of endearment for the very special and relevant people in an Italian-American family.

Presently in our village, grandparents are referred to in proper Italian as *nonno* and *nonna*, but in the old days where dialect ruled, other words were used: *Mamma* for mom, *Papà* for dad. But sometimes, and especially when a father was older, he was sometimes called *tatà* by some villagers. We usually called our grandfathers *tatuccio*. Great-grandpas were sometimes called *tatone* and grandmothers were called *mammuccia*.

In the Italian language, where feminine and masculine references rule, there is only one word that indicates granddaughter and grandson: *nipote*. Even more of an oddity is that the same word also refers to niece and nephew. Many refer to their small grandchildren as *nipotini*. For me the reference denotes affectionate, sweet, tender little creatures to who we give endless unconditional love.

Contents

Dedications
Acknowledgements
A Note To My Readers
Foreword
Introduction

Per i miei nipotini, for my grandchildren:
Anthony, Gianni, Avery, Sofia,
Aubry, Dominic (Nico) and Olivia

My mom and other women of the village would sit around mourning the death of another villager and, during their conversation, a familiar comment would be repeated: *"Kaeshta vita è na affaciata deh na fineshtra"* (*Questa vita è solo un'occhiata fuori di una finestra*, This life is just a look out a window).

May the window you choose in life be immense and crystal clear with a magnificent view!

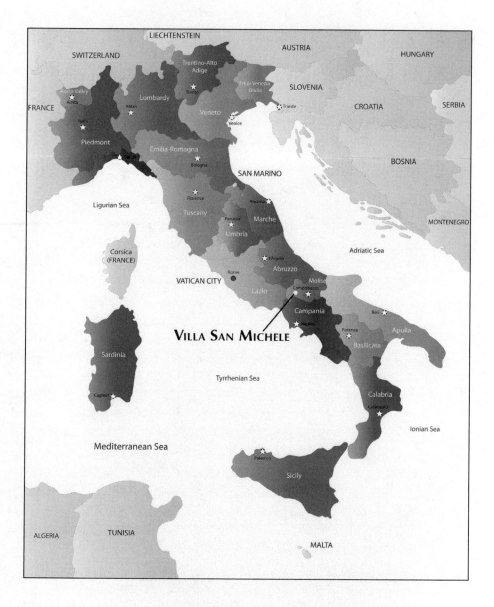

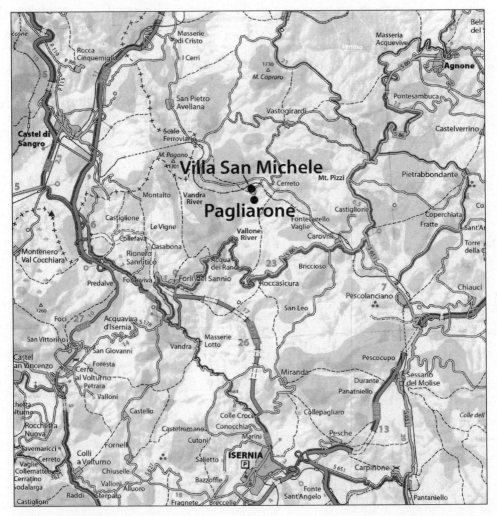

Alto Molise

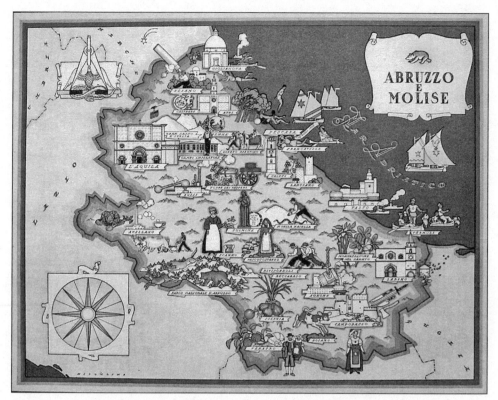

Abruzzo e Molise (pre-1963)

*Road sign near the railroad station in
San Pietro Avellana with cousin
Louie Lombardi*

Welcome to Villa San Michele

Villa San Michele in summer and in winter

ACKNOWLEDGEMENTS

They left their families behind in search of a better life. Long ago those men from our little remote backward village traveled far in search of bread. Their families followed them to those new, different places. Some of those men were short-term immigrants, choosing to go back home after saving some hard-earned money. Most of those early immigrants overcame many obstacles, but endured and paved the way for the later *paesani*. To people mentioned in this book and also to the many not mentioned who touched my and my family's lives, your contribution was enormous and appreciated greatly by all of us: Italians, Italian-Americans, American-Italians, Americans.

My parents and many others seized the opportunity and took the big risk of coming to America; not for themselves but for their children, their children's children, and generations that followed — that will follow. To them I say "*mille grazie*," a thousand thanks. I write these words in their honor.

Our children complete our lives. To ours, Daniella and Dominic, I say thank you for more than completing ours. Thanks for pushing me to complete this book when I doubted myself. To my son-in-law, Frank, and my daughter-in-law, Michaela, thank you for allowing me to immerse our grandchildren in the many Italian traditions of our culture.

Grandparents sometimes joke that the reason you don't kill your kids is so they can give you grandchildren. Thank you, my children, for our seven beautiful grandchildren. Every day they make our lives more complete. I dedicate this book to many, but most of all to you, my *nipotini*. You truly inspired me to write these stories. No matter how many times I told you a story, you wanted to hear it again and again. I hope that you remember and repeat those stories to your children.

The Italian phrase '*ti voglio tanto bene*' literally means 'I want so much good for you.' The real meaning is 'I love you very much.' When you love someone, you want all the goodness in the world for them. You wish only good for them in academics, in sports, in careers... in life. To each of my seven grandchildren, "*Ti voglio tanto tanto, tanto bene.*"

To my brother, Ezio, and his wife, Bambina, and sister, Maria, and her husband, Vittorio, thank you for all the help, for filling in all those blurred or forgotten memories. You were instrumental in providing information about our family, our village, our journey.

To my aunts and uncles, most of whom have departed this world, to my nieces and nephews, to my numerous cousins, there were many times that I was inspired by you from the mere mention that you "can't wait to read my book." Lots of pressure! To my nephew, Vic, the celebrity in our family — a Denver sportscaster — your suggestions and your insight helped greatly in completing this book.

To my large extended family, thank you for listening, for asking, for contributing. To all my friends, especially the *morra* group, the Mount Carmel men's club group, and the soccer groups: One way or another you all gave me motivation to finish my book.

To Ronald A. Busse, I feel blessed to have found you. Your editing, proofreading, and formatting skills, along with your many useful suggestions, have definitely helped in making this book readable.

To Marilee Heiss Wehde, thank you, *mille grazie, tausend dank*. Your editing, suggestions, assurance, and clarifications helped tremendously.

To Mark Tweed, my longtime fellow soccer player, first thank you for putting up with me all those years on the soccer fields and secondly for the incredible job on making sense of my pictures and documents. Your graphic design knowledge and professional input worked wonders on all parts of this book.

To Gianfranco and Pamela Marcantonio, *mille grazie* for your accurate translations, your help with putting our dialect into written words and the numerous other suggestions and corrections that greatly clarified my Italian as well as the rest of the book.

To my wife, Jackie, ever since our wedding night and our 40 years of marriage I can count on my hand the nights that I have not shared a bed with you. Together in those beds we loved, we created. We dreamed, we planned. We contemplated, we debated, we decided. We laughed, we cried. We grieved, we prayed. We complained, we accepted. We discussed, we resolved. We watched our children and grandchildren sleep like angels. We reminisced. We wrote this book!

Your common sense, your honesty, your undivided love has made my life worth living. Thank you for being a perfect wife to an imperfect husband.

amore sempre.

To my readers, thank you for plowing through this book, for your mercy, for your understanding of the errors and oversights. I hope you are as thankful as I for being fortunate enough to look out my window and see the greatest place on earth to live a life, *l'America.*

A NOTE TO MY READERS

I have included many Italian words and phrases within my story, and the Italian is written in the especially suitably named style, italics. My usual format is to put the actual spoken words in our *Molisano (Pagliaronese)* dialect first. This is followed many times by the formal Italian word or words, which is followed by the English translation. When just a word or short phrase in Italian is used, I simply put a comma after the italicized Italian to say it again in English (or the English first and Italian second).

Because the local dialect in which we speak is not a formal written language, I have taken some license in creating the spelling of what was said. I struggled at times as to whether I should write it the way an Italian speaker would read it, or the way an English speaker could read it as the words are pronounced. Many times I did a bit of both. Usually I wrote the words the way an English speaker could read them, although I sometimes hesitated using the letters *j*, *k*, *w*, *x*, and *y* because they are not in the original Italian alphabet. But for some words it seemed the best option.

Many times I took the liberty of paraphrasing the Italian into comprehensible English, rather than translating the literal meaning of the Italian words. I might have erred in my translations, and some might even say that "That's not how we say it in our town, or province or region," or "That's not how we did it in our village," which is all true. Throughout Italy's villages, cities and regions, local expressions are just a little different and, sometimes, much different.

My distant cousin, Roberta Iannacito-Provenzano, Ph.D., is a professor and lecturer of Italian linguistics in Toronto, Canada. She did an admirable job with her research for the very detailed book about our village's dialect, *Il Dialetto Molisano Di Villa San Michele, (IS)*. Hopefully the audio version of this book will help with pronunciation and accents, slangs and clarification of the many adages.

The inclusion of pictures, documents, and letters will hopefully assist in clarifying my frequent unclear accounts.

FOREWORD

I was six years old when my uncle taught me how to read.
Think about that for a moment.

Is there anything more powerful than the gift of reading? Is there anything more liberating than allowing your imagination to take you places you've never been? And how convenient that you can find those places in the corners of the written word.

This book is about the journey from old country to new. It's about a family's passage from a tiny mountain village in the Italian Apennines to a bustling mountain city in the American Rockies. Exactly 5,672 miles separate Villa San Michele, Italy from Denver, Colorado but the cultures, the opportunities, the way of life — those things are worlds apart.

The Italy that thrives on tourism — the Italy of picturesque beaches, historic landmarks, sprawling canals — that's not the Italy you'll read about in this book. This is about the workingman's Italy, a land of hillside farms, plush forests, ancient chapels, dilapidated train stations, stray dogs, and bearded old ladies. This is my uncle's Italy. It's where the journey started just a half-century ago.

Truth be told, I was often ashamed of my family's humble beginnings. As a child, I would lie awake at night yearning for normalcy. My family was anything but normal. As the first-born of Italian immigrants, I often bore the responsibility of introducing my parents to the customs of a new land. You're not allowed to haggle with salesmen at Montgomery Ward. You don't get a better deal on school tuition just because you're willing to pay cash. Throwing shoes at your children in the middle of a shopping mall is often frowned upon in America.

I didn't realize how blessed I really was. I was taught how the power of a sturdy hand could take you places you'd never dream. Whether I was mowing lawns with my grandfather or painting apartment walls at my father's side, there was always some type of work to be done. Work never wavers. For most, it's a necessary evil. But for those immigrants who had to beg, borrow and steal just to survive, the thought of steady work was a bountiful opportunity. That's why they came here. That's why this book was written.

I hated working because it always interfered with my first passion — sports. I fell in love as a kindergartener, the day my mother dropped me off at my first football practice with the Rough Riders at Horace Mann middle school. I lined-up at running back, even though I had no idea what the hell I was doing. But it taught me discipline. It forced me to adapt. It encouraged me to communicate. Participating in sports is how I assimilated to a new culture. Best of all, it was fun.

In the 7th grade, my uncle bought me a subscription to *Sports Illustrated*. That's when I knew. That's when I immersed myself in my books with the same tenacity my father applied to his various jobs. I'll never forget the conversation I had with my parents during my senior year of high school. I told them I had plans of going to college. Not just any college — the University of Notre Dame. Undeterred, my parents would pay for everything, even though they had no idea what it would cost or where it would take me.

People often like to slap you on the back for "making it" in life. What the hell does that mean? What is "making it?" How could my career as a local television sportscaster even compare to the courageous road my parents took? It's simply mind-blowing to know that 50 years ago, my father and uncle were stacking bales of hay on an angry donkey in the hills of Italy, and here I am typing that very sentence on my iPhone.

For my parents, just like their parents, the ultimate goal was to make life better for their children. How can I possibly top what they've already done? I can only imagine the angst my grandfather felt when he moved halfway across the globe at the age of 48 with a young family in tow. Nothing can possibly compare.

Anytime I had a question about my family's journey, my uncle had an answer. I encouraged him to write a book about it. He did. And I can't read it without laughing and crying. Hopefully, you can relate to some of these stories. Everything you're about to read is true. You couldn't possibly make this stuff up.

Thank you, Uncle Tony. This book is a precious gift, even better than the first one you gave me some 40 years ago. (Every Italian has an Uncle Tony. If you don't, sorry, you're not a real Italian.)

Vic Lombardi
Denver sportscaster

INTRODUCTION

Italian fairy tales and some fictional stories begin with *C'era una volta*, There was one time, or most commonly in the English version, Once upon a time. These stock phrases have been used for many centuries in storytelling. Both the Italian and English versions don't really add up. *C'era una volta* means that there was one time. Certainly there are more than one and different times in a story. The English version is even more puzzling. Once upon a time literally means 'one time on top of a time?' As with this and other expressions of our lives, we follow certain customs and traditions without ever questioning what and why.

I will begin my story with this phrase. It is a safe beginning, since my story will probably be as many times puzzling as the aforementioned phrases, perhaps because I have forgotten most of the Italian grammar and never really grasped the English rendition.

"You should write a book." I don't know how many times I have heard that comment when telling stories of my childhood to family, friends, and whoever would listen — including, at times, total strangers. *Mille grazie a tutti*, a thousand thanks to all of you for encouraging me to write these stories. My wife had to remind me continually that I had already told a particular story to the captured audience and whispered to me not to tell it again. God knows how many times she has been present as I recounted these stories.

When I attended Metropolitan State College, I enrolled in a Colorado history course. The professor, Stephen J. Leonard, who is the current department chairperson, gave us a choice for the final: Either take the test or write a paper. A no-brainer for me, I would write a paper. I wanted to tell my story, "The Long Journey to Colorado." Dr. Leonard's thesis at Regis University had been about Como, Colorado, a town named after Como (a town in the Lombardia region of Italy), from where the founders of the Colorado town had immigrated. I knew that my story would interest him. I wrote a rough twelve-page typewritten paper with many pen corrections that I had found after re-reading it, but I was too lazy or too late to type it again! This paper would be worth 30 percent of my grade for that class. I included some pictures to hopefully bolster my chances for a good grade. When Dr. Leonard handed the papers back, he made remarks to the class about how interesting mine was, and so on. He gave me an 'A' and asked for permission to make a copy so he could contribute it to the Denver Public Library's Western History Department. That was in 1974.

$\frac{1}{L} = 30\%$ of grade

A

ANTHONY PETER LOMBARDI

12 pgs +

An excellent paper
I enjoyed reading
it. You express
yourself very well

Peter, I would like to make a
copy of this for The Denver Public
library. It is very interesting

"The long journey to Colorado"

Life in the small town of Pagliarone (later renamed Villa San
Michele) wasn't very rewarding to most of its inhabitants. My grandpa
had learned the shoemaking trade but with seven children and an ill
wife, he had a hard time finding enough work to feed and keep them.

In April of 1930 along with his older daughter and her husband,
he left for Argentina. The shoemaking business in Buenos Aires,
with a tropical climate and the custom of the natives of that city
was not even to make much use of shoes other than on their holidays,
made it even more difficult for my grandfather to earn a living
there. And my uncle (his son-in-law) being unable to find work of
any consequence at all, left the responsibility for grandpa to
keep himself along with his daughter, son-in-law and a grandson
which had just joined the family.

One day, while walking the docks of Buenos Aires' port, my
uncle came upon a sailor that listened to his problems. He said
he would help him by taking him to North America. Grandpa tried
to immigrate to the U.S. but at that time it was impossible.

Thinking very hard about it, my grandpa and uncle decided
that going to America del Norte would be the best thing for them
to do. Grandpa had two weeks to sell whatever he possessed to make
possible the equivalent of $100 payment to the sailor which he
demanded for his risky services. As the day of departure neared,
grandpa possessed only the clothes that he wore.

On January 22, 1933, well after twelve o'clock A.M., in the

Years went by before I picked up the paper again. My nephew, Vic Lombardi, wanted to read it and use it for one of his classes. My son, Dominic, and daughter, Daniella, also used my paper during their high school days, as did my other nephews, Adelio, Mario, and John. I cringed when I reread it, as I saw the numerous grammatical mistakes. I also noticed that I had skimmed through my journey and that there was a lot more to tell.

For years I thought about writing the long version of my story, but I could never find the time or the impetus to start the process. When God blessed us with our grandchildren and when my parents passed away, I finally found the energy, the will, and the urgency to begin. Whenever I read a book to the first two of our seven grandchildren, Anthony and Gianni, they always asked me to tell them a story about when I was a little boy in Italy, rather than reading them another children's book. They never tired of the same or new stories about our animals, our lives, and our village. So I realized that I needed to put those stories down on paper for them, for their children, for my brother's and sister's families, or risk that they would be forgotten.

I thought I had asked my parents everything about their lives, but as I write I wish that my mom and dad were still alive to answer so many more questions I have for them. How could I have forgotten the details to a certain story after I had heard it many times? What were their grandparents' names? How quickly names and places are forgotten. When I meet some Italian-Americans and they mention that their ancestors came from Italy, but they don't have any idea when or from where in Italy, it scares me to think that someday my descendants might not know our family's story.

Now that I have found my motivation, I begin. Of all the material things I will leave to my family, I think that this story will be the only thing that might stay with them for more than one generation. Money will be spent; properties, cars, and other things will be sold. And because this book will always contain the story of the roots of each successive generation, I hope the chances are good that it will be handed down.

The village of Pagliarone, where I was born, is already slowly turning to ruins, and the future of the new village of Villa San Michele does not look very good. The young people left town to look for work and a better life in other parts of Italy and abroad. Most of what is left is older residents who will eventually fade away. I hope I am wrong, but the probability of Villa San Michele becoming a ghost town is very real.

Our house being overtaken by weeds 50 years after we left it, as my brother, sister and I revisit with our spouses. 2014

Although this is a story about my family's beginnings in a tiny remote village in Italy and their travels to the new world of America, it is very similar to the lives of many other immigrants from our village, our region, our country, and other parts of the world. They endured many of the same heartaches and adversities as my family encountered. Thankfully for most of us, our futures became brighter with perseverance and hard work. Many immigrants who came from nothing now have something. Having experienced a meager life in Italy, once in America with a chance, they seized the opportunity with all the energy they could muster and saved enough money to buy their own piece of the American pie.

With no grants or research assistants, let it be known that a lot of the historical information might not be accurate and is based on my findings, perceptions, and opinions. Much of the information is from stories handed down by the people of the area, mainly from my parents, grandparents, other relatives, and friends. I have heard similar stories told in many contrasting ways, some with completely different endings. Many of the stories I pass along could most likely fall under the headings of legend, folklore, myths, and old wives tales.

Chapter I

C'era Una Volta · Once Upon A Time

C'*era una volta*... Once upon a time there was a small remote village deep in the Apennine Mountains of south central Italy, where a few families lived...

It was June of 1958. The sun was already beating down on our heads as my sister, Maria, and I were standing next to our mom, waiting by the fountain, *la fonde deh Lvg, la fonte di Luigi*. On that early summer morning, the people from our little hamlet of Luigi, a hillside section of the town of Pagliarone, were bringing their sheep to the predetermined location of the hamlet's fountain for the daily trek up the hillside, and to the mountain fields for the daily grazing. It was our family's assigned week to *pascie le pecore*, graze the sheep.

Fountain of Luigi, Jackie and I on our honeymoon with Luigi residents Lina and Vittorio Lombardi, 1975

The longstanding tradition was to combine the town's sheep into one herd, with families taking turns watching the sheep as they grazed. Every spring the men of the town would meet and hold a lottery, *il sorteggio*, the draw, to determine when and how many days each family would be required to graze the sheep and cattle of the town. The number of days a family was responsible for the herd was determined by the number of sheep they owned. Forever ingrained in my memory are the utterly confusing gatherings, men talking loudly all at once about the issue at hand. There were always complaints about the number of days and the dates assigned to them. All the men would assuredly try to falsify the number of sheep or cattle that they owned, hoping to be assigned fewer days. But giving inaccurate counts was just part of the process, because in our village everybody knew everybody's business. Even a child like me knew how many cows and sheep our neighbors owned.

Eventually, after they all attempted to get into good position for counting off, each man took numbers for each of the days he would have to take responsibility for the grazing. Then the men would *mehnà ar tuock* (*menare a chi tocca*, throw down fingers to determine turns). This was something like casting lots. Every man would throw down his hand and expose fingers from one to five, and all the fingers casted would be added up. The man counting up the numbers would be watched closely by the rest of the group with their gruff and serious faces. They would make sure that no mistake was made during the important count. Tension would build as the tally was added up. If, for example, the sum of fingers added up to 75, the man who had ended up with 75 during the count off would get the first day of the grazing season. The men would repeat this process again until only one man was left, and he was assigned the last spot on the schedule. The kids, mostly boys of various ages, would watch as the heated discussions lasted into the night, but finally an agreement would be reached and a schedule finalized. *La partita*, the herd, was compiled and finally the men headed for their homes, most still complaining about the draw and the days they received. As the crickets sang out and the fireflies lit up the spring night, my brother and I followed our dad home, where my mom and sister were waiting for the results of the *tuock*, lottery.

The 8th of May was a special day. That was when government owned lands would be opened up for public grazing. On that day the livestock were taken out of the barns and led to the fresh, new spring grasses for the beginning of the grazing season. The sheep were gathered and the assigned shepherds guided them up the path to the mountaintops for the daily grazing. As our family's turn loomed on that early June morning, my sister and I were by the fountain waiting for the herd to gather.

My brother, Ezio, was already gone, having left before dawn. He had headed for the *tratturi* to milk our cows on that spring morning. The *tratturi* was a stretch of land, more or less 100 meters wide and over 200 kilometers long. It was called the *Celano-Foggia tratturo* because it started near the town of Celano in the central region of Abruzzo and ended near the city of Foggia in the southern region of Puglie. This was just one of many *tratturi* all over Italy. That grazing path has existed since before Ancient Roman[1] rule. In earlier times, shepherds came from as far as the Puglia region of southern Italy, herding their sheep, goats, and cattle through these grassy tracks. The herds headed up the Abruzzo mountains for the summer grazing and then came back down to the lowlands in the fall. The *tratturi* had areas that were designated as overnight resting points. They were called *la mandria*. One of these campgrounds was at a location near our village. My sister and brother vaguely recall the shepherds and their herds resting for the night. By the late 1950s the shepherds had abandoned that ancient tradition.

My brother was older and experienced in herding cattle, and he absolutely loved doing that work over any other. Watching over a herd of cattle was more of a man's job, and Ezio possessed those traits even at a young age. He was an absolute workaholic and would work all day until nightfall, when he was forced to quit — not because he was tired, but because he could not see anymore. My brother never showed any symptoms of being tired. On our assigned grazing days he would watch over the herd, and at nightfall he would lead them into *la mandra*, a pen that had been constructed by the men of the village. The herd stayed at those faraway grazing lands throughout the summer, but every morning at dawn people would walk to those locations with buckets made of zinc or aluminum. With those canisters in hand, the villagers milked the cows and then headed back to their homes to make a variety of cheeses, such as *caciocavallo* and *scamorza*.

📖 *Caciocavallo*, literally meaning 'cheese on horseback,' is stretched and shaped by hand. It is then hung by tying a string to the top of its pear

---

[1] *The Roman Republic, circa 500 BC to 27 BC; the Roman Empire, circa 27 BC to 500 AD*

shape. As it ages, it changes from a soft to gratable cheese. It is generally mild in taste with a somewhat salty bite. *Caciocavallo* is popular in central and southern Italy, particularly in the Apennine Mountains. Usually a dish of this sliced cheese is part of our table, especially when guests visit.

Caciocavallo

📖 *Scamorza* is a smaller version of the *caciocavallo*. It is a semisoft white cheese that is chewy and stringy, similar to *mozzarella* but just a bit firmer and with more flavor. The name is derived from *scamorza*, an expression

that means beheaded in central and southern Italy. The idea is that when you go to eat it, the first thing you do is cut off head of cheese. It is usually eaten fresh, although our family's favorite is fried *scamorza*.

Scamorza

My sister and I were not as interested as was Ezio in spending time in the fields, so our parents had to force us to do our part. Early one morning we reluctantly began the trek up the mountain with the herd of sheep. My sister, Maria, was barely eleven years old and I barely six, but we were relatively mature and grown up for children our age — not by choice, but by necessity. I think that children of our village in the past usually matured faster compared to today's urban counterparts. A five-year-old usually exhibited the maturity of a ten-year-old, or at least had to perform tasks that normally an older kid would do.

My mother gave us the worn, patched, grayish *tascapane* (a canvas bag with a shoulder strap, literally meaning 'pocket for bread'). In it she put the only food left in *la misella* (*la madia*, the cupboard), a chunk of bread. She also included a small aluminum pot about four to five inches in diameter and three or four inches deep with a handle, battered from years of use, to get water at one of the nearby watering holes. It was also handy for gathering wild berries when the sheep rested under the huge beech trees.

Il tascapane

My mom would always warn us about the wolves. If we saw any come out of the forest searching for a meal, we needed to scream loudly, *"Il lupo! Il lupo!"* so that nearby farmers could come and help us; and also in hopes that the loud screams would send them back into the forest. These wolves were a menace to our livestock and every time someone killed one in the area, the wolf hunters would skin it and come to town with the animal's hide wrapped around their shoulders. The ladies would give the great hunters a treat for killing the evil beast. His *tascapano* would be filled with bread, eggs, grain, fruits, nuts, and sometimes a few *lire*, money.

As Maria and I tended the sheep this day, the wolves stayed in the woods; maybe not willing to come out in that hot summer sun, but probably because they had already made a kill and were content for another day.

i lupi, the wolves

Mamma also warned us about rain storms. If it started to rain, we were instructed to find a rock to shield us, and absolutely stay away from trees.

A year earlier my sister and her friend, Maria di Viduccio, were watching their sheep. Maria was the daughter of a man named Viduccio. This reference was crucial because many people had the same name and had to be identified by the family to which one belonged. Even in legal documents, a reference was made to a person's father. My father was referred to as Vittorio Lombardi *di* Pietrantonio, of/son of Pietrantonio. If his father was dead, then he would be known as Vittorio Lombardi *fu* Pietrantonio, was/son of deceased Pietrantonio.

The two young girls were watching over the sheep when the sky went from blue to almost black. Lightning and thunder swept through the mountain and a heavy thunderstorm came down on the two scared teenagers. So they ran under the nearest tree for cover. Suddenly, a few meters away, lightning struck a tree leaving only the smoking trunk intact. The girls were temporarily blinded and dazed by the lightning. After they regained their senses, having been in great panic and crying uncontrollably, the girls forced the unwilling sheep to head back down the mountain towards town. The people were in an uproar seeing their sheep at their barn doors in the middle of the day. My parents endured the ire of many, and scolded my sister for bringing the sheep home so early. They warned her never to do that again, no matter what.

As the hot sun shone directly over our heads and the sheep gathered under the shade of tall trees for their afternoon rest, we knew that it was time for us to have our lunch of bread and water. We searched for some ripened berries nearby, but could not find any. We had been warned not to eat the unripened ones, or surely we would suffer great stomach distress. We were hungry and were tempted to go searching farther, but thoughts of wolves taking our sheep kept us near. We were very hungry and wanted more than just a chunk of bread. My sister came up with a solution: Find a sheep that was feeding her lamb and try to milk the sheep so we could have a nice lunch of bread and warm milk.

I remember the struggle we encountered getting the sleeping sheep to stand, and even more problems trying to get milk to flow into the battered small aluminum pot. I could not keep the sheep calm long enough for my sister to milk the uncooperative, woolly animal. We finally gave up. Exhausted, we sat there sad and hungry. We would have to eat that chunk of dry bread and be thankful that we had at least that.

As we walked towards the location of the *tascapane* where our bread was stored, we noticed some of the sheep gathered around it and as we got closer, we saw one of the sheep eating the last piece of our bread. We both frantically pushed the sheep away, but the bread was gone. We both started to cry. My sister held me in her arms as tears flowed down our faces.

We endured the rest of the day and as the sun began to set in the western horizon, we knew that it was time to start heading back down the mountain towards home. We pushed the lead sheep with *la campana*, the bell, hanging on her neck towards the road to lead the herd home. We counted them as they went by to make sure that none were left behind. Usually the older women of the town, who were no longer able to do the heavy field work, stayed home to care for the family's children and to prepare dinner. When they heard the sound of the bell, the women would head to their barns to let their sheep in for the night.

It would be almost dark when my mom and dad arrived home from their work in the distant fields. There was nothing in *la misella*, the bread box, to quiet our hunger. *Mamma* came home and we told her of our misfortune. She cried, *"Figli mia muert deh fame"* (*I miei figli morti di fame*, My children, dying of hunger). She went to Rosa's house, just below ours, to hopefully borrow a loaf of bread, but Rosa did not have any to spare. All of the villagers' wooden wheat containers were almost empty and the wheat fields were not quite ready for harvest. Families would have to rely on other foodstuff until the wheat containers were full again.

La misella, our bread box still in our kitchen in 1975

Mamma quickly cooked some *minestra* (soup made with a mixture of greens and grains) for dinner. As our family sat there eating that humble meal she began to cry, asking my father, *"kaeshta vita non seh puo fa kiù (Questa vita non si puó fare più), quando arrivano le carte di chiamata per l'America?"* We can't live this life anymore, when are the immigration papers for America going to arrive?

Papers had been filed by my paternal grandfather, *Papà* Pietrantonio, on April 20, 1955. My parents waited and waited and years went by before the documents arrived. In 1965, ten years after the initial official paperwork was filed to begin the emigration process to emigrate to America, the good news arrived — thanks to the new U.S. Immigration and Nationality Act of 1965. But by 1965 life was better for our family, and the decision to leave for another world would not be as easy as it would have been 10 years earlier.

April 25, 1507 was the first time the word America was written by German geographer, Martin Waldseemuller. Amerigo Vespucci was a Florentine merchant who owned a shipping supply store in Seville, Spain and he made many journeys to this New World. He was one of the first to think that those lands were *mundus novus*, a new world. After Waldseemuller read letters about the New World, he suggested the name for this world be made in honor of Amerigo Vespucci, and not Christopher Columbus, *Cristoforo Colombo*. Europe eventually adopted this suggestion and the new continent discovered by Columbus was named America.

My *Mamma* would always say *"ma seh Cristoforo Colombo scoprette l'America, perchè non zeh parla Italiano qua?"* If Christopher Columbus discovered America, why isn't Italian spoken here? She was obviously very upset with Columbus for making life miserable for the Italian immigrants as they struggled with the English language! For them, the official language should not be English or Spanish, but Italian — and preferably the Italian they knew, which was their hometown dialect! Because of this and other issues facing the Italian immigrant, my *Mamma*'s and most Italian immigrants' favorite adage was: *"Mannaggia l'America e chi la scoprette,"* Darned/damned America and who discovered it.

Eighteen hundred years before Christ, nomads wandering about in what is now southeast Europe came to settle in an area that is now called the Calabria region of southern Italy — the area that looks like the toe of Italy's boot shape. These people came to be called *Itali*. This name is derived from *vitulus*, meaning 'veal' or 'calf' in Latin, *vitelli* in Italian. The area was rich with bovine animals and thus the name. After the Greeks colonized the area, they called it *Italoi*, meaning 'veal' in Greek. The Romans kept the name and eventually called the whole Peninsula *Italoi*. The present name, Italia, appears on a coin found in the Abruzzo region, dating back to the 2nd century BC.

Italia, as it eventually came to be known, did not unify until 1870. Unification would require a movement called *Il Risorgimento*, literally meaning 'a revival.' The political movement spearheaded by Giuseppe Garibaldi (comparable to America's George Washington) freed the Italian peninsula from centuries of Bourbon and Papal rule. I remember learning in school about all the independent states that made up the Italian peninsula. The political party of *I Guelfi*, the Guelfs, sided with the pope, while *i Ghibellini*, the Ghebbelines, supported the emperors. The two factions were always battling one another and nothing ever seemed to be accomplished or changed. Some think that it is the same situation in Italy's present government!

The new Italy installed Rome as its capital, as it was during the Roman Empire. Modern Italy would go through some tumultuous periods. Discontent, poverty, and prejudice by northerners towards the *Mezzogiorno* (meaning 'midday,' it references Italy to the south of Rome because of the intense heat in that area during midday) were just part of the reason for the turmoil that unified Italy would endure. This also included Italy's economic distress, resulting in most Italians being fed up with the new government. The result was that the new nation saw one of the largest exoduses in history. Many Italians would either venture north to the northern European countries or across the Atlantic Ocean to South America. But the biggest number of migrants headed for North America — mainly the United States — swearing to never go back to that land called Italia.

Italy's land area covers 116,347 square miles, with a population of over 60,000,000[2]. In comparison, the state of Colorado covers an area of 103,730 square miles, with a population of just over 5,000,000. Italy is just a bit larger than Colorado, but with more than ten times as many people!

Italy was comprised of nineteen regions (roughly equivalent to our fifty states) until 1963 when the regions of Abruzzo and Molise separated, giving Italy twenty regions. Presently there is a move to combine the two regions again in order to cut down on the duplicate and excessive spending for government administrators and services. Molise is the second smallest region in Italy with 4,437 square miles of land area — smaller than the state of Connecticut. The smallest region is Valle D'Aosta, which is tucked in the Alps of northern Italy. Molise has two provinces, Campobasso and Isernia. Isernia will more than likely be removed as a province, also in an effort to eliminate duplicate services.

There is evidence of *homo sapiens* living in the areas of modern day Abruzzo and Molise over 700,000 years ago. These areas were populated by many different peoples, but the Samnites, *Sanniti*, were the people generally associated with it in the pre-Roman era. There are many locations throughout Molise with names with *Sanniti* roots. It is thought that these people were descendants of the Spartans. They spoke

[2] *Population in 2010*

9

the Oscan language, which was similar to Latin. Although they mainly cultivated land and raised animals, they were also great mountain warriors, and there is evidence that the Roman gladiators emerged as a result of the many battles between the Roman legions and the Samnites. The Romans emulated a lot of the dress of these hill tribes and also used the captured Samnites as combatants in public bouts. The participants eventually became known as gladiators.

Isernia, a present day province of Molise, was a Samnite town called Aesernium. The town of Pietrabbontante was also a Samnite center, which was called Bovianum. Both towns were a few miles from of our village. When the Romans ruled the area, these towns became important colonies. Hannibal destroyed many of the theatres and temples in those colonies when he came down through the Italian peninsula with his army that included elephants. A close look at the route he took clearly shows that his army was in our area during the invasion.

As a child in school in Pagliarone, I recall teachers talking about Samnite warriors, Roman legions, Hannibal's invasion, Germanic tribes, Crusaders, and centuries later, Allied and German soldiers who came through that same area where I lived. It did not register then, but now as I reflect, I find it fascinating that I roamed the same area as these ancient and not-so-ancient historical figures. The *Sanniti* people fought many wars with the Romans and if they had been better organized, they might have won. But eventually after decades of battles, the Romans defeated them and began ruling the area.

Some historians believe that the name Molise is derived from a Norman warlord named Hugo I of Molhouse, who ruled the area, and at his succession he gave the name of Molise. It is also thought that it could be derived from the name of a castle in the area. Others think that the name originated from the Latin word *mola*, which means grinding. The thought is based on the fact that there were a lot of mills, *mulini*, in the area. But there are many other schools of thought on the subject, and to this day scholars of the history of the region are not in agreement of its origin. The name Abruzzo appears to derive from the Latin word *Aprutium*, probably contrived from *Praetutium*, the name of the people from Praetuti, what is the present-day Abruzzo city of Teramo.

The northern part of Molise is referred to as Alto Molise (Upper Molise), bordering the region of Abruzzo. Early immigrants to America from the area think of themselves as *Abruzzese* (one who hails from Abruzzo), because they remember only the time when the two regions were one, *Abruzzo e Molise*. People from Molise are referred to as *Molisani*.

There are small villages scattered throughout the valleys and mountaintops. Vastogirardi is one of the larger towns and serves as the *comune*, much like a township or municipality. This is where inhabitants of our area go for basic administrative needs, such as registry of births, deaths, deeds, etc.

Town of Vastogirardi

The present-day lands of Molise were under a feudal system for centuries. Noble families owned the land, and the peasants worked it and then paid the landlords their share of the harvest — just as my parents did with some of the land that they cultivated.

About eight kilometers south of Vastogirardi lies the village of Cerreto, and two kilometers west of Cerreto lies Villa San Michele. This is our *paese*, our town. A couple of kilometers southwest of Villa San Michele on the other side of a hill, there is a scattering of old houses and barns where the remnants of the old village struggle to survive. One of those run-down crumbling houses is where I begin our story and that of the other families with roots in Pagliarone.

Remnants of Luigi hamlet, 2014

Section of old Pagliarone. Our house barely visible in the background.

Contadini, dirt farmers, came to this area looking for new land to cultivate and for their animals to graze. They came, for the most part, from a town six kilometers to the south called Forli del Sannio. The name *Sannio* suggests Samnite, *Sannito* influence. Forli is derived from the Latin word *forum*, which means marketplace. Forli was likely a principal post for the Roman legions as they traveled through the area to and from other occupied lands. Sometime in the 6th century, the Germanic tribe known as the Longobards, *I Longobardi*, also known as the Lombards, *Lombardi*, occupied the area in and around Forli. The surname Lombardi is very common in Italy and in our village, and probably originated from the occupation of that area by that Germanic tribe.

These farmers from Forli del Sannio ventured north in the early 1700s to cultivate new lands. They worked the land during daylight and went back home to *Fuorla* (our dialect pronunciation of the town Forli) at night, where they felt safe from any harm that might come their way by way of intruders. During the Middle Ages when many European towns were founded, towns were built on a hillside or mountaintops whenever possible. These usually walled towns provided considerable safety for their inhabitants during armed conflicts. In comparison, American settlers were forced by larger spaces to build homes on their remote lands, leaving them exposed to attacks from enemies, mostly native Indians.

Eventually for these farmers from Forli del Sannio, the walk back home each night became arduous after working hard all day deforesting, preparing, and cultivating virgin lands. So they started building shelters in which to spend the night. They built these primitive huts by dry stacking *pietre*, stones, for walls and gathered *paglia*, straw, for roofs. Eventually these pioneers laid claim to specific areas, and small hamlets began to emerge throughout the valley and surrounding hillsides. These small separate clusters of houses were referred to by various names, usually the names of men who initially settled the area.

Forli del Sannio

It is said that the first farmers were four brothers who ventured north from Forli del Sannio and began a new life. Their names were Pasquale, Gaetano, Pietro, and Luigi Lombardi. I have also heard of different names and a different number of brothers from our elders, but these four are most constantly mentioned. Others would follow and eventually, many structures began to emerge. Some of the names given for these small hamlets that emerged are fairly easy to determine, but for some it is unknown where the names originated or what they mean. A few of the names were and are to this day: Pasquale, Zirri, Pietro, Ciacariangio, Cordisco, Bastimento, Peppa, Luigi, Bartolomeo, Zarrafino, Castra, Cambeste, Scialitto, Cioccaro, Cesevecchie, Giarrocca, Ramicuozzo, Ciacolitto, Trebbante, etc.

The collection of all those small hamlets was eventually given the name Pagliarone, loosely translated to mean a big hay barn – probably so named because of all the straw roof houses and the big barn that could be found there. The barn was more than likely built by Benedictine monks who roamed the area at an earlier time. The hamlet that was our family's home was called Luigi, named after one of those first brothers that settled the area.

Glimpses of Pagliarone

Descendants of Luigi Lombardi improved the area and constructed many stone houses. There were four brothers who were instrumental in the progress of that small hamlet; their names were Luigi, Michele, Pasquale, and Antonio. But ancestors have mentioned that another brother existed and he was referred to by the nickname of *reh matteh* (*il pazzo*, the crazy one). Evidently he was not insane, rather just a bit deviant from the norm, different, eccentric.

Because of that one crazy resident, our hamlet's other residents were sometimes referred to as *reh miatteh deh Lvg* (*I pazzi di Luigi*, the crazy ones from Luigi). And on one of our recent visits to our village, I asked an elderly resident about the *matti di Luigi* reference. He not only reinforced the idea that we were sort of crazy; he also said when other residents of Pagliarone passed through, the presence of "outsiders" resulted in something of a war zone. He informed me that Luigi was sometimes also called *fronte Tripoli*, referring to the World War II North African battlefront near the city of Tripoli.

Our hamlet was the first of Pagliarone to have an actual stone fountain with a reservoir, where animals could go for a drink, *la fonde deh Lvg* (*la fonte di Luigi*). I guess the residents did not view too fondly the villagers from the valley below coming up to our fountain to water their animals. They would try to keep others away with some bizarre actions to solidify our "crazy" label. I remember the heated shouting matches that took place with the other villagers as they came through our hamlet to water their animals, or to simply use the dirt path of our neighborhood that led to many grazing areas up the mountain. I even recall as a small child throwing rocks at animals and sometimes at other people who encroached on our territory.

That reputation has followed us to America because our immigrant friends from Pagliarone will sometimes refer to us as *reh miatt deh Lvg*, the crazy ones from Luigi.

Centuries ago, all the men who made the decision to relocate their families to the area of Pagliarone worked long and hard to make sure that the existence they carved out there would survive. The ingredients for basic survival were there. The pioneers would just have to put it all together. Water was plentiful with two rivers bordering the area: Rio di Penne, referred to as Vallone by the locals, and another not so far away river called Vandra. Stones for building were plentiful — too plentiful! There were some tough years when there were droughts, and the stones seemed to be the only thing growing out of the parched ground. The farmers continually gathered and piled rocks to have more usable land to cultivate. As time passed, stones along with trees and shrubs were cleared to plant seeds to grow food to sustain the families and their livestock. Fruit and nut trees were planted to add to the area's natural richness of a variety of trees and plants. But utopia it was not!

In 1824 the area was visited by Prince *Francesco di Borbone*, the heir to the throne of Naples, *Napoli*, and the two Sicilies. As he traveled around Molise to survey his realm, he kept a diary. He wrote about the area of Vastogirardi, the spectacular forests, rivers, and green valleys. He stated that Vastogirardi had approximately 1,500 inhabitants and the remote village of Pagliarone had 150 souls. He mentioned that those peasants lived in deplorable conditions and extreme misery.

The ruling government at the time made Pagliarone part of the *comune*, municipality of Vastogirardi. This meant that the people of Pagliarone would have to go to Vastogirardi for all their legal and social needs; from registering their newborns to burying their dead, and of course for paying taxes to that municipality. It was difficult making the uphill walk to Vastogirardi, which was done on foot, on donkey, by mule, or on horseback, almost ten kilometers and 1,200 meters above sea level. Requests by the inhabitants for a change went unheard and ignored by the authorities in Vastogirardi and the Province.

In the late 1800s representatives of the village went to Campobasso, a provincial capital of Molise to protest and to persuade the Provincial Council to let them become part of the *comune* of Forli del Sannio, which would take them with open arms. The protesters complained that they paid the same taxes as the people of Vastogirardi, but were continually left out of any benefits coming their way. Their reasoning for their detachment from Vastogirardi was that Pagliarone was closer and more accessible to Forli del Sannio and, after all, they were descendants of that town. Forli is where they went to find spouses, to buy supplies, and to visit relatives. They just felt more comfortable with the people of that town. The Provincial Council agreed with the neglected inhabitants of Pagliarone.

In September of 1887 the Council members gave a unanimous decision to allow Pagliarone to become part of the *comune* of Forli del Sannio. But the federal government rejected the proposed move, claiming that such a move would create new and bigger problems for the State. But at least the federal agents gave the *comune* of Vastogirardi a directive to provide Pagliarone with some of our people's requests. Eventually, Vastogirardi pacified the complainants of the *Pagliaronesi* (people from Pagliarone) by awarding them basic essentials such as their own cemetery, a priest for their church, and they were also given additional land to cultivate. Life became a little better, but not by much. Living was still harsh for the *Pagliaronesi* and to add insult to injury, they continually had to deal with nature's fury, with the likes of heavy snowfalls, torrential rains, scorching summers and droughts.

In December of 1933 it rained for days. The river and creeks swelled, causing flooding in most of the low lying areas. Houses started to shift and eventually started to collapse as a result of the rain-soaked ground. Landslides destroyed parts of the town and many people in the low lying areas lost their homes, their barns. The *comune* asked for help and the provincial government did provide some relief, but these landslides continued. Finally the Italian government, under Benito

Mussolini, approved funds to start building new houses on the other side of a mountain called *Colle dei Noci* (hill of walnut trees), where the land seemed to be more stable and also much closer to the *comune* of Vastogirardi and the railroad, *la Ferrovia*. That railroad was a godsend. The rail line, put into service in the late 1800s, was the only modern mode of transportation for the villagers and it became a blessing for those who could afford its service. Others would have to keep relying on the donkeys, mules, horses, and their own two feet.

The new town was built on an area called *Campanello*, literally meaning 'small bell,' but no one seems to be sure why it was named so. One old timer thought that the name originated as a result of the abundance of the *campanella* flowers (bellflowers) in the area.

The new town of Campanello, circa 1955

The present name of Villa San Michele was introduced in 1959, an idea from the town's priest, Don Nicola, and *il sindaco*, the mayor, who was my father's younger brother, Umberto Lombardi. The name was given in honor of the patron saint of the town, *San Michele Arcangelo*, Saint Michael the Archangel, who is the angel of God who battled and defeated the fallen angel, Lucifer, and the other renegade angels. The hope was for Saint Michael to battle for the survival of our town and protect it from evil.

Eventually a real town began to emerge. We had *la Chiesa*, a church, *la scuola*, the school, *i negozi di alimentari*, grocery stores, *la cantina*, a bar, *lo scarpaio*, a shoe shop, *il macellaio*, a butcher, and other small enterprises. Some of the streets were even paved with stones. On my way to school, I would stop and watch in amazement as workers, seated on short wooden stools, laid the gray cobblestones on top of the dirt streets of our town. They moved so fast and with such ease. They would throw stones around to each other, where they would fit them into a slot on a bed of sand, and the huge puzzle emerged as our street. I would sit there and watch and listen, as they spoke and sang in a different dialect. It was *Napoletano*, as they were from the area of *Napoli*, Naples.

On most days after school we would hang around and play *calcio*, soccer, or *goccetto*, marbles. We either gathered behind the school to play soccer on a small asphalt area or made our way to the marble hill to play marbles. There was a series of holes and paths in the dirt that we would hit our way through with marbles, and if your marble was the first to go into the last hole, the reward was the other players' marble. Marbles were won and lost daily, but we all had our favorites and they were never, ever put at risk in the game for someone to win. I sometimes wonder what happened to my marble collection, especially the two big, shiny red ones that won many games for me. We played hard and fast because most, if not all of us, needed to go to our barns and help with the needs of the various animals.

Grandsons Gianni on the left and Anthony playing marbles in our backyard, 2015

Our town was coming of age, and out of the Stone Age! We even had paved streets, which were clean and pretty, but not easy on the knees while playing our games of *calcio*, soccer, *guerra*, war games, and *nascondino*, hide-and-seek. Some kids would ride their bicycles, if they were lucky enough to own one, up and down those cobblestone streets. We also played a form of modern day baseball, *mazzeh e cuzzeh*. A stick about three feet long and an inch or so in diameter would be used as a bat to hit a smaller stick that was about a foot long and approximately an inch thick. The smaller stick was thrown to the batter from about ten yards away. After batting the smaller stick, you would run to a base and then run back to home base.

Grandsons Anthony, on the right and Gianni playing mazzeh e cuzzeh, 2015

The new houses of Campanello were outfitted with a sink, toilet bowl, and bidet (a basin-like bath which was used for washing the genital area), but the water system hardly ever worked. To gain enough pressure, the water system had to be turned off for most of the day until the water reservoir filled, and from the natural water pressure we would get some water flowing into our homes at night and in the morning. There was plenty of water around, but we needed the pumps to get crystal clear, fresh water into our homes. This was not to be feasible anytime soon, as the *comune* did not have the funds to install the technology. We did have electricity – barely.

In 1951, after many years of anticipation, the lights came on in Campanello and Pagliarone. Two brothers from Forli del Sannio, who were proprietors of an electrical company, were awarded the contract to bring electricity to our town. Their family name was Lerza, a name that will be etched in my memory forever. During evenings when we were eating dinner or doing our homework, the crude lone light bulb hanging down from exposed wires would begin to flicker and eventually go out, sometimes not coming back on for days. "*Disgraziato di Lerza, puozz'ess maledetto Lerza*", *Puozz'avè un tocco Lerza, volesse uccidere quelli mostri di Lerza*, Damned Lerza, may he be cursed, may he be stricken by some ailment, I wish I could kill those Lerza monsters). These were some of the comments my parents and all of the townspeople would continually make about Lerza. Although they sounded harsh, they were just harmless complaints.

Thinking back, it could be that we, the kids, were the culprits. From the balcony of our house, if you had long arms, you could actually reach out and touch the electrical wires. We would throw metal objects at the wires just to see them spark! We finally had electricity, probably the most important invention in the world that would take us out of the dark ages and into the modern age, but in our world it would always be a struggle to keep the lights on.

There were countless cold nights sitting in front of the fireplace on small chairs with their rush seats, made with cattails and woven by my mom's brothers, who were very skillful. The chairs were low to the ground so we would be closer to the fire. Most of the time, the fire was the only source of light and heat. The front of your body would be hotter than the hottest sunny day, while your back was colder than the coldest snow. And the wool knee-length socks that *Mamma* seemed to be always mending would hardly ever come off your legs during those cold winter nights in Pagliarone.

The fireplace in our home, Mamma smiling for the camera. 1966

The town persevered through many struggles, and its people continued to work the land to survive. But the dream of many was to leave for a better life *all'estero*, abroad. Some had gone to the new colonies in Ethiopia and Libya in the early 1930s, but eventually came back to Pagliarone, where at least they had water.

Going up to northern Italy, Switzerland, Germany, France, and even England provided temporary work for many. But the dream world for the *Pagliaronesi* was to go to *l'America*. Although that is the name for the whole continent, when someone spoke of *l'America*, they usually meant the United States of America. Many emigrated to Canada, Brazil, Argentina, and other countries of Central and South America, but we referred to those countries by their names and usually not by '*l'America*.'

In 1954 my parents almost emigrated to Argentina, where my father's younger brother, Alduino, and older sister, Rosanna, lived. But they opted to hold out for the hope that someday my grandfather, Pietrantonio, would send for us from that land of opportunity and wealth called *l'America*. This was a wise move because that same year we received immigration papers that were filed by my grandfather in Denver, Colorado for us to join him. There was some hope that we would be allowed, but immigration was still closed to us. As we waited for the immigration process to be completed, we went on with our same difficult lives in Pagliarone.

Copy of document filed by my grandfather

Through the centuries the land around our village had been chopped up as a result of inheritances. So we were left with a bunch of tiny pieces of farmland scattered throughout the area. There were six children in my father's family, a typical size, if not small, for that era. All of those

2. The name(s) of the prospective immigrant(s) for whom I petition is/are: (See instruction No. 9)

	Full name	Relationship	Marital status	Birthplace	Birth date
(1)	Vittorio Lombardi	SON	MARRIED	ITALY	SEPT. 1, 1918
(2)					
(3)					
(4)					

3. Present address of prospective immigrant(s):

VASTOGIRARDI   CAMPOBASSO   ITAly
(Street)   (City)   (Province)   (Country)

4. The prospective immigrant(s) __HAVE NOT__ at any time been in the United States. (If ever in the United States
(Have) (Have not)
give information requested below):

Name	Alien Registration No.	Place of entry	Date of entry	Date of Departure

5. If admitted to the United States, the prospective immigrant intends to reside at __DENVER__ __Colorado__
2915 W. 25TH AVE.
(Number and street)   (City)   (Zone number)   (State)

6. I acquired United States citizenship (Check appropriate box below):

☐ By birth in the United States.

☒ Through my naturalization by CouNTY OF McKINLEY on NOV. 19 1945
(Court)   (Month)   (Day)   (Year)
at GAllup, NEW MEXICO   Certificate of Naturalization No. 6113698 [See
(City)   (State)
instruction 9 (d) as to cases in which naturalization certificates must be submitted.]

☐ Through the naturalization or citizenship of my _____
(Father)   (Mother)

_____
(Husband)   (Former husband)

NOTE.—If you have been issued a certificate of citizenship by the Immigration and Naturalization Service in your own name, show the number
here: _____ If you do not have such a certificate, be sure to attach the required documentary evidence. [See instructions Nos. 9 (b),
9 (c), and 9 (d) and answer item 7 or 8 below.]

7. Fill in this block only if you claim citizenship through a parent or parents, and have not been issued a certificate of citizenship by the Immigration and Naturalization Service, or are petitioning for a brother or sister.

I was born on _____ at _____
(Month)   (Day)   (Year)   (City)   (State)   (Country)

My father _____ was born on _____
(Full name)   (Month)   (Day)   (Year)

at _____ and resided in the United States from _____
(City)   (State)   (Country)

_____ to _____ He _____
(Was) (Was not)

naturalized in the United States. (If naturalized): His naturalization occurred on _____
(Month)   (Day)   (Year)

by _____ at _____ Certificate of Naturaliza-
(Court)   (City)   (State)

tion No. _____ (If your father was a citizen): He _____ lose his United States
(Did)   (Did not)

citizenship. (If citizenship was lost): He became expatriated on _____ by _____
(Month) (Day) (Year)   (Show manner in which

citizenship was lost)

My mother _____ was born on _____
(Full name, including maiden name)   (Month)   (Day)   (Year)

at _____ and resided in the United States from _____
(City)   (State)   (Country)

_____ to _____ She _____ naturalized in
(Was) (Was not)

16–62563-1   2

40

heirs would someday expect and receive a piece of their parents' land. Essentially, what was once a large piece of land was divided into equal amounts for the heirs of the family. This created a mosaic landscape with different families owning small strands of land in various locations in the surrounding area of our village. One might ask why not trade lands with others so that everyone could have larger plots. Although it

12. Fill in this block only if you are petitioning for your wife or husband or child [see instruction No. 9 (e)].

I married my _Wife_ (Wife) (Husband) on _Feb. 27_ (Month) (Day) _1915_ (Year) at _VASTogiRARdi_ (City) _CAMpobASSo_ (State) _ITALY_ (Country) by _CHURCH_ (Civil) (Church) (Proxy) (Common law) ceremony or marriage.

How many times have you been married? _TWO_ How many times has your husband or wife been married? _ONE_ If either of you have been married more than once, fill in the following information for each previous marriage.

Date married	Date marriage ended	Name of person to whom married	Sex	How marriage ended (Death or divorce)
(a) 1935	1951	JOSEPHINE LombARdi	F.	Death
(b) 1915	1931	BAMPINA LombARdi	F.	DEATH
(c) 1935	1951	JOSEPHINE LombARdi	F.	DEATH

13. Fill in this block only if you are petitioning for a brother or sister.

The parents of the prospective immigrant _____ the same as my parents. (Are) (Are not)

(If you answered "are not") give the following: The prospective immigrant's father is _____ (Full name)

and mother is _____ (Full name) they were married on _____, 19_____,

at _____ (City) _____ (State) They _____ (Were) (Were not) previously married, as follows:

Date married	Date marriage ended	Name of husband or wife	Sex	How marriage ended (Death or divorce)

I am able to and will support the immigrant(s) for whom I petition, if necessary, to prevent such immigrant(s) from becoming a public charge. I do swear that I know the contents of this petition signed by me and that the statements therein are true and correct.

NOTE.—If you are outside the United States, your statements must be sworn to before an American consular officer.

Antonio Lombardi
(Signature of petitioner) (See Instruction No. 7)

Subscribed and sworn to before me this _12th_ day of _April_, A. D., 19_55_

at _Denver, Colo._

[SEAL] My commission expires _____

J. C. Chandler _22._
(Signature of officer administering oath) (Title)

16—52883-7   4   43

Last page of the document filed by my grandfather

was practiced, this was usually not an agreeable option because everyone wanted to trade either for the prime, flat, fertile locations or for the lands closer to the village.

My father had many quarrels with his relatives about land ownership.

Many arguments took place over land boundaries; some so heated that physical altercations erupted, causing families not to speak to each other for months, if not years.

Many of our parcels of land were close to home, but others were very far away and it took much of the day just to reach them. My mother was given a piece of land by her parents as part of her dowry called *La via la Rocca*, so named because it was located on the way to another town called Roccasicura. Although it was far away, it was a fertile piece of ground and one of my favorite places to go. I actually enjoyed going there with my family because my uncles also owned parcels in the area and the lands were rich with various fruit trees. We enjoyed a variety of fruits when in season and usually ate too many, making us sick to our stomachs.

There are many happy memories of the hamlet named Trebbante, where my mother was born. The hamlet was also referred to as Trebande or Trebbande, but for us the name of that most favorite place was known as Trabiand. The name apparently stemmed from accounts that the first man who settled the area within the same valley as Pagliarone, liked to continuously travel, sort of a globetrotter, a *trebande*. Whenever we went to visit *Mammuccia Genoveffa*, my maternal grandmother, we made a beeline for her bedroom, where an old hope chest took up a corner of the room. Opening it, we hoped to see the sugar squares, the ones sent from America from her sister, Cosima, who lived in Denver. Cosima and her husband, Salvatore, owned a grocery store on Mariposa Street, and my grandmother's family would have surely followed them if the immigration restrictions had not been put in place by Congress in 1924.

Road sign for Trebbante, 2012

My mother, Maria Lucia, born July 15, 1921, was the eighth child and only daughter of Genoveffa Lombardi and Fiorindo Carmosino. Her brothers were named Michele, Cosimo, Giovanni, Salvatore, Domenicantonio, Giuseppe, and Angelo. All but one lived out their lives in Italy. My uncle, Domenicantonio, and wife, Bambina, emigrated to Canada in 1960, following their two sons who had made the move a few years earlier. Most of my uncles lived into their late 90s, and one, Giovanni, died at the age of 101 in Villa San Michele.

My mother worked hard during her young life, but she was also protected and spoiled by her older brothers. She usually helped her mother, Genoveffa, with household chores while her father and brothers worked, but during important planting and harvesting cycles she was also expected to help out.

My mother told me stories of my grandfather, and what a wonderful, gentle man he was. He had a sharp mind, although very little education. He was a builder by trade, but also dabbled in money lending. He had one axiom when he made a loan: he would not lend money to relatives. A smart man indeed, but his potential clientele was diminished greatly. Of course he had a soft touch for my mom, his youngest and only girl. I never got to know *Nonno* Fiorindo, as he died of some unknown illness in 1952, a year before I was born.

Mamma at the age of 13, standing by her father, Fiorindo with hat and some of her brothers, and other kids of Trebbante, 1934

My father, Vittorio, was the second of six children born to Bambina Lombardi and Pietrantonio Lombardi. He was born on September 1, 1918. My grandfather broke away from tradition of the firstborn son being given the name of the father's father. Instead, Pietrantonio chose to name my father after the King of Italy, Vittorio Emanuele. The firstborn was a girl, Rosanna; next came my father, and then Umberto. My grandfather again chose to name his second son after an Italian king, Umberto I; then came Claudino, Alduino, and Leontina.

Standing from left my mother's brother zio Salvatore Carmosino, my aunt Leontina's husband Flavio Carmosino, my father's sister Leontina Lombardi Carmosino, my uncle Salvatore's wife Michelina Carmosino. sitting Jackie Lombardi and my mother's brother Giovanni Carmosino. 1975

My father had a much harder life than my mom. His mother, Bambina, died on the sixth of January, 1936 at forty years old from probable heart disease. Rosanna was twenty, my father eighteen, Umberto sixteen, Claudino fourteen, Alduino eight, and the youngest, Leontina, was only six.

My grandmother, Bambina, was born in 1896 to Domenicantonio Lombardi and Teresa Morelli, who was from the bordering town of San Pietro Avellana.

My paternal grandfather was Pietrantonio, whose grandchildren called him *Papà* Pietrantonio. Others called him by his given name, but through the years – including those in America – he accumulated many nicknames such as Antonio, Toni, *cininn* Toni, Little Tony, and *reh shemecca*, the shoemaker. He was the only son of Giuseppe Lombardi and Carolina Lombardi. During his younger years, Pietrantonio dreamed of a better, more exciting life than that of *il contadino*, a dirt farmer. At the start of World War I he was drafted into the army, and soon after he was put on a train headed north to the front in Northern Italy. He spent many weeks there in a trench near the Piave River, fighting for Italy's cause.

My grandfather, Pietrantonio Lombardi, with his father, Giuseppe, and mother, Carolina, circa 1910

According to *Papà* Pietrantonio, life in the trenches was miserable most of the time. Hygiene was at its worst in those crowded trenches. Soldiers sometimes stood shoulder to shoulder waiting, peeking over the trench into no man's land surrounded with barbed wire. During his duty in the trenches, he was usually wet, muddy, cold, and bored. During the day, fighting was sporadic, and at night there would be some movement on either side, but nothing seemed to be gained or lost. The men tried to keep their morale somewhat high by telling stories of home and playing the game of *morra* (an addition game using your fingers, explained in detail in a later chapter) because they had at least their fingers to do so.

He was thankful that he survived the trenches when many of his comrades did not, usually dying from infections and diseases. Towards the end of the war he was sent back to Caserta, the same army camp at which he trained in a town in the region of Campania, bordering Molise to the south.

On the way, looking out the train window, he recognized the familiar landscape. He and his companions were near his home, where his young wife, Bambina, waited with their small baby girl, Rosanna, wondering if and when her husband would come home. Feeling homesick, he decided to hop off the train and walk for half a day towards home. His superiors wished him well. He could have been at risk of being labeled a deserter, but he did not care at all — he longed for his family, his village.

The Italian authorities did not pursue any legal action against him. After all, he had fought and endured the miserable conditions of that war and likely would have been discharged once back in Caserta. Pietrantonio felt that he did the authorities a favor by hopping off that train.

Once back home in his small hamlet of Luigi, Pietrantonio struggled with the backbreaking work of *il contadino*, a dirt farmer. Deep inside, he still dreamed of a better, more exciting life for himself and his growing family. So he decided to learn a trade. He traveled by mule to the town of Castel di Sangro everyday to apprentice at a shoe shop. There he learned the skills to be a shoemaker, a cobbler. Unfortunately in Pagliarone, with its few inhabitants that included other shoe repairmen, business was scarce. Most people could not afford to repair their worn shoes, much less order new custom-made shoes. At that time most people wore a combination of wood and leather sandals. He utilized anything he could think of to make footwear for his family, for the villagers.

Pietrantonio often dreamed of immigrating temporarily to America; of going to work there for a few years and then coming back home with enough money saved to provide for his family. That hope was dashed by the passage of the U.S. Immigration Act of 1924 by the United States Congress, which limited the number of emigrants allowed entry into the United States through a National Origins quota. Also, the rise to power by Benito Mussolini and his fascist regime resulted in the passage of an Italian law, prohibiting most Italians from leaving the country. The U.S. immigration quota allowed immigration visas for up to two percent of the total number of people of each nationality living in the United States, according to the 1890 national census.

Starting in the early 1800s, about 5.5 million Italians would immigrate to the United States. But many arrived after 1890, so the percentage of Italians living in the United States in 1890 was low. This meant that the Act seriously restricted emigration from Italy and other undesired countries. This was a definite and calculated move to restrict Italians and other southern and eastern Europeans, along with potential emigrants from other continents of the world who wanted to immigrate to the United States. This was a deliberate move to keep emigrants who did not fit the Caucasian profile out of the United States of America. The Act clearly favored emigration from western and Scandinavian Europe, which had the largest number of residents in the country in 1890 and thus, a higher number of new emigrants allowed from those countries.

Pietrantonio reluctantly decided to immigrate to Argentina, instead. In late 1931, he and his son-in-law, Lorenzo Lombardi, *Zia* Rosanna's husband, went together. My grandfather left his wife and six children, and my uncle left his young wife and baby daughter, Ida.

On one of our trips to Toronto, Canada, I visited Cousin Ida, who had immigrated there years before with her husband Vincenzo and daughters Giuseppina and Rosanna. As I asked questions to gather more family information, I asked her why her father's family was referred to as *keer deh Chunn* (*quelli di Cian*, from the area of Cian). I wondered about the name Cian. She mentioned that a patriarch had immigrated to America. His name was Giovanni, but while in Denver he was called John, English for Giovanni. When he came back home to Pagliarone, people started to call him and his family's area by the American name, Cian, *Chunn*, the villagers' dialect pronunciation of the English name John!

In Argentina, an uncle, Pasquale Lombardi, waited for my grandfather and Uncle Lorenzo. Pasquale had immigrated there years earlier. My *Nonna* Bambina, with the help of *Papà* Pietrantonio's elderly parents, took care of the other six children. My father, the oldest son at thirteen years old, had to assume somewhat the role of the man of the house. And they waited patiently for the letter from their father, Pietrantonio, with good news; news that life was better in Argentina than in Pagliarone and that he would send for them soon. But that letter never arrived. It was never sent.

Shoemakers in Buenos Aires were not in great demand, and other work was also scarce. It was just a big city with the same problems as our small village, including that there was not much work. So again, Pietrantonio contemplated a move. Or, was this the excuse of a man whose two feet wanted to keep moving towards the next horizon; was Pietrantonio destined to be a vagabond?

My Uncle Lorenzo would often walk the docks of Buenos Aires to look for work and to think. He would engage in conversation with the various sailors working on the docks and on the numerous cargo ships. Eventually he befriended two men who worked on a freighter that made voyages to North America. The sailors were not Italian, but Argentinians of Spanish descent. The weathered sailors were friendly, although they had a look of menace. *Zio* Lorenzo would tell them that he had family and friends in America, in Colorado, *Denva*, Denver. He wished that he could go there because he heard that there was of plenty of work in timber, mining, and railroad in the nearby mountains.

One summer night in December of 1932, my uncle was approached by the two sailors, who informed him that for a fee they could take him to North America, to New York. My grandfather and uncle, after much contemplation and discussion, decided to sell all of their meager possessions to raise enough money to pay the sailors for passage to New York.

On the hot and muggy night of January 29, 1933, my grandfather, Uncle Lorenzo (Rosanna's husband), Lorenzo's brother, Salvatore, and another friend, Guerino – all originally from Pagliarone – went to the docks after midnight and were sneaked onto a freighter on the docks of Buenos Aires. They were taken deep to the depths of the ship and ushered through a hole, just big enough for them to fit into that could be accessed when a large piece of machinery was pulled away from a wall. That small, dark room would be their home for the next thirty days, as the cargo ship stopped at various ports while making its way to New York.

The incredibly long days and nights were occupied by dreaming and anticipating life in *Denva*, Denver. The sailors would appear every three days with water, some food, a clean refuse bucket, and any other supplies they could gather. *Papà* Pietrantonio told me these stories many times and they were retold to me again by my Uncle Lorenzo when he and his wife, *Zia* Rosanna, visited us in Denver in early 1980s. While reflecting on that difficult voyage, he casually mentioned that the only thing they seemed to have plenty of were cigarettes!

Finally, on a cold and foggy day, the freighter docked in New York. They waited for what seemed to be an eternity, but finally the screeching noise of the large machine that was used to wash clothes was heard, as it was pulled away from the wall. The two sailors, with their index fingers in front of their noses as a gesture for silence, motioned for them to crawl out. They were somehow sneaked off of the cargo ship and whisked to a hotel near Little Italy in the heart of Manhattan, where the sailors had a room. Plans had been made for my uncle's brother, Benny Lombardi, and another distant cousin, Salvatore (Silver) Lombardi, to be waiting there for them.

Panic set in when Benny and Salvatore were nowhere to be found. The group waited anxiously for two days. The sailors were becoming very anxious and impatient, as they would have to get back to the freighter soon for the return trip to Argentina. On the third day there was a knock on the door. The sailors hid the four illegals and opened the door. Benny and Salvatore introduced themselves and my Uncle Lorenzo heard the voice of his brother for the first time in many years. Tears of joy flowed as they hugged and kissed each other. They also apologized for being late, as they encountered some car and road problems on the way from Denver to New York.

I knew that Salvatore (Silver) Lombardi was somehow related to us, but did not know much about him until one summer day in 1998. A car pulled up in front of my upholstery business on 52nd and Marshall Street in Arvada, Colorado. The car was older, larger, and longer than the other cars in the parking lot. Originally it was probably rust in color, but now it was a faded rusting color. An elderly gentleman struggled out of the vehicle and slowly made his way to the door. It took him a few seconds to get his bearings and as he surveyed the room, I waited for the usual questions that I would get from some seniors: They were lost and wanted to know where the emission shop was located! Or they had a chair that they purchased at the Denver dry-goods store many years ago for $39.95 and wondered if it was worth reupholstering. This usually meant that they hoped the upholstery work could be done for about that same price!

Instead he asked me if I were a Lombardi. He then asked me if I knew a man nicknamed *Cininn Toni*. *Cininn* is dialect for little, small, short. I thought he was asking me about someone living and I mentioned that I knew a Tony who was referred to as 'Shorty,' but then I realized that he was talking about someone of long ago. He went on to say that he had known such a man, and as a matter of fact he recalled *Cininn Toni* standing in the same location of the room where I was standing! He informed me that my property was once a bar owned by a man named Silver Lombardi and that *Cininn Toni*, a shoemaker, was related to him! My hairs stood up on my neck when I suddenly realized that this old man was talking about my grandfather. I had a very long, interesting talk with the nice 92-year-old man, who was a good friend of my grandfather.

His name was Bill (Guglielmo) Ghillarducci. He came to America at the age of ten from the Tuscany region of Italy. He owned a farm in the area, but now just a sliver was left as commercial and industrial buildings supplanted it. As Bill recounted stories about my grandfather and Silver, my mind floated back to 1933, to a hotel room in Manhattan.

Sometime in March 1933, my grandfather, Pietrantonio, *Cininn Toni*, and his fellow travelers left New York and headed for Denver in Silver's big black car, probably a Model A Ford. The road trip was going well until one morning somewhere in Kansas, when they would encounter trouble. My grandfather recounted the story. A big truck full of hay swerved in front of their car, and as Benny tried to avoid the collision, their car also swerved and went off the road and rolled. It seemed as though it rolled forever, but in a few seconds it came to a stop in a cornfield, a short distance from the road. Except for some scratches and bruises, everyone seemed to be in one piece.

The car was upside down and would have to be uprighted and probably towed to the nearest town for repairs. People would come to investigate, including the authorities. A quick decision was made to walk to the nearest town — about ten miles away — to get help, leaving Benny with the car. Eventually in some remote Kansas farming town, they were able to board a bus that was headed west, towards Denver, Colorado.

The four men, accompanied by Silver Lombardi, finally reached Denver, where they were welcomed by friends and relatives from Pagliarone who would help them establish a new life there. The new arrivals stayed with my Uncle Lorenzo's relatives, and all worked odd jobs where proper immigration papers were not required. Pietrantonio did not work in his shoemaking profession for some time. Instead, he started making cheese from the back of a residence on 35th and Shoshone, and sold his *scamorza* and *caciocavallo* cheeses in the Little Italy neighborhood of north Denver.

A family friend, Frank Amato, remembers walking by that address as a young boy on his way to school with his friends, and usually the man there would give Frank and his friends a taste of his cheese. Frank also remembers occasionally seeing another man with Pietrantonio, and my grandfather seemed to be teaching this other man all he knew about making fresh *scamorza*. Frank insisted that this other man was Mike Leprino, the man who later started what would eventually become the empire of Leprino Cheese!

Eventually Pietrantonio would work in the trade that he learned in Italy: shoemaking and repair. He rented a storefront on 19th and Champa and started his venture as a business owner. In his spare time he designed and made colorful cowboy boots. Finally some luck would come Pietrantonio's way, as he discovered a demand for his custom-made cowboy boots in the Denver area. He worked day and night to keep up with the cowboy boot orders. He was making money and stashing it in many different hiding places, hoping to someday send some back to his family in Italy.

In Pagliarone, life was difficult for my father's family, and it became even more so when *Nonna* Bambina, my father's mom, became ill with probable heart problems. I say probable because it seemed that when someone had an unknown disease, it was eventually diagnosed by non-experts, the villagers, as *mal deh coreh* (*male di cuore*, heart disease). It could have been a variety of other unknown illnesses. There was hope that somehow Pietrantonio would figure out a way to get his wife and family to America, where hopefully they could get Bambina the medical help she required to diagnose her illness and hopefully treat it.

The family kept waiting for some news, but none ever came. Yet they would not lose hope while anxiously waiting for some good news from America. Pietrantonio would periodically write letters; he also sent some money on holidays, and when compatriots returned to Italy from Denver, he sent money with them to give to his family. He reassured the family that he hoped to somehow figure out a way to bring all of them to America — a difficult task as an illegal alien. Unfortunately he wasn't able to accomplish that difficult feat, and sadly he would never see his wife again. Without proper medical help, her heart stopped. As my dad recalled, the heart stops with all causes of death, and in 1935 she died, leaving six young sons and daughters without parents.

Many men who came to America without their wives and their families were surely lonely, and eventually sought some company. I suspect that some fell in love and some got married, living a double life. Some abandoned their families in their homelands forever. It seems to me that my grandfather was a lady's man, but whether or not he was an adulterer, that went with him to the grave. Sometime after his wife's death, he did remarry, although only in common law. The woman was fourteen years older and wiser than he; her name was Giovina (Josephine) Lombardi. Although her last name was Lombardi, she was not from Pagliarone, but from L'Aquila, a town to the north and the capital city of *Abruzzo e Molise*. Her husband had passed away in 1933. Giovina was the grandmother of Frank Amato. Our family and his would become good friends many years later, when my nephew, Vic, and Frank's son, Gino, attended Holy Family grade school together. They became close friends and eventually our families figured out the relationship!

One evening my Uncle Lorenzo, one of his brothers, Salvatore, and their friend, Guerino, were at Ernie's Supper Club in north Denver, east of 44th and Federal Boulevard. After drinking too much and not mentally sharp and deep into conversations, these men told some of the patrons the stories of their lives, including their illegal entry into the

U.S. That proved to be a life-changing mistake. The conversation was overheard by someone who called the authorities, and Uncle Lorenzo, Salvatore, and Guerino were arrested by immigration agents.

Many attempts were made by my uncle's relatives to keep them in the country, including begging for clemency to the then Colorado Governor Edwin C. Johnson. Sadly, they were eventually deported. My Uncle Lorenzo and Guerino were sent back to Italy, as they were citizens of that country, and Salvatore back to Argentina because he was a naturalized citizen of that country. *Zio* Lorenzo would eventually return to Argentina in April of 1951, with the help of his brother. Lorenzo's wife, Rosanna, and their children, Giovanni, Lina, and Bambina, would join them in 1954, leaving behind their eldest daughter, Ida, who was married. Guerino decided to stay in Pagliarone. He was tired of the long, grueling, and cruel misadventures of America.

During numerous interrogations by immigration agents, one of the men broke down and eventually divulged that Pietrantonio Lombardi was the other man who had accompanied them on the illegal journey to New York. In the following days, while my grandfather was at work in his small shoe shop at 1961 Champa Street, two men dressed in dark suits walked in asking questions. The agents asked him his name, where he came from, when, how, and so forth. And then they asked him for identification papers. He calmly told them that he had his passport and would get it for them in the back room. With his work apron on, he bolted out the back door and ran towards what was called the Loop Market, near 15th and Larimer Street. There he mingled with the crowd. He did not see the two men anywhere and felt a little bit at ease. Then he realized that he was still wearing his work apron. He immediately took it off and tossed it into a garbage can. Still with no sign of what must have been immigration agents in sight, he boarded a streetcar headed for north Denver.

It was not safe for him to stay in Colorado. Eventually the immigration agents would track him down and arrest him, so he decided to leave town — with the help of a friend, a man named Wesley Lunon. Wesley and my grandfather drove to Yuma, Arizona, where they stayed for about a month. Hoping that things had cooled down back in Denver and tired of hiding out, they decided to return home. On the way back they stopped for a short rest in Gallup, New Mexico, and my grandfather immediately fell in love with the area. It reminded him of home; home in Pagliarone, Italy. After a few days in Gallup, they headed towards Denver.

Back in Denver, relatives and friends warned Pietrantonio that eventually the immigration agents would catch up with him and deport him back to Italy. It crossed his mind that maybe that idea was not so bad. After all, his kids were there and without parents to care for them and support them. But with his ultimate dream to somehow, someday bring his family to America, the decision was made to move to that town in New Mexico that he found to be to his liking, while on the run from the law. Also, his wife had a relative there who would help him get established. He was told that there might be a demand for his cowboy boots in New Mexico. He and Giovina packed up as many belongings as possible and boarded a train to Gallup, New Mexico, for once again, a new life in a new place amongst strangers.

In Gallup they moved into a storefront at 249 West 4th Street, where they would live for eight years. He opened a shoe repair shop and began making cowboy boots. In the back of the storefront they made their home. There was a backyard that was turned into a vegetable garden. His cowboy boots were a hit around town and throughout the surrounding area, where ranchers lived amongst native Indians. The sheriff of Gallup also ordered a pair of boots. This sheriff and Tony (his given name of Pietrantonio was now just a memory of a prior life gone by) would eventually become very close friends.

The Italian-American sheriff, who would also become a five-term mayor of Gallup, was Domenic Mollica, born in Floridia, Sicily, Italy in 1889. The two men were *paesani*, about the same age with similar traditions and interests. Mr. Mollica visited Tony often and they enjoyed some of Tony's homemade wine. Someone suggested to Tony that when customers came in to pick up their shoes and boots, that Tony should offer them a glass of his homemade wine. People enjoyed his wine and started buying it. With the sale of his wine and custom-made boots, Tony amassed a nice nest egg. But the best part of his life in Gallup was the fact that Mr. Mollica assisted my grandfather in obtaining legal residence. With his influence he helped Tony to somehow procure a green card, making him a *legal* resident of the United States of America. As soon as he was able to, Tony applied for citizenship and eventually, on November 19, 1945, he became a naturalized American citizen in McKinley County of Gallup, New Mexico, USA.

Life was good for Giovina and Tony. They would not have to be anxious anymore. Every time a customer walked into their shop, they no longer had to wonder if he might be the immigration agent who would finally take Tony away to jail. There would be no more nerves being rattled over that. With their legal residency, they were able to travel freely, making trips back to Denver usually for Christmas and Easter. Tony and Giovina brought back gifts for Giovina's children and grandchildren, many of the items made by the Indians and Mexican-American artisans of New Mexico. Not only had Tony learned the English language, but he also grasped a bit of Spanish and various Indian words of the Navajo, Zuni, Hopi, and other tribes of the area.

Giovina missed her family, and after eight years they had had enough of life in Gallup. Once the citizenship certificate was in hand, they were ready to go back home to Denver. Just before the Christmas holidays of 1945, they gathered their belongings and boarded a train for the final trip back to Denver.

They moved in with one of Giovina's nine children, Carlo Amato, Frank Amato's father. Tony reconnected with old friends and relatives, and even traveled to Louisville, Oak Creek, Phippsburg, Ladora, and Tolland to visit *paesani*. He would take custom-made cowboy boots and sell them to the men working in the timber and mining camps. In Tolland, he visited with people who he grew up with in Pagliarone. These *paesani* had found work in and around the town, about fifty miles northwest of Denver, working in the timber camps. They had signed contracts with the railroad and worked long hours, seven days a week.

Prosper Lombardi, a close friend of Tony, was a foreman for one of the camps. On Tony's many trips there, he would spend nights as a guest of Antonio and Adelina Iacovetta and their two sons, Joe and Alex. Their conversations would always include whether or not they had made the right decision in coming to America. The long, hard work days and their small one-room cabin were not much better than the hard life in Italy. But they would endure and hope that their hard work would someday be rewarded with an easier life, at least for their children.

One of the operators of the timber camps was Gaetano (Charles) Zarlengo, a successful immigrant originally from a town near Pagliarone named Pietrabbondante. He would be a constant example and inspiration to the other fellow Italians, that hard work might also bring success to their families. Mr. Zarlengo (Zarlenga) more than likely recruited the first laborers and thus, the first immigrants from Pagliarone, to work the timber and mine establishments in Colorado.

Frank Amato also recalled his father, Carlo, trying to teach my grandfather how to drive a car. Carlo took Tony to open fields, where he would attempt to teach him how to drive. In his early 50s, learning how to drive a car was not as easy for Tony as it would have been when he was a young man. As he contemplated his next venture, Tony decided that he would buy a car, even though he did not have a driver's license. Learning to drive turned out to be more difficult than he had ever envisioned. Carlo became frustrated and many times, Mr. Amato told Tony that he was not destined to drive a car and to just give up. But Tony would not concede, realizing that in order to advance with life in America, driving a car was essential. Finally, after many near-collisions and actual collisions along the sides of a curve and other obstacles, Tony learned to drive – although not very well, but well enough to get a driver's license. In Italy, driving a car – much less owning a car – was only a dream of the *signoria*, the privileged. With his new mode of transportation, my grandfather made it a point to visit every relative and friend in Colorado.

Tony and his wife were enjoying the fruits of their hard work in Gallup. They sent packages and money back to his family in Italy and traveled all around Colorado. Giovina had a brother in Pittsburgh, Pennsylvania, whom she had not seen for forty-five years. Tony and Giovina hopped on a train and took off for Pittsburg for a short visit. They came back home a year later! A question that I would pose to my grandpa, if he were alive, would be if he ever considered leaving Giovina in Pittsburgh to go back to Italy to see his children. As a citizen he could travel freely and maybe while in Italy, he could somehow figure out a way to get them all to America. World War II was over, he was a little closer to Italy, and that would have been a great opportunity to reconnect with his family back in Pagliarone.

That thought might have crossed his mind, but he did not go back then, nor did he ever set foot on Italian soil again. His family would have to come to him in America. Tony was a hard worker, an artist in his trade, but he was also a free spirit, a bohemian. He enjoyed the good life: traveling, dining out, theatres, nightclubs, dance halls, and corner bars. Long road trips were part of his life, whereas his counterparts from Pagliarone had never set foot inside these places of entertainment. They never left the confines of north Denver unless work necessitated it.

Frank Amato recently told me a story about going to the train depot to pick up Tony and his grandma, Giovina, when they came back from Gallup. Among the many pieces of luggage was half of an oak wine barrel that took two people to pick up and put into the car. Back home at 3525 Osage, Frank gazed into the barrel. It was full of gold and silver dollars. One morning Tony was busy making a pair of his custom boots, when two masked men walked into his store and pointed shotguns at his head. They knew exactly what they were looking for; they wanted the wine barrel. They quickly loaded the loot into a car and took off. They had an Italian accent but Tony did not recognize them. Talk around town was that it was an inside job done by a relative of his wife, Giovina. That relative is said to have despised Tony and Giovina's family. Without any evidence, it was difficult to confirm the perpetrator and the case went unresolved. Their nest egg was gone. Grandpa Tony worked day and night, and slowly began to fill coffee cans with money. Opening a savings account at a bank was strictly out of the question. He did not trust the banks and would never use their services throughout his life.

Sometime in the late 1940s, my grandfather *Cininn Toni* (meaning Little Tony), a nickname he had inherited because of his small stature opened up a store on 21st and Larimer. He named it Denver Ranchmen's Boot Shop. There he made and sold cowboy boots. Governors, mayors, and other dignitaries was his clientele. His most lucrative two weeks of the year were during the yearly January Stock Show at the Denver Coliseum.

In 1946 Tony and his wife, Giovina, also bought a house on 2915 West 25th Avenue. It was not in the heart of north Denver's Little Italy, but it was close enough. They moved into the small flat-roofed, one-story building and slowly transformed it into a comfortable Italian home with a vegetable garden and a small cantina (wine cellar).

Sometime in 1951, Tony went to see why Giovina was not getting up and found her dead in their bed. He had lost his soul mate of many years. He thought of his family in Italy, his grandchildren whom he had never met, and thought maybe this was the time to go back and see his family. He considered taking a trip back to Pagliarone, though never seriously. He moved on with life in Denver, but he was lonely. He frequented north Denver's bars and beer joints. His favorite was the Columbus Inn on 39th and Navajo. Antonio (Sperry) and Giustina Lombardi were the proprietors, and also immigrants from Pagliarone. There he met a woman, Esther Dinicola (DeNicola). She became his new girlfriend. Esther died a couple of years later. He was alone again.

At a local dance club he then met a woman, Dorothy (Mazzocco) Smith, who was many years younger than he. Her family also hailed from Pagliarone. He married her a short time later and a daughter was born to them in 1957. The marriage was volatile. The age difference probably played a role in their conflicts, but the main antagonist was alcohol. They divorced, and a short time later Dorothy died after collapsing in her kitchen, as her five year old daughter stood by.

My grandfather, in his early 60s, would now have to care for a small child by himself. With his young daughter, Colette (Coco), he continued living and working in his shoe shop on 25th Avenue. He had closed the store on Larimer and set up shop in the front section of his modest house. Working at home made it easier to take care of his young daughter. He would take her everywhere with him, including the Columbus Inn lounge. Friends, mostly immigrants from Pagliarone, would try to help him, to advise him. The women, especially, would suggest methods of raising the little girl.

He did the best he could. He bought her anything she desired, probably out of love, but maybe also out of guilt. Tony spoiled his daughter. That probably was the only thing he knew or could do to keep some semblance of a family, of raising a small child at his advanced age. People would try to offer advice to him, warning him that spoiling her was not the right way. He didn't care. She was all he had and would have until 1966, when two of his sons and their families from Pagliarone joined him in his small house. The reunion brought the feeling of a real family to his household, but eventually it created some turmoil and resentment for all.

My paternal grandfather, on the left, Pietrantonio Lombardi, circa 1946

❦

Chapter II

La Guerra · The War

While my grandfather, Pietrantonio (also known as Tony, *Cininn Toni*, or Little Tony), was living out his adventures in America, his family in Italy was living a difficult life. Since their mother had died in 1936 and, prior to that, having been sick and not able to work, all she could provide was motherly and moral support. After her death, the kids felt lost and deprived of most family purpose. Thankfully, their paternal grandparents were still alive and offered some semblance of a normal family unit. *Mammuccia (Nonna)* Bambina had a sister, Ernestina, and together with her husband, Cosimo, widely known as *Cosmo deh Zirr*, this aunt and uncle helped the orphaned kids as much as possible. The other inhabitants of the Luigi hamlet, relatives, and many of the villagers also offered and gave some assistance. The older brothers were given the insurmountable task of providing for their younger siblings and elderly grandparents.

Armando Lombardi, Zia Leontina Carmosino, Jackie, and Zia Ernestina Lombardi, 1975

To make matters worse, the three older brothers — Vittorio, Umberto, and Claudino — were drafted into Mussolini's Italian Army in 1938, as tensions in Europe were heading towards World War II. In the 1930s, Mussolini was the fascist dictator of Italy, as was Franco in Spain and Hitler in Germany. As Nazi Germany began its expansion of power, Mussolini sided with the Germans, the Axis powers.

My father, Vittorio, age twenty, was drafted on May 10, 1938 and sent to an army base in *Caserta* for basic training. That is where he learned such basics as how to tell time on a clock. He was instructed and eventually grasped the basics of a medic. My Uncle Umberto was sent to the Slavic regions to fight the war, was injured in Albania, and was eventually given a discharge. His injured foot gave him problems throughout his life.

Vittorio Lombardi di Pietrantonio,
the soldier, circa 1939

Many other young men from our village were drafted into the Italian military, while thousands of miles away in America young men who were born in the same village in Italy were drafted into the United States military. These young men, not so many years earlier in the hills of Pagliarone, had played war games of Roman gladiators using crudely made wooden swords. And now there was a real possibility that they could be firing real guns at each other while fighting on opposing sides in a real war.

Vittorio Lombardi, son of Salvatore (Sam) and Bonina avoided the possibility of shooting a childhood playmate by being deployed to the Pacific theatre. Uncle Olindo (Bill) Lombardi was also fortunate, as he was sent to the Pacific to fight the Japanese, but not so lucky to be shot in the shoulder when his unit was ambushed while crossing a river on an assignment. Some of his comrades died from gunshots or drowned in

Bill Lombardi, Violet Meloragno Lombardi, Frances Welch Meloragno,
Dominic (Babe) Meloragno, circa 1948

the water of the river. He spent the night in the water until daylight, when he was taken to a hospital and treated. The doctors could not find the bullet.

In the early 1950s Bill felt a lump in his back. An X-ray showed an object that turned out to be the Japanese bullet! In 1952 Uncle Bill, his wife, Violet, along with her brother, Babe (Dominic) Meloragno, and his wife, Frances, were driving to Columbus, Ohio to see relatives. When they stopped to use a restroom, Aunt Violet left her purse unsupervised on a counter while using the toilet. The purse was stolen and, among its contents, the bullet.

Other American soldiers such as Giuseppe (Joe) Iacovetta were sent to Italy to fight against the Axis powers. Giuseppe fought in the battle of Montecassino and on the island of Sardegna, where he met his future wife. Sadly, as these Italian-American soldiers fought for the Allies, if their parents were not naturalized citizens of the United States, they were asked to register as 'enemy aliens' and were at risk to be taken to internment camps by the United States government.

My Uncle Claudino was sent to the Russian front and as the war ended, he was listed as missing in action. In the last letter the family received from him, he asked for wool socks and wool undergarments because it was extremely cold in Russia. Upon returning home from the Russian front, a soldier from our town related to the family that he last saw Claudino hunkered down near a bush on a snow bank, complaining that he could not feel his feet anymore. With the Russian army advancing, the situation became chaotic and Claudino was most likely captured.

Our family always wondered if Claudino was alive somewhere in Russia. Did he start a new life there? Did he have a new family, as depicted in the movie *Girasole* (*Sunflower*) with Sophia Loren and Marcello Mastroianni? That question was answered many years later when the Communist Party in the Soviet Union fell in the 1980s and World War II records were finally released. The *Carabinieri*, the State Police of Italy, hand delivered a letter to my Aunt Leontina in Villa San Michele in 1993. The official letter was from *Il Ministero Della Difesa*, Minister of Defense, stating that *Zio* Claudino was captured by the Soviet Army on the front, in the former *U.R.S.S.* (U.S.S.R., the Soviet/Communist Russia) and interned in a hospital. Claudino died there on March 15, 1943, more than likely as a result of hypothermia. He was buried in a mass grave and his remains will never be recovered. Of some 235,000 soldiers of the Italian 8th Army in Russia, nearly half of them lost their lives.

My father, Vittorio, was sent to Africa where he worked as a medic. He treated soldiers for spider and snake bites more than he treated them for war wounds! He told us that on a daily basis, the Allies would send bombers for air strikes. The Italian soldiers would all scramble for cover, praying for the bombs to miss their area. One early evening as he and two other soldiers were walking on a road somewhere near Tripoli, they heard the planes on the horizon. Suddenly they saw them appear over some mountains, headed directly towards their position. They all ran for cover. My dad hid under a nearby horse cart and the cart tipped over, pinning

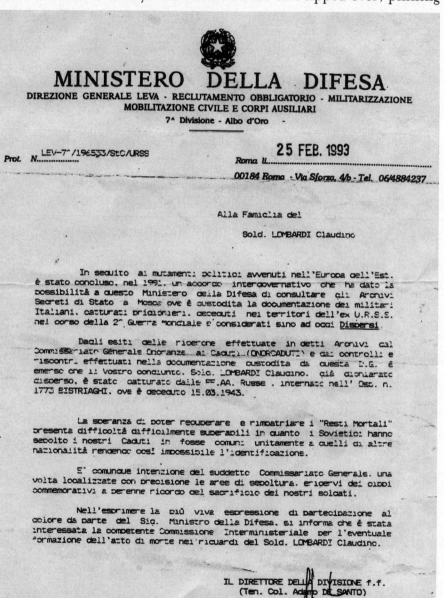

Copy of document from the Italian Ministry of Defense confirming that Zio Claudino did die in 1943

his hand. The planes flew over their heads, low enough where he could see the pilots. My father could not move, and just prayed that no bombs would be dropped near him. He was spared that night, and with his companions he walked back to the base. They had to keep quiet about his injured hand because they were in an area that was off limits, and he would surely be reprimanded by his superiors.

MINISTERO DELLA DIFESA

COMMISSARIATO GENERALE PER LE ONORANZE AI CADUTI
Direzione Storico–Statistica - Ufficio Estero e Rimpatri – Sezione Caduti in Stati Europei

Indirizzo Postale: Via XX Settembre 123/a - 00187 R O M A
Posta elettronica :
Posta elettronica certificata :
Pdc: Ass. Amm. Massimo Palleschi – tel. 0647354289

Oggetto: Soldato LOMBARDI Claudino, nato a Vastogirardi (IS) il 03.07.1922.
Prat. C.G.O.C.G. n° 93798.

Al   Signor Antony LOMBARDI
e-mail:

****
Rif. e-mail del 10.02.2014
****

1. In esito a quanto chiesto con la lettera a riferimento, La informo che agli atti di questo Commissariato Generale il Soldato LOMBARDI Claudino, già effettivo al 278° Reggimento Fanteria – Divisione Vicenza, risulta deceduto il 15 marzo 1943, nel lager - ospedale n. 1773 di BISTRIAGHI (Russia).

2. La speranza di poter recuperare e rimpatriare i Resti mortali dei nostri Caduti, sepolti a BISTRIAGHI, è praticamente nulla, atteso che nella predetta località - come avvenuto in altri campi di prigionia - gli Stessi sono stati tumulati dai Sovietici in sepolture comuni, unitamente a quelli di altre nazionalità. Tutto ciò rende impossibile procedere all'identificazione dei singoli Caduti che rimangono accomunati, per l'eternità, da un unico tragico destino.

3. Le sia di conforto sapere che mai potrà venire meno la riconoscenza e la doverosa ammirazione verso Chi ha donato la vita per la Patria.

4. Per maggiore informazione e conoscenza, Le invio, in allegato, copia della scheda notizie relativa al summenzionato campo.

Con i sentimenti della massima comprensione.

IL COMMISSARIO GENERALE
(Gen. D. CC. Silvio GHISELLI)

Letter from Italian Defense Ministry detailing my uncle's burial site in Russia

MINISTRY OF DEFENCE
COMMISSIONER GENERAL FOR THE HONORABLE FALLEN
Historical Statistics Directorate - Foreign Office and Repatriation – Section: Fallen in European Countries

Postal Address : Via XX Settembre 123/a - 00187 ROME
E-mail:
Certified e-mail :
Pdc : Adm. Asst Massimo Palleschi - tel. 0647354289

Subject: Soldier LOMBARDI Claudino, born in Vastogirardi (ISERNIA) on 03/07/1922 .
Prat . C.G.O.C.G. n° 93 798 .

To: Mr. Antony LOMBARDI
e-mail:
****
Reference: e- mail of 10/02/2014
****

1. In response to the inquiry made in the referred letter, I inform you that, resulting from the registered documents at this General Commissariat, the Soldier LOMBARDI Claudino, attached to the 278th Infantry Regiment, Vicenza Division, died March 15, 1943, in the BISTRIAGHI camp hospital #1773 (Russia).

2 . The hope of the mortal remains of our fallen buried at BISTRIAGHI being recovered and repatriated is virtually zero, since in the above location - as it often happened in other prison camps – those Fallen were buried in mass graves by the Soviets, together with those of other nationalities. All this makes it impossible to identify the individual Fallen, who now remain united for eternity by a single tragic fate.

3 . May it comfort you to know that one could never diminish the gratitude and the right and proper admiration towards those Who gave their lives for their country.

4 . For further information, I am sending you, in the enclosed attachment, a copy of the information sheet relating to the aforementioned camp.

With sentiments of the highest understanding.

THE INSPECTOR GENERAL
(Gen. D. CC . Silvio GHISELLI)

OSPEDALE n. 1773

Località : BISTRIAGHI
Provincia : ORICIJ
Regione : KIROV
Repubblica : RUSSIA

Nell'ospedale speciale n. 1773 sono deceduti 243 soldati italiani.

L'area cimiteriale è composta di due gruppi di Sepolture:

Il 1° gruppo, formato da circa dieci fosse comuni, è completamente ricoperto da una fitta vegetazione che non consente la precisa numerazione dei tumuli. Le fosse contengono le Spoglie dei prigionieri morti fino all'agosto del 1943 per la maggior parte italiani.

Sepolture di 2 o 3 prigionieri sono comprese nel secondo gruppo che si trovano in un boschetto poco lontano.

Tutta l'area cimiteriale è situata nel territorio del comune di Tarasovo.

Bistriaghi e quindi Tarasovo si possono raggiungere da Kirov in auto, in quanto la stazione di Bistriaghi rimane isolata e non è facile trovare un mezzo per portarsi verso i cimiteri.

La distanza da Kirov è di 52 Km.

Life goes on, even during a World War. Our parents' wedding picture, Vittorio Lombardi and Maria Lucia Carmosino, January 28, 1942

Another hardship he endured in Africa during the war was the period when all the soldiers had to drink their own sanitized urine for fear that the Allies had poisoned the water supply.

In 1942 Vittorio returned to Italy on leave via the port of Naples. Making his way back to Pagliarone, my father married Maria Lucia Carmosino of Trebbante on January 28, 1942. Because of the war, the celebration was very simple and quick. After the ceremony at Pagliarone's original church, located in the Pasquale hamlet, the families gathered at my mother's parents' house in Trebbante for a meal and a bit of music and dancing. A few days later he returned to Africa to treat the wounded and sick Italian soldiers.

In 1943 Vittorio was shipped back to Italy to his base in Caserta, a city south of Pagliarone in the Campania region of Italy. He waited there for his next orders that would never come. Mussolini's army was in disarray. My father also learned that the ship from which he had disembarked in Naples was bombed and sunk as it was on its way back to North Africa.

In July of 1943 Benito Mussolini was arrested and soon after, the Fascist Grand Council gave him a vote of no confidence. King Vittorio

Emanuele III replaced Mussolini, with Marshal Pietro Badoglio as prime minister. Mussolini was moved around to various islands and other areas of Italy. Eventually he was held captive in the Hotel Campo Imperatore at a ski area in the Gran Sasso Mountains, within the region of *Abruzzo e Molise*. Acting on personal orders of Adolf Hitler, Mussolini was rescued during a daring raid by German Commandos and flown to a military airport near Rome, and then to Vienna, Austria. Hitler informed *Il Duce* (the name that Mussolini gave himself, meaning 'the leader') that Hitler was forming a new Nazi-backed Italian fascist State. It would be called the Italian Social Republic, later referred to as the Salo Republic. It was named after the town of Salo, its de facto capital on Lake Garda in northern Italy.

In nearby Naples there was an uprising against the German army, which was retreating north through Italy. The Italian resistance fighters were all around, and many Italian soldiers began to fight alongside the Allies as a result of the publication on September 8, 1943 stating that an armistice had been signed on September 3, 1943 in Cassibile, Sicily between the Kingdom of Italy and the Allies. The armistice presented a total surrender of Italy. But part of the Italian army ignored the surrender and remained loyal to Mussolini. As a result of this division, Italy was plunged into a civil war. Of course Hitler was very upset by the situation in Italy and sent several divisions there to officially protect it from the Allies; but in reality Hitler intended to control the country.

Days before the Germans appeared in our village, passenger trains and freight trains coming from the north were jammed with Italian soldiers trying to make their way back home from various fronts. They were hungry, thirsty, and some very ill as a result of smoke inhalation from the long railroad tunnel just north of the village that filled with smoke from the locomotives. Women of the village gave bread, potatoes, and whatever else they could, but this was not nearly enough to feed the numerous pleading soldiers.

Disenchanted and confused with Mussolini's war, my father, Vittorio, decided to throw down his weapon and make his way back home — hopefully before the Germans got there — so he could protect his family. He borrowed an army pack mule and headed north for home. He sought the help of rural farmers for directions and for some food. He spent the nights near farmhouses, sleeping with one eye open, making sure that the stolen mule would not be stolen! This mule was used primarily to carry supplies and was not very interested in being mounted by people. So my father walked the fifty-plus miles, as the mule carried his personal belongings and some other items he had "borrowed" from the base; items that would be very useful back in Pagliarone. My father justified taking as much as possible because the Germans would have eventually loaded everything on the trains that were headed for Germany.

Vittorio was always on the lookout for the enemy, but who was the enemy? At this point he decided that everyone he encountered was an adversary. After a few days and nights of dodging numerous hostile soldiers, he was back with his family in Pagliarone. The people of Trebbante were the first to see the soldier pulling a mule on the walking path leading to their small enclave. Fiorindo Carmosino was overjoyed to see that it was Vittorio, his son-in-law. His family and friends were glad that he was home safe and alive. But the pains of war were not far behind, and would revisit him in his own house.

My mother told many stories of those difficult and terrifying war years. 1944 was an especially difficult and horrible period. The village had already been stripped of the most able-bodied people who would normally till the soil. Those strong young men were now in some faraway front fighting a war. My mom remembers the long winter of 1943-44, the heavy snowfalls, the loud noises, and the bombings just across the mountain, and wondering what was going on at the other side of those peaks. When I mentioned to her years later that it was probably the bombing of the Abbey of Montecassino, she vaguely remembered people talking about it. I wonder if any of them were aware that a young man from their village – someone's nephew, cousin, or friend – was there fighting against the Italians and the Germans. That young man was an Italian-American immigrant named Giuseppe Iacovetta.

📖 The Abbey of Montecassino was founded on a hilltop near the town of Cassino in the year 529 by Saint Benedict of Nursia, *San Benedetto da Norcia*. The Abbey had been home to many monks including Saint Thomas Aquinas in 1230.

Normally the Germans, especially the top brass, looted everything they could get ahold of throughout the countries they conquered. They shipped the treasures back to Germany and Switzerland to add to their private collections. Adolph Hitler and Reichsmarschall Hermann

Göring coveted and were the recipients of some of the greatest pieces of art in Western civilization. Surely the treasures of Montecassino were on their list. A German captain, Dr. Maximilian Becker (a doctor and an art aficionado who was assigned to the elite Hermann Göring Division) realized that because of the strategic location of the Abbey, it was in grave danger of possible destruction and the probable loss of the irreplaceable treasures that it contained. Without authorization, Dr. Becker, with the help of Colonel Julius Schlegel, put a plan in motion to remove some 1,400 artifacts from the Abbey, away from danger.

For over two weeks, the numerous pieces of art were crated and then, during nighttime, over 100 trucks full of artifacts delivered the items to an undisclosed storage location in Rome. During the process it was revealed to Dr. Becker that the Abbey also contained most of the city of Naples' art treasures, as they were taken there for safekeeping during the German retreat. Dr. Becker and Italian art officials became suspicious of the Germans' intention of the final destination of the art collection. Becker and the Italians feared that the whole collection would eventually make its way to Berlin and other secret locations. They pleaded for help, and with the steady stream of newspaper stories from abroad, the Germans, against their usual practice, gave in to the strenuous requests and finally delivered the treasures to the Vatican. Later it was found that two trucks full of handpicked artifacts from Montecassino never made it to Rome, but instead arrived in Berlin, just in time for a birthday gift for Hermann Göring.

Regrettably, a decision by the Allies was made to bomb the monastery because they were convinced that the Germans had occupied it, and the Abbey was a strategic part of the German "Gustav Line" of defense. The German commander-in-chief ordered German units not to occupy the Abbey or make it part of their defensive positions, and allegedly informed the Vatican and the Allies of this. This was definitely out of the ordinary for the Germans; the Allies obviously did not believe them and carried out their bombing. Thankfully, most of the monks and civilians had evacuated the structure. By February 15, 1944, only Abbot Gregorio Diamare, a few monks, and about 250 civilians were inside the monastery when Allied air force bombers – the largest concentration of bombers the Allies had ever sent against a single structure – flew over the Abbey. The 1,150 tons of explosives and incendiary bombs reduced the entire top of the mountain to a mass of rubble.

Later investigations confirmed that there were no German soldiers in the Abbey at the time of the bombing, but they did occupy the ruins after the bombing, which made great defensive positions. By the end of the battles around Montecassino, a total of 185,000 casualties were recorded. The abbot and some monks survived the bombing by hiding in the deepest crevices of the Abbey.

Nowadays, as we drive down *l'autostrada del sole*, motorway of the sun, the *A1* — a highway that connects Milan with Naples up on the north side of the highway — the massive white stone structure comes into view. After the war, the Abbey of *Monte Cassino* was rebuilt to its original scale. With the Abbey in view, we knew that soon we would get off the highway and head east-northeast for Isernia, towards our village.

Monte Cassino in ruins, February 1944

In 1944 the Germans were retreating from Africa and southern Italy, heading north towards Germany, and Pagliarone was in their path. My mom recalls the horror as the Germans bombed bridges and tunnels. The final blow to our beloved railroad came one day when the people of Pagliarone heard a racket coming from the south, past the village of Cerreto. As my mom told the story in our dialect, "*neh treneh keh nah cosa anniand tagliava tutte le traverse della ferrovia*" (*un treno con qualcosa davanti tagliava le traverse*, a train with a devise in front of it cut the railroad ties). The German soldiers had orders from their commanders, from their Führer, to go for total destruction of train tracks, bridges, factories, and when necessary, whole towns. The famous railroad ten-column bridge of our town was saved by a courageous act of a young man, Carlo Carmosino, who

Monte Cassino rebuilt, 1964

had explosives experience. He sneaked onto the bridge and dismantled the explosive charges that had been set by the Germans before they headed north.

The Germans forced the villagers out of their homes, ate what little food they had, and loaded even their simplest possessions on trains headed north for Germany. The people of the town were hiding their livestock and other possessions in caves in the nearby forests. My dad and his brothers, Umberto and Alduino, hid theirs in our land called *Friatt,* *Fratte* (meaning an area with a

One of the railroad bridges of Pagliarone, 1975

dense growth of trees and shrubs) avoiding German soldiers patrolling the railroad nearby. They prayed that a cow would not moo or a sheep would not bleat, because certainly the Germans would hear them and take the livestock and possibly shoot my dad and uncles dead and leave them in the remote cave. During my childhood I would often visit the caves, the place where my family had spent many days and nights protecting their animals, waiting for the German soldiers to leave.

One morning, shortly after sunrise, my father and Uncle Umberto, thinking that there would not be any German patrols, took the army mule to gather some wood. They came around a bend in the road and saw four German soldiers walking towards them. My father and uncle quickly turned and began to run, as gunshots rang past their ears. They stopped and waited for the Germans to approach them. They realized that their mule would be taken, but also feared that they would be shot or arrested and then taken to some faraway war front. The soldiers took the mule and then started shouting something in German at my dad and uncle; waving, pointing their weapons at them, and finally motioning for them to go.

My father and his brother quickly walked away, looking over their shoulders for fear that they would be shot in the back, but they only saw a soldier attempting to mount the mule. This mule was not happy with the idea of being ridden and started to buck, throwing the soldier to the ground. It galloped away with the Germans in chase, but the soldiers eventually gave up trying to catch him. My father and his brother were hiding behind some bushes on a hilltop. They eventually sneaked around the patrolling soldiers and began their search for the mule, finding it grazing in a field nearby. Then they quietly went back to the cave where they were hiding.

During those anxious days people stayed in hiding most of the time, but eventually they ran out of food and other supplies. One afternoon, my mother and Rosa, a neighbor, decided to walk to the neighboring town of San Pietro Avellana to attempt to buy some sugar and salt. The Germans had moved on, so *Mamma* and her friend felt that it was safe enough to travel. As they walked on the dirt pathway towards *Sand Pietr*, San Pietro, ten kilometers north of Pagliarone, they heard noises. The noises got louder and louder, and then the women realized that something was flying over their heads. They were in the midst of a cross fire between the Germans and the advancing Allies. The women crouched down in fear as the battle ensued, watching trees being cut down as though they were twigs. This seemed to last an eternity but finally subsided, giving them an opportunity to run back towards Pagliarone, ignoring the warning given by my father to keep an eye out for land mines set by the Germans. Luckily they made it back home safely, but badly shaken.

Later that week the people were shocked to hear that *i Tedeschi*, the Germans, had pretty much destroyed nearby towns. In San Pietro, only a church stood in the rubble. The nearby town of Castel di Sangro was also leveled. The German S.S. even shot some men in the town square, accusing them of housing Allied paratroopers and/or Jewish families. My mom told me that many of the resulting homeless people from San Pietro Avellana took refuge in our village, where the locals took in some of those shattered neighbors. She remembered the look of despair on their faces, their only possession being the clothes on their back. Some of the refugees mentioned that it would have been better to be entombed under the rubble of their homes, because now the hope of a better tomorrow looked hopeless. I recall her mentioning that the lost souls they took in were somehow related, probably relatives of my grandmother, Bambina, whose mother hailed from San Pietro Avellana.

To avoid aerial attacks, the Germans had decided to take back roads, as opposed to main highways, during their retreats. They set up fortification lines in the area where Pagliarone lay. To the north was the German Gustav Line and to the south was the Barbara Line. Our village lay right in the midst of these defensive lines. These fortification lines were designed mainly to keep the Allies from reaching Rome.

As the Germans retreated north, the Allied Fifth Army followed. Only one third of the army was American soldiers, another third was English, and one third was comprised of soldiers from Brazil, Belgium, France, India, New Zealand, North Africa, Canada, Poland, and other Allied nations. Visions of soldiers handing out chocolate bars might come to mind, but in my family's experience, this did not take place very often. Some of the soldiers actually took up unwelcomed residence in the town's houses and made themselves at home, just as the Germans had done earlier. The concerned mothers kept their daughters hidden, just as they had done with the Germans for fear of their being raped.

As the allied chase of the Germans moved north, Pagliarone and its people began to return to some sort of normalcy. But sad news would come daily of badly wounded and dead soldiers from our town. The number of women dressed in black dresses and men in black shirts, ties, black buttons and armbands was growing, as they honored their dead relatives. Black was the only color many people would wear for many years, and the wives and moms wore black for the rest of their lives, honoring their husbands and sons. Seven young men never returned home from the war, either dead or missing in action, a rather large number for a tiny remote town in the mountains of south central Italy.

Screams of joy and screams of terror could be heard intermittently, as news came to our town about the young soldiers who had been fighting in the war throughout Europe and its surrounding areas: Either a mother holding a letter to her heart, yelling sounds of joy after reading that her son was alive and coming home soon, or a mother holding a letter over her head, crying as loudly as only a mother can after reading that her son was dead or missing in action. That terrible war dug broad wounds, even in a small remote village deep in the Apennine Mountains of Italy.

The tragedy of that awful war would not end with the death and injury of young soldiers; rather it also took the life of a young boy, Giovanni Iacovetta. In the winter of 1944, a group of young kids was playing in

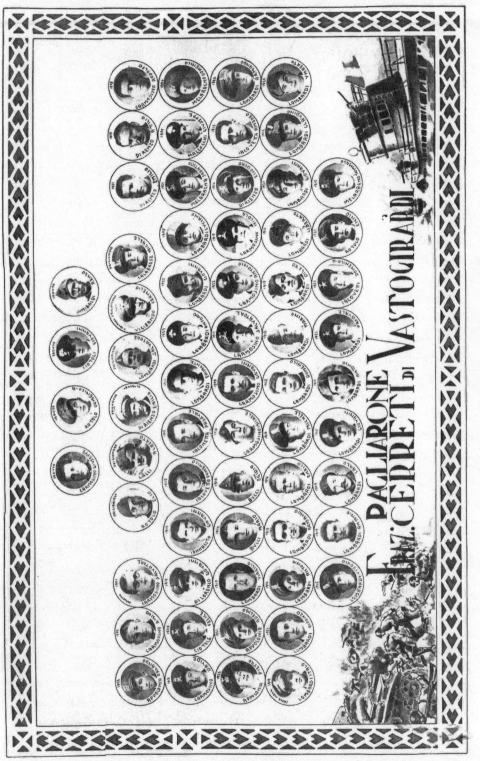

The WWII soldiers of Pagliarone and Cerreto, circa 1940

a field near our town, when a girl, Maria Carmosino, found a shiny object. The kids gathered together and inspected the beautiful, strange toy that had a chain hanging from its casing. While a boy was holding the object between his legs, another decided to pull on the shiny chain. The explosion was heard by most residents of the town and they ran to the area where it came from. The explosion of the hand grenade caused injury to most of the children. One little girl lost an eye and one boy suffered devastating leg injuries that would affect him for the rest of his life. And Giovanni Iacovetta could not overcome his numerous injuries. He died a few days later in the hospital.

As a child I remember a commotion around town when a farmer, while plowing his field, unearthed a bomb! Fortunately it did not explode and the authorities hauled away this reminder of World War II. Farmers would find unexploded bombs and other war reminders in their fields well into the 1960s.

The railroad and most roads were destroyed in the war, neighboring towns leveled, and lives ruined. The physical and mental rebuilding process would take years. The rail line that connected Castel Di Sangro to the north and Carovilli to the south would not be rebuilt until 1960. I recall vividly as *la lettorina*, *littorina*, the small passenger train, wound its way over the bridge, stopping for the first time in a long time at the tiny train station of Villa San Michele. People were waiting anxiously to celebrate the occasion, and some waited to board it for a ride to the next town. Quality of life improved tremendously with the trains running again, as the isolated village once again started its journey to modernization. My father even landed a part-time job with the railroad and our family actually experienced, for the first time, some real monetary income.

La lettorina, the small passenger train

It is inconceivable to think that my parents and other married couples of the village were able to marry and start a family during those tumultuous war years. My parents were blessed with their first child, a baby girl named Bambina, born on September 28, 1942. Sadly, she died on the 29th of

January 1943, at only four months old. My father was not there for her birth or her death; he was in Africa fighting a war. She became ill and died on a very cold winter morning. Periodically we would ask *Mamma* how sister Bambina died, and she always replied that she got sick and there was no doctor available. Even if one could be found, he would not have come to Luigi in the cold, snowy weather. So a few days after she became very ill, she died.

On June 14, 1944 a son was born and my parents named him Ezio Giovanni. My brother thinks he was named Ezio because he was born on *il Giorno di Santo Ezio*, Saint Ezio's Day, but probably not, because *Santo Ezio's* Day was on March 6. He was named so because my father broke the longstanding tradition of the firstborn son of a firstborn being named after the paternal grandfather. My father had not heard from his father, Pietrantonio, for many years and assumed that his father had abandoned his family back in Italy. In protest, my father refused to name his first son Pietrantonio, his father's name.

On February 2, 1948 a daughter was born, whom they named Maria Bambina, in honor of my father's deceased mother.

While trying to put the war and its devastation behind them and working hard to raise a family, my parents were hit again with more painful memories of World War II. On November 22, 1951 my father was served and charged by the Military War Tribunal with desertion. They were very worried that my father could possibly go to prison. On May 28, 1952 he and other war veterans from the village had to present themselves at the Military Tribunal in the southern city of Bari. Thankfully they were all acquitted of the crime, the Tribunal stating that due to the extreme circumstances during those last days of the war, the soldiers did not commit the crime of desertion. But my father would have to wait until 1963 to receive an honorable discharge from the Italian Army. In June of 1972, *Caporalmaggiore*, Corporal Major, Vittorio Lombardi was presented in absentia (he was in America) with a *Croce di Merito*, Merit Cross, for his almost six years of service in the Second World War.

During the Christmas season of 1952, my siblings — Maria, age five, and brother Ezio, age nine — were excited in anticipation of a new addition joining the family. A month earlier, their mom, Maria Lucia, had become increasingly ill and finally had to be rushed to the hospital in Agnone, a mountaintop town about 26 kilometers (15 miles) northeast of Pagliarone, where she eventually had her gallbladder removed. The operation was a dangerous procedure in those days and it was compounded by her late term pregnancy. The operation was successful and the surgeon jokingly told my father, "*Auguri per un figlio maschio,*" Congratulations on a baby son. The two children would ask every night where their mother was, and *Papà* would reassure them that she was fine and would be home soon. But she would spend more than a month in the hospital.

On the cold and snowy night of January 9, 1953, my mother and

Croce di Merito, Merit Cross

the village's midwife, *Zia* Vincenza, a sweet elderly relative, sat around the fireplace trying to stay warm. They would spend most of the night there, dealing with labor pains. Finally at 5:30 a.m. on Saturday, January 10 a baby boy was born. "*Si nat prupia attuorn ar fuoke, (Sei nato propio attorno al focolare,* You were born literally in front of the fireplace), my mother would tell me. My cries woke up Maria and Ezio, and they joined *Mamma e Papà* around the fireplace with the new addition. The doctor was correct in predicting a boy. That morning my father walked through several inches of snow to Trebbante to give my mother's family the news of the birth of the baby boy. All babies born in Pagliarone were delivered at home with the help of only a self-made midwife. My mother told me stories of babies born around the same time as I, about how she and other new mothers would share their full breasts of milk with the babies of mothers whose breasts had little milk.

In those days there was still a practice of wrapping babies from neck to toe with *fascia*, cotton strands of fabric, believing that this would avoid deformities and make bones grow straight! Also, these swaddling wraps allowed the babies to adjust to their new environment more gradually, since they were used to their confined space of the womb. At about three months old, the arms would not be wrapped, allowing movement. The rest of the body was sometimes wrapped until the baby started to walk. Thank God my mom did not wrap me with *fascia*, as the practice was fading. Surely it caused physical and emotional damage to numerous babies. Although I remember seeing some babies wrapped like mummies, the practice eventually was abandoned.

My grandfather, Pietrantonio, living in Denver, had reestablished contact with his family back in Pagliarone and was even sending money and packages with assortments of desperately needed supplies to his family. So his oldest son, Vittorio, would honor his absent father by naming his second son Pietrantonio (PeterAnthony), in honor of his father. Priests, nuns, and teachers called me Pietrantonio, but around our village I was known as Toni or Tonino (meaning small or young Toni). The nickname was extracted from Pietran<u>oni</u>o and the more popular An<u>oni</u>o.

I do not recall any birthday celebrations for me or other residents in our village. I doubt we even knew what day of the week it was. My first birthday celebration was my sixteenth, in America. The birthdays before that are just a blur. The only thing I remember is my mother saying, "*come vuoieh siveh nateh,*" *a questo giorno sei nato,* reminding me that on that day I was born; and my birthday gift was her telling her story of that special night of my birth! More importance seemed to be placed on one's name-day, *onomastico.* I actually recall my sister and other kids wishing me *buon onomastico* on June 13, Saint Anthony Day.

My mother and all other pregnant women of the town were hardly ever examined by a doctor, and the babies were usually not seen by any medical professionals. I recall a nurse giving me and the rest of the children of the village a smallpox vaccine in the late-fifties, and that was as close as we got to being examined by a medical professional. The permanent scar on my left arm is a constant reminder of the day we all lined up at school to receive the vaccine. The usual lack of trained medical care meant there were unfortunately many times when babies were stillborn or died during or soon after birth. Sometimes both mother and baby would lose their lives.

Chapter III

LE SCUOLE · THE SCHOOLS

From an early age, my older brother, Ezio, showed no interest in formal education. The nuns who taught school in Pagliarone would tell my parents that Ezio had difficulties focusing, that his mind was somewhere else. That "somewhere else" was our fields and our livestock. My sister remembers the total non-interest in education by our brother and many of the other older boys when they were in school in the Castra neighborhood of Pagliarone, a hamlet about one kilometer east of Luigi.

The construction of the school was made possible by the hard work of the town's priest, Don Edolo Casacchia. He was able to raise enough funds to build the schoolhouse. He was also instrumental in bringing in three nuns to run the school. The school was named *Immacolata Regina di Pace*, Immaculate Queen of Peace. The sisters were able not only to teach the children, but also the many other inhabitants of the town, who looked to them for help with medical and social needs. Parents were able to leave the small ones in the kindergarten all day while they tended to the fields.

The school in the Castra neighborhood of Pagliarone, 1990

My brother, Ezio, and sister, Maria, have fond memories of one of those sisters. Her name was *Suora Mattia*, Sister Mattia. They remember her making visits to our house to give advice, but mostly to talk about Ezio. He just did not like school. On one school day, Sister Mattia called on Ezio to come to the front of the classroom and write a letter on the *lavagna*, blackboard. My brother stood up and informed the nun that this whole school thing was a waste of his time and that he had better things to do. There was a lot of work in the fields and his animals needed attention. So instead of going to the front of the class, he headed for the door and calmly walked out of the classroom and headed towards Luigi.

That night the nun paid my parents another visit. As a result, my brother had to endure the pain from slaps delivered by my father. Crying and very upset, the twelve-year-old ran out the door. Normally he would go hide in the barn, but knowing that that would be the first place my mom would go to find him, he hid under a woodpile down the hill from our house. He fell asleep and spent the night there while my mom spent the night awake, waiting for him to come through the door. He unwillingly returned to school, but his lack of interest and concentration robbed him of any real education. He was a very happy boy when school was finally over for him after the fifth grade.

The school teachers who came to Pagliarone were presented not only with the job of educating us, but also with the monumental task of breaking us from using our dialect by teaching us an almost completely different language, formal Italian. The Florentine dialect was adopted by Italy as proper Italian, as a result of the widely read writings of the Late Middle Ages poet, Dante Alighieri, in his epic allegorical poems titled *Commedia*, Divine Comedy. Some of the students and parents were not very interested in learning this new language. That language was only for the people who were high on the social ladder, such as politicians, priests, doctors, lawyers, and teachers. What need was there to waste all this time learning this strange language, when the fact of the matter was that most of the kids in town would grow up to eventually plow fields and look after animals, which certainly did not necessitate the use of proper Italian.

My sister continued her education after fifth grade. The school in our village only offered education up to the fifth grade. If students wanted to continue with higher education, they would have to take the train or bus to schools in bigger neighboring towns. My sister decided to attend *le scuole medie*, the middle school, in Castel di Sangro. I went there once and it seemed more like an orphanage for girls than a school, and indeed it was also an orphanage. It was operated by our priest, Don Edolo Casacchia, who had also been the pastor of the church in our village from 1943 to 1949. He was instrumental in attempting to take our town out of its archaic past and into the modern era. He even installed *l'altoparlante*, a loudspeaker, on top of *Colle dei Noci*, the hill that separates old Pagliarone from the new town of Villa San Michele. Every morning and evening, Don Edolo would play music and inform the people of Pagliarone on a variety of subjects; information that they would otherwise never be aware of or even know existed.

Many girls from our village attended school in that edifice, which in an earlier time was a *birreria*, a brewery, for their continuing education. But many returned to Villa San Michele to work the land and wait for the next aspect in their lives: find a mate and marry. At the age of fourteen my sister continued her education and went to a school in Roccaraso, a ski town north of Villa San Michele. She wanted to eventually work in the ski resort industry. My mom and I went to visit her there a couple of times. That was the farthest place from our village I had ever been to as a young boy. It seemed so far away, but in reality it was a distance of only about twenty miles. Maybe it seemed so far from home because it was so different from our village. Roccaraso was a beautiful ski resort, with fancy cars and elegant people. My sister quit that program after she met Vittorio Ienco, the man who would become her husband.

Our parents were happy to be informed by the nun teaching *l'asilo*, kindergarten, that their youngest son, Pietrantonio, was doing very well, and suggested that he should be moved up to first grade. So at the tender age of five, I skipped most of kindergarten and went on to grade one. According to a loving mom's account, even though I evidently did well in first grade, my parents decided to keep me in grade one for another year, mainly so I could be with kids my own age. Schoolwork seemed to be easy for me. I did not necessarily love it but, unlike my older brother, I embraced it. Watching my brother doing all that hard work in the fields and taking care of our livestock, I opted to milk the education angle for as long as possible.

On a cold, wintry afternoon at the age of nine, a moment of fame developed for me that would cause my young life to take a drastic turn. A substitute teacher had been teaching the fifth grade class. The students were given a math assignment for homework by their regular teacher, who was at home in another town, ill. None of the students in the class, including the substitute teacher, could solve the math assignment. Someone suggested that Tonino in the fourth grade be given a shot at the solution because, supposedly, I did well with that subject. I solved that math problem and the next day at the *edificio*, our schoolhouse, I was paraded to the fifth grade classroom where I showed the regular teacher how I solved the math problem. I don't remember what it was, but I recall something about a train leaving a rail station at a certain time and traveling to another location at some distance, at an average speed, etc. News spread around the small village and from that day on, I was sort of thought of as *lo studioso*, the studious one.

Unfortunately, that tag indirectly cost me two years of my young life away from my family and friends, as my father's godson and my future godfather, Davide Carmosino, kept urging my father to send me away to a school, a monastery, operated by Franciscan monks, where I could be challenged.

I enjoyed school, at least more than I enjoyed working the fields and looking after our animals. But every morning before we left for school, we had a number of chores that needed to be performed. I recall feeding our chickens and getting eggs from the chicken coop below our house, while my sister fed the pigs. We would then go to the barn and help my brother milk the cows, carrying the pail of milk back to the house where my mom was waiting. Mom would warm the milk in a pot that hung from a chain in our fireplace to begin the process of making cheese.

Our chores differed according to the time of year and temperature, but for sure, some work needed to be done before I could put on my *grembiule*, apron, that was dark blue with white ribbons sewn on the front left chest. Each ribbon represented a grade. For example, when I was in third grade there were three ribbons sewn to the *grembiule*. With *la borsa*, a school bag, off to school I went. All of the students looked basically the same with the *grembiule*, uniform, not that any of us had the opportunity to differentiate ourselves with better clothes or fancier shoes. For the most part we were all in the same economic status: poor. We were in school for most of the day, including Saturday, from eight in the morning until two in the afternoon, which left enough time in the day to go home and help the family with chores. We all studied hard, knowing that the difficult exams awaited us at the end of the school year.

Third grade class, 1963, and our teacher, Matilde Spina.
I am to the right of the priest, Don Antonio Di Lorenzo.

As summer approached, we all anxiously awaited *gli esami*, the final exams. A member of the provincial school board would come to Villa San Michele to administer tests to all the students in every grade. These exams were both oral and written. The oral part was the most challenging. The students would be asked to solve a math problem on the blackboard, fill in countries on the African continent, recite a poem, and so forth.

The whole village was anxious during these exams. Three different scenarios could materialize: One, if a student performed well on the exam, he or she would be *promosso*, promoted, to the next grade. Two, if you did not pass all of the tests, you were *rimandato*, sent back, and given the opportunity to go to summer school to improve on the failed subjects and be re-tested again in September. Then if you passed, you would move on to the next grade; if not, you would have to repeat the grade. Three, if you failed the exam miserably, you would be *bocciato*, failed, and would have to repeat that grade in the coming year. Of the three, *rimandato* was the worst scenario because it meant that you would not be able to help the family with the hectic summer chores while attending summer school.

The week before my fifth grade exams, I came down with mumps, *orecchioni*. Mumps is a viral infection that attacks the salivary glands, causing fever, lack of appetite, tiredness, and swollen salivary glands. It seemed that no child in town was spared. Everyone at one time or another had swollen glands and jaws. The day before the exams, my teacher walked the short distance from *l'edificio*, the schoolhouse, in Villa San Michele to our *barracca*, our tiny house, to see me and urged my parents to send me to school for the exams the next day. The teachers wanted to make a good showing at these exams, as it would show that they were doing a good job. So with my swollen neck, I went to school and passed the exams with flying colors, earning a huge hug from my *maestra*, teacher. Primary school was over and now I had the opportunity to go on to *le scuole medie*, middle school.

L'edificio, The elementary school, photographed in 2012,
is now a community center called Il Circolo, The Circle.

I looked forward to summer, although it meant a lot of hard work in the fields and tending to our animals. It would also be a very anxious summer, because my parents awaited news from the Franciscan monastery in Todi, a town in the north central region of Umbria. My godfather assured them that the monks would take me with open arms because of my excellent school grades. So I was worried about the possibility of leaving the safe and simple life of my village for a Franciscan monastery in the faraway and different world of Todi.

Schoolmates from top left: Giuseppe Flagiello, Michelina Carmosino, Franca Lombardi,
Lucia Lombardi, Carmelina Melaragno, Giuseppina Lombardi, Natalina Lombardi,
Sabatino Melaragno, Sandro Lombardi, Salvatore Lombardi.
Bottom left: Pietrantonio Lombardi, Giulio Carmosino, Antonio Melaragno, Pasquale Lombardi,
Maria Carmosino, Adelia Carmosino, Luisa Melaragno, Ilde Carmosino,
with our teacher Maltilde Spina in the back, 1964.

Chapter IV

LA BOTTIGLIA D'ACQUA
THE WATER BOTTLE

The bottle was scratched and chipped. It had a dark green tint and an old cork top that had seen better days. It was a two-liter size, but it seemed bigger and heavier than that in the eyes of a six-year-old. Every night my dad would send me to Luigi's fountain to get fresh cold water for our dinner. The water in the *conca*, basin, which was perched on a concrete corner counter in our modest kitchen, was warm and stale. I carried the bottle down the stairs from our *loggia*, balcony, making a sharp right turn down past our chicken coop. Then I headed down the dirt footpath. The path was scattered with stones, which caused people to twist their feet; although the stones became handy during rainy and wet days, when we stepped on them to keep out of the mud that seemed to be all around. The fountain was a couple hundred yards west, at the end of our *borgo*, hamlet.

The water is flowing stronger fifty years later. Pietrantonio Lombardi, Ezio Lombardi,
zia Leontina Lombardi Carmosino, Maria Lombardi Ienco. 2014.

As I had done many times before, I carefully lifted the bottle and held it under the spigot that spit out that natural cold water. It took all my strength to hold the bottle, which was getting heavier and heavier as it filled up with *acqua fresca*, fresh water. Wrapping my small hands around the wet, slippery bottle, I headed towards home where my family was gathering for our simple dinner. At times I would envision dropping the bottle and breaking it. This caused me to be extra careful, watching every step I took.

On that hot summer night, as the sun dropped behind our mountains and nightfall loomed, I noticed my friend, Pasqualino, sitting outside his house. He wanted me to go with him to shoot our slingshots before it got too dark and hopefully, for once in our lives, we would hit a bird. I told him that I would hurry and be back as soon as possible. As I turned to run home, the bottle slipped out of my hands and as I tried to catch it, I saw the rock next to me. The bottle smacked that rock, shattering it into what seemed a hundred pieces.

Spot where I dropped the bottle in 1959. The stone that broke the bottle
was barely visible after fifty-three years when I photographed it in 2012.

The noise brought neighbors outside, all staring at me and the broken bottle in amazement. I knew I was in big trouble when I saw Pasqualino's mom, Giulia, grasping her hands and lifting them over her head, the gesture meaning big trouble. In today's world, that incident would be equal to a kid getting into a car and driving it through his family's closed garage door! I was petrified, scared, and ashamed for what I had done. There was no way I was going home, so I ran to our barn and hid in the hayloft.

I could hear my mom calling my name, *"Toni, Tonino."* I sat there in stifling heat, worried about snakes that might slither by and about my impending punishment, as darkness engulfed the barn. That bottle was an irreplaceable item in our scarcely equipped kitchen, a useful commodity — and I broke it. As darkness totally took over the barn, I had to choose between the scary, dark barn and the snakes, or the pain of the sure beating from my dad. Hearing a strange sound from the depths of the barn, I scrambled out of there and ran the short distance home. My mother, my savior, smoothed things over and saved me from the *schiaffi alla faccia*, slaps to the face, from my father.

Unfortunately, my mother would have to go every night with *la conca e la spara*, the copper basin, and the labrum (a round, doughnut-like cushion to balance *la conca* on top of the head) to get water. Carrying the heavy load on top of her head was not easy after a long day working the fields. This task was off limits to males. It would be the equivalent to a man wearing a dress in today's American culture. Later on that summer I was sent to fetch fresh water in an aluminum bucket!

Girls from our village with la conca e la spara, the copper basin and the labrum

I remember *il piattare*, the pots and pans vendor, yelling at the top of his lungs. You could hear him a mile away, singing a catchy phrase that would hopefully motivate the masses to buy his wares. Each vendor had his own unique, catchy phrases that we usually memorized and repeated at some opportune time. My mom and I walked the short distance down the hill to the rough dirt road where he had all his wares laid out on a canvas tarp: pots, pans, forks, spoons, dishes, bottles. My mom would look at all of them. She could have used a new pot to make her *polenta* or a new bottle to fetch water.

My son, Dominic, finds our coffee pot under some debris, 1990.

This memory, as with many others, is a reminder to me of the extent of poverty in our village and how important every little item that we possessed was to our survival.

In 1975 my wife, Jackie, and I traveled to Italy for our honeymoon and visited my hometown. It had been nine years since my family had left Italy, left that old farm house. Jackie and I walked into the kitchen and the aluminum bucket still sat on the corner counter in the empty, abandoned, dusty house. The bottle incident came back to me as I walked with her to the fountain. I stopped on the very spot where the bottle had broken, right in front of Giulia and Ginuccio's house. A large rock was sticking out of the ground, bigger than the rest. Was that the same rock? I stared at it for a moment and my wife gave me a confused gaze. I told her the story as we sat on the worn rock ledge of the fountain. *Antonio la fonde*, as he was called because he lived near the fountain, and his wife, Lucia, were watching us curiously from their old house above Luigi's fountain.

Back at our weathered house, I was surprised that *la cundra*, the cradle, made by my great-grandfather, was the same cradle that my grandfather and father slept in as babies, as did my siblings and I. The cradle was nestled under spider webs in the bedroom, next to the taller, larger *cundra*. Somehow my wife convinced me to take the smaller cradle back to Denver. She also wanted the taller one, but I did not want any part of the hassle of hauling it back home. I now regret that decision. We could have shipped it back, and that was our plan when we went back to Italy in 1990, but unfortunately the big *cundra* was gone. We gathered all that was left in the house: some pots and pans, an old picture hanging on a crumbling wall. A faded green jacket

I am sitting on la cundra, the cradle, in 1975, Jackie next to me with friend Valentina Flagiello, her son, Michele, and Cousin Adelia Carmosino. The small rush seat chair is sitting in the same place as I remember it.

hanging in the bedroom brought back vivid memories of my brother, Ezio, walking behind our cows with that jacket on.

My kids and their babies have slept in that small cradle, the one made by my great-grandfather, Giuseppe, so many years ago. I look for it every time we go to our son's house, making sure that it's being preserved for future generations.

la cundra

Chapter V

La Terra · The Land

The first recollection I have of leaving the surroundings of Pagliarone was when I followed my mom as we walked on the railroad tracks and other pathways, on our way to another town. It seemed to take forever as I lagged behind on my short four-year-old legs. I could not keep up, and my mom would turn and wait for me with her arm extended, waiting to give me her smile and her hand in support. We finally reached our destination, Carovilli, a town about eight kilometers southeast of our town. I recall her handing a man some coins, and he in return handed my mother a bottle. Years later I was reminiscing with my mom and I learned that she had traveled to Carovilli for *la penicillina*, penicillin. Before then, my world consisted of only our valley and the surrounding mountains.

On the long summer days of the late 1950s, all of the kids from the small hamlet of Luigi would gather and sit on some stone wall and we would stare at the tall mountains surrounding Pagliarone. We often wondered what we would encounter if we climbed to the top and looked on the other side. Would it be different than this side or just more of the same? The few square kilometers of landscape around our village was all we knew, all we had experienced. As a small child, I had no idea what lay beyond those mountains. And for some of the adults of the town, the wonderment was the same as mine. Their village and the land surrounding it was the only life they knew, the only place they were accustomed to. That land was their world. They did not even have the opportunity to learn of other people and places from an old, battered geography or history book, because most of them never went to school. Some could not even sign their name. The only signature they knew was the one they put on their piece of Pagliarone's dirt on a daily basis.

Pagliarone's mountains, 2012

My father and my older brother, Ezio, would leave the house at dawn, as all the roosters sang their wakeup call to the village. They headed for some plot of land, many times hours away, with our dependable donkey loaded with whatever tools that were needed for that day's work. If it was early spring, they would bring *zappe*, hoes, and usually a load of cow or sheep manure to fertilize the plot of land that was going to be prepared for planting. *Grano*, wheat, *orzo*, barley, *patate*, potatoes, *barbabietole*, beets, *granoturco*, corn, and fava and garbanzo beans were the basic plants we cultivated. Years before, these plots of land had been cleared of most of the naturally abundant rocks. Many rocks remained, though, and some new ones seemed to grow during the long winter months, inviting us to stack them onto *la macera*, the stone stacks that littered the landscape.

One of the many rock walls decorating Luigis' landscape, 2012

Throughout the summer months, days were long and hard. We would be out in the fields from dawn to dusk, tending to the many small patches of dirt that we owned or rented. Late summer/early fall was an important time in our daily quest for survival. God forbid if one of the worker bees got ill and was unable to contribute during that very important harvest time. Wheat had to be cut, gathered, and brought to harvest. Hay had to be *faviciata*, cut, gathered, bundled, loaded onto our donkey, and taken to our barn. Hopefully it was enough to sustain our animals through the cold winter months. Later, potatoes and beets would be unearthed, put into sacks, loaded onto our donkey, and brought to storage. Many times we would split up and go to different locations to perform the various tasks and endless work.

If the donkey was not overloaded, my brother would ride to the fields as my father led or followed it. That donkey seemed to always know where to go. As a small child, as young as three years old, I would sometimes tag along and help out in any way I could. Usually I would be given the job of watching over our donkey as she grazed. But as a very young child, most of the time I stayed behind and helped out at home. While my mother and sister, Maria, prepared the meal of the day, I fed our chickens and our pig.

As mid-morning approached, we would gather all the essentials and depart for the piece of ground that my father and brother had been working since dawn. My father would remark that Ezio's eyes were falling out of their sockets, straining to look up to see if we were approaching with the food. My mother would find a level, shaded spot under a tree and lay out a tablecloth on the ground, where she carefully placed our meal. Usually it would be *polenta* or pasta with *le polpette*, the cheese balls, not meatballs or *salsiccia*, sausage. Meat was very scarce, and the meatball was introduced and widely used by Italian-Americans in the United States, where meat was plentiful. In Italy, at least in our village, meat was a rarity. Of course bread was always included, as was some sort of fruit at the end of the meal.

Sometimes my father and brother would take a short nap, although they very rarely did so in the heat of harvest season. My sister and I would walk around the wheat field and pick up any loose wheat stalks that had fallen when the wheat was *mietuto*, reaped. There would absolutely be no waste; every grain was collected. We would do the same with our corn fields, walking up and down the rows of corn, making sure every ear of corn had been picked. The corn was transported by our donkey to our *fondaco*, storage room, and piled in a corner. Later, the whole family and friends gathered to help with the corn husking. All of the kids would sit on top of the pile and watch the huskers, primarily women, as they took the husks off the corn and then threw the ears into a bushel. Stories were told, songs were sung, we played, we helped, we listened, we learned.

If we were at a field where hay had been *falciato*, cut, we would all help rake the hay into a bundle and onto *la rete*, the netting, held together with a wooden pole on each end. These poles would be pulled together and tied, creating a large round bale that held the dried hay. The bales would then be loaded onto our donkey, one on each side, tied down with ropes on the saddle. These bales would have to be close to the same weight, or else when mounted onto the donkey they would cause an imbalance. I remember times when the saddle would turn completely to one side of the donkey, bringing the poor animal down on its side. Or, if these bales were too heavy, it would be very difficult to load, and the donkey's very strong legs would start to buckle from the excessive weight.

Donkey loaded with bales of hay on our ara, aia, looking west from our house in Luigi, 1975

My brother had difficulty recognizing when enough was enough. He and I were at *La via la Rocca*, the piece of land near Trebbante, my mom's hamlet. That piece of ground was part of the dowry she had received from her parents when she married my father. It was fertile land and hay was bountiful that year. We raked the dried hay all day, gathered it, piled it on to the net and baled it, as I kept a keen eye out for snakes. I remembered the year before when our family was at that same location raking hay. While piling the hay, Ezio noticed a snake tangled in his rake and he promptly killed it. Knowing the fear that my mother had of snakes, he placed the dead reptile on top of a pitch fork, topped with some hay, and then beckoned my mom to grab that last pile of hay under the fork, while we waited by the bigger pile under the netting. As she lifted the pitch fork the dead snake seemed to come slithering down towards her body. She let out the loudest scream and ran off. We laughed, she yelled at my brother, and then we all went back to work.

That late summer day, my brother wanted to finish that job; he was not interested in going back the next day to finish hauling the hay. He proceeded to make the biggest bales of hay I had ever seen and we barely had enough rope to tie the nets together. As a seven-year-old, even I realized that this was not going to be possible. I went to get the donkey as she napped lazily under a shade tree. Her only movement was her tail swatting the annoying summer flies away. I'd swear that she even had a puzzled look on her long, large face as I positioned her between the two rolls of hay. Ezio positioned himself behind one of the bales and attempted to lift it onto the donkey, with me ready to secure it with the saddle's ropes. He barely got the bale a few inches off the ground.

Ezio tried and tried again. With every attempt his cursing got a little louder and more descriptive. God and saints were invoked, the worst being *porca Madonna*, Virgin Mary the pig. It sounds terrible, but it was just a phrase invoked by even the holiest of our villagers, with no thought ever given to the actual meaning. When I asked my dad or brother why they invoked holy names when they cussed, they brushed it off and explained that it was just something to say when they were upset about something. *Porca Madonna*, *mannaggia Cristo*, and *porco di Dio* were some of the more popular cuss phrases.

My very frustrated brother then instructed me to take the donkey under *la macera*, a pile of crudely stacked rocks. Ezio then barely rolled the bales on top of the rocks and attempted to load them onto the donkey's back, as I held on to the confused animal. After repeated attempts, the donkey became frustrated and did not want any part of the unfamiliar undertaking. She became agitated and stopped cooperating, pulling away from the wall as I tried to make her stand still. My brother became very angry, screaming at her and me as he came down from the stone wall. He grabbed the bridle and yanked it wildly, causing the donkey's big eyes to become even bigger and more alarmed. As panic set in, the donkey pulled away from my brother's hold and ran around the hay field. Ezio finally caught her, but he was now crying and very upset. He then proceeded to bite the donkey on her face! The donkey let out a bray of surprise and pain. I immediately ran away from the chaotic scene, thinking that surely I would be his next victim.

The commotion beckoned one of my uncles working in a field nearby. He was able to calm my sixteen-year-old brother and our donkey. He shook his head in disbelief as he gazed at the enormous bales of hay. As dusk approached, with the help of my uncle, the smaller manageable bales were loaded onto our donkey and we headed back to Luigi, where my mom's eyes and ears were straining for any sign of her two sons.

When we got home, she yelled the usual at my brother, "*Mi si fatta ushì gl'uocchi*" (*Mi hai fatto uscire gl'occhi*, My eyes came out my eye sockets from straining), searching for any sight of him. Many times she would lament that although she could make out a donkey on the horizon, she hoped that the people following it would be us, but it usually turned out to be someone else. Those donkeys, they all looked remarkably alike. And the little boys following the donkeys all looked like her Tonino, until they got close enough to see it was another mom's Tonino. Tonino was the most common of the village's boys' names. Ezio was by far the most uncommon; in fact my brother was the only boy in the village with that name. Unfortunately for him, when someone said that it was Ezio who did it, there was no guessing which Ezio they were talking about.

Reminiscing back to those tough times, I can't help but think of the injustice that our forefathers bestowed on us. In an attempt to be fair to their heirs, they created a real mess of our land. What used to be a large piece of land, good for cultivation, was reduced to tiny little plots that were divided between sons and daughters through the many generations. All the wasted time walking to all the small pieces of wheat fields and hay fields made our lives even more difficult. I chuckle when I think of the miniscule pieces of dirt that we would cultivate. Some were as small as maybe six feet wide by thirty feet long.

With no real visible boundary lines, there were always conflicts with neighbors, usually with close relatives. I can easily awaken the memories of those anxious moments when my father had a dispute with one of his siblings because someone had cut some of the other's wheat, corn, or hay; or had even dug up some potatoes that belonged to the other by trespassing inches into the other's field. Worse yet were the confrontations as to the ownership of a certain piece of ground. Frequently the disagreements escalated into full-blown altercations, usually verbal but at times physical, which would cause families to go into the '*non si parlano*' mode, not talking to each other for months if not years.

The wives, the women of the families, would try to keep some sort of relationship going. The younger children were not affected by the conflicts, but as they got older they would have to take sides and respect their fathers' implied directives not to talk to some relative. The nerve-racking situation was taxing on whole families. It wasn't so easy to avoid someone whom you did not talk to when we all lived in a small, confined area. I can see my father walking past a relative on some narrow walking path and avoiding eye contact. Thankfully a family member or close friend would bring the quarreling siblings together to work out their differences, and all was good for a while — until the next conflict.

The most dependable of our animals. Donkeys were our trustworthy mode of transportation, shown here loaded with dried kindling and a wood container used to transport manure.

Trying out il falcione, 2014

Chapter VI

I Serpenti · The Snakes

Imagine a hot summer night, trying to sleep in the stifling heat, you look down and next to your bed a snake is slithering by. My sister and I screamed in horror, beckoning my father. The snake scurried away into the next bedroom with my father in chase. Under our dad's bed it went, escaping out of sight through a small hole between the wall and the wooden floor. Needless to say we hardly slept that night. I envisioned the snake crawling between our sheets.

The next morning my mom was demanding that the snake be found. She summoned my brother, Ezio, who was the only one in our household who had no fear of snakes. My brother made the small hole a little bigger by knocking away some of the plaster. I was in a panic for him as he peeked in the hole. No snake in sight.

Outside my mom was recounting the events to the other women of Luigi. All were clasping their hands and putting them over their heads, signaling disbelief and despair. Rosa, our neighbor, with her house right below the bedroom where the snake made its escape, was also in a panic as she wondered if the snake had made its way into her house.

Ezio, about sixteen years old, was still hunting for the snake. He suddenly pointed towards the roof of our houses. Just below the red tiles and the stone wall, the tail of the snake was dangling. My brother ran to the get a ladder, quickly climbed up towards the dangling snake and with no reservation, grabbed the snake, yanked it out of the wall, and slammed it to the ground. The stunned snake tried to regain control of its green and brown three-foot-something frame, but my brother hurried down the ladder, grabbed the *zappa*, hoe, next to the house, and with one swift strike he cut the snake in half. The snake went into convulsions and soon lay there dead. My brother summoned for a pitch fork and tossed the snake over a nearby wall and into some bushes.

Snakes in Italy are plentiful, fortunately only a couple are poisonous: the *vipera aspis* and the *vipera berus*. Both are a smaller and less poisonous version of their cousin, the rattlesnake. There are about ten types of snakes in south central Italy. Most of them are not poisonous and usually timid, and will do their best to avoid people. But at times this is not possible because usually people invade their space.

As a young girl, my Aunt Leontina was bringing lunch to her brothers working their wheat fields. She put her basket down and then she lowered her hoe to the ground right on top of a snake, prompting it to bite her lower leg. She screamed in pain and horror, summoning her brothers as the snake slithered away. Upon examination, they noticed the snake bite mark on her leg. My aunt described the snake as being not very long and greenish-brown in color. Fearful that it could have been *la vipera*, the viper, they loaded her onto their donkey and walked a few kilometers to see a doctor in the town of Vastogirardi. She was given anti-venom. The fact that her leg was swollen and discolored for weeks confirmed that indeed, it must have been a viper bite. She complained of discomfort in her leg for years.

That story was told around the fireplace many times during those long winter nights, which instilled in all of us — with the exception of my brother — a fear of these creatures.

My mother and I once saw a snake crossing a footpath in front of us. "*O Mamma mia, la serpa!*" she screamed, pulling me close to her, clutching my small hand to protect me from the menacing reptile. The next day as we again walked the same path, she took a detour to avoid the spot where we last saw the green serpent, straining her eyes to see if it was waiting there to attack us! Yes, she did a great job of instilling a great fear of snakes in us. It did not seem to sink in for Ezio.

One summer morning when I was six or seven years old, I was holding on to the lead rope of our donkey as she grazed. I decided to pull up some tall grass and feed it to her with my hand. The donkey latched onto the fresh grass, along with my small hand and would not let go. I screamed in pain so loud that my mother and father heard my cries as they were hoeing a potato field down the hill. They both ran up the hill towards me screaming, *"Che success?"* (*Che e' successo?* What happened?) As I was trying to pull my hand loose from the donkey's big mouth, I looked down to grab a stick to hit the donkey with, and right next to my feet a snake was taking in all the commotion, causing me to scream even louder.

My father, out of breath, quickly surveyed the situation with the donkey and smacked her on the side of the head, causing her to release the gentle grip. I screamed out *"la serpa, la serpa!"* while pointing to the ground. In a quick and swift motion, my father kicked the snake away from me. Unfortunately the snake's flight passed directly in front of my mother as she approached us. The scream she let out was much louder than mine, causing other farmers to run over to check out the commotion. My mother absolutely hated and was terrified of snakes, any snake, no matter what size or type.

One afternoon, all the people of our Luigi hamlet were minding their own business and performing their various chores. My cousin, Terenzio, my friend, Pasqualino, and I were playing on top of a cow manure hill with our homemade *carro armato*, war tank. It was made with a wooden thread spool with notched grooves for traction and rubber bands bound around with a small twig, causing the spool to move. Our war tank! Suddenly we saw *Zja* Ida, Terenzio's mom, run out of the storage room right below our houses, screaming in fear, *"la serpa, la serpa!"* My brother, tending to our cows in the barn nearby, ran to her rescue. The snakes were wrapped around each other in a cubbyhole in the room, slithering and hissing in pleasure. Ezio was ready to go in and chop the creatures into pieces but Massimino, our neighbor, stopped him in his tracks, telling everyone that the snakes were mating and would get really pissed off at anybody who disturbed their session!

Il guardiano, the forest ranger, Luigi, stopped by to investigate the commotion. Peering through the small window, he took a step back as he removed his rifle from his shoulder and placed it on top of the window sill. He took aim towards the cubbyhole where the snakes were mating, he pulled the trigger, and the rifle emitted a loud, unfamiliar noise that scared most of us. The men went in first and then slowly the rest of us made our way into the storage room. I was amazed at the carnage; pieces of snakes everywhere, some still moving. The women cautiously cleaned up the mess. Whenever I passed that small window, numerous times a day, I would always recall that scene, hesitantly peering inside to make sure that other snakes had not taken up residence.

The small window where Luigi, the forest ranger shot the snakes, 2014

There were many tales centered on snakes in our village. There were rumors of two-headed snakes, giant ones, and all sorts of aberrant types. I can still hear the animated discussions by the women of our neighborhood as they sat around the fire, knitting and mending. They would recount how a hen clucked insistently, and upon entering the chicken coop a snake was seen making a move for the hen's eggs.

Of all those stories there is one that still blows me away. I vaguely remember the women with their hands clasped over their heads, a sign of disbelief, as they were lamenting in unison about what happened to the new mom of the village, Elena. *"Povera Elena!"* Poor Elena! Her breasts were plump and full of milk for her new baby, but somehow during the night she would lose her milk.

One night the poor husband woke up to check on his wife when he heard her moaning. He tried to wake her but she seemed to be in a trance, under a spell. As he pulled away the blanket, to his astonishment a snake was sucking on her breast. Yelling out in panic, he fetched his sleeping parents from another room and they, too, witnessed the horrifying scene. Supposedly the snake put the poor young woman into a hypotonic state and then sucked her breasts dry! The husband slammed the snake against the wall, killing it. Henceforth the baby had plenty of milk.

The former version was my mother's. After coming to America I heard another version of the milk-thirsty snake, as told by Bonina Lombardi, an early immigrant to Denver of 1920s. As the legend goes, a woman had recently given birth. After a few weeks, she found she could not nurse her baby in the morning. No one could understand the problem until one of the women suggested they sprinkle flour on the floor of her bedroom to see what or who was taking her milk during the night. The next morning, they did find there were tracks on the floor leading up to her bed — the tracks of a snake.

On another of those summer days, my mom and I made our way past Luigi's fountain and up a hill. My mother was carrying a rush basket full of food. The aroma of freshly cooked *polenta* and sausage beckoned a dog that followed us for most of the trip up the footpath; a path that would take us to a piece of land in a place called *masseria*, or as we called it *la masseria*, the old farmhouse. I hated helping my parents work that small piece of earth that ran straight up a steep slope, making it difficult to even just stand there, much less hoe the soil. At the bottom of that slope was a somewhat level area with a large fig tree. There my mom set her food down and spread a tablecloth on the ground, as if to set the table. My mom and I waited while my dad, brother, and sister made their way down the slope, where they had been cutting wheat all morning.

We all sat around the legless table and began feasting on the still warm *polenta*. To all of our surprise, a big black snake literally slithered across our tablecloth, even slowing down to take in the scent of the *polenta*. My mom, with help from me and my sister let out a scream that did not seem to bother the uninvited lunch guest. Ezio sprang to his feet and ran towards the hoe, but by the time he came back the creature had sought refuge under a thorn bush. My dad and brother ate their lunch and got back to the wheat field. My mom, sister, and I were not able to eat anything, and as we cleaned up we all kept one eye on the thorn bush.

Of all the creatures on this earth, the snake scares me the most. I can thank my mom and my village for that. A combination of reality and myth rendered the snake an evil creature in our town. All the other critters roaming our countryside were of some use to us, but not the snake. My mom would always warn us whenever one of her dreams included snakes, that something bad was bound to happen. She had an explanation for every one of her dreams. Each dream meant something: clear water, muddy water, wine, trees, daylight, darkness, and of course the ever-present dreams of a dead family member. "*Mi song sennat a Mamma e meh ditt...*" (*Ho sognato Mamma e mi ha detto...*, I dreamed of mom and she told me...). How many times I heard that from my mom. Even though these people were dead, they were a part of our daily lives. Our elders always talked about them, and asked them for guidance, protection, and advice.

As a young boy I assumed that these dead relatives crawled out of their tombs at night and actually helped with whatever our family needed. We did not have to worry much about cattle rustlers because *tatuccio o mammuccia, nonno o nonna*, some grandparent was there watching over our animals. Oh how I wished I had eyes in the back of my head because I always looked behind me to see if a dead relative was following me, protecting me, but actually the thought of them being near scared the hell out of me. I did not care how many times my mom reassured me that the dead were not going to hurt me and that they protected me, I really wished that they would stay in their tombs. Only the living will hurt you, my parents would tell us.

Of course all the reassurances that our parents gave us about our dead were instantly negated by the tales told by the older kids while we sat around some stoop. We would be huddled together as they told stories of some dead old man who was seen roaming around at night, waiting to grab some kid who disrespected him when the old man was alive. Those evenings of 'let's scare the hell out of the younger kids' brought back memories of *Zizi, Zio* Michele Lombardi, my father's uncle and the father of Armando and Massimo, who lived a few steps from our house on that hillside cluster of homes and barns we called *Lvg*, Luigi.

I remember Uncle Michele dressed in his best clothes: his gray fedora hat, a dark dress shirt and dark jacket, with a gold chain hanging out of his gray pants that secured his gold watch. He could no longer perform

The house to the left of ours where Zio Michele lived with his son, Armando, and family, 1990

any of the work, but always seemed to be there giving suggestions. He always gave us orders rather than suggestions, we thought. Waving his cane at us, he would reprimand us about something we were doing that he deemed to be bad. How I wished that I had never grabbed that cane from him as he waved it at me that day in the *aia*, barnyard, and then foolishly threw it over the wall on the path below. When my father caught wind of my disrespect towards the old man, the eldest, the patriarch of our enclave, he gave me a couple of swift hard slaps in the face and forced me to go to Armando and Lucia's house and apologize to *Zio* Michele. I thought of and dreamt of *Zio* Michele many times after he died, waiting for him to appear next to my bed and beat me with his cane.

Even with my parents' reassurance that our dead relatives were protecting us, I wasn't so sure, and it seemed that even my mother didn't feel they protected her from snakes. How badly did my mom hate snakes? Whenever one appeared on her TV here in America, she would scream and shriek and run out of the room mumbling, "*O Mamma mia, o Mamma mia.*"

Although I don't scream when I see snakes, thanks to *Mamma* and my village I loathe snakes. I don't care about the alleged benefits that they have in our environment; when I see one, whether poisonous or not, I usually take a shovel or a rock to it. Recently I did that to a snake slithering nearby, as I pulled weeds out of our flower garden near our waterfall. And when I examined it, I noticed the three rattles! A baby rattlesnake, said to be the most dangerous because they cannot control the amount of venom injected when they strike! Could it be that my mother had a sense of the perils for which she should prepare her children? Did mine know that some fifty years later I might actually be in danger of being bitten by a snake?

Chapter VII

SALE E TABACCHI · SALT AND TOBACCO

As young as six, I would have to walk to the *Sale e Tabacchi* store to get my father five unfiltered *Nazionale* cigarettes and to get *Mamma* things like salt, sugar, and other staples we couldn't grow ourselves. Our hamlet of *Lvg*, Luigi, was situated in the foothills on the south side of the *Colle dei Noci*. A dirt road was carved right into the side of this small mountain, and it wound around all the way to the other side where the new houses were. We were the last of the residents of Pagliarone to be awarded a new house, because our old house had not been directly affected by the numerous landslides that were slowly destroying the houses in the valley below.

The *Sale e Tabacchi*, Salt and Tobacco, as these stores were called, was a tiny room with the bare essentials: cigarettes, wine, salt, sugar, and a few other items such as candy. Today's *Sale e Tabacchi* stores throughout Italy are the equivalent of American corner convenience stores. The hole-in-the-wall store we had was on the eastern end of the hill in Castra, one of the hamlets of Pagliarone. It was just about halfway between our old house in Luigi and the new town of Villa San Michele.

This area called Castra was very important before the building of the new town. It was where vendors gathered to sell their merchandise, mainly because the gravel road ended there. It was the nerve center of town. New houses had been built there, thanks to money coming from America, where husbands were working. The area was given a nickname by one inhabitant, *Vincenza dell'asina*, Vincenza of the donkey, so named because Vincenza had received a donkey as part of her dowry. She proudly renamed Castra as Piccola Napoli, Little Naples. Naples it was not. Right across the way from Castra was also where we brought our wheat to be thrashed by the combine.

The *Sale e Tabacchi* was owned by a man named Annibale, but we called him *Nibiluccio*. For some reason at that age I was a little scared of him. Maybe he was annoyed because I never had money when I was sent there to buy things. Instead I would tell him to add it to my father's name in the book of credit. He would reluctantly open his worn notebook and add the purchase price to our total. Money was a scarce commodity in our remote village, but eventually my father would pay *Nibiluccio* a few *lire*[3] after the sale of one of our animals.

I had made the walk with my sister and brother many times before, but at the age of six I was allowed to make the walk on my own. Later I would make that walk daily because I attended first grade in the schoolhouse near the *Sale e Tabacco* store. *Nibiluccio* was also an experienced carpenter and stone mason. I am sure he created many different products, but the only memory that remains with me is that of the simple wood coffins that he built when someone died.

The old schoolhouse and Annibale's Sale e Tabacchi store, 1990

I remember one warm summer night vividly as I walked past houses and people asked me, "*Andò vià?*" (*Dove vai?* Where are you going?) "*Accattà le sigarette peh Papà*" (*A comprare le sigarette per Papà*, To buy cigarettes for my dad). *Nibiluccio* handed me the five unfiltered *Nazionale* cigarettes and sent me on my way. I had watched my dad put a cigarette in his mouth and so I thought I would give it a try. For some reason the cigarette started to fall apart as I played with it in my

---

[3] *Lira, plural lire, was, as is the Dollar in the United States, the traditional monetary unit in Italy. The still rather recently formed European Union, the E.U., consolidated the currency of all its participating member nations into the Euro. Since 1999, the Italian lire, French franc, German Deutschmark, etc. have been put to rest.*

mouth, so I put that one in my pocket and tried another and the same thing happened. A woman passed me on my way home and she scolded me for having a cigarette in my mouth, and she informed me that she would tell my parents that I was smoking. I don't remember how long it took me to get home, but I delayed it as much as possible because all I had in my pocket was crumbled up paper mixed with tobacco.

Advertisement on Nazionale cigarette pack,
circa 1960s: 'Smoking relaxes!'

"Andó schtian le sigarette?" (*Dove sono le sigarette? Where are my cigarettes?*), my father asked me as I walked in the house. As I pulled out a handful of what was left of the *Nazionale* cigarettes, I felt the wrath on my face. I was not given that chore again! That was just fine with me because I always dreaded facing *Nibiluccio*. In reality he was a gentle, intelligent, although a bit eccentric man. When we became next-door neighbors in the temporary barracks, he and I became close. He would tell me about my grandfather Pietrantonio. They were the same age and they were in World War I together. Our close relationship continued, as we were also next-door neighbors in our new homes. His grandchildren, Luigi, Lina, and Nino became good friends of ours.

Annibale as a WWI soldier, circa 1915

Buying a pack of cigarettes was usually out of the question. My father didn't have money for five, let alone a whole pack. In fact we did not possess any money at all. *Nibiluccio* usually bartered with customers for various merchandise or services.

Bartering was prevalent in those days within our community. When the fruit, apparel, hardware, utensil, etc. peddlers arrived, they screamed, and when they replaced their horses and carts with vehicles, they honked their horns and yelled out loud for everyone to hear that they were in town with their wares. These vendors preferred money but also welcomed trading as consideration. They would usually accept grains, chickens, and/or eggs.

One day while my parents and Ezio were out in the fields, my sister and I heard the fruit peddler bellow out, "*Un chinacchione di fichi per ni chinariello di grano*," A big kilo of figs for a little kilo of wheat. So my sister and I, craving one of our favorite fruits, went to our storage facility, *il fondaco*, and scooped grain out of the large wooden bin. We traded what we thought was wheat, but it was only *biava*, *l'avena*, oats. *Mamma* scolded us for buying figs, but also complimented us for at least being wise in not offering our wheat for barter.

Some things never change; my wife Jackie buying fruit and vegetables with Cousin Maria Carmosino Lepore, 2014

Nibiluccio was still alive when I went back to Villa San Michele in July of 1975. It was our honeymoon and Jackie, at twenty-one years old, was in culture shock. The first morning when she woke up in our house in Villa San Michele, she cried; she missed her family. I heard commotion outside and heard my Aunt Leontina call my name. I looked out the window to see what the commotion was about. My aunt said they were all worried about us. They did not want to disturb us, but it was one o'clock in the afternoon. We had slept for over twelve hours. We got dressed and walked out the door to go to my aunt's house, just around the corner, above and across the town's fountain. Jackie noticed some elderly women clad in dark clothes and scarves walking into the house next door, *Nibiluccio's* house. I dreaded telling her what was going on. Letizia, *Nibiluccio's* daughter, had died and her body lay on a bed in the house, and people were coming over to give their condolences.

That news put Jackie over the edge. She was in a strange town with strange people, a different language, and there was a dead woman next door! Thankfully the next day there was a funeral service for Letizia, which we reluctantly attended, but it was the right thing to do. I vividly remember the funeral services I had attended as an altar boy, and this wasn't going to be pretty. It certainly was not one of the things I had planned for my new bride to experience on our honeymoon.

Nibiluccio was sort of a free spirit; he was different, although he was very sad for his daughter's passing. He also realized that it was what it was and life goes on. He had made the coffin long ago for his daughter to be buried in. He had to go down to his old farmhouse in Castra to dig it out of storage. When he opened the coffin, snakes slithered out of there.

Annibale in front of his tobacco store; our new house is on the right, circa 1964

After the church services, people lined up behind the coffin for the long walk to the cemetery for the burial. And as I had anticipated, as soon as we walked through the iron gates, people scattered to the graves of their own loved ones, some crying, some screaming. Jackie and I were left there with the grieving family, a few other villagers, and the priest. Jackie wondered why my cousin Adelia's husband, Peppino, was crying so loudly by a grave. It was his mother's grave, as she had died in her forties just a few months earlier of heart problems. Eventually the service ended and we headed back to town. I promised my wife that the rest of our six-week stay in my beloved town and country would be more enjoyable.

Chapter *VIII*

LA VENDEMMIA · THE HARVEST

My childhood memories include those of the very hectic times during the hot days of summer. The hayfields were lush and tall and ready for harvest. Men of the town could be seen all around our landscape wielding their *favicione*, *la falce*, the sickle, as they steadfastly swung back-and-forth, cutting the hay. After the hay had been cut and dried on one side and then turned to dry the other, it would be gathered and transported to our barn. The hay was stored up in the loft of the barn and then used to feed our animals during the winter.

La falce, the sickle

In the meantime the wheat fields, thanks to the hot summer sun, had turned golden. Actually the top of the wheat plant, which is part of the grass family, died, telling the farmers that it was ready for harvest. The whole month of July and part of August were devoted to the reaping of the wheat fields. My mom and dad, with my brother, sister, and I, would set out early in the morning and cut wheat until dark, usually seven days a week. We went to different plots of wheat fields in the countryside and cut the wheat with sickles. My left little finger is a constant reminder of the sharpness of the sickle (or the misuse of the sickle by a kid). The scar is still very visible. It should have been stitched, but only a wrap to stop the bleeding was administered by my dad.

The whole village seemed to move to the wheat fields during harvest. Wheat was a most important crop in our village, as it was included in almost all of our daily diets. You would see babies sleeping under shade trees and people singing popular songs as they grabbed the wheat plants and hacked them off with their sickles. Because my parents did not trust me much with the sharp half-circle knife, I was usually given the task of gathering the bundles of wheat and dragging them to an area where they would be stacked in a way that protected them from the weather.

After all the harvesting was completed, the stacks of wheat were put into *le gabbie*, the wooden cages, loaded onto donkeys, and transported to our *aia*, barnyard, for thrashing. One might ask why a wagon was not utilized. The numerous walking pathways that snaked all around the countryside were barely wide enough for an animal to fit through. They were usually so bumpy, muddy, and rocky, that a wagon wheel would never work. When I see Indians in those old western movies with their wooden A-shaped skids being pulled by horses, it brings back vague memories of men doing the same thing in our village.

Donkey carrying wheat in le gabbie,
the wooden cages, July 1975

As you came down the stairs of our house in Luigi and looked out to the east, there was a somewhat rounded open area outside that was decorated with other smooth and primarily white stones. We called it *l'ara*, *l'aia*, the barnyard. Some of the most vivid memories of my childhood took place *ingoppa á l'ara*, *sopra l'aia*, on the barnyard, where every summer we would have *la tresca dl iraneh*, *la trebbiatura del grano*, the threshing of wheat. Horses or mules would go around and around, as the animals were guided by a man who was standing in the middle of the wheat, which had been piled in a large circle. The horses would trot in a circular pattern and their steel shoes would extract the grain from the wheat plant.

The families worked together to harvest what would be their main source of food for the coming winter. Kids as young as four years old were expected to help, and although it was work, it was also fun to see the horses go around and around. Men with their pitchforks would pick up the wheat and fling it into the air to loosen it up, so that the majority of it would be extracted. Usually some of the wheat was extracted by hand by the women and kids. The women collected the grains in rush baskets, and then put them onto sheets laid out on the ground to begin the drying process. The men piled the straw and stacked it. The shape of a Christmas tree comes to mind when I think of the stacks of hay on our *aia*. The straw would be used as bedding for the animals.

Recreating La Tresca, la trebbiatura del grano, the threshing of wheat,
in the Molise town of Carovilli, 1990

In the early 1960s *la trebbiatrice*, the wheat thresher or combine, had finally come to town, and the old way of threshing wheat was becoming just a recollection of the past. Every late summer all the kids would listen for that sound, a sound we hardly ever heard except when *la trebbiatrice* wound its way down the only road that led to Villa San Michele. The combine, which was owned by a private company, had probably just finished threshing wheat in a neighboring town, and our village was the next of many stops in our area.

I remember *la trebbiatrice* being a faded orange color. It looked enormous as it was pulled by the tractor with its gigantic tires. As soon as we saw it coming out of *la pineta*, the pine forest — hardly a forest, just some pine trees that lined the road between Villa San Michele and Cerreto, a town two kilometers to the east — we would run up the road to meet it. Not only did we love the noise of the tractor but also the smell of the fumes it emitted from the diesel engine. All the town's kids would follow the tractor, breathing the fumes as it slowly made its way to the area where the stacks of wheat awaited. *La chiana campesto*, the flat field, where all the wheat awaited the combine, was across from Castra, where the *Sale e Tabacchi* store and the elementary school were located. This area was about halfway between the original scattered town of Pagliarone and the new town of Campanello (later renamed Villa San Michele).

Me holding a bundle of wheat 1975

To our parents this modern marvel represented a respite from the backbreaking work of the old way of threshing wheat. The satisfaction of knowing that a machine was going to extract the grain from the wheat, fill the grain into burlap sacks, and then bale the straw, was magic; it was a miracle. The men and women of the village had worked from dawn to dusk cutting the wheat, bundling it, and hauling it to the threshing site. They loaded it onto wooden cages that were tied to the saddles of our donkeys and mules. This process created a procession of donkeys, mules and horses being pulled by their owners, loaded with wheat on their way to the holding area.

The farmers stacked the wheat there and then went back to the fields for another load of the golden wheat. The bundles were stacked as high as possible, in multiple rows. This was done because the area was not very large and each family was allowed only a small plot for their harvest. The wheat was also stacked in such a way to protect the head of the stalk from the weather, while at the same time allowing the drying process to continue. *Le reglie,* the stacks, varied in size and each stack belonged to a different family. Men would create colorful geometric designs and it became a competition to see who could create the best *reglia,* stack.

That great maze of stacked bundles of wheat fashioned the most perfect location for us to play our games of *nascondino,* hide-and-seek, or *la guerra,* war. This was also the perfect area for kids to test their skills in archery with their bows and arrows. These bows were made of wooden sticks that we had painstakingly searched for in our forests. When we found the perfect piece, we would cut it down, peel off the bark, and then bend the pole into shape while it was still green. We then tied on the string, which was not a readily available commodity. Most of the time these strings were crudely pieced together with whatever we had that resembled string.

The arrows were also made out of wood, but because these perfectly straight, hard twigs were very difficult to find, we discovered a better way. We took apart old umbrellas and used the metal rods as arrows. We painfully sharpened one end by grinding it on a stone and made a groove in the other end so we could hook it to our bows. It was so much fun to shoot those arrows into the bales of straw to see how deep we could sink that steel rod into those rectangular targets. Sometimes it went too deep, and we'd lose the arrow forever. The older kids continually attempted to ditch the younger archers, threatening us with physical harm. We would eventually leave them to find our own stack of straw victims.

One hot sunny day, bored with the usual routine, we decided to have a competition to see who could shoot their arrow the highest. I remember pulling back that steel rod that was hooked to my bow as hard as possible, aiming for the sky. I looked up as I released the sharp steel bullet that was quickly lost in the rays of the golden summer sun. That same bright, golden light blinded me. The steel rod came back down as quickly as it went up, and at the last second I saw it above my head. I attempted to move out of the way but was only able to turn my head slightly, as the arrow whizzed by on its way back to the ground. Instantly I felt a terrible pain in my leg and as I looked down, I noticed the arrow embedded deep into my right calf. The other kids watched in horror as I screamed in agony. In a panic, I grabbed the arrow and instinctively pulled it out of my right leg. Surely blood would gush out, but only a few drops appeared. That small hole in my leg created tremendous pain. The other kids looked on in dismay as I cried in pain, and as if they had seen a ghost, they all ran away from me, looking back to see if I had fallen over dead.

I eventually limped my way home, constructing a story in my mind that I would offer to my parents as to why I was limping. I would say that while playing soccer I got kicked by one of the other kids. The next day I could hardly walk, but forced myself to leave the house to do my chores of feeding the chickens and the pig. I limped for weeks, my mom always asking me why, as I hid the black-and-blue leg under my sock. As summer came to an end, my leg was finally back to normal and I walked with no pain. Looking back I am thankful that my Guardian Angel worked overtime to protect me. Was the arrow rusty? Yes. How close did the arrow come to my head? Very close. Should my leg have become infected? Yes. Was I lucky to be alive? Absolutely!

Grandson Nico trying to shoot with our homemade bow and arrow, 2015

As an adult, when I have gone back to Pagliarone, I have walked to Luigi from Villa San Michele. Along the way I have stopped and looked over the threshing field, trying to recreate those wheat and straw stacks in my mind, but seeing only a variety of weeds. But the memory of that fateful day would quickly return as I looked up at the same blue sky and bright sun that blinded me and almost got me killed on that hot summer day, long ago.

Taking a water (wine) and cigarette break from the wheat cutting. Antonio (La Fonte) Lombardi on the left with fellow helpers. Circa 1960's

Chapter IX

I Cani · The Dogs

My brother, Ezio, was coming back from *La Rocca*, Roccasicura, a town about seven miles south of Pagliarone. While riding his donkey, he noticed she was getting a bit agitated, perking her ears up and turning her head to stare at something behind them. My brother instantly had visions of a wolf ready to harass them. He forced himself to look back and saw a black dog a few meters behind, cautiously following them. Ezio made repeated loud noises to make the dog go away. This worked temporarily, but then the dog suddenly reappeared and eventually followed him all the way home to Luigi. I immediately fell in love with that stray dog. My brother named him Ali. Ali went everywhere with us and was the perfect companion during those long days of working the fields or grazing our animals. With the exception of sheepdogs and some hunting dogs, these animals were usually just another burden and another mouth to feed, and were mostly ignored and neglected.

Ali regrettably developed an appetite for eggs that he found when he crawled into our *shtrella*, *il pollaio*, chicken coop, as he chased our alarmed chickens around the barnyard. My father tried everything to break him from that very bad habit. Those eggs were a crucial ingredient of our daily diet. *Mamma* usually added eggs to almost all of her cooking and baking: pasta, soups, breads, and of course *polpette*, cheese balls, made from eggs, cheese, bread crumbs, and parsley. She would mix the ingredients and then make individual balls with her hands, flattening them a bit before baking them. Later she would add them to her sauce. Our meatless meatballs!

polpette, meatballs without meat

Before school my mother would go to our chicken coop just below *la loggia, il balcone,* our balcony, and bring up the freshly laid eggs. She would punch a small hole about a quarter inch in diameter in one end of the egg and punch a bit smaller hole in the other end. Then she carefully handed me the freshly laid warm egg to suck the raw egg out of the shell and into my mouth. It was a quick breakfast with no dirty dishes to wash!

I dreaded swallowing an egg that way and always gagged and sometimes heaved, which was followed by a crying spell as I lamented the torture she was putting me through. *Mamma* would say that *quell'uovo,* that egg, would make me smart and make me strong; and so the torture would take place every morning. And then one certain special morning, *Mamma* broke the egg and put it in a cup, filled the rest of the cup with some Marsala wine, added a tablespoon of sugar, stirred it and handed it to me to drink.

Marsala is a fortified wine produced in the area around the city of Marsala, Sicily. If the sweet Marsala wine was not available, she would whip the egg and sugar and offer me the mixture to eat. Finally I had graduated to the same breakfast as my sister and brother. That was my breakfast of champions as a small boy; the fresh egg, sweet wine made sweeter by a spoonful of pure white sugar, and off to school. When the chickens refused to lay eggs, my breakfast included a slice of bread dipped in a cup filled with a bit of coffee and mostly warm milk and sugar. Looking back I wonder how I wasn't bouncing off the schoolhouse walls!

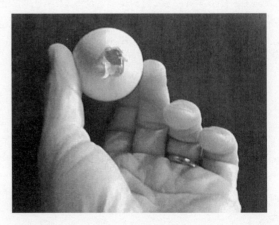

Two holes punched in the ends of an egg so the contents could be sucked out

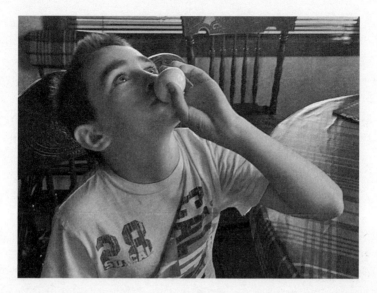

My grandson, Gianni, demonstrating how I drank an egg as a child. I proposed that he actually try sucking out the yolk and the white, but he said that was definitely out of the question! 2015

Eggs were important to us, and our dog was not in harmony with this. Dogs in our village were towards the bottom on the list of fundamental farm animals. Cats roamed our town and I don't remember who owned them, if anybody. They were sort of community property and were welcomed guests around the barns, haylofts and homes, where mice liked to roam. The village dogs were more of a luxury for the people who could afford to feed them. Our dog could only hope for some food if we had any leftover scraps that we hadn't fed to our pigs which seemed to have a constant appetite. Essentially, most dogs of the village were undernourished. The only dogs that looked healthy were the hunting dogs owned by the few hunters. And when you're hungry, you will eat things that are not normally part of your diet. Ali was forced to make that choice.

That choice to eat our eggs would be Ali's demise. So the decision was made without my consent that he must go. My brother took up the task. He tried to leave him at different faraway places in hopes that the dog might latch onto someone, but he always came back home.

I don't know Ezio's reasoning, but one day we were on the mountain grazing our cattle. I was just a seven-year-old boy with his black lab playing in the forest. My sixteen-year-old brother and his friends came up with a grand idea: Take the dog and carry him up the tallest tree that they could find and leave him there. For sure the dog would not be able to get down by himself and follow us home. I cried and cried, begging my brother to bring our dog down from that gigantic tree. I anguished for Ali as he tried to balance himself on the large branch. As the sun started to go down, we made our way down the mountain with our cows.

I prayed that someone would see my dog and rescue him from that tree branch. My mother consoled me when we got home, but I cried and lamented for days. One night a few days later we were eating dinner and my dad heard a commotion outside our door. When he opened it, Ali was there wagging his tail, very happy to be back home. I was also very happy to see him, as was my sister, and my mother was a bit relieved. My dad and brother were frustrated. How he got down from that tree we never knew, but I was elated that he did.

Unfortunately, we could not keep Ali out of the chicken coop. He became more aggressive about chasing our chickens. My mother worried that he would eventually kill one of the hens. Our chickens roamed freely around the area near our house. They never ventured far away from there. When we wanted to feed them we would make a combination of sounds that beckoned them to run to us for their feeding. They seemed to recognize the sounds we made because the other chickens in the area would generally stay away. The residents of our small hamlet knew exactly to whom the numerous roaming chickens belonged, and usually left others' chickens alone unless the roaming chickens ventured too close to their houses.

Whenever la zingara, the gypsy, Maria, came around Luigi to beg for whatever, I recall her asking, "signò fammi na grazia," for any food that we could part with. When there was a zingara sighting, people would all be on guard. Even though we all knew her to be for the most part friendly and fascinating to the younger populace, there were unconfirmed reports of gypsies putting a needle through a kernel of corn and throwing it to chickens. When a chicken ate the corn and started to choke, the gypsies would catch the chicken and hide it in their seemingly bottomless gypsy pouches. One older zingara, dressed in the traditional gypsy garb of a long colorful skirt, would actually sit in our kitchen and talk with my mom. She usually overstayed her welcome and would eventually leave only when Mamma put a link of sausage, a couple of eggs, or a piece of bread in her bag. Maybe my mom should have offered her our dog!

The word *zingaro*, male gypsy, is derived from the Greek word Atziganoi, who were members of a sect living on Mount Athos. The sect was committed to murder, thus providing the strongly negative connotation associated with the name. The legend of the origin of the word gypsy is that these nomadic people came to Europe posing as rich Egyptians and that 'gypsy' is a derivation of the word Egypt.

The appropriate name for this ethnic group of people was Roma or Romani, not to be confused with Romanians nor with modern or ancient Romans. They originated from the Punjab region of northern India. It is said that they were expelled from the area as undesirables by the Afghan conqueror, King Mahmud. The Roma then ventured to the Middle East and Eastern Europe and finally into Western Europe, including Italy, in the 14th century. Throughout the centuries the Romani people suffered from discrimination and hatred, and during the Nazi campaign to eliminate the *untermenschen* (inferior humans), approximately one million gypsies perished.

As children we were warned to stay away from gypsies and not to trust them. Many tales were told about them stealing anything in sight, including small children. Our village resident gypsy, Maria, was actually nice and never a threat.

I worried that la zingara, the gypsy, would take me and hide me under her flowing skirt

That summer my brother and sister and I were leading our cows and our donkey to a faraway place called *la posta*, possibly named so from a postal stop from days gone by. We grazed our cows in those fertile green pastures. While crossing the river Vandra, my brother, with the urging of the other teenage boys who were also on their way to *la posta*, decided to throw our dog into the river, hoping that he would swim to the other side and run away. Ali quickly swam back to shore, where my brother and his friends were waiting to throw him back in. At first my sister and I were amused, but as the dog struggled to swim back to shore, we became worried. His belly was getting bigger as a result of swallowing water. We begged the older kids to stop. Finally they did. Another attempt of ridding the family of that nuisance went awry. But eventually the decision was made to ultimately unburden the family of the menace, of my beloved friend, Ali.

Enea, my *Zia* Ida's brother, was in Luigi helping the family with *la tresca, la trebbiatura,* the wheat threshing. That afternoon I noticed him with his rifle at his side, strapped around his right shoulder. My brother followed him with Ali in tow. They were walking towards *la padula,* probably derived from *la palude,* the marsh or the swamp, it is a small chunk of land where we had our *orto,* vegetable garden. From outside our house, I watched Ezio tie Ali to a tree and walk away, wondering what was going on. *Mamma* noticed me observing what was taking place and quickly picked me up and started to take me up the stairs of our house. Near the top on *la loggia,* the balcony (landing), we heard a loud pop. My mom squeezed me and gave me one of her loving kisses. Ali was shot and left somewhere where wolves and foxes would make a meal out of him. I missed my dog and begged my dad daily for another.

Finally in December of that year, my father gave in to my constant requests and one day brought home a puppy that a friend from a neighboring town gave him; a shiny, golden, cuddly dog that I immediately fell in love with. I also named him Ali.

At that time we lived in the barracks, a temporary public housing next to the new village, until our new house in Campanello was ready. This tiny place had no fireplace or brick oven, only a tiny propane stove. My mother used the fireplace and oven at our house in Luigi for most of her baking. For Christmas, it was a tradition to make *scherpelle,* a pastry made with dough, fried in oil, and sweetened with sprinkles of sugar. *Mamma* put the *scherpelle* in a large round rush basket, covered them with a red and white checkered cloth, and placed them on a chair near the fireplace. Meanwhile my father had put a box of poison nearby for the annoying mice.

Our parents wrapped me, my brother and sister like mummies for the half-hour or so journey to our *baracca*, our temporary housing in Campanello. Ali with his wagging tail waited patiently by the door hoping to join us on our trek, but he would be left behind in our old and faithful home in Luigi.

As usual, early that following morning my dad and brother, Ezio, headed *capaball*, down below, to Luigi to tend to our animals. When my dad went inside our house he noticed Ali near the fireplace, stiff and motionless. With the rat poison nearby, my father quickly realized what had happened; that Ali had helped himself to some of the poison. He broke the bad news to us when he came home that evening, and my mother again comforted me as I cried. My sadness was appeased a bit by the expectation of the upcoming Christmas holidays and the anticipation of *La Befana*.

Hunter with his hunting dogs in Villa San Michele, 1975

Chapter X

NATALE E LA BEFANA
CHRISTMAS AND THE EPIPHANY

Christmas was a special time of the year in our tiny village. The religious aspect of it did not take a backseat to anything else, but for the kids of the village other things seemed to be more important than the midnight Mass! It was one of the few times of the year when we actually experienced the taste of chocolate, tropical fruits such as oranges, and a variety of nuts.

I recall one particular Christmastime as a small boy. My father had been ill for what seemed to be in my young mind a very long time. I was confused and saddened when I saw my father in bed and not in the barn tending to our animals. Those chores were left to my poor mom and hardworking brother, with my sister and me pitching in. I don't remember if he was suffering from any physical illness, but these many years later as I recall my father in bed with that despondent look on his face, I can now surmise that he was suffering from a bout of depression. He would struggle with this ailment during other times later on in his life.

In past years my father would be the one to bring home a tree for Christmas. That particular year, during what was usually a blissful time of year for us and our small, remote, humble village, we were struggling to survive, with much less to celebrate. But my frail and tender *Mamma* would have no part of the gloom and doom written on my father's face. She summoned my teenage brother to find a tree for the family.

113

It was on a cold and snowy morning that my brother decided to go out and cut down a tree for our home. I begged to go with him and so, reluctantly, my mom wrapped me in numerous layers of various clothing and allowed me to go with Ezio. With an ax resting on his shoulder, my brother and I made our way up the mountain. It was the perfect setting for Christmas with the freshly fallen snow, crystal white, mostly undisturbed except for some animal tracks. I recall the determined and focused look on Ezio's face as we made fresh tracks in that snow, searching for that special tree. He was determined not to disappoint and embarrass our family, so we kept looking even though we had walked past many small evergreens that seemed sufficient to me. My brother thought otherwise, so we kept trekking through the deep snow, searching for the perfect Christmas tree.

Surely by now my mom was becoming concerned about her sons. It was a bitter, cold winter and danger lurked up on that mountain. My earliest recollection of our small hamlet of Luigi is of a past winter when the snow was so deep that the town was isolated and running out of food and other provisions. I wasn't much older than three or four and the vision of helicopters hovering over our village, dropping sacks of much needed supplies to the stranded residents, stayed with me forever. Those mountains were home to *lupi*, wolves and *cinghiale*, wild boar, and they could be aggressive towards a couple of kids if their space was invaded.

By now my mom was contemplating going down the stairs to my uncle's house to ask *Zizi* Umberto to go search for us. With her eyes firmly straining through the small kitchen window, *Mamma* hoped to see her two sons. Glancing up and down the path west of our house towards the mountain, her eyes hurting from the glistening white snow, she finally saw someone coming towards Luigi from that direction. As they got closer, she noticed a large object following them. To her surprise, her elder son was struggling to drag a huge tree, as I followed closely behind.

Even as a child, I realized there was a problem with this tree. It seemed taller than our house, but by now I knew how my brother operated. He always went overboard on everything he did. So I helped him as much as my little body could in dragging this tree down the hill towards Luigi. I hoped and prayed that *il guardiano*, the forest ranger, would not see us, because we cut down the tree on government protected forest land.

The people of our small hamlet coexisted as they coped with each other, and although most of the residents were harmonious neighbors, there were some who were envious and distrustful of others. Someone would surely question where this tree came from, and we would get slapped with a hefty fine if it came from government land, which would surely make that Christmas even worse.

As we dragged the tree up the stairs and onto our *loggia*, it was obvious that it was not going to fit through our door. *Mamma*, with our sister Maria at her side, opened the door. At first she scolded my brother for staying out in the cold snow for so long, and then she pulled us in the house as her voice changed from a worried sick to happy crying mode: *"Povr figli miie, muert deh fridd"* (*Poveri figli, morti di freddo*, My poor sons, freezing to death). After conferring with my ill father, she instructed my brother to cut off the top of the tree and bring it into the house, and then cut the rest of it up and hide it somewhere near the wood pile below our house.

Tradition in our town, as in the rest of Italy and some other European countries, was to hang a Christmas tree from the ceiling upside down as a representation of the Holy Trinity. Legend has it that a monk traveled around the Devonshire area of England preaching religion and used the triangular shape of a tree to represent the Father, the Son, and the Holy Spirit. I recall the tree being scantily decorated with edible things such as dried figs, nuts, apples, and sometimes candy.

So we hung our tree between our fireplace and the bread oven and decorated it with the few treats that my mother had saved up. My father forced himself out of bed to see it and his sad face was wet with tears. *Mamma* followed with tears of her own but was determined to stay strong, to make sure that her three children experienced some happy moments during the festive season of *Natale*, the Birth, Christmas. Below the hanging tree, next to the fireplace was our *presepio*, manger scene. Mostly made out of wood, the *presepio* was carved by my mother's brothers. A log burning in the fireplace warmed the house, representing *il ceppo*, the yule log.

One of the clearest memories I have about our kitchen is the Christmas tree that hung upside down in its warm and cozy corner, 1975.

I don't have any recollection of *Babbo Natale*, Santa Claus, during my childhood years in Pagliarone. Christmas morning for us meant dressing up in our best clothes, which for me meant my brother's hand-me-downs, and going to church. After church there was a meal that, if we were fortunate, included something more than pasta or *polenta*. Maybe, if we were lucky, we would experience the taste of meat and sweets.

Our remote village was not privy to the travel plans of Santa Claus on Christmas Eve. On Christmas morning we did not have a bunch of toys and other presents, but we had that special Christmas spirit that engulfed the small village. I'd swear that to a small child, it seemed as though even all of our animals also received that special gift; the one where poverty and other hardships were put on hold and the whole village was aglow with joy, if just for a short while. As we celebrated the Christmas season, the kids of the village anxiously waited for a special morning, the morning of the twelfth day of Christmas.

The morning for which the children of Pagliarone anxiously waited was January 6, *La Befana*, Epiphany[4], or Three Kings Day, when *La Befana* would come to our house and hopefully leave us treats.

This legend has many different versions, but the most accepted is that of an Italian old woman who was busy cleaning and scrubbing her house when three travelers stopped by to rest and ask for directions. It turned out that they were the Three Wise Men, who were following the bright star that would lead them to *Gesù Bambino*, Baby Jesus. They invited the elderly woman to join them but she refused, saying that she was too busy. Later that same evening a shepherd came by and asked her to join him in his journey, but again she refused. That night she saw a bright light in the sky and changed her mind. With a sack of treats and her broom in hand, still wearing her apron, she decided to go looking for the Wise Men and for the Baby Jesus, but she never found them.

Time has changed her itinerary. In hopes that she might find Baby Jesus, *La Befana* flies every Epiphany over the rooftops of Italian homes, leaving treats to all the good children of Italy.

As I snuggled next to my brother on that cold and snowy night of January, I can vividly recall hearing someone in our kitchen. It had to be

[4] *Epiphany celebrates the manifestation of Christ to the gentiles. According to the Bible story, the Three Wise Men (also known as the Three Kings or Magi), who were the first non-Jewish (gentile) visitors, arrived with gifts twelve days after Christmas as they met the infant Jesus.*

La Befana. I looked over at my brother and he was sound asleep, and my sister was doing the same in her bed next to us. I just lay there motionless and prayed that this time *La Befana* would fill my stocking with goodies. The next morning I dragged my sister out of bed and into our kitchen, our bare Christmas tree still hanging there until the day after Epiphany. The wool stockings that we had worn the previous day had been left that night to hang by the fireplace. They did not look full as I had hoped.

La Befana

As I dug into the sock, I pulled out an orange, a walnut, and a piece of burned wood; not at all what I had hoped. Disappointed, I wondered if I would ever get something that resembled a toy. I questioned just how good of a boy did I need to be to get a toy. I never did get a toy from *La Befana*. But on that morning of *La Befana*, my father got up and went out to help Ezio with the animals, and when they came home we all gathered around our little table and ate our simple lunch together. As we sat around the fireplace, my father took me in his arms and held me tight. As I looked down at my stockings, I forgave and forgot about *La Befana* not bringing me a toy and realized that having the rock of our family healthy and happy again meant more to me than all the toys in the world.

As the 1960s emerged, *La Befana* somehow came into a bit of good fortune, because she started putting a few more sweet goodies in our stockings including *torrone*, a nougat sweet popular in Spain, France, and Italy. Some historians say that it originated from the Middle East, but of course Italians claim that it originated in the northern city of Cremona. In 1441 during the wedding of Francesco Sforza and Bianca Maria Visconti, members of the powerful families of Milan introduced a dessert made from nutmeats, honey, and egg whites as part of the wedding buffet. The candy was shaped like the famous tower of Cremona known as *Torrazzo*, hence the name *torrone*.

The southern city of Benevento in the Campania region also lays claim to its creation. Some suggest that the name *torrone* comes from the Latin *torrere* which means to toast. A main ingredient of *torrone* is toasted nuts, usually almonds. *Torrone* has been part of the Italian palette for centuries. Presently there are many different versions of the popular Christmas candy, but my all-time favorite is the one enveloped in dark chocolate!

Torrone

Sometimes *La Befana* would leave a *panettone* next to the fireplace. The dome-shaped sweetbread originated in Milan in the early 20th century. It is made with a type of sourdough, mixed with dried fruits such as candied oranges, citron, lemon, and raisins. The fluffy bread is also a favorite in Italian homes during the Christmas season. A favorite for our family is the *panettone* that is infused with dark chocolate cream.

Panettone

As I snuggled next to my brother and sister and the cold winter winds howled through the dark, snowpacked landscape, my sister softly hummed in my ear:

La Befana vien di notte,
con le scarpe tutte rotte,
neve, gelo, tramontana,
viene, viene, La Befana!

La Befana comes at night,
wearing her ruined shoes,
snow, ice, winter winds,
she will come, she will come, *La Befana!*

Ezio and Maria assured me that no matter how severe the weather outside, *La Befana* would stop at our house and put something in our socks or in our shoes, which were neatly placed near our fireplace on the night of January 5.

After *la Befana*, we wanted the snow and the cold to go away. We waited patiently for spring and all the flowers that would engulf the landscape.

Chapter XI

PASQUA · EASTER

As the cold weather subsided and the accumulated snow started to melt, it meant that spring was just around the corner. The religious holiday of Easter was something that the whole village looked forward to, because that feast also denoted the approaching warmer days.

Pasqua comes from the Hebrew word *Pesach*, meaning 'Passover.' The corresponding English word Easter is derived from the Teutonic[5] goddess of fertility, Eostre. The holiday itself is, I think, a combination of pagan festivals and religious celebrations, as are most of the holidays that we enjoy. But before *Pasqua*, our village prepared for *Carnevale*, Carnival, and *Martedì Grasso*, *Mardi Gras*, Fat Tuesday. This was the week of partying until Ash Wednesday, the beginning of Lent.

I recall those bitterly cold Februaries, sitting in front of the fireplace trying to keep warm. *Carnevale* was something to look forward to; the huge fires, food, and games. I particularly recall one game that we played year-round, but it was enjoyed most around *Carnevale*. Kids were blindfolded and given a stick. Taking turns, we would have to hit a potato that had been placed on a table. If you were successful at smashing the potato, a treat was in order, such as an apple, a walnut, or maybe a candy if it was available.

---

[5] *Teutonic means 'Germanic.' Germania was the name the Romans gave to the tribes of the North. Around the year 1000, the Germans eventually referred to themselves as Deutsch (derived from the Middle High German word meaning 'common'), as the collective name for all the tribes: Franks, Saxons, Burgundians, Lombards, etc. 'Teut' and 'Deut' are essentially the same root. And it is from the 'Teut' root that Italian takes the word tedesco.*

In our own tiny section of Pagliarone, *Lvg*, Luigi, the families all gathered at someone's house for the celebration. Adults and children alike would dress in something different from the norm. Without fail, our neighbor Matilda would knock on the door and rush in, wrapped in a sheet, her face coated with flour and her mouth filled with *cumbiett*, *confetti* (white almond-filled candy). For us little ones, we thought that certainly she was *reh spiriteh*, *fantasma*, a ghost. Whatever it was, it scared the hell out of us.

Carnevale was a lot of fun for adults and kids, and we made the best of what we had. We ate a lot of food, mostly soups and pork, which was plentiful from our pig slaughter a couple of months earlier. If we were lucky we would consume some sweets in anticipation of the total abstinence of it in the coming weeks. This would be the storm before the calm of *Quaresima*, Lent.

The forty days of *Quaresima* followed *Carnevale*, and these were the slowest, most boring forty days of the year for a catholic boy like me, as it was for my brother, sister, and the rest of the youngsters living in our remote village. We were expected to pray continually, to fast, to reflect, and to do nothing but good deeds. There were numerous trips to church, where we would be bombarded with sermons about the meaning of *Quaresima* and the forty days. We were told to do penance, just as Jesus did for forty days in the wilderness. Noah, with his wife and all the pairs of animals, spent forty days and nights on his ark. The Israelites spent forty days wandering the desert. Moses spent forty nights on Mount Sinai. And a baby spends forty weeks in the womb. I got tired of hearing about *quaranta giorni*, forty days.

The Wednesday that marked the beginning of Lent was *il Mercoledì delle Ceneri*, Ash Wednesday. The priest would make the sign of the cross on our forehead with ashes, reminding us to repent and to be sorrowful for the next forty days. But the priest also gave us something to look forward to: Those long, dark days of winter would soon be replaced by the new light of spring.

As time got closer to Easter, the young adults of the town would put on a theatrical performance in the schoolhouse. The narration of the Passion was anticipated by all the residents of the village. We all crammed into the small schoolhouse in the Castra neighborhood of the village to watch the performance. I will forever remember when Jesus, played by

Salvatore Iannacito, son of Felice of Trebbante, was put on the cross. With thorns on his head and blood dripping down his face, his body was finally nailed to that wooden cross by the Roman soldiers. It seemed very real to us, but obviously Salvatore was not literally nailed to the cross. But with his eyes closed and motionless, he scared the crap out of all the younger kids. We thought that he had died on the cross, just like Jesus. My mom had to keep reminding me and my sister that Salvatore was alive and well.

I did not really believe her until I saw Salvatore walking behind his cows when I went to visit my *mammuccia*, my *nonna*, Genoveffa, in Trebbante. I was always frightened of Salvatore, envisioning him on that cross. Years later when I saw him again while visiting my sister in Toronto, Canada, the Passion play in Pagliarone reappeared in my head. I reminded him of it and mentioned that he came a long way from being nailed on the cross to owning a concrete finishing business with his brother, Dominic, and my brother-in-law, Victor, in Canada.

During the days before Easter, it seemed as though we took residence in the church. We started off with *La Domenica delle Palme*, Palm Sunday. Jesus rode into Jerusalem on a donkey which represented peace, as opposed to a horse which represented war. This Sunday was different from the others. We were given olive branches, not palms. I suspect this was because olive branches were more readily available to us, and olive branches were also more available in Jerusalem; so the road that Jesus traveled to make his triumphant entry into Jerusalem was probably lined primarily with olive branches. As I held my branches, sitting next to my *Mamma* and my siblings, safe and content, who knew some fifty years later that this day, Palm Sunday, would become the most tragic day for our family, in some faraway land.

The following week was the holiest of the year. On *Lunedì Santo*, Holy Monday, *Martedì Santo*, Holy Tuesday, etc., we were in church every night performing some rite. On *Giovedì Santo*, Holy Thursday, I recall twelve men having their feet washed by the priest. Some of these men I had never seen in church before. As a young boy I thought that was a bit odd, but my mom explained to me that *Gesù*, Jesus, had washed the feet of the Apostles before the Last Supper as a sign of humility. Evidence of this practice is found in ancient writings, with hosts removing the sandals of men and washing their feet. I just could not understand why that priest had to wash those feet that probably had not been washed for months.

At the end of the night, we (the altar boys) would help with basically stripping the altar of most items: candles, missals, linens, and everything else that adorned the church. They were removed to make the altar bare and dark, just as Jesus was stripped of everything before crucifixion. The altar and the church were transformed into a dark, solemn space. We were in mourning until the Resurrection.

Venerdì Santo, Good Friday, was a national holiday in Italy. We would again spend a lot of time in church, helping the priest and his mostly female assistants get ready for the procession that would take place that night. It would begin at the church. Most of the townspeople who were able to walk would gather outside, and the priest would lead the flock down the road. Women would recite the rosary. The men would lag behind with their hands clasped and hanging against their lower backs, resting on their buttocks. Some pretended to be praying but probably most were actually thinking about their livestock or other impending work. But realizing how important this tradition was to their family and the town, they participated.

Older Italian men, especially, are seen in this stance. 2014

The procession wound its way out of town on the road that led to the old village of Pagliarone. On a hill, halfway between the old and the new town, were three crosses. The young and the old climbed the hill where the three crosses stood. The priest would lead the flock in prayers, until sunset had turned into the dark of night. We would then go back to church for some more prayers. The streets were dark, as the town had hardly any outside lighting. Candles were the only lights that guided us down the pitch-black dirt road. People would fall, stumbling over rocks sticking out of the ground. Most obstacles were avoided with the knowledge of where they were located, because we all had walked that road countless times. Kids would grab onto their mothers a little tighter if a howl was heard in the distance, thinking that a wolf or a ghost was watching from beyond *reh cierr, gli alberi*, the trees.

By late-night the services were complete and families made their way back home. As we tried to sleep in our straw beds, all we could think of were the sweets already being prepared by *Mamma* that would be ready for us on Saturday.

By the time we opened our eyes on Saturday morning, the sweet smells had already engulfed our modest home. The very same smells were in every home of the village. All the moms, grandmas, aunts, older sisters, and pretty much every female of the town were all busy making Easter goodies. Our favorite was the sweet bread. *Mamma* baked many loaves and she always included special treats for us. She would take boiled eggs and carefully place them in the sweet dough and created different shapes. *Mamma* made one for my sister that looked like a doll, and for us boys she made something more manly — unless we were under the age of five and a *pupetta*, a little doll, sufficed.

I can easily recall those memories of Easter, when *Mamma* would lift the tablecloth laid over the food on the table to reveal the assortment of sweetbreads she had prepared while we slept. That warm, sweet smell from the kitchen was like heaven to us. The reality that we were very poor and barely making it was forgotten on those Saturday mornings before Easter, when we had all and more than we ever needed.

Pupetta di Pasqua, little Easter doll

One of the traditional treats of Easter in our remote village was *sciatone*, called by many other names all over Italy. *Pizza rustica* or *pizza ripiena* are the conventional Italian names. It was a combination of dough, eggs, cheese, and sausage that was a couple of inches thick and either rectangular or round in shape. Because of the rather salty taste, I did not care for it so much, but the adults ate it in abundance.

When Easter Day finally arrived and we got the church obligations over with, the townspeople went to visit their relatives and friends. This was my favorite time because aunts, uncles, *compare e comare*, godfathers and godmothers, would always put something in our hands; maybe a chocolate, a coin, an Easter egg, or some other treat. By the time we got home, my stomach was full and my pockets were bulging with goodies.

Eventually, families had gathered and celebrated the day with as much food as they could afford. Our meal had even included some meat: *pollo*, chicken, *agnello*, lamb, or maybe even *carne di vitello*, veal. When I was ten years old I remember receiving the traditional Italian Easter egg — a huge chocolate wrapped in colorful foil. When we cracked those chocolate eggs, some of which were larger than a football, various small toys appeared. One that I cherished was a simple spinning top.

We did not wake up on Easter morning to see what the Easter bunny had brought us. We saw the eggs and bunnies as representations of fertility all around, reminding us of the approaching *primavera*, spring.

Uovi di Pasqua, Easter eggs, some were huge as compared to a wine bottle!

Although *Pasqua* was a great day for the town, for the kids there was an even more fun and exciting day ahead: *Pasquetta*, little Easter, Easter Monday. This was just another Monday in America, but in Italy it was another day of celebration. This day was one of *scampagnate*, picnics. The word *scampagnata* is derived from *campagna*, meaning 'countryside.' Urban Italians headed out to the countryside of Italy for the springtime picnic. Even though we already lived in the countryside, it was nevertheless a truly fun day for us. We would gather all the leftover food from *Pasqua* and head out to someplace — up to a mountaintop or down near a river, and sometimes to a place farther away — for a day-long picnic.

I remember one such *Pasquetta*. At thirteen years old, this would be my last *scampagnata*. Whether by train, by bike, or by car, all of the kids of

Villa San Michele headed out for *la stazione di San Pietro Avellana*, the train station of San Pietro Avellana, which was a few kilometers east of the actual town of San Pietro. The only soccer field in the area was near the station, on the way to San Pietro. That field was our destination for our day-long picnic.

That day, food was abundant. My mom had packed *panini* for me, along with bread and *prosciutto*, *formaggio*, cheese, and a boiled egg, all enclosed with her sweetbread. She also packed some sweets such as *biscotti*, cookies, and some dark chocolate, leftover from my Easter egg. She had nothing to send with me as a drink, but along with the train fare money, one hundred extra *lire* — equivalent of around ten cents — was proudly put in my pocket by my loving *Mamma*. And with a smile she told me to go to *Mamma* Linda and *Papà* Giulio's *negozio*, a tiny convenience shop across the road from the soccer field, and buy something to drink.

A group of us waited at the tiny train station of Villa San Michele. We could see *la lettorina*, the small passenger train, stopping at the Vastogirardi (Cerreto) station, two kilometers east of ours. Not the fastest train in the world, it seemed to take forever to reach us. The conductor was happy to hear that we would be getting off at the next stop, San Pietro Avellana. We were loud and hyper, probably as a result of our sweets intake of the day before and of that morning, as we waited for the train. A half-hour or so later we were at San Pietro Avellana. Some of our friends traveling by car were already there. No sign yet of those riding bikes, as it would take them a while to go up the mountain road to Vastogirardi and then loop around to reach San Pietro. We all walked down the road towards the field, stopping halfway there at the roadside store.

The proprietors of the tiny shop were a dear elderly couple originally from Capracotta, a town southeast of Villa San Michele. They were childless; maybe that was why they were always so pleasant to us. We called them *Mamma* Linda and *Papà* Giulio. The 'mom' and 'dad' were in reference to their motherly and fatherly personalities. She was slender and always dressed simply but stylishly. He was plump, also neatly dressed with his red suspenders holding up his clean and pressed pants. Their shoes were clean and shiny. Later in my life, memories of *Mamma* Linda and *Papà* Giulio would come back to me as I read books to my children about Santa and Mrs. Claus. They did not mind the invasion of all the kids of Villa San Michele. On the contrary, they loved to see us. They were patient with us, and I am positive that they charged us less than the actual price for the goodies that we wanted. They were truly the salt of the earth.

During my two years of school at the Franciscan monastery in Todi, I was introduced to a soft drink called *chinotto* when we were on a summer-break outing. The carbonated drink was made from the fruit of the myrtle-leaved orange tree, called *chinotto*. The dark-brown soft drink had an herb-like, bittersweet taste. I hated it at first but eventually grew to like it and even crave it. In the store, I rushed to grab a *bottiglia*, a bottle, of *chinotto*, about the same size as a Coca-Cola bottle. To my surprise, *Papà Giulio* gave me back change. At the monastery I had become an avid stamp collector, as were the rest of the boys there, so with my change I purchased a pack of stamps to add to my collection. *Mamma* Linda and *Papà* Giulio bid us farewell, with a warning to be careful and to enjoy ourselves.

We, the boys, played soccer on the mostly dirt soccer field for most of the day. The girls went for walks, picking early spring flowers and ultimately sitting in a circle laughing, whispering, pointing at us, and surely talking about whom was *innamorato*, in love, with whom.

We boarded the last train to Villa San Michele, getting home just before dark. One of my favorite holidays of the year was over. The next day all would be normal again; school for most, work for others. But for me that year, there was a trip to *Napoli*, Naples, with my parents for our physical and mental exams at the American Consulate, in advance of the long journey to America.

Chinotto

Chapter XII

Le Mucche · The Cows

Our two milk cows, Romanella, and her offspring, Paunella, provided a mainstay of our diet during my childhood in Pagliarone. Our two cows were different than most cows in the village. They were mostly gray, splotched with some white and charcoal. I remember my father mentioning that these cows were from northern Italy; the *Grigia alpina* breed comes to mind. My brother, Ezio, loved these cows and treated them well — sometimes better than he treated me and my sister. He was obsessed with them and risked my sister's and my well-being for theirs. He worked overtime to take care of them, forcing us to do the same. He could always be found in the barn tending to our animals, feeding them, and removing straw and manure by shoveling it out the door and piling it up in the field across the barn where, in the coming spring, it would be put into sacks, loaded onto our always dependable donkey, and hauled around to our various lands to enrich the soil.

My brother riding our cow
Romanella as Paunella
looks on, circa 1960

Ezio put down fresh, clean straw on top of the stone and cement floor. Then he would sit on a wooden stool as he milked the cows. When he and I were the only ones there, Ezio would always give me a milk shower by squirting the precious milk at me as I scrambled to hide behind the other cow. Aside from walking in the rain, that was as close as I got to experiencing a shower. I can still see Ezio laughing uncontrollably as he nailed me in the face with warm milk. I enjoyed helping him brush their coats until they were smooth and shiny. Ezio would climb onto the second floor of the barn where the hay was stored and with a pitchfork, he threw the hay down through *la cataratta*, the hatch, into *la mangiatoia*, the trough, for their daily feeding. The *mangiatoia* took up the western wall of our barn, which was about fifteen feet in length.

The animals always lined up the same way, with the cows closer to the door and our donkey at the end. Every morning Ezio would lead them out the door for the walk to the fountain of Luigi for their daily drink. If other animals were there we would have to wait our turn and be careful not to involve our animals in any skirmishes with the other cows, although my brother welcomed it. Someone would always complain about the wait or the length of time other cows took for their drink from that cold natural spring. During those gas wars in the U.S. during the 1980s, memories returned to me of how similar those long lines of cars at the gas stations were to the long lines of cows at our village fountain, waiting to fill up. I was always worried about our cows and/ or my brother getting into a fight, but my brother looked forward to it and enjoyed the possibility of any of that happening. Our cows were well taken care of and very healthy, making them the odds-on favorite to win any confrontations with other cows. My brother made sure of that, and usually he would have to be reprimanded by our dad for allowing our cows to bully our neighbors' animals.

Ezio tended to go over the top when it came to tending to our livestock. We had a beautiful *vitello*, calf, a gift from our dependable and reliable cow, Romanella. Hopefully the new calf was going to fetch enough money *alla fiera*, at the fair, to sustain our family for the whole year.

These markets were held in bigger towns around the region at a predetermined time of the year. Everybody knew when a certain *fiera* was taking place. The markets I remember most were those in Castel di Sangro, *la fiera di Maddalena e la fiera di Tutti i Santi*. We would walk the fifteen or so miles loaded down with food for us and for the animals. Since one of those markets was a two-day event, we stayed overnight, sleeping in makeshift beds on the ground near our animals.

There were other markets near our town such as Carovilli, Forli di Sannio, and Roccasicura. Our village was too small to hold such an event, so every time we had to sell or buy animals and other supplies, we would have to walk — sometimes very long distances. Farmers from all of the various surrounding towns would come to buy or sell their animals. The scene was similar to a present-day flea market, where there were the usual vendors selling apparel, shoes, fruits, vegetables, and other provisions. And then there were the numerous vendors selling all sorts of items they either made or had at hand, that they were selling for cash or barter.

Also at the markets there were obviously artisans who brought their products, which were usually related to farming or ranching, such as saddles and farming tools. But the majority of the vendors were there to sell or trade their livestock. The bigger, healthier, and stronger an animal was the more money or barter it fetched. Our calf was going to fetch a lot; my brother was going to make sure of that. He meticulously cared for this bull calf, keeping it well fed and groomed. My father would always warn him not to overfeed it with fresh *erba medica*, alfalfa, to avoid bloating.

One fine spring morning my brother took the calf out for a fresh feeding. Once back at the barn, my father noticed that our calf had bloated and began to panic. Somebody would have to fetch Amico, my *Zia* Ida's father in Campanello, because as a licensed butcher, Amico somehow qualified as the town's veterinarian. I recall all the people who were not out in the fields gathered outside our barn, waiting with us anxiously for the arrival of Amico, who was summoned by one of the older kids who could run the couple of kilometers to Campanello the fastest. There was no time to wait for a real veterinarian to come from the neighboring town of Carovilli; something would have to be done quickly. So the tall and neatly dressed Amico (at least that's how I remember him) walked towards our *pagliao*, barn, to release the gas created by the fresh alfalfa, or the calf would soon die.

Amico did not guarantee success, and mentioned that he had seen this procedure being performed by vets and had only attempted it a few times with some success. My father gave him permission and with a knife, Amico cut a hole and inserted a small tube into our baby bulls' belly. I was standing by my worried brother, mother and sister as the calf's legs soon became weak and he suddenly tumbled to the ground in obvious distress. His mouth was foaming and his breathing became heavy and irregular. His belly filled like a balloon, ready to explode. Finally he took his last breath, causing my dad to weep and my mom to wail with her hands grasped together above her head. As a young boy I did not fully comprehend the tragedy. Amico suggested that we quickly butcher the young bull and sell the meat to the villagers at a discounted price; and hope that it would not be reported to the authorities, who would otherwise force my dad to bury the carcass.

When my mom put her hands above her head, it signaled some sort of anguish. I wish we had a photo of the familiar pose. My sister remembers it well, 2015.

The news quickly traveled throughout the village and people came to buy some of the meat to help my distraught parents with their loss. My brother was devastated and also had to endure my father's wrath. If he was sort of a loner before this tragedy, I think he went deeper down that road. The embarrassment caused Ezio to stay away from people and spend more time with his beloved animals and the land. Not once did I see him play soccer or other games. He loved our little hamlet of Luigi and spent as much time as possible away from Campanello, our new home. He would always leave the house before dawn and come home after dark. Many times my father would have to go out looking for him at our scattered pieces of grazing fields and bring him and the animals back home to our barn in Luigi.

Soon after the death of our calf, our other cow, Paunella, became pregnant. My job that summer was to take our cows to *la posta*, a land that was fairly far from Luigi. It could be reached by following a path along the railroad track that wound its way towards San Pietro Avellana, a town northwest of ours. I did not mind that route. Although longer and a lot of it uphill, it was the passage I preferred because the other easier and shorter path was haunted! This "haunted" path that followed the river Vandra was densely wooded with many different types of trees, some very tall, which denied the summer sun to peek through, rendering the rocky pathway dark and eerie. Whenever I was enticed by my dad to take the shorter, safer road with no trains to worry about, I became very agitated and would only go that way if accompanied by someone else.

I recall that late summer morning of 1962. As a nine-year-old, I was burdened with the job of taking our two cows to that faraway land for their daily grazing. This was a difficult and strenuous undertaking for a young boy, but for the adult population of the village it was just another routine part of their workday. That day I was to meet up with *Lino di Zirr*, a boy from the hamlet downhill from Luigi called Zirr. Lino was about four years older than I and I hoped that he would be able to help me with my cows, especially Paunella, our very pregnant cow.

After about one hour we reached the grazing lands of *la posta* and the cows went to town grazing on the fresh green grass. Lino and I set up our camp under a big shade tree, where we could keep an eye on our small herd. As the sun shone its hot rays on the cows, they sought refuge under some shade trees, where they lay down for their afternoon nap and battled the ever-present flies by swatting them away with their tails. Lino and I ate our plain lunch of bread with *mortadella* and cheese and decided to follow it up with some dessert, maybe wild berries or some hazelnuts. We searched the surrounding area for them and found a hazelnut tree that we promptly climbed to look for *villane, avellane,* hazelnuts, that were ready for consumption. The ripe hazelnuts were those with a brownish color and not the green ones. We stayed in that tree and enjoyed the few hazelnuts that were ripe and played on the limbs as if we were Tarzan. Of course as young kids normally do, we lost track of time.

Suddenly a panic came over me as I looked over to where the cows had been resting and saw only Paunella lying down, in distress. The other cows were up and grazing again, gazing at Paunella. We ran over to her and to our amazement we saw two feet sticking out of her vagina.

I screamed in fear. Lino ran away from the cow, choosing not to deal with the situation. Left there by myself, I had to make a choice, and one of them was surely not to assist the cow by pulling on those two feet, as I recalled men doing during past births. My hands were too small and weak. Scared and stunned, I began to cry uncontrollably. Lino was watching me from a distance, pacing back-and-forth, expecting me, the younger kid, to resolve the situation.

I decided to hit Paunella with my walking stick and force her to get up, in hope that the baby calf would go back into her belly. This upset the cow greatly and as she struggled to her feet, she turned towards me with her head down, ready to charge me and gore me to death. Waving her head back-and-forth in a frenzy, she put the fear of God in me. I backed away and started to run towards Lino. Paunella started after me and as the two of us boys screamed with fear, she ran right past us faster than I had ever seen that pregnant cow run. She was headed towards the trail to Pagliarone. Lino urged me to follow her while he looked after Romanella, our other cow.

I could hardly keep up with Paunella. I was huffing and puffing, but I had to keep up with her. If I lost her, that would be the end of me. As we reached the fork in the trail, I prayed that she would go left, the northern route that followed the railroad tracks. I tried in vain to catch up to her and hopefully steer her towards the northern trail. She must have known that the quickest way to the barn was the southern route because she didn't even hesitate in heading for the heavily wooded and haunted route.

I froze when I reached that fork in the road. I had never walked that path by myself, and even when I walked it with my parents, I was very apprehensive. And now I was in the most difficult situation of my young life: Either follow the cow and deal with what that forest had in store for me, or just walk home along the tracks and hope that the cow makes it home. Tales of bandits lurking inside that forest, waiting for opportunities to steal animals and sometime kids ran through my head. If the pregnant cow vanished, I would without a doubt suffer some major punishment. As tears filled my eyes, I made the decision to enter that dark and mysterious forest.

I was running as fast as I could but could not see or hear my cow. Sounds of birds singing in the trees brought temporary peace in my mind, but as I went deeper into the woods, the sound of the rushing waters of the river Vandra rang in my ears. The trail paralleled the northern banks of the river. I had never seen it and never wanted to, but I heard the story countless times about a part of the river that formed a whirlpool and if you got too close to the bank, the undercurrent would pull you in and swallow you into its bottomless hole. Visions of Paunella disappearing in that hole entered my already crowded mind. As the sound of rushing waters got louder, I moved as far away from the river as possible, also being careful not to enter the deep forest and deal with its secrets.

Suddenly I envisioned a man hanging from a rope around his neck, swaying back-and-forth and staring at me and then reaching for me. It was that same man about whom my *Zia* Ida narrated to us during those fireside stories, which she did with as much vigor and enthusiasm as that of any modern day orator. Our parents, grandparents, aunts and uncles were our books. Not having many books to read, our families read us books that were stored in the memory files of the computers of their minds. The storytellers were our children's books. Some of those stories would not be suitable by today's standards for our children, but for us there were no guidelines. We were expected to be tough, yet we were children.

In one story, the two *briganti*, bandits, forced a poor man deep into that forest, hanged him on the tallest tree, and stole his beautiful black horse. That man now haunted the forest. There were stories of people walking on that same path on which I was walking now all alone, and they would hear the pounding of a horse's hoofs. While turning their heads to see who was coming up behind them, they would get only a glimpse of the horse and his rider as they disappeared into the forest. Some people reported seeing only a horse suddenly appear and then disappear. Or they would only hear a galloping horse without ever seeing it, even after an extensive search of the deep forest from where the noise was coming.

I was faced with a multitude of problems while running as fast as I could through the heavily wooded hell. The sun's rays forced their way through the tall, dense trees periodically, creating shadows that my mind confused with a man dangling from a tree or a black horse galloping towards me to mow me down. I did not dare to look behind me. Surely someone was following me, waiting for the right moment to take me into the forest or throw me into the rushing waters of the river, where the whirling pool would suck me into the deep, black, bottomless hole. I had no more tears to shed; I just wailed quietly as I waited for my demise.

I wondered if my pregnant cow had wandered near the whirlpool and was sucked in, or was she way ahead of me and close to home? Hopefully one of us would be spared. My family would at least have plenty of cow's milk, along with the money that a calf would fetch at the fair.

Although in reality that stretch of deep, dark backwoods was not that long, for me it seemed to be never-ending. I was sure that I would never make it out of there alive. As I struggled through this nightmare world, a loud and chilling lightning and thunder roared through the trees, causing me to stumble and fall onto the dirt pathway; and now my ordeal included being in a cold wind tunnel. Surely this was the perfect moment for that horseman to reach down and swiftly scoop me up onto his big black horse.

I remember mumbling the word *Mamma* and for a moment, I saw my mom coming towards me to save me. I closed my eyes for a second and focused on that figure coming my way. It wasn't my mom. My mom would have her hands outstretched, ready to take me safely in her arms. This figure was waving her arms up and down and every which way, screaming at me, telling me that Paunella almost ran her over as she raced past her. It was Fonzina, Sestino's wife, neighbors from the Pietro hamlet below Luigi. Their barn was located near our house. I sometimes played with their daughter, Natalina, who was a couple of years older than I. Fonzina rambled on and on, admonishing me about the runaway cow as she balanced her rush basket on her head with one hand and pointing at me with the other. I hardly heard anything she was saying; I was just delighted to see a living person in that hell hole. And I was absolutely elated to know that my cow was safely out of there and still bolting towards home. As Fonzina walked deeper into the forest, probably on her way to bring her husband food and to help him with his day's work, she warned me to hurry home because the sky was dark and soon it would rain.

I looked up as I came out of the woods and into a clearing and the sun had disappeared, replaced by dark clouds. Lightning lit up the sky in the distance. I wondered why God was punishing me with this deplorable day. As the houses of Luigi came into view, I strained my eyes to look for any sign of Paunella. All I could see and hear were the trees swaying back-and-forth from the strong winds that had suddenly made a presence with the black clouds above. I rushed towards our barn and as I turned the corner of the row of stone structures, I saw Paunella at the door of our barn. She was pacing back-and-forth, nudging the door with her horns. She seemed to be in a great panic and in distress.

I ran as fast as my short legs could go and opened the barn door, at the same time keeping an eye on my pregnant cow in case she decided to punish me for putting her through this ordeal. I had never seen her or any other cow in such a state before and it scared me. She rushed inside and promptly lay down. Not knowing what to do next, I ran out of there in a panic.

In that same cluster of attached structures was also the location of the house and barn of Luigi, *il guardiano*. The forest ranger must have heard the commotion. I noticed him walking towards me and that alarmed me even more. In a low, calm voice he asked me, *"Che è succiess?"* (*Che è successo?* What happened?) I pointed to the door of our barn. He peeked inside and then walked towards his own barn, faster than I had ever seen him walk, and returned with a rope. He rushed back inside our barn.

Hesitantly, I peered inside and noticed that Paunella was in great distress, and then I saw two little legs emerge from her backside. Luigi proceeded to tie the rope around the tiny legs. He got down to his knees directly behind the cow and while wrapping the rope around his arms, he began to pull. The cow turned her head towards Luigi, breathing heavily, her mouth foaming. I worried that she would attack Luigi (I don't recall anyone calling him by his given name, always *reh vardianeh*). The cow turned and gave him a gaze. I was positioned by the barn's door, ready to run if Paunella decided to turn on the forest ranger. But as her head moved up and down, I knew that she was thankful for the help. Finally after what seemed an eternity but was actually a few minutes, the young baby calf was out and immediately struggled to stand on her feet. Her mother got on her feet and turned to see her newborn, and began to smell and lick the baby calf.

Luigi continued to help, putting fresh straw down for the mom and baby, making sure that there was hay in the *mangiatoia*, the feeding trough, and water in the bucket. I had not moved an inch from my position by the door, still scared to death from the day's experience and also apprehensive of the forest ranger, the man whom most people in town feared. He looked at me and asked me, *"Andò shta patrteh?"* (*Dov'è tuo padre?* Where's your dad?) Before I could answer him the barn door opened and my dad hurried in, soaking wet. I peered outside and noticed a downpour coming from the dark sky.

It seemed as though all the moisture in the sky was being released onto our little village, nestled in the Apennine Mountains of Molise. My father quickly went over to Paunella, giving her a couple of pats on her back, and then to the new baby calf that was now trying to latch onto her mother's teat. My father told Luigi, "*Parabuone ca che shtiv tu*" (*Che fortuna che c'eri tu*, Good thing you were here). He did not profusely thank him for the help; it would almost be an insult. It was assumed that help would be given to a neighbor, even when those neighbors may not see eye to eye.

Neighbors, brothers, cousins, fathers, and sons could be in the biggest argument and not talk for years, but if one needed help at a crucial moment, they would give each other help. And that helpful occasion might end what was usually a silly argument, or it might just suspend it momentarily and then it would be back to warring again. My father, or more so my brother, had had clashes with the forest ranger. As a result of my brother's numerous trespasses on government lands, my family thought that the forest ranger — our relative and neighbor, Luigi — had it in for my brother. But I think that all the other families of the village thought the same way when Luigi hit them with a fine. Needless to say, after that day I had a different opinion of the man with the huge rifle and his big German shepherd.

My father finally turned his attention to me, asking me where Romanella, our other cow, was. She was at *la posta*. Hopefully Lino would bring her back home if they did not drown in the *diluvio*, downpour. I am sure that deep down he was anguished about what I went through that day, but he did not communicate that to me in any way. After all, I was accountable and responsible for the safety and well-being of those cows, and if I had jeopardized that, then for sure my father would have communicated that to me by giving me a lecture, followed by a couple of smacks to my face. My mother, on the other hand, kept saying, "*Povr citr mieh*," *Il mio povero bambino*, My poor baby, bragging to the listening ears how smart I was to get Paunella home for the birth!

Later that afternoon my family had gathered, along with relatives and friends, to check out the new addition to our stock and to give a helping hand. I felt important that day and surely my actions would be another notch towards manhood. My brother, Ezio, would have been so proud of me. I wished I could have talked to him, to tell him all about our new calf, but he was in the faraway land of Switzerland tending to someone else's cows.

Lino did guide Romanella back towards our hamlet, because as the sun was going down over the rain-drenched mountains she appeared at the barn door, peeking in and wondering what the hell all the commotion was about. I had instantly connected with our new baby calf and would spend most of that summer attending to her every need. As I left every morning for different grazing lands, our little baby calf would line up behind her mother and make the journey with us, and if she fell behind, Paunella would pause and wait for her to catch up to us. She would playfully run up to us and fall in line again. At times she would decide that she was hungry and wanted to feed, but I would have to push her away from her mother until we reached our destination, and then she could nurse while her mother grazed on fresh grass.

Calf trying to feed while en route to pasture, 1975

We had many different animals while growing up in Pagliarone. Our two cows, Romanella and Paunella, bring back some of my most vivid memories. They were an integral part of my family's well-being, providing us with plenty of milk, which was essential to our daily diets. My mom and dad made cheese almost daily. *Caciocavallo* and *scamorza*, cheeses typical of the Molise region, were always hanging in our kitchen to dry. Those two cows also provided us with many healthy heifers and bulls that my father usually brought to markets, near and far, to sell or trade for other animals and/or goods.

Normally a male cow that had been castrated was used for heavy work in the fields. I have vivid memories of my father, with the help of my Uncle Umberto, tying the testicles of a young bull with a string, causing the testicles to dry and eventually fall off in a few weeks. That bull became *reh vove*, *il bue*, an ox. These animals were bigger and a lot more docile than a breeding bull. The oxen were used to pull *l'aratro*, a plow, to break the usually hard ground for cultivation. These animals needed to be strong and durable for that hard work. Two oxen would be put side by side, harnessed together with a yoke. The yoke was a wooden bar with two U-shaped poles that went around the oxen's necks, with another long pole attached perpendicularly that went back to the plow. The oxen were controlled by attaching steel prongs to their nostrils, but sometimes an additional worker would guide them by pulling them with a rope.

Most female cows were not strong enough for this task, but our strong, dependable Romanella and Paunella were exceptions. With their help, my dad and brother plowed many fields. When the cows got tired and slowed their pull, a long pole with a sharp nail at one end which we called *la vertica* was used to poke their butts, to make them keep on pulling that plow.

We did not like seeing our two cows with their behinds speckled with pricks and dried blood that had dribbled out of the punctures. We would wash the wounds, eventually they would heal, and the cows would be ready for another round of poking and urging them to pull that plow harder.

Some might think that there were some activities that bordered on animal abuse in our village. Anywhere or anytime in this sometimes cruel world of ours, where a choice has to be made between human survival and a heavy burden placed on work animals, one would think that human survival would be the option chosen all of the time.

Our cows were the most important part of our family possessions. The number of cows a family owned affirmed their standing and social status in town. We always owned at least two cows, probably average for our town. Some families did not own any cattle and it seemed that either they were involved in some other employment enterprise, or they just could not afford to own that very important commodity.

l'aratro, the plow

Chapter XIII

LA CHIESA E LA PIAZZA
THE CHURCH AND THE SQUARE

I remember, vaguely, an old church at Pasquale, a hamlet in the valley below our hamlet of *Lvg*, Luigi. The old church was deteriorating as a result of the landslides. When a new church had been built in the new part of town, the old structure was torn down in the early sixties. Some of its old parts were reused at the new church in Campanello, the new town on the north side of the hill that we called *Colle dei Noci*. Built on the west side of the village and set slightly higher than the houses, the church was certainly the centerpiece of the village. It seemed to oversee

Villa San Michele's church

everything that went on in the town. And the priest was the eyes of that stone structure and what it represented. All of us respected and most of us young ones feared the priest and the Church. The man in the black robe manifested the clear and obvious power that has existed in the Italian Catholic Church for many centuries.

Ever since Simon Peter established the Catholic Church in Rome, it has played a major role in the lives of Italians. Every tradition that exists in Italy takes part in some way in its churches. From the beginning of life with a baptism to the end with a funeral, the church is involved. The only aspect of our lives in the new world in America that was somewhat the same as the one in Italy was the Catholic Church.

The word catholic is derived from the Greek word *katholicos*, meaning 'universal.' The early Roman citizens referred to this new religion that followed the teachings of Jesus as catholic; as its followers could be found throughout the Roman Empire[6]. In the faraway lands of America, the Catholic Church had established itself and the universal liturgy of the church here was similar to that in our small remote village and throughout Italy. The physical structures were for the most part analogous, making us feel at home when we attended functions. But there was also one glaring difference that could not be ignored: the language. Aside from the few Latin words, all functions were conveyed in English by mostly English speaking priests and other lay people.

In our village as a small child, I would attend church with my mom, brother, and sister. As my brother, Ezio, got older he suddenly was missing from most church functions, as my dad had been ever since I could remember. Some of the village's men could be seen outside of the

---

[6] *There was only one official institution of Christianity for its first thousand years, which is why it was the universal church. The word 'catholic' (small c) means universal. Then in 1054, the Roman Catholic Church, as it is called today, split from the Church of the Eastern Roman Empire, Byzantium (its capital, Constantinople, is today's Istanbul in Turkey). The Byzantine or Eastern Church is today referred to as Orthodox Christianity, which includes the Greek Orthodox and Russian Orthodox Churches. The Roman Catholic Church continued its sole control of Western Christianity until the mid 1500s when its monopoly was fragmented during the Reformation, out of which came the Protestant (those who protest the pope's ultimate authority) denominations (Lutheran, Episcopalian, Presbyterian, Methodist, etc.). For the most part, those countries in Europe farthest from Rome, such as Northern Germany, England, and all of Scandinavia broke away from Catholic control, while those countries closest to Rome remained Roman Catholic.*

church, sitting or standing by its steps, usually arguing about something related to the state of our town, region, or country. Sometimes the arguments or discussions got so loud that they could be heard inside the church, annoying the hell out of the priest. Most of the town's men were actually nowhere to be found within the confines of the church, but were somewhere working some piece of land or tending to their animals. Unless there was an important ceremony such as a baptism, communion, confirmation, wedding, or funeral, men were usually not part of the daily religious functions, such as Mass or reciting the rosary. Women and children and elderly men made up the majority of the congregation. Most of the time the priest and the *sagrestano*, sacristan, were the only adult males inside the church.

*Jackie and I posing next to l'edificio, our school with la chiesa,
the church overlooking the village, 1975*

Being an altar boy, I was involved with many of our church's functions. I recall serving Mass for many marriages and funerals. I and the other altar boys had many other assignments in addition to serving Mass. My worst fear was not having the correct vestment ready for the priest when he came into to the *sagrestia*, sacristy. I recall checking a book to see what color and type of vestment was required for that day, and those priests were very meticulous when it came to their vestments. The priests that I recall being altar boy for were Don Nicola D'Amico, Don Antonio Di Lorenzo, and Don Felice Fangio, who is the present-day priest.

I would practice ringing *le campane*, the bells, after every Mass and finally I was given the job of ringing the bells during Mass. During consecration, when the bread and wine were prepared and blessed by the priest for Holy Communion, the altar boy would ring the bells.

Our bells were fashioned with a handle at the center of four arms, with each arm reaching out a few inches to one corner of a square, with a bell on each arm. Their shiny gold color gave them the appearance of being priceless. One ring was easy enough, but when the priest presented the host and the chalice, the bells would have to be rung three times in three very distinct and sharp rings. If the rings were muffled or not separated with a short silence, the priest would give the ringer a quick discontented stare. Practicing endlessly on the wrist action required to properly ring the bells paid off, as this job was given to me by Don Felice. I really did not know the exact reason for ringing the bells, but when I rang those bells, it awakened some of the napping parishioners, so I assumed that ringing those bells was to wake them up and alert them that Holy Communion was going to be bestowed to them. I kept that important and prestigious job until we emigrated to America. I was among the elite of the altar boys.

le campane, the bells

There was another big bell job for which we, the altar boys, were responsible. Between the church and the priest's residence stood *il campanile*, the bell tower. It seemed to be as high as the moon to my young eyes, but it was just slightly taller than the church. Looking up at the huge bells hanging, dangling on top of the tower, I was mesmerized and frightened. With the help of other altar boys, we would grab onto the enormous ropes and pull as hard as possible. The bells were much heavier than we were. They seemed to pull us up, and I feared that they would pull me to the top and then release me to the stone floor, smashing my small body into million pieces. My even greater fear was that for sure, one of those times the ropes would come loose and the huge bells would come crushing down on us, flattening us like pizzas.

The responsibility of ringing those bells was extensive. The loudness and interval of the sounds signified different functions that were about to take place in the church. A mistake might falsely inform the town that a funeral was about to take place instead of a wedding or the usual celebration of Mass. A mistake such as that would enrage the priest. If there were only a couple of us little guys pulling on those ropes, the mistake was inevitable, summoning the priest who would scold us and then help us with the ropes.

When we were back in the village during the summer of 2014, I visited with Don Felice.

il campanile, the bell tower, 1975

He had just celebrated fifty years of priesthood, all in our small village. As I visited with him and we spoke about the church of some fifty years ago, he mentioned that when he was eight years old he was ringing the bells in his town, and a stone did fall from atop the *campanile* and struck his foot; and he hopped around on one foot for days. He also took me inside the *campanile*. The ropes were gone and the area where we pulled the ropes was now occupied by a boiler that provided heat for the church and his living quarters. The bells were now rung electronically; the modern age of electronics had even changed the ringing of church bells.

My favorite memory of the church was actually its piazza, the square. Many of the boys of the village gathered on the church's piazza to play *calcio*, soccer, because it was the only *pianura*, flat ground, around. Before 1960 soccer was almost nonexistent in our small, remote village. The game was played by kids in the cities, by those who could afford a round ball to kick around. We could not even kick a can, as anything that resembled a can was used for something more productive than soccer. With the advent of television, the game would evolve in every nook and cranny of Italy's landscape. In our old town of Pagliarone, we played with rolled up rags or whatever we could fashion into something round. We played in every conceivable small space we could find.

My brother, Ezio, came back from Switzerland, where he had been working on a farm owned by German speaking cattle farmers. One summer in one of those early years of the 60s, he brought me a huge Swiss chocolate bar and an actual ball; the elastic rubber beach ball type, not a real soccer ball, but my friends and I rejoiced over that perfect round ball.

I immediately gathered my friends together for a soccer game on our *aia* in Luigi. How great it was to kick that ball around. We did not mind that the ground was uneven and littered with rocks and cow plop. We were in heaven, playing and learning the tricks of the game. And then the unthinkable happened. Someone kicked the ball over the edge of the terrace, sending it down below. The soccer ball rolled and bounced down that hill faster than anything we had ever seen. We all started the descent down the slope to rescue our prized possession. The ball took one last big bounce and was headed directly for a bush, a thorn bush.

We all froze as we heard the 'swoosh.' When we reached the bottom of the hill, I carefully made my way into the bush, scratching my legs and arms, but I had to get to my ball. I finally saw it. It was a mere shell of the beautiful sphere that my brother proudly handed me the day before. It had shrunk into a tiny, wrinkled-up, bumpy shape; it aged a hundred years in an instant. I immediately began to cry as I pulled the tiny plastic blob out of the thornbush. The other kids were as equally disturbed as I, some also cried. We lumbered back up the hill, and with our heads down, we all went home.

I carried my punctured ball up the stairs and into my house. My mother let out an *"eeeehhh e mò! La sete bucata," e adesso! L'avete bucata*, now what! You punctured it. My brother promised me that he would buy me a new one when he returned to Switzerland. The next day we cut a hole in the ball's shell, stuffed a bunch of rags inside, and resumed playing our beloved sport.

My brother was almost ten years older than I. He had never even kicked a soccer ball. His athletic endeavors were minimal, as they were with most other older kids of our town. Whatever games they played involved sticks and stones. Balls of any kind were absent from our village. When those older kids saw us kicking something, they would come over and give it a try. They were all either very unskilled or uncoordinated and clumsy. Disgusted, they would walk away, lamenting that we were wasting precious time playing that silly game and that we should go help with the important things, like shoveling manure out of the barn!

The church's piazza was the only fair-sized area where we could actually play a semblance of a soccer game. The town did not have a soccer field, it never did. In the 1980s a small soccer field was built on top of *Colle dei Noci*, the hill just south of Villa San Michele. But before that, the asphalt surface of the church was our field. We used to play on the cobblestone streets of town, but after a few broken windows we were driven out of there. Men such as *Toni di Fuorla* from Forli threatened to kill us all if we played in front of his house and, God forbid, if we broke one of his windows. *Toni* never even touched us; he just loved to yell and harass us, but I think deep inside he enjoyed watching us kids play soccer!

Unfortunately, we would be continually ousted from the church grounds by the priest, his mother or sister, or by others that did not want us playing that silly game. But we kept going back until they got tired of sending us away. Our parents would forever wonder why we were not as persistent when it came to homework or farm work.

During one of those cold winter days, a group of us waited in front of the church for our friend *Peppino*, Giuseppe Flagiello. We called him *Peppino di Totò* because his father's name was *Totò*, a Napolitan nickname for Antonio. *Totò* and his brothers were traveling clothing and shoe vendors from Napoli. He met Esmeralda Iacovetta, a girl from our village, and married her. *Peppino* would later become my cousin when he married my cousin, Adelia Carmosino. He was also related to me on his mother's side of the family. *Peppino's* grandpa had immigrated to America, to Denver. *Peppino* received a letter from his grandpa notifying him that he had sent a package, and in that package he had included among other things, a ball.

Peppino and the rest of us waited for that package for what seemed an eternity — it was actually a couple of months. Finally the package arrived. His father collected it from the post office and brought the package home with *Peppino* in tow. He told us to go wait at the church and he would bring the ball over so we could play soccer. We anxiously waited there, keeping an eye on the stairs that led to our houses, from where *Peppino* would come up to the piazza with the brand new soccer ball.

Finally *Peppino* emerged from down those stairs and as he approached us, we noticed that he was a bit disappointed. We noticed the brownish ball he was carrying, and as he got closer we all stared at the misshapen ball with pointed ends. It looked like a huge brown egg. *Peppino* lamented that it must have gotten crushed in the package during its long journey from America. We all tried to push on each end, hoping to massage it back to a round shape.

That ball was all we had, so we started to kick it around. I recall the frustration we all had trying to keep that ball in front of us, to make our dribbling moves and take our shots on the goals consisting of two rocks a few feet apart. I don't remember if we ever learned what that ball was, but we kept playing with it, controlling it as best as possible. That oblong ball probably made us better soccer players, as it bounced every which way but straight.

When I came to America, on that first day of school, at recess, I saw the exact same balls as the one *Peppino's* grandpa had sent him. The American kids were not kicking those balls, they were throwing them. That funny ball that we played soccer with in our village was a football, the American football! The ball that is not kicked, as the name implies, rather it was usually thrown.

But in Italy, as we got a little older, we still played in the churchyard of our village, although we would also go with the older kids to the only soccer field around our area. It was right near the railroad station of San Pietro Avellana. We would take the *littorina* train there most times, but we would also walk or ride bikes, which meant going all the way to Vastogirardi and then back down to San Pietro, a long loop-around. We were exhausted by the time we reached the soccer field. Today there is a much needed asphalt road that connects Villa San Michele with San Pietro. It follows the rail line and takes just a few minutes to reach the town of San Pietro Avellana.

As a boy, the church and its piazza were central gathering spots for the townspeople. While I was an altar boy for many funerals and weddings at our own church, Don Felice would put me on the back of his scooter and we would go to Cerreto, an even smaller town about two kilometers east of ours, where I would serve Mass at the Church of San Felice.

I enjoyed being an altar boy, and that might have given certain people the misconception that I might want to follow the calling and become a priest. My brother and sister certainly thought that. Every time they put together make-believe plays in our little hamlet with the rest of the kids, I would always be elected to play the part of the priest. I resisted playing that part. I wanted to be the father, the doctor, or somebody else, but eventually I got stuck with the part of the priest.

I was not always a good altar boy. I remember opening a drawer of a cabinet in the church and seeing a lot of coins, money collected at Mass. I figured that a couple of coins would not be missed, and not being able to resist the temptation, I helped myself to two 100 *lire* coins (equal to about twenty cents) and invited my friends to play *bigliardino*, foosball, at the small rec room adjacent to the church. When asked by my friends where I got the money to pay for the many games we played, I said that I found it on the piazza. Of course I had lied and I felt very guilty for taking the money. In the back of my mind I always wondered when God was going to punish me for stealing from the Church. I don't remember whether or not I confessed my sin to the priest, but if I did, I am sure I did not offer the details!

Some things never change, most older women in church are usually dressed in black, mourning a loved one. Pietrantonio Lombardi, Donetta Lombardi, Silvia Lombardi, 2014

Chapter XIV

IL BATTESIMO · THE BAPTISM

There are seven sacraments in the Catholic Church: *Battesimo*, Baptism; *Eucarista/Comunione*, Eucharist/Communion; *Confessione*, Confession; *Cresima*, Confirmation; *OrdineSacro*, HolyOrders/Ordination; *Matrimonio*, Matrimony; and *Unzione degli infermi*, Anointing of the sick. These sacraments, or gifts from God, were derived from ancient pre-Christian rituals that marked the stages of life. The sacraments were an important aspect in the lives of the people of our village. They were taken very seriously and were acted upon in the strictest accordance with the Church.

Presently, baptisms are performed when the baby is a few months old, but this was not so in our village. Life in the Catholic community began with the first of the seven sacraments. As newborns were baptized, immersed in water, the original sin committed by Adam of disobeying God, was removed. This purification removed the original sin, signified us as united with God, and made us members of the Catholic Church. In our village, babies were baptized within a week of birth. The urgency for this rite was out of fear that a baby might die, which happened many times. If a baby died before baptism, then there was the belief that he was doomed for Limbo[7] because of the original sin, with which we were born, thanks to Adam.

I was born on January 10, 1953. I would always ask my mom and dad if they were absolutely sure that that was indeed the date of my birth. Stories often circulated in our village about the authenticity of someone's age. My dad told me that on Monday, January 19, 1953, the day after I was baptized, he and friends Giovanni Lombardi and Salvatore Lombardi walked in deep snow to Vastogirardi, to *il comune*, the municipality and

---

Lombardi Ezio Giovanni: nato il 14.6.1944
battezzato il 30.7.1944 don Edolo Casacchia; Padrini: Giovanni e Dalinda Lombardi
cresimato il 4.6.51 da mons. Epimenio Giannico; Padrino: Gatta Emidio

Lombardi Pietrantonio: nato il 10.1.1953
battezzato il 18.01.1953 da don Pasquale Lalli; Madrina: Carmosino Linda
cresimato 4.7.65 da mons. Pio Augusto Crivellari; Padrino: Carmosino Davide

Lombardi Maria Bambina: nata il 2.2.1948
battezzato il 3.2.1948 da don Edolo Casacchia; Padrini: Giovanni e Linda Iacovetta – Lo...
cresimato il 22.6.58 da mons. Pio Augusto Crivellari; Madrina: Carmosino Maria

Non esistono i registri di Prima Comunione.

Villa San Michele, 4.2.2011

Il parroco
don Felice Fangio

Don Felice Fangio

Baptism and confirmation dates of my brother, sister, and me.

[7] *The medieval Church constructed a detailed plan of Hell, which can be seen in Dante's Inferno. It was understood to be a descending vortex, with Satan at the bottom. Those closest to him in the pit of ice were the betrayers who committed sins of the spirit including, among others, Judas. Above them were those who committed violent acts. Above them were the thieves. The top level of Hell was for those who gave in to the sins of the flesh, such as the gluttons and adulterers. Just above them, at what was considered to be a halfway point between Heaven and Hell, Dnate's Purgatory. It wasn't bad, but it wasn't Heaven. This is where unbaptized babies, the likes of Socrates and other good pagans (those who never heard the Gospel, not to be confused with the heathens, who heard it and rejected it) would spend eternity. In 2007 the Catholic Church did away with its official teaching of a belief in Limbo.*

applied for my birth certificate. His friends acted as witnesses to the fact that I was indeed born on January 10. My godparents were Linda Carmosino Iacovetta and Giovanni Iacovetta. This was the same couple who had baptized my brother and sister. Only Linda was present for mine because her husband, Giovanni, had emigrated to Canada, and Linda awaited the paperwork to follow him there.

By the time I was nine years old I was a full-fledged altar boy. I looked forward to serving Mass when there was a baptism. I hated being there during a funeral. There seemed to be an equal number of the two rites. That wheel of our village kept turning: one would fall off and one would get on. The saddest piece of life in our town was when there was the baptism of a baby, soon followed by a funeral for that same baby. My mom reminded me many times that, for sure, all the joy that you experience during a celebration is all paid back during times of sorrow. She was so overjoyed when my sister and her family came to visit from Toronto and almost at the same time, she would mention that that joy would have to be all given back the day they went back to Canada. I would tell her that with that attitude, it was better if they had never come, and she would quietly say, "Oh no." The day that my sister, or for that matter any other relative, had to go back home, my mom would put on this long, sad face and we would all anticipate her crying for days after their departure.

Present-day baptisms are not celebrated as in years past, here in America or in Italy. The sacrament, typically performed on a Sunday, is attended by close family, and the sponsors or the godparents are usually family members. In the past, the godparents were chosen out of the immediate family circle, and they were referred to not by their names, rather by *comare* for the woman and *compare* for the man. The more colloquial dialect references were *cummà* and *cumbà*. The parents, as well as the godchildren, would respectfully refer to their godparents by those names.

Since Louie and Elaine Lombardi baptized both of our children and in turn, my wife and I baptized all three of their children, we are double *cummàs* and *cumbàs*. And we are committed to fulfilling our obligation to be there for those kids at any time, for whatever need might arise.

When our friends from England, John and Cheryl Bickers and their kids, came to visit us in Denver and spent time with us and *Cummà* Elaine and *Cumbà* Louie, the Bickers would refer to them as *Cummà* and *Cumbà*, thinking that those were their given names. With the combination of their English accents and their proper articulation of the words, we did not tell them that those were not their given names because we enjoyed hearing them say the names. They became confused when other people called them Louie and Elaine, and the confusion became more confusing when Louie and Elaine called us *Cummà* and *Cumbà*. Finally we clarified the confusion for them.

Comune di VASTOGIRARDI	
Provincia di ISERNIA	

UFFICIO DELLO STATO CIVILE

ESTRATTO PER COPIA INTEGRALE DAL REGISTRO DEGLI ATTI DI NASCITA
DELL' ANNO 19_____ · Parte I. · Serie A

Numero__ Due

Cognóme__ LOMBARDI

Nome__ PIETRANTONIO

Sesso__ maschile

Al margine del presente atto si trovano le seguenti annotazioni :

N U L L A

L' anno millenovecento cinquantatre

addì diciannove del mese di gennaio

alle ore sedici e minuti quindici

nella casa Comunale di Pagliarone

Avanti di me Lombardi Salvatore, Consigliere Comunale

Ufficiale dello Stato Civile del Comune di Vastogirardi, per delega= zione avuta

è comparso Lombardi Vittorio di Pietrantonio

di anni trentaquattro residente in Vastogirardi

e

alla presenza dei

testimoni Lombardi Giovanni di Salvatore

di anni trentasette residente in Vastogirardi

e Lombardi Salvatore di fu Domenico

di anni cinquantotto residente in Vastogirardi

mi ha dichiarato quanto segue :

Il giorno dieci del mese di gennaio

dell' anno millenovecentocinquantatre

My baptism certificate

Chapter XV

LA COMUNIONE · THE COMMUNION

"*Ti raccomando, non fà tardi massera,*" *Ti raccomando, non fare ritardo stasera,* I am warning you, don't come home late tonight. Those were the words my mother spoke to my brother as he and I left for *La via La Rocca,* the land that she had received in her dowry from her parents.

On that summer morning before my First Communion, I thought about that important Catholic sacrament and what I had learned during catechism classes. I would need to go to confession to be free of any sins before receiving Communion, and that scared me to death. I was confused about what exactly a sin was. In 1960 Italy, a sin was different than a sin of today. Would I have to tell the priest that at times I hated him and I disrespected the nuns? That at times I would daydream during Sunday Mass or catechism class? I think I decided that I would take my chances and not divulge any of that to Don Nicola. The risk of getting slapped outweighed the risk of hell. But no worries, when that host went into my mouth, all sins would be forgiven and all would be well again. I wondered how that thin, round, white wafer would taste. Was it sweet or salty? Would I remember all the rules of the rite? If I ate something before Communion, I would surely be doomed for hell. But as much as I tried to focus on what was going to take place that coming Sunday, I could not help thinking about what had happened the week before.

My mother and I had walked from Luigi to the tiny train station in Campanello, where we boarded the train bound for Castel di Sangro, a neighboring town of about 5,000 inhabitants. It seemed huge to my young eyes. Castel di Sangro was the place to go to buy merchandise. Walmart they were not, as most *negozi*, stores, were just a cubbyhole stuffed with things the vendors were selling. My mother's mission that day was to buy my outfit for my First Communion.

We went to the larger main store in town, and with the help of the wife and husband owners of the establishment I tried on many different dark jackets. The owners were becoming annoyed. There was no need for pants or a white shirt; I would wear my brother's hand-me-downs. My mom finally decided on a jacket and after a valiant effort to bargain for a cheaper price, she finally gave in and paid the proprietor 1,000 *lire* for it. That was all the money she had. I would guess that it was the equivalent of a few dollars, but in those days it might have been a big expense for my family.

As we were walking back towards the train station, we ran into another woman from our village who was also there to buy a suit for her son's Communion. She had found a much cheaper jacket at another store. My mother and I went to the other store and sure enough, we found a similar jacket for 500 *lire*, half the cost of the one we had purchased.

We walked back to the store where we had bought the jacket and my mother practically begged the owners to take it back so we could buy the cheaper one. The owners eventually grabbed my mother and escorted her out of the store. She was crying and I, confused and scared, joined her with tears of my own. The other woman from our village assisted us and also started yelling at the owners of the store, causing a commotion. A small group of people, mostly from our village, vowed not to ever shop at that store again. I can still see my mother shaken, being consoled by the other women. They told my mom not to ever buy anything else from *quireh Giudea, quell' Ebreo*. I always assumed that *Giudea* was the name of the owner. Years later I realized that it was in reference to their Jewish ethnicity.

Memories of that unfortunate incident in Castel Di Sangro came back to me with a fury in the late 1990s while reading a book about a soccer team from Castel di Sangro, a book that put the town on the map. The town had become well-known to all of Italy by the miraculous climb of their local soccer team in 1995 to the heights of the *Serie* B league of Italian soccer. For such a small town, that was a monumental conquest and it got the interest of an American author, of all things! Joe McGinniss moved to Castel di Sangro in the fall of 1996 and followed the town's now famous soccer team around for nine months, as it played for *la salvezza*, to save itself, to stay in the *Serie* B league.

The league included much bigger cities than Castel di Sangro, such as Bari, Brescia, Lecce, Empoli, Genova, Torino, Pescara, Chievo, Ravenna, Reggina, Foggia, Padova, Venezia, Lucca, Salerno, Cosenza, Cesena, Cremona, and Palermo, all large cities. After numerous delays, the team's 7,700-seat newly completed stadium would have 2,000 empty seats if each and every resident of the town attended the game!

In the ever-changing rules of *Serie* B, the three teams with the most points moved up to *Serie* A, the top division of Italian soccer, one of the best leagues in the world. The teams that finished in the middle of the table remained in *Serie* B, and the three teams that finished at the bottom of the table were relinquished to *Serie* C, a lower division.

Mr. McGinniss wrote a book, *The Miracle of Castel di Sangro*. Now the town would be known to the rest of the world! Much to my surprise, my son called me sometime in 2001 while he was attending school in Perugia, Italy and said, "Dad, guess who's teaching a class at Umbra Institute?" It was none other than Joe McGinniss! I quickly purchased four more copies of his book and sent them to my son, so that the famous American author could autograph them — which he did graciously, adding nice comments.

The town that left me with a sad memory was now world famous. I told my mom about the soccer team and its owner, and she got a look of contempt when she heard the name Pietro Rezza. He owned a construction company, Ditta Rezza, which built some houses in Villa San Michele. Mr. Rezza supposedly arrived in the area on a donkey from Napoli with nothing, and built an empire. My father, along with many of the town's men, worked for him. *Signor* Rezza did not treat his employees well. He continually shorted them on their wages and allegedly committed many corrupt exploits. And he became very rich as he built structures all over the region.

The ending to the town's story was still in the future as I prepared for my First Communion. My workaholic brother ignored my mother's warning to bring me home early so I could participate in that night's rehearsal to prepare for the next day's celebration. Later that Saturday afternoon, my brother gathered his tools used to cut that early hay crop and disassembled *il favecione*, *la falce*, the scythe, removing the cutting blade from its long wooden handle. He pulled *il battifalce*, the scythe-sharpening tool, out of the ground. The sharpening tool was a steel peg about ten inches long with a two-inch cubic square block on top. A hammer was attached to it by a couple feet of rope or chain. The scythe's blade would be placed onto the steel block and then hit repeatedly with the hammer to sharpen its cutting edge.

il battifalce, the sharpening tool

After loading all of our stuff onto the saddle of our donkey by either tying it with ropes or putting things in canvas bags, my brother finally climbed in the saddle himself. Then he pulled me up behind him and by jerking the reins, our donkey headed out *per la via*, to the path, for our journey back to Luigi, about an hour-long ride barring any distractions. As we headed towards Trebbante, my brother noticed a cherry tree brimming with cherries, many of them red and ripe and ready for picking. Ignoring or forgetting that my mom had warned him that morning not to be late, Ezio decided to climb the tree for a treat of cherries, inviting me to do the same. When neither one of us could not eat another cherry, my brother decided to pick some to bring home to *Mamma*. So we began to fill two burlap sacks with cherries, while still forcing some more into our mouths.

After filling the two sacks and somehow tying them onto the saddle, we headed towards the cluster of houses in the western horizon, where the sun was ready to drop out of sight. I felt sick to my stomach and prayed that I would not throw up the numerous cherries gurgling in my belly.

The first house that we passed on the way through the quaint little hamlet of Trebbante was that of my Uncle Michele. He was sitting on a chair by the door as we came around the bend. My brother hesitated and almost turned the donkey around, but my uncle grabbed the reins and felt the burlap sacks. He must have watched us pick the cherries from his cherry tree because he calmly asked my brother to unload the sacks of cherries. Michele and his son, Armando, poured most of them into rush baskets, leaving some in the sacks for us to take home to his beloved sister, Maria Lucia. He chastised my brother, then thanked us for picking his cherries and sent us on our way home.

By the time we got to Luigi and put the donkey to rest in the barn, the sun had disappeared over the mountains. Darkness soon fell as we made our way towards Campanello. As we came around the curve of the road where the Stations of the Cross were located, we saw my father coming towards us with his right arm extended and pointing in our direction. I had seen that gesture many times before and that meant big trouble for my brother. Grabbing his arm, my dad proceeded to spank him continuously on his butt, while asking him if he did not hear my mom's clear instructions to get me home on time so I could participate in the rehearsal for the next day's Eucharistic rite.

I missed the night's proceedings, and all night long my brother endured a continual scolding, resulting in a heated argument between my mom and dad, who blamed each other for Ezio's behavior. That Sunday morning began badly. My mom, sad from the night before, began to dress me. Finally she put the jacket on me, which renewed our memories of a week ago of the problem in Castel di Sangro. I cannot recall if I did it because I now hated that jacket, but while drinking my coffee and milk, I spilled the hot *caffè e latte* all over the newly purchased, overpriced jacket and the white shirt. My mom tried frantically to quickly wash and dry it, but there wasn't enough time — so we went to church with me sporting a huge wet mark on that jacket. I could not wait to take it off. I was convinced that the jacket was now a curse.

Details of the actual celebration are vague, except for the memory of the priest putting the host in my mouth, where it instantly stuck to the roof. Having no clue as to how to dislodge it, I tried to pry it off the roof of my mouth with my tongue, but no luck; it remained there until it slowly melted away.

The only other memory of that celebration is of my *Zio Peppino* (Giuseppe Carmosino), my mom's brother who lived in nearby Cerreto. With his jacket thrown over his shoulder and sporting a fedora hat, his signature fashion, he began searching his pocket and pulled out a 20 *lire* coin. I recognized the amount instantly because that coin was bronze colored, whereas the rest of the lira coins in Italy were silver. Later Italian coins included some that were silver, inlaid with bronze. He handed me the coin as he was walking out of our *baracca*. That coin was worth enough to buy a couple of pieces of chocolate candy at the tiny grocery store around the corner. The pleasure of opening the bright aluminum wrapping was as enjoyable as actually eating the small, dark chocolate confection. The memory of that dark brown chocolate was the catalyst for my addiction to that sweet to this day.

Italian 20 lire coins

Chapter XVI

LA CRESIMA · THE CONFIRMATION

I was allowed to return to Villa San Michele from Todi twice during my stay at the Franciscan monastery: once for my *Cresima*, Confirmation, and the other for my sister's wedding. On the Fourth of July, 1965, Bishop Pio Augusto Crivellari came to our town to perform one of the seven sacraments, during which I would reaffirm my belief in the Church and become an adult member of the Catholic Church. Of course for us, that date was just another Sunday.

The Friday before, my *compare*, godfather, Davide Carmosino, picked me up from the monastery. I remember being very shy, nervous, and hesitant about seeing him. Had the monks already trained me to feel

A group photo of confirmation and communion participants
(I am to the left of Don Felice, the priest), 1965

comfortable in the monastery? I had not been home for over a year. *Compare* Davide had chosen my father as his *compare* on his confirmation. He was very well-respected by us and the village.

A few years earlier, *Compare* Davide had been within a couple of weeks of becoming an ordained priest. He came back home to Villa San Michele for a brief vacation before the monumental day for him and his family. While home he fell in love with a beautiful young lady, Adelina Lombardi. Although many tried to change his mind, Davide was not ordained a priest, choosing instead to marry the woman he loved. Another good priest lost by the Catholic Church.

Numerous debates, arguments, and conferences take place on this subject of priestly celibacy. There are disagreements as to whether it should be a Church law or a rule that priests cannot marry. The origins of Catholic clerical celibacy began in 1139 at the Second Lateran Council, under Pope Innocent II. The written reason for these laws was for the priest's purity and holiness, but some argue that the real reason was for the desire of popes that the Church would inherit priests' property, thus enlarging and strengthening papal power. Land owned by priests had been passed on to the married priests' heirs, but now those holdings would remain in the possession of the Church. Out of the 265 popes to date, 39 were actually married. I suspect that this touchy argument will be a precarious subject for years, if not centuries, to come.

Compare Davide ushered me out of the monastery's front door and into his Blue Fiat 500. The trip home for me was very nerve-racking. I was bashful, scared, and quiet. Davide asked many questions in an attempt to get me to open up. I answered most questions he asked. I wanted to ask him things but just could not muster enough nerve to do it. A major question I had was whether or not he was happy with his decision to leave the priesthood. Did he enjoy teaching middle school in the nearby town of Chieti? Had his family forgiven him?

When we reached Castel Di Sangro and realized that we were close to home, I asked him to stop at the newspaper stand. With my 1,000 *lire* that I had kept hidden for so long, I bought many packs of stamps for my collection and to trade with the other kids at the monastery. Davide had a look of surprise when I pulled out the rolled up 1,000 *lire* from inside my tie, where it had been hidden and out of the reach of the always searching monks. I always wore the tie when the monks took us on outings, but they never left us alone long enough for me to use it to buy stamps or a Tex Max (the American cowboy) comic book.

When we reached Villa San Michele I was happy, anxious, and scared. The hugs and kisses from *Mamma* and my sister, Maria, put me at ease a bit. My brother, of course, was not at home at our new house in Campanello; rather he was *capaball*, down at the old house, in Luigi tending to our animals. I remember waiting and waiting for him to get home. He finally came in the door and although excited to see me, he looked pensive and preoccupied. He was the father figure because my father, along with other men of the town, was away working in some factory in St. Moritz, Switzerland.

On that hot Friday afternoon of early July, many people were outside, most adults sitting on stoops talking, children were playing, some were friends my age. I longed to play soccer with them again, to show them my many new skills, to show off. All eyes were on me when I got out of the car. I felt embarrassed and awkward, not knowing whether to walk over and say 'ciao' or to go inside the house and hide. I opted for the latter. As relatives and friends eventually came in to see me, I started to feel a bit more at ease. *Mamma* made dinner and I just could not eat the salted bread. I had become accustomed to the unsalted bread served at the monastery.

The Saturday before the celebration, all the candidates for Confirmation met at the church, where Don Felice, the parish priest, gave us directions and information and reviewed some of the questions that the bishop might ask. At the monastery, the kids who were going to be confirmed went through extensive learning about the Sacrament of Confirmation. Many of the kids seemed nervous and scared that the bishop might ask them a question and, God forbid, they would not know the answer. Don Felice and the rest of the kids hoped that I would be the one picked to answer questions, as they assumed that coming from a Franciscan monastery I knew everything about *la Cresima*, Confirmation. I noticed that my friends already looked at me differently, as if I were already wearing the habit of a Franciscan monk.

The warm and sunny Sunday morning of my Confirmation included me getting dressed in a nice blue suit and *Mamma* in a woolen skirt and top that was more appropriate for winter, but I am sure that that was her best and newest outfit. Her hair was pulled back tight and into a bun. I noticed a lot of gray around the edges and her frail, skinny body that did not fill out her gray outfit. As her bony hands held mine, she told me with a soft smile, "*Come si biegl*," *Come sei bello*, How handsome you look. And then she resumed her more pensive, sad face. I suspect that she was sad because my dad was not there for my special day and that my older brother was not back home from his chores in Luigi. My seventeen-year-old sister looked like a woman in her nice floral summer dress.

Ezio was gone when I woke up. I was upset because I wanted to go with him. He had too many chores to perform in Luigi and could not be bothered with the onus of my Confirmation. I felt the same way. I wanted a break from church, praying, and studying continually. Shoveling cow manure sounded much better to me.

My mom, me, and my sister on my Confirmation day, 1965

Cumbà, Godfather Davide and his wife *Cummà*, Godmother Adelina came over with their parents, along with other relatives. My *Zio* Angelo was excited for me and was glad to see me again. My grandma, *mammuccia*, gave me her always loving hug. After coffee and sweets, we joined the other townspeople in their Sunday best heading towards church, where *il vescovo*, the bishop, awaited our arrival.

Luckily it was hot and the bishop seemed to want to hurry things along. He did ask me a question. I can't recall what it was, but I answered it and got a look of approval from Don Felice. It seemed that our priest had suggested to the bishop that he put his questions to me. The bishop also wanted to know the name of the saint I had chosen for my confirmation name: Francesco, what else?! Everything was going great until for some reason some of us started giggling and could not stop. Don Felice gave us the look, the one that meant there would hell to pay, like pulling on our ears until they fell off.

Eventually we calmed down and thankfully the ceremony was over. That day I realized that the village had come a long way from just a couple of years before, materially and intellectually. Some people even had photo cameras, and we were photographed.

My mother hurried home for the final preparations for the *pranzo*. As the guests arrived and took their seats in *il salotto*, the parlor/dining room, my mom kept going to the door. She would open it slightly and focus on the road leading to our old house in Pagliarone, hoping and praying to see my brother walking towards home. He never came and the celebration went on without my two most favorite men in my life: my dad and my twenty-year-old big brother, Ezio.

A couple of days later, *Cumbà* Davide showed up at our door to take me back to school in Todi. I cried as I looked back towards our house, where my mom and sister were waving, tears flowing down their cheeks and mine.

My Godfather Davide and me,
fifty years later, 2015

Chapter XVII

Il Matrimonio · The Wedding

As stories are told about weddings in Italy, I can easily conclude that, as with other traditions of Italy, *lo sposalizio*, the wedding has more customs and differing regional practices than any other of the multitude of ceremonies of Italian culture. Our small village has or had its own specific traditions and practices that will forever be etched in my memory.

I served at many marriage ceremonies during my years as an altar boy. My cousin, Lina, my *Zio* Giovanni's first daughter, presented me with a picture when we were back in Italy in 1990. She asked me if I recognized the little boy serving Mass at her wedding. As my wife and I stared at the picture, I told her that it was my son, Dominic! But it was me, at age nine. I was a *chierichetto*, an altar boy. I served as an altar boy before I left for the monastery, during my two years at the monastery, and even after I came back to Villa San Michele, waiting for our voyage to America. I especially enjoyed being an altar boy for weddings, as everybody was generally in a festive mood.

I was the altar boy for my Cousin Lina Carmosino marriage to Palmerino D'andrea, 1963

The church wedding was preceded by a celebration *al Comune*, the civil ceremony. The couple would go to the *comune*, the city hall, and fill out the proper documents to receive a legal marriage certificate. Usually the civil ceremony was performed a few months before the religious ceremony. This day was also an excuse to have a celebration; not at the same level as the party that followed the religious wedding, but nonetheless a dinner with the families of the future bride and groom.

Of course the big day was the church rite. In our village all marriage ceremonies were held on Sunday, considered the luckiest day. There were no weddings during Lent or Advent, nor in May, which was dedicated to the Virgin Mary. I served Mass during many of these ceremonies and I recall the brides' white dresses and the grooms' dark suits, no tuxedos. Most of the village also dressed in their best and came to church for the ceremony.

We, the altar boys, could not run fast enough after the wedding Mass into the sacristy to shed our vestments and dash out the door to take our positions on the steps in front of the church. As the newly married couple walked out of church, members of the families would throw *confetti* (white sugar-coated almond candy) and coins on the newlyweds. It signified good fortune, prosperity and fertility for the couple.

All of the kids scrambled to gather as much *confetti* and coins as possible. This brief scene of diving for candy and money caused some chaos, as we would wrestle underneath people's legs for those delicious candies and small coins. Some of the older ladies held on for dear life as we crawled between their legs to get to the loot. Suddenly we would stop in our tracks as four hunters of the village fired their guns in the air to wish the newlyweds good luck. The loud sound was deafening and even though I knew it was coming, it still scared me. The girls also took part in this treasure hunt, but usually they were overpowered by the boys. We would have pockets full of candy and coins, whereas the girls had only a few in their hands. Male physical prowess started very early in that remote mountain town.

Sadly, there were some wedding celebrations where the bride did not wear a white dress. As if not enough shame and embarrassment had been brought upon the couple already, more was bestowed on them as a result of the bride having become pregnant out of wedlock. There was no way that the priest would allow it. Wearing a white dress was a sign of purity, and only those brides who did not have premarital sex would have the honor of wearing white. The disgraced families arranged a quick wedding as soon as

*Group picture in front of church before Maria Lombardi and
Vittorio Ienco wedding ceremony, February 1966*

the young lady mustered enough nerve to tell them about the pregnancy. All the usual traditions were eliminated from the brief ceremony.

There were times when the boyfriend, usually with pressure from his family, refused to marry the pregnant young woman. His parents deemed her unfit to marry their son, even though it was their son who put her in that shameful situation. Usually, blame was placed on the girl and she would be the one marked for life. This happened to girls who more often than not had out-of-town boyfriends. Men from our town who intended to keep living there were more apt to take responsibility for their actions with a girl from our village. A young woman whose boyfriend wouldn't marry her would be left to raise the child on her own, while living with grieving but always helpful parents. Single men would avoid her like the plague. She was almost treated like a prostitute, although she was far from that. But she was now viewed by the community as flawed, used, not pure.

Some women who had just come out of church, now finished with their daily prayers and commitment to being good Catholics, would start their gossiping on the walk home, talking about some young woman, usually a friend of their own daughters. Maybe those daughters were even in contention for the same available young man. The older women would criticize a young woman for kissing that young man in public or worse yet, if she was seen going into a barn and coming out disheveled, with hay on her clothing.

Yes, gossip was huge in that tiny remote village and young women usually bore the brunt of the slander, most of it dished out by members of the same sex. Whispers of young women behaving badly were at times rampant. As a young boy I heard and digested only bits and pieces. It seemed that all the young women of the village were or would surely become pregnant. The rumor mill was alive and well about any and all aspects of our lives. The one that hurt the most was the suggestion that a young woman was promiscuous. I vaguely recall gossip about the town's priest being involved with some young woman.

If a young man was sought after by many, it gave that man celebrity status. Men, boys, women, and girls of the town seemed to throw accolades his way, admiring him for his prowess with women. Men most definitely were given preferential status in our village. Even as a little boy, I was allowed to go out at night and hang out in front of the town's only small bar, sitting on the steps as men played cards, drank wine and argued inside. Younger kids sat and listened to older kids as they concocted scary tales just to see us get scared half to death. There were no girls in sight; they were not allowed in that man's world. Rarely was any criticism cast upon those men, rather only on the young women, whom the men most likely took advantage of while the women attempted to win them over another girl who was probably her friend or a relative.

When we immigrated to America I remember watching a soap opera called *Peyton Place*. In many ways it brought me back to our village. My mom watched it too, even though she did not understand a word they were saying, but somehow figured out what was going on. Surely some episodes reminded her of the soap operas of our town.

For a wedding, there was always the ever-present question of the amount of dowry that the parents of the young woman could provide to the groom, to his family. Dowry, la *dote* (we called it *la dodda*) was an important part of this rite of passage. *L'usanza*, the custom, in our village was for the bride's family to give some livestock, along with a piece of land as dowry, a gift, to the groom's family. My mom always mentioned that the nice fertile piece of land that we owned near the hamlet of Trebbante, where she was from, called *la via la Rocca*, was from the dowry from her family. Her family also provided another plot of land that was by the river Vandra, called *Malpasso*, as well as a couple of sheep for my dad and his impoverished family.

Thinking back on those weddings, it seemed that most were arranged by others. It seemed that the wedding was promoted by the family by way of putting pressure on the potential bride and groom. An uncle, an aunt, a cousin, etc. would start the process. Then the young man would ask for permission to go to the home of the young woman, *va peh Maria*, *va per Maria*, he is going to Maria's house for her, the literal meaning; the real meaning was that that certain young man was 'going out with Maria.' Those words I remember most about the courtship of my sister, Maria, by Vittorio Ienco. Vittorio was a handsome man; he had dark wavy hair, dark eyes, was muscular, and he was always nicely dressed. He was eight years older than my seventeen-year-old sister, something my parents initially frowned upon. Not only was his age a concern, but so was the fact that he owned and drove a car!

Rumors started to make their way around town that Vittorio *aveva lasciato*, broke up with another girl in our town. My sister remembers sitting on the steps of the church with other girls of the town on a Sunday afternoon during *la festa di San Rocco*, the feast of Saint Rocco. Antonio di Ginuccio, a friend from our old town of Luigi, approached her and informed my sister that Vittorio would like to meet her. My sister resisted as she was well aware that the other girl might still be involved. Maria was living in Roccaraso, a ski town in Abruzzo, where she was attending school. Vittorio went with Salvatore Iannacito, his sister's husband, to see her and again ask permission to come to our house to formally make it known to all that he wanted her to be his girlfriend.

Vittorio lived in San Pietro Avellana, the town just northwest of ours. He lived and worked with his family in the forests in our area as a *carbonaio*, charcoal burner. I remember seeing Vittorio, his father, Giovanni, and mother, Carmela, in our forests, where they built a hut with a mud roof. They lived in that hut as they closely attended their work. They would pile long pieces of wood in a large cone shape and then bury the wood pile with dirt. They made a chimney hole on top and other smaller holes around the bottom. They would then light the wood on fire and let it burn slowly for days. This process needed close monitoring to make sure that the wood did not burn too fast and turn into ashes. The holes were covered up to restrict oxygen and slow the burning at the right intervals. If the burning occurred without any problems, the process would produce a generous amount of charcoal. I recall going to the different locations in our forests with other kids just to watch these strangers perform that odd craft.

And so it began when Vittorio visited Maria. My sister would fix herself up in the afternoon, comb her hair, wear a pretty dress, clean the kitchen, and put some chairs around the fireplace. As nightfall approached we would hear a car pull up in front of our house, followed by a knock on the door. My sister would push me or my mom to open it. And with a *buona sera*, good evening, Vittorio would come in to court my sister.

There was no theatre for a movie, no restaurant for dinner, no park bench to sit on, and no bowling alley. There was no venue for courting other than our kitchen with its warm fireplace. And if these amusements had existed, I doubt very much that my sister would have been allowed to leave our house, at least not without a chaperone.

I was away at school for most their courtship and while there, I received a letter from my sister saying that Vittorio had asked her to marry him. I was happy and sad, knowing that more than likely I would not be allowed to go back home for her wedding.

The wedding date was set for February 20, 1966. My sister wanted me, the consummate altar boy, to serve Mass on her wedding day. My father, with help from my sister, wrote a letter to the director of the monastery, pleading and begging to allow me to return to the village for the ceremony. At first the director refused, but my godfather, Davide, wrote another letter and finally the director agreed to let me go home.

The director informed me that I could go back home for my sister's wedding under one condition: that a monk — who had helped out from time to time at the monastery but lived at a monastery in Perugia — would accompany me. The director informed me that the monk was from the neighboring town of Carovilli, and that it would be very convenient for the monk to bring me back to Villa San Michele on the train so he could visit his family.

I liked that particular friar and I was delighted to hear the good news. The director also asked me if he could help with the writing of a letter that I would read to my sister in the church during the wedding ceremony. That letter would have the whole church crying when I got on the pulpit and read it. I wish that I could remember it word for word, but the years have erased most of it from my memory. I vaguely remember it telling about the importance of matrimony and of parents' hope and wishes for their children to find and live a life with someone they love and care for deeply. And it spoke to the nobility of our commitments to another person and to God!

The morning of my sister's wedding my father actually swept the whole cobblestone street from our house to the church, the equivalent of a couple of blocks! My sister, with her white dress and a veil covering her face to keep evil spirits away, walked with our family and friends to church for the very important wedding ceremony, and I had the perfect view as I assisted Don Felice as the altar boy.

The church ceremony was followed by a multiple-course dinner, usually at the bride's parents' house. My sister's dinner was held in the empty house of a family that had recently emigrated to Canada. Relatives and friends were the cooks, the servants of the elaborate meal. I remember a sign crudely made by my father out of a white sheet and some black ribbon. It hung on a wall behind the newlyweds and read: '*W GLI S*,' *Viva gli sposi*. Loosely translated, he wanted to say 'Long live the newlyweds.'

My sister's wedding waitstaff, from front left going around: cousin Nicola Carmosino, cousin Pasquale Carmosino, my brother, Ezio, Zia Michelina Carmosino, friend Antonio Lombardi di Massimo, cousin Irma Carmosino. Behind her is her husband, Alfredo Iannacito, Zia Giuseppa Carmosino, cousin Ersilia Carmosino, Zia Pompilia Carmosino, my father, Vittorio, and cousin Elvira Carmosino, February 20, 1966.

Viva gli Sposi, 1966

That evening the whole town was invited to our house to dance the night away in our kitchen and wrap the bride and groom with colorful, thin paper ribbons to reinforce their bond. I did not take part in the dancing and eventually went upstairs to sit in a bedroom, the transformation by the monks was starting to take place. My mother came up and forced me downstairs, where the ever-watchful eye of the chaperone monk was present. A couple of days later the monk and I boarded the train that would take us back to Todi, to inside the massive walls of the monastery.

My father dropping white almond candies, confetti, on my sister and her husband for more good luck, 1966

My sister went to live with her husband in San Pietro Avellana, a town a few kilometers up the road. For my mom it might as well have been a thousand miles away, as she felt she had lost her daughter to a husband and his family. Maria would be true to her vows to her husband: to be his wife for better, for worse, for richer, for poorer, in sickness and in health, and for mostly all new wives of the village, to stay with the husband no matter how difficult life would be living with his parents!

When they married, firstborn sons usually brought their wives to live with him in his parents' home. Many situations evolved from those arrangements. Daughters would cry to their mothers that they wanted to come home, that they were tired of being a slave to their mother-in-law, who thought that her son could do no wrong. And sometimes a story would make the rounds around town about a daughter-in-law and her husband mistreating a poor mother-in-law. But no matter how difficult a marriage was going to be, divorce was out of the question. In our village it was not an option, as divorce wasn't even legal in Italy until 1970.

My brother, Ezio, didn't court anyone seriously in Italy before we emigrated. Although there were some attempts at hooking him up with a village girl, no real courtship ever materialized. After we moved to America, he got a modern dating opportunity. He enrolled in night school at Emily Griffith to learn English soon after he arrived here. It was essential for him to learn the language in order to land a job. The class was composed of people from many different nationalities, all trying to learn English. My twenty-two-year-old brother befriended a Korean girl from that night class. One day he asked me to go with him downtown to meet the young woman so I could help with translation, because his English was very limited. I reluctantly agreed. After all, I was a shy, introverted, reserved barely fourteen-year-old.

We met the short, thin, shy, dark-haired twenty-something Korean girl on some corner on 16th Street in downtown Denver. Ezio mumbled out something that vaguely resembled the fact that I was his brother. She kept nodding. My brother asked me to ask her if there was something she wanted to do or see. At fourteen years old and fresh out of a Franciscan monastery, I hardly had any communication skills when it came to girls. But I quietly asked her the question while we were walking in downtown Denver.

She reluctantly made eye contact with me and mumbled something that did not sound like any English I had heard before. I repeated the question, and to my surprise I realized that she did not have any idea what I was talking about. She knew less English than my brother. He seemed confused when I told him that she did not understand much of what I was telling her. Could it be that the reason she was in the English class with him was to learn English? Did that ever occur to him? He did not have any idea that she could speak less English than he, because he could not understand any of the language himself — so he thought that she understood and spoke some English. Korean and English probably sounded exactly the same to him, foreign!

We both grew tired of the nodding and the permanent smile on her face, and finally we said goodbye and went home. Many years later, my brother confided in me that he went out with her a few times when both could speak a bit of English.

For a year or so my brother went out with a few different young women. Some he met on his own and some were suggested by others, mostly relatives. None of these relationships worked out and were deemed not acceptable to him for marriage.

In February of 1968, Ezio decided to go back to Italy and find the right girl to be his bride. I recall my parents being somewhat opposed to it. Arguments ensued many nights over the idea, as they wanted him to wait a bit longer, to save some money. But as usual, my brother's mind was made up and no one could change it.

My mom prepared a couple of suitcases that were bulging and ready to explode at any time for my brother's trip back home. Everything you could think of was stuffed into those suitcases. Gifts from America for all the relatives: cigarettes, gum, those great American potato peelers, electric blankets, wool sweaters and other varieties of apparel. The suitcases were ready, tied with a rope to make sure they did not explode, but to me they looked like they would burst at the seams at any time.

Without fail, friends and relatives came to wish my brother well. They all came with envelopes, some bulging with money. Others came with packages that were taped and tied, some neatly covered in a white fabric that was sewn shut. These were not gifts for my brother but for their families in Italy. My mother would have to tell her friends that there was no room in the suitcases, but they all tried to make their case. "*Ma è na maglia pe Mamma*," But it's a sweater for my mom, and surely you can find room for that. These people were some of the most insistent people I knew. *"E iamm, fammeh quisht favore,"* *Dai, fammi questo favore,* Come on, do me this favor, they all barked out — and they would not take no for an answer. My poor mom ended up taking some of her own items out of the suitcases to make room for some of the packages of our *paesani,* but most of those packages were left behind. She would have to call them after we came back from the airport and give them the bad news.

Ezio boarded the TWA flight loaded down like a donkey, his coat pockets bulging with envelopes full of money for the expectant relatives in Villa San Michele.

Back in Italy, my brother stayed with my sister's in-laws, Giovanni and Carmela Ienco. They had purchased our house, and so my brother was back in his old surroundings. My brother recalls his first courting of a girl. She was from the neighboring town of Castel di Sangro. He was accompanied by two men: Giovanni Ienco, a robust, thick man with a Hitler-like mustache, dark eyes, and salt-and-pepper hair and Felice Iannacito, a friend from the Trebbante area of Pagliarone. He was the father of Salvatore, who was married to Ida Ienco, Vittorio's sister. Felice was a slight, little man with a gaunt face, sunken eyes and mouth, and some missing teeth. His body revealed years of backbreaking work. He was a simple man, always with a smile on his sun-beaten face, and I remember him being very funny. Both were in their Sunday best: suit, tie, and hat. Laurel and Hardy, the comedy pair of the 1920s, could have been their twins.

These two in-laws sat with my brother and the girl's father at their dining room table making small talk, drinking an espresso. The young girl seemed very nervous and stayed with her mom in the kitchen for most of the visit. The father finally informed the trio that his daughter was not interested in marrying Ezio or anybody else at this time, but appreciated the visit.

Giovanni knew another family who had an available daughter. Ezio was accompanied by only Giovanni on this other courting visit. The girl was pretty and nice, but panicked when she found out that she would have to move to America. There was no way that she would leave her family. My brother was getting discouraged and wondered if he had made a mistake.

A dance was planned on a Sunday evening in the *edificio,* the town's schoolhouse. Ezio attended the dance, with music provided by Clemente Ranalli, the town's longtime official accordion player. He remembers dancing with a few of the town's young single women. Someone suggested that he dance with Bambina Lombardi. They danced many more times that night. The next day, rumors were already going around the village that Ezio had found a bride.

Bambina with her father, Adelio, ready for the gun salute and avoiding kids scrambling for their loot, April 16, 1968

On Sunday, April 16, 1968 the town of Villa San Michele prepared for *lo sposalizio*, the wedding, of Ezio Lombardi and Bambina Lombardi. My mom was sad and worried on that Sunday morning. Her oldest son was getting married and none of us would be there for him. Only aunts, uncles, cousins, and friends would attend. Hopefully his new bride's family was going to give him some comfort and support. We went to the post office to send a telegram, wishing the bride and groom best wishes on their special day.

The celebration continued well into the night, and most of the town jammed into Adelio and Maria's (Bambina's parents) house to drink and dance the night away. The newlyweds were wrapped in paper confetti as people danced around them, another way to wish prosperity and fertility to the newlyweds.

Dancing the wedding night away to accordion music by Clemente Ranalli,
as my brother, Ezio, makes a toast, 1968

My brother came back to Denver a month after the wedding, leaving his new wife in Villa San Michele. He filed the proper immigration papers for her and six months later she came to Denver to join him. She was noticeably sad in the beginning, missing her parents and three younger sisters. My parents honored them with a wedding reception soon after Bambina arrived from Italy. The party was held at the Slovenian Hall near Interstate 70 and Washington Street. It was an old, dark place, but fun was had by all the *paesani* and friends. Apparently no one thought that it would be nice to take some pictures!

Bambina and Ezio lived in our house with me and my parents. She seemed lost and missed her family. With the help of a relative, she found work at Pagliacci's Italian restaurant. Bambina did a little of everything and for others it might have been hard work, but for her it was easy. It was certainly not as hard as what she had to do back home. Hauling buckets full of pig feed up a steep hill on cold, wet mornings was much harder than cooking pasta in a warm place.

Family picture in our kitchen on my sister's wedding day, from right: my father, Vittorio;
Pietrantonio Lombardi; the bride, Maria Lombardi; the groom, Vittorio Ienco; my mother,
Maria Lucia Lombardi; my brother, Ezio Lombardi, 1966

Chapter XVIII

Il Maiale · The Pig

The pig was a tremendously important part of our diet while we were living in Italy. Every family would raise at least one. Ours was kept *nella stalluccia*, in the small stable, *stalla* meaning 'stable.' We fed our pig a mixture of barley and many other things that we now usually refer to as garbage. We called this *viverone, beverone,* mash. One of many chores I had as a child was to walk up the hill to the *stalluccia* and feed the pig, or pigs. I would watch in amazement as the pig devoured this concoction and when it was all gone it would attack the empty pail looking for more. Our pigs were our version of the garbage disposal!

The piglet would grow before my very eyes and at the beginning of every year the fattened animal was ready for slaughter, one of the most dreadful events of my young life. Having taken care of the pig throughout the year, I became very attached to it. And then with the help of other Luigi men and relatives, my dad would take it out of its stall and walk it down the hill to the area in front our house, where the men would grab the pig and put it on a wooden bench. While they held it down, one of the men would insert a long knife in its neck until it reached its heart. The pig would squeal and move violently and then go limp and die. In the meantime, my mom and other women would scramble to catch all the blood in a pail. Every piece of that pig was saved and used to make some sort of edible staple.

My brother, Ezio, helping with the slaughtering of a pig on
one of his returns back to the village, circa 1985

Soon after, I would stop crying and resign myself to the loss of my pet, and then I would help with the rest of the process. A combination of hot water and burning dried weeds was used to remove the hair from the pig. The men shaved it with their knives and then carried it into our kitchen, where it was hung with its hind legs to the ceiling. Men and women frantically moved about doing different tasks in preparation for the cut down the middle of the pig's belly. All of its organs would be removed, cleaned, and saved.

While the men tended to the slaughter, my mom and her helpers already had a huge pot on the fire to cook the blood that had been collected. My mom added sugar and walnuts as they made *sanguinaccio*, blood pudding. If something was sweet, I would eat it. We feasted on *sanguinaccio* all day and night.

When all the work was completed the families would gather for a big meal. We ate many different dishes prepared with the meat of the freshly slaughtered pig. I especially remember the *polenta* sprinkled with fresh *cicuri*, bits of pig meat. The celebration would last into the night, and then on another January day it would start over again with another family's pig as the victim.

The pig would hang from the rafters of our kitchen for a week or so to dry out a bit. I don't know how many times we ran into it as we moved about our small kitchen. It became an annoyance and we couldn't wait for the day when my dad and the other men would take it down and cut it up for the *prosciutto*, bacon, sausage, etc.

Pig hanging from kitchen rafters

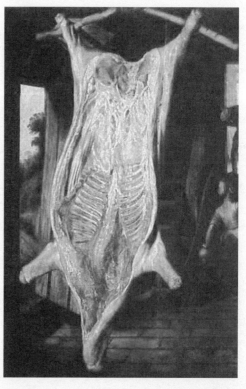

One of my jobs was to help make sausage. We saved, soaked, and washed the pig's intestines to use for the casings. Since we used the pig's hind legs to make *prosciutto*, dried ham, other parts of the pig were used for sausage – usually the shoulder and some belly fat. After the meat was cut away from the bone, it was then cut into smaller pieces and ground with a hand grinding machine. A variety of spices was added, usually black pepper, parsley, sweet basil, salt, and I recall my mom adding a bit of sugar. The ground meat was then put into the same grinding machine and while turning a handle, the meat was stuffed into a wet casing, which was a washed length of intestines that had been pushed onto an aluminum tube. I can vividly recall the slaps on the head if I lost my concentration and allowed too much meat into the casing, causing it to burst. My sister and brother would have sort of a competition to see who could stuff the longest sausage without a break.

After the regular sausage was stuffed and placed on a table, my parents would then make liver sausage. For some reason they enjoyed their liver sausage, claiming it to have some sort of medicinal value. For their children, not so much.

In the morning my dad would carefully place the sausage on poles hanging from the ceiling of our kitchen to let it dry. After the sausage dried, the women would cut it into two inch pieces. These were put into jars which were then filled the rest of the way with melted lard. These sausages and the rest of the meat would all be consumed, as they were essential components of our daily diet.

Every part of that pig would eventually be used for human consumption. *Mamma* would scrape every bit of meat from all the bones, and then put those bones in a pot of boiling water. As the broth simmered, she added some vegetables and a great winter soup would be created. I drew the line with pig's feet, ears, and tongue. When these parts appeared on our modest dinner table, I would settle for just a hunk of bread.

I could not wait for my father to cut into one of the two *prosciutti*, cured and dried ham. During hot days those pig thighs would be hung in our kitchen or in our storage area, where it was cooler. Every year he would make two more *prosciutti* to replace those he made last year that we had by now eaten. And the thigh bone was surely used by *Mamma* to add flavor to one of her soups. My parents knew exactly what to do to prepare those hams for curing. Washing them in water which had been salted — eventually my father would apply salt to every part of the meat — he would then hang them with a hook from the ceiling in a corner of our kitchen. Those hams greeted me every morning and they seemed to be a permanent part of our small kitchen as the old ones were replaced with the new.

The *prosciutto* was a delicacy and *Mamma* would slice some primarily on special occasions. A dish of thinly sliced dried ham was always part of a special meal. Because we did not have any refrigeration, the delicacy was consumed for the most part during the cold winter months, or else it would spoil in warmer temperatures. In the cold months we ate many pork products and in the hot months we ate primarily pasta, fresh produce, and fruit. If we were lucky we would have a taste of some lamb meat during the spring.

Prosciutti and other home made delicacies in my sister's cantina (wine cellar) in Woodbridge, Canada, 2015

Freshly made sopressata (an Italian dry salami) hanging in my sister's cantina. 2015

Chapter XIX

Le Pecore · The Sheep

The stony slopes of the mountains and hills of our area was the ideal environment for sheep. These animals could graze in rocky, barren, and difficult to reach areas. Cows and other animals would not, could not venture onto that steep incline where the fresh grass awaited. Goats were even better climbers but would eat anything in sight. Because goats were almost a nuisance, very few were painted into our landscape.

It seemed that every family had sheep. Some did not have cows or a horse or even a donkey, but sheep and chickens were very essential to every family's subsistence. We always had at least five sheep in our flock, some years more and some less. In the barn, we had an enclosure where they would spend the summer nights and the long winter days and nights.

Only a few sheep were grazing in the lush fields of Pagliarone in 2014.
Giacinto Lombardi one of the last of the town's shephards.

With our cows, we would clean up after them every morning and night. But with our sheep we would not bother, letting the manure build up all year long. In the spring we would have to break up the tall mound of manure and load it into two wooden barrels. Each barrel attached to one side of our donkey's saddle and we would haul it to various plots of land which were going to be cultivated that spring. Of all the many chores we had to perform as kids, that was one of the most detested. Shoveling that manure that had been sitting there all winter was difficult, and the smell and the fumes were atrocious. I am surprised we did not blow ourselves up with all that methane gas coming off of the decomposing manure.

As dreadful as that work was, I enjoyed being around our sheep. I especially looked forward to them giving birth to their baby lambs in late winter and early spring. I recall constantly going to the barn to watch them, hold them, and pet them. We loved to watch them nurse. Their mothers didn't seem to mind the attention we gave them.

The small kids of the village were allowed to be around sheep without supervision. These animals were usually very docile and non-aggressive. I especially enjoyed rattling *reh mrtale*, *il mortaio e pestello*, the wooden mortar and pestle. That sound would get our sheep to come running to eat the crushed salt we fed them to help them stay healthy. That same mortar was used to crush salt for our own use, and I have no recollection of it being washed after the sheep licked it!

Jackie and I rescued our mortar and pestle along with the coffee grinder from our house in 1975 and they are now proudly displayed in a showcase in our home in America.

Sometimes news would circulate around town of a ram butting someone, injuring some part of his or her body. We were not allowed to be around rams during breeding season, because they sometimes became aggressive if we got in their way. I remember sneaking up to flocks of sheep with my friends to watch the rams perform their breeding work. We were amused by the activity, not fully realizing what was taking place. We called our rams *reh mondone, il montone,* the mounter!

The lambs were a substantial part of a family's yearly income. They were sold at markets to brokers who would bring them to various butcher shops. I cried many times when our lambs were taken away to markets. They were taking away our pets, the same animals that greeted us every morning with their welcoming bleats, licking our hands, and giving us a friendly nudge. I vividly remember my father carrying one of our lambs to Campanello, to the church, to donate it for the feast of Saint Anthony. It was an honor for a family to make such a donation.

During the winter months, sheep would keep their woolen fleece to protect them from the cold. As spring approached there would be a rush to shear all the sheep. This was done with a hand shearer. There were men around town who were very fast, accomplished shearers. They would be in great demand.

We gathered around in the barn, or if it was warm the sheep were taken outside one at a time, where the shearers would begin removing their woolen coats. What was once a large, rotund sheep was now reduced to a skinny, feeble-looking animal. With their clean, white, shaven bodies they would be led back to the pen, where their baby lambs gave them a smell. They seemed to be confused and upset by their mothers' naked bodies.

Most of the time my father, with the help of family and friends, sheared our sheep. The usually calm animals resisted the men as they put the sheep down on one side. Some would squirm violently and escape from the grip of the shearers. Young and old scattered to chase the runaway sheep. Cornered and tired, the sheep would be dragged back to the barn. It was those agitated ones that were speckled with blood. Some speckles were tiny, but some were large enough to cause the blood to flow freely from their wounds caused by the shears. Many times my father had to give my brother a scolding for nicking the skin of the sheep as he learned to give them their yearly shave.

The women sat around gathering the wool, taking out the bad pieces and stuffing the rest into burlap sacks. The wool was sold to wool merchants who came through town with trucks. After the sacks were weighed, they were loaded onto the back of the trucks and taken to a site where the raw fiber would be cleaned, scoured, and finally woven into wool yarn. I vaguely recall women gathered around a fireplace spinning the wool into yarn. But most of the town's wool was sold to commercial weavers. Clearly the sheep were a valuable commodity. Families who owned large flocks seemed to be more affluent in our village.

My brother, Ezio, recalls the discussions he heard around the fireplace when he was thirteen. The decision was made to use the money that *Mamma e Papà* had saved to buy more sheep. My father traveled to Vastogirardi where he was able to make a deal on three sheep from one of the vendors *alla fiera*, at the market. Our flock had now grown from five to eight sheep. More lambs, more wool, and more milk meant more money, and that meant a better life for their children. It was all about the children. They did not mind suffering as long as the children had clothes on their backs, enough to eat, and a place to sleep.

My brother remembers the difficulty he had with the three new sheep. They were hesitant to be part of the flock. They missed their old flock and were not used to their new surroundings. As Ezio and his friend, Pasqualino, headed up the mountain to graze the flock, they literally pushed our new sheep into the group. But the smell of the group told the newcomers that this flock was not where they belonged. My brother kept an eye on them and continually urged them to join the flock. This was a new problem for Ezio. He was used to seeing animals follow the leader, usually a ram, to wherever they were directed. If the lead sheep went down a cliff, the rest would follow, no matter what the consequences. Staying close together with the flock was their way of protecting themselves from predators. These animals were dumb but not stupid.

Our new sheep seemed to miss their old flock and were intent on finding their old friends. As Ezio and Pasqualino played, the three new sheep wandered away from the flock. By the time my brother realized that they were gone, there was no sight of them on that mountaintop.

Panic set in, crying followed. He ran home to get help. He and *Mamma* hurried back up the mountain to search for our three sheep. My dad would later join them as they frantically looked behind every rock and rummaged through every bush. In the distance they saw something that resembled our sheep, but as they got closer they realized that it was just a cluster of white rocks. The sheep were nowhere to be found. As nightfall came my parents and Ezio went home, where my sister waited anxiously as she kept an eye on four-year-old brother, Tonino.

Days later my father found some remains of all three sheep deep in the forest. Wolves had feasted on all three. Family and friends stopped by our house to console my parents, but the loss was devastating. At the age of four, I am glad I don't have any recollection of that tragic part of our lives. Though heavily depressed, my family would not let that loss defeat them. They marched on with their daily battles to assure our survival.

The lead sheep

Me sitting at a favorite spring from which our sheep would drink on the way to grazing lands called la fonte vregna, 1975

191

Shepherd in Pagliarone, circa 1934 (photograph courtesy of Lillian Lombardi Bertollt)

Chapter XX

LE BARACCHE · THE BARRACKS

Our little hamlet of Luigi was the last of Pagliarone's various neighborhoods to be moved to the new houses in Campanello. Luigi was perched on the side of one of the hills of the town, and not initially affected from the landslides caused by rushing rain waters. But eventually the whole area of Pagliarone was deemed to be in some sort of aquifer fault that was responsible for the slow movement of the soil. The rest of old Pagliarone's residents were moved to our *edificio*, schoolhouse, in the new town and then to the wooden barracks that were hastily built for the displaced residents. Rows of these small houses resembled army camps; we called them *le baracche*, the barracks.

Plans were also in place to build more new stone houses. 'Slow' is an understatement for the progress of the construction of those houses. So we were in those barracks longer than expected. We endured living there for almost three years. Thank God for our old house in Luigi that seemed to be stable and not moving. We went there daily, where all of our animals were in their stables. We, especially my brother, went there to escape crowded Campanello. The small propane stove in the barracks wasn't going to cut it. We needed our fireplace and the wood-fired oven to make our bread; without them we could not manage.

Villa San Michele with barracks shown at the lower left; ours is marked with an X, circa 1960

In the *baracca* we walked up three tiny steps and into the tiny kitchen with a small propane gas stove. There was a table with chairs and not much more. We also had a little *sala*, parlor, with two adjoining bedrooms, no bathroom. The first bedroom was for the three of us and the next was for my parents. Of course there were no hallways, so to get to my parents' bedroom you had to walk through the other rooms.

The most vivid memory I have of that little house is of a night in August 1962. We were awakened from our sleep by the movement of our small metal bed from one side of the wall to the other. Screams and panic followed as my family ran out of the *baracca*. The town had been rudely awakened by an earthquake. Afraid to go back inside, the villagers spent the rest of the night outdoors. As morning approached, men surveyed the town and found that major damage was avoided. Later news started to reach us that the other nearby towns had not fared as well. I don't think many people slept well that following night, fearing a repeat of the night before.

While living *alla baracca*, my mother had purchased a few kilos of beautiful, big green grapes from *il fruttivendolo*, the fruit vendor, on his weekly stop at our village. She had locked the delicious grapes in the china closet of our small *salotto*. She hid the key in her room under the mattress. (Did she think that as a nine-year-old I would not figure out that every time she went to the china closet it was preceded by her lifting her mattress?) The big bowl of grapes was carefully placed in the back of the china closet, so as not to tempt my eyes and those of my siblings. I don't recall the special occasion, but one was coming up because my mom had also purchased other foods that were not normally part of our daily diet.

Every day after school, while my parents and brother were working out in the fields and my sister was outside with her girlfriends, I would sneak into the china closet and take only a few grapes. I was sure my mother would never notice. I kept helping myself to a few grapes until there were finally just a couple left on the last stem. As my sister and I walked down to Luigi to help out with the numerous chores, I began to worry, to regret consuming the majority of the sweet fruit.

A few days later, for some special occasion, my parents hosted *una cena*, a dinner, for an important out-of-town guest. My brother seems to remember that an official from our province, Isernia, was friends with my dad and occasionally came to visit. After dinner, as espresso coffee was brewing on our small propane stove, my mother went to her bedroom. She appeared with a key in her hand, and when I saw it I quickly realized that she was going to get the grapes to serve to us and our guest. When she reached for the bowl, deep in the back of the closet and pulled it out, she was surprised that it was almost empty; just a lonely stem with a few grapes barely clinging to it remained. She removed some dishes and looked for the grapes. The grapes were gone. She was upset and my father, noticing her distress, was fuming.

That night I suffered one of the most memorable lectures and disciplinary acts from my parents, which included a couple of slaps from my dad. I had embarrassed them and vowed not to do that to them ever again; although I think I might have suffered a relapse a few times.

The most anxious time in our *baracca* came late one night in early August of 1964 when the whole town was awakened by the news that Emilio Lombardi, our relative and neighbor from Luigi, was being brought back home from the hospital in Isernia, where he had died. A strong man in his late-thirties had died unexpectedly of some unknown illness. The doctors at the hospital performed some sort of exploratory surgery; they made a huge cut in his stomach and supposedly he died on the surgery table. When the family was informed of the awful news, they were surely deeply distraught; and they were also informed that the doctors would have to keep the body there for an extended period, so the authorities could perform all the legal procedures involved with a death.

The family, especially the heartbroken mother, Gasperina, begged the hospital staff to allow them to take their beloved son home, so they at least could give him a proper and timely burial. The hospital authorities reluctantly agreed, but advised them to do it in the middle of the night to avoid being seen and stopped by the regional authorities.

My father was the designated town nurse. People came to our house to get an injection of penicillin (the cure-all medicine) always in the butt, and they also came for other minor procedures. That night he was summoned to help get Emilio ready for burial. In the middle of the night, the townspeople gathered to mourn the death of the young father who left a wife, Gilda, and two young daughters, Rina and Maria.

My mother did not want me to join them at Emilio's house. At eleven years old she did not want me to experience the bedlam. I could hear the crying, screaming, and wailing as I sat up in bed in the darkness of night. Suddenly I began to hear voices near me, followed with silhouettes of people around the bedroom. I sat there frozen and surrounded. Surely I would be taken away by all those ghosts to the deepest crevices of the cemetery and kept there for the rest of my life.

As the ghosts were about to engulf me, I heard a voice outside. It was the welcome familiar voice of my sister, Maria. She was coming back home to stay with me. I asked her where our parents were and she told me that *papà* was cleaning and shaving Emilio and *mamma* was consoling the family, along with many other villagers. She also told me that *Papà si era quasi abbilit, svenuto, Papà* almost fainted when he removed Emilio's hospital gown. She did not tell me why on that scary night, but later I was told that either in haste or due to shabby work Emilio's cut across his stomach had not been stitched, but rather stuffed with gauze! When my father regained his senses, he wrapped the dead man's stomach and then dressed him in his burial suit.

We lived in that wooden matchbox of a house for about three years, before we finally moved into our new home at the other end of the main street. It was a proper house made of stone. Sometime in the 1980s the barracks were torn down when most of them were destroyed by a fire. People suspect that it was started by a man of the town who had lit a fire on the floor in one of those firetraps. It was also discovered that the barracks were built with carcinogenic materials and were deemed to be unhealthy for inhabitants. This was not good news, considering we lived there for an extended period. But we were not surprised by the findings, considering that many government contractors were corrupt. Their bottom line was to line their pockets with as much money as possible. They felt confident that those dirt farmers from the remote villages were not educated enough to question the inferior materials, shabby work, and the use of unskilled workers. But some of the strangers who came to town did have skill and some stayed around town for longer than expected.

My brother, sister, and I in front of la baracca. My siblings dressed well, I in my hand-me-down high-water pants and shoes without laces! Circa 1960

Chapter XXI

Il Toscano · The Tuscan

He came to Pagliarone in the late 1940s to work as a cobblestone cutter and setter for the streets of Villa San Michele, and he never left. His name was Domenico, but we called him *il Toscano* because he came from the region of Tuscany. A woman of the town took him in to help her with chores! I remember her as being a bit different from the other women of the town. She had a son but was not married, and talk around town was that she kept men. I did not have any idea what that meant. One day she kicked *il Toscano* out, not needing his services anymore. With no place to call home, he just roamed our new village, but he was usually seen in the Pagliarone area and the surrounding countryside.

Il Toscano was our modern-day homeless man. During the summer he would sleep under a tree or a rock and during the cold months he would sneak into a barn or an old empty house and bed down for the cold nights. I always saw him hovering over a small fire built with branches that he had gathered while aimlessly wandering the countryside. Whenever I ran into him by myself, I would turn the other way or keep walking, staying as far away as possible for fear that he would grab me and throw me into his sack that he carried with him at all times. I wondered what he had in that sack that he held on to so dearly. Later I realized that all his life's possessions were inside that canvas bag.

Decades later in America, a diminutive Asian man came around my business location every morning carrying a sack on his back, roaming the parking lot and rummaging in the trash bin looking for aluminum cans. He seemed to be *il Toscano* reincarnated. When I first saw that little Asian man, I thought for sure that after many years of searching, *il Toscano* had found me here in America.

Many times *il Toscano* was seen performing some menial job for a family, a job that usually no one else wanted any part of. He did the work for a warm meal. The work that he had probably apprenticed for as a young man in some distant place, the honorable trade of stonecutter, had not been part of his life for many years. And now this beaten man was a lost, homeless soul.

As a small boy, I was afraid of my father, the man who would teach me most of life's lessons. I feared the priest; he unleashed the fear of God in me. I was scared of Luigi, the forest ranger, with his huge gun and big German shepherd. All my teachers had unlimited authority over me, making them very intimidating. Also very high on the list of people whom I feared in our town was this homeless man, dressed in rags and moving very slowly in a non-threatening manner. But for some reason I was always afraid of *il Toscano*. Something about him made me and most of the young kids uneasy whenever he appeared. He would simply disappear for days and as suddenly as he vanished, he would reappear. His Tuscan dialect and his scruffy appearance – with his very soiled and torn clothing, old hat, and unshaven, sunken face – gave him a ghostly appearance. Whenever I saw him coming in my direction down a road, I would run in the other direction and pray that he did not chase me down and take me away to his world. But when I was in the company of friends, some of them being older than I, we would make fun of him. Some of the kids even poked at him with sticks, infuriating him.

I often wondered where exactly he was from and if he had family. I felt sorry for him because even though we didn't have much, he had nothing. Why did he choose to live such a miserable, lonely life? What kept him from going home to Tuscany? Surely someone missed him. He chose to roam our town and the surrounding hills with no real purpose to his existence, relying on the townspeople to give him anything that resembled a meal. It was rumored that, following a romantic breakup, he became disillusioned and moved away from his home.

One day *il Toscano* was discovered in a rundown house. Edilia Lombardi, while discussing the subject here in America, informed me that she and her cousin found *il Toscano* in the abandoned house. He had died there, all alone, his few possessions next to him in a bag. The people of the town gave him a proper funeral and burial. The location where he died was on the road that my brother and I had taken every night from our old house and barn in Luigi to our *baracca* in Campanello. Ezio knew how frightened I was of *il Toscano* and took full advantage of it. I hoped that nightfall would stay away until we got home to Campanello, but that was not the case every day. My brother would linger at Luigi, creating chores for the both of us. I would continually remind him that it was getting dark and that we should go home, where my mom was surely waiting with *la cena*, dinner. It was obvious that my brother hated Campanello and would rather stay in Luigi with his animals. As the sun disappeared over the mountains and most of our neighbors had already headed up the hill, towards our new house, Ezio reluctantly decided to start our trek to Campanello.

I already knew that we would have to stop at the little fountain for a drink, the same fountain where *il Toscano* had often been seen filling his water jug. I anticipated what was going to happen and no matter how I prepared for it, the result was always the same. As my brother took his drink from the tiny fountain, I surveyed the hillside behind the fountain, straining my eyes in the darkness and listening carefully for footsteps. Although I was not thirsty, my brother invited me to take a drink anyway. And then like clockwork he would yell out, "*Mo vè il Toscano,*" Here comes *il Toscano*, pointing to the tiny path behind me. And then he would take off running, leaving me there by the small fountain, waiting in fear for *il Toscano* to come for his drink, as he did when he was alive. When my sister, Maria, was with us, she offered some protection. That was until she, too, looked around in panic, anticipating the appearance of *il Toscano*.

Maybe this was the night that I would finally face this ghost. In a way, I wished that he would finally appear and I would deal with the consequences. I was tired of dealing with that fear every time we walked by that little fountain. No matter how much I begged my brother to take the road down below the possessed fountain, he would have nothing to do with that. He needed his nightly drink of water. In reality, he needed his nightly entertainment of scaring the shit out of his younger brother, and some nights his younger sister.

Il Toscano would always return to claim my frozen body, yanking my hand that was firmly grasped to the fountain's faucet, as I anticipated

My sister Maria with cousin Antonio Carmosino posing in August 2014 by the still-functioning fountain where il Toscano roamed.

his attempt to pull me away and take me up that path that disappeared into the unknown, behind the small hillside. Then with a snickering smile on his face and the expression that said, "I got you again," Ezio would lead me home where I would complain to my mom. And she would tell me not to be afraid of *il Toscano*, that he would not harm me. But she never reassured me that he was not out there somewhere in the darkness.

Talk around town of sightings of *il Toscano* did not help to ease my fear of this dead homeless man. *Il Toscano* sometimes occupied my dreams during those long winter nights. And during the summer, he would occupy my mind as I walked in places where he frequented. As I turned my head to make sure he was not behind me, my brother would say, "*Mo t'accappa!*" He's about to grab you! How I wished we had owned one of those big, fast horses that only a few of the village residents owned. And surely *il Toscano* would not catch me if I had one of those la *cinquecento*, Fiat 500, cars that we occasionally saw in town. Or at least if I had a bicycle, I could easily pedal away from him!

Chapter XXII

LA BICICLETTA · THE BICYCLE

It was old and rusty with no tubes or tires, just wheels, but that old bike did have a bell. It was my brother, Ezio's, bike. But now that he had gone to Switzerland at the age of eighteen to work on a farm, that bike was mine. Of course that old racing bike was much too tall for my short legs. My friends and I would drag it next to some steps, I would get on, and with a push from the other kids I would attempt to pedal by swaying from side to side so my feet could reach the pedals. The metal rims going over the cobblestone street shocked my entire body, but I was determined to keep up with Luigi and Domenico as they rode their shiny new bikes up and down the main drag of our village.

Luigino (Little Luigi) and I had been playmates until he emigrated to America with his brother Domenico and their mother Ida. Her husband, Nicola, had been living and working in Philadelphia for a couple of years. They lived in the Luigi hamlet with their grandparents, Luigi (the forest ranger) and Vincenza.

Luigi and I used to spend our days playing and chasing chickens and our summer evenings trying to catch fireflies. The five of us — Luigi, Domenico, Terenzio, Pasquale, and I — were the youngest boys of the Luigi clan. We could hold our own against kids from the other neighborhoods below, and we were especially deadly in rock throwing wars. However we sometimes misfired, as Pasqualino did when he hit me in the head with a rock meant for the enemy. As I ran down the hill to chase someone, Pasqualino pelted me in the forehead, creating a good-sized gash that seemed to bleed for days. I can easily recall that day when I look in the mirror today and the scar looks back at me.

It was a sad day when the crazy team from Luigi was broken up, as two from the group left for America. Now my cousin, Terenzio, and friend, Pasqualino, and I would have to defend the hillside where Luigi stood. We did our best to uphold our nickname: *matti di Luigi*, the crazy ones from Luigi!

Three years later, Luigi, Domenico, and their mom, Ida, returned to Villa San Michele for a visit. My mom and I were at *il negozio*, the little grocery store, owned by distant relative Angiolina, which was located in a tiny room in the front of her *baracca*, barrack. Ida walked in, hugged and kissed my mom and commented on how much I had grown. (I was actually a midget and even my nickname implied it, *Tonino*, Little Toni.) Ida opened her purse and handed me a small yellow packet and as I looked at it strangely, she told me that it was *gigomma*, gum, from America. I would have to share the five individually wrapped pieces with my sister, and the older kids would help themselves to the rest as I foolishly showed it to them. I chewed and re-chewed that gum for weeks.

The next day I saw Luigi and Domenico again as they rode their beautiful, new, shiny bikes around our cobblestone streets. The rest of us just watched them in envy. Some of the kids actually had bikes. They were old and rusting but had tires, and even though the tires were flat, they tried to keep up. That's when I decided to take out my brother's monster bike. I gave it my best, but was no match for the new fast bikes of Luigi and Domenico. They sort of taunted the rest of us and spoke to us in their weird language as they sped by on their bikes. They declined our invitation to join us in our street soccer game, where we would surely show them some skills only possible by Italians. Instead they went inside a relative's house and from the upstairs window they began to throw coins onto the cobblestone street. We left the soccer game and scrambled to collect as many coins as possible.

That day, Luigi and Domenico reinforced in us kids what we had heard about America; that you could have anything you wanted there, like new bikes, and that maybe money did grow on money trees or fall from the sky. We all wished we could go to America.

Many years later I found out that the new bikes that Luigi and Domenico flaunted were bought for them in the bordering town of

Castel di Sangro by their uncle, Don Camillo, the priest. And the coins launched from the window also belonged to the priest! I wished that I had an uncle who was a priest. I did have many uncles for whom I was thankful, and one special uncle who was my favorite.

la bicicletta

Chapter *XXIII*

ZIO ANGELO · UNCLE ANGELO

My mother's brother, Angelo, was the youngest of six brothers. Always with a smile on his face revealing a few missing teeth, his sunken cheeks and large nose made him look older than his actual age. A French beret-style hat was always on his head, I don't remember ever seeing him without it. He was slightly hunched over, making him seem shorter than he was. His thin build, slight limp, and over-sized clothes made him look frail and weak, but he was actually as strong as an ox.

When delivering Angelo, my *Nonna* Genoveffa went through a distressed and prolonged labor. The baby was having a difficult time because of his abnormal position and both the baby and mother were in danger. The midwife and other women of the area tried to help her, but the mother and baby's conditions were getting grave. A couple of the older brothers, my uncles, got on their horses and rode to Roccasicura, about ten miles east of Trebbante to seek the help of a doctor.

My uncles, with the doctor in tow, hurried back to the tiny village to assist the mother and baby, who were in dire condition. Something drastic had to be done soon or both mother and baby would run the risk of death. The doctor was able to get ahold of the baby with forceps, and with some struggle was able to pull the baby out. The family was alarmed by Angelo's misshapen head, but the old doctor assured them that the baby would be fine and that the mom should have a long bed rest.

Zio Angelo, 1975

During the early years of *Zio* Angelo's life he was a bit slow in developing, but otherwise he seemed to be normal. He was a smiling, happy baby boy. Unfortunately as he got older there were definite indications of mental retardation. In order to save both baby and mother, the doctor may have squeezed the forceps too hard and caused brain damage. At the age of ten, *Zio* Angelo also developed a very high fever and with no doctor around to treat it, more than likely this caused additional brain injury. My uncle would live his life facing all the same problems that every other mentally challenged person has to deal with in this world of ours.

I loved *Zio* Angelo very much and have so many fond memories of him. He would do anything without any complaints or expectations for his beloved sister, *Marialci* (Maria Lucia) and her family. There were numerous times when he carried me on his back from Trebbante, where he lived with my grandmother, Genoveffa, to Luigi where we lived. This was not an easy trek. It included navigating a river crossing and climbing narrow and steep muddy paths, but he did it without ever complaining. He would endure ridicule that kids would throw his way. He would just smile at them and gently push them away as they tried to take his favorite knife or piece of string. If they knocked his hat from his head, he would simply pick it up and put it back on his head, all the while making sure that I did not fall off his back.

As the other kids teased him, I hurt deeply inside but as a very young boy there was nothing I could do. They would mock his impaired speech and awkward stature. Many times the older kids, and even adults, made fun of him, mocked him.

My mom and the rest of the large extended family endured it, but I never forgot who the culprits were and tended to be bitter towards them for many years. At times kids would call me *Angeluccio*, making the reference that I was dimwitted like my uncle. Those memories are sometimes triggered when I see these same people, now adults, in Italy and here at home. For a moment I get angry but then I remind myself that kids can sometimes be cruel, as I am sure I was at times.

My mom was Angelo's favorite person on earth. She treated him well. He ate with us at our table and not by himself around the fireplace, as he liked to do at other relatives' houses. Unfortunately even his relatives took advantage of his disability and made him perform chores that no one else cared to do. I would always try to get him to walk away from his work and play with me, and usually he complied.

Zio Angelo and me, 1975

My uncle was one of a number of people in town who was afflicted with some sort of birth defect. I recall a man and a woman getting around town by dragging themselves on a small wooden chair, a wheelless wheelchair. One boy lay in a crib continuously, only moaning some words. When my mother and I visited him, the boy would talk to me, smile at me, but I just held onto my mother's skirt while staying as far away from him as possible. I was very afraid of him, but *Minguch*, Domenico, was a boy who just wanted to be my friend. As years went by, his head grew to a somewhat normal size while the rest of his body stayed small like a child's. He spent his days in the crib by a warm fireplace and at night in his bed. The only request he would make to his mom was to change the picture on the wall occasionally, just so he could look at something different.

Many people were born with some disability, while others were stricken later in their childhood. Nobody knew how or why, there were no doctors to diagnose or treat their illnesses. Families merely accepted the cross that God had given them. When a family member was stricken with one of the numerous diseases such as polio or tuberculosis, they lamented it but accepted it as the will of God. Not knowing any better, their loved ones were kept in bed all day and night, thinking that this was the best way to get them back to good health; not realizing that those extended stays in bed actually aggravated their illnesses.

When I heard stories of the many "crosses" that people of the village had to bear, as they were recounted by my mom during the multiple long walks behind our donkey, I thought that those stories were fictitious; just my mom's way of keeping me near, quiet, or maybe to scare me about certain dangers. Later I realized that most of the stories were true. There were too many tragedies for such a small village. One such tale was told and retold by my mom as we walked near a house on the way to Trebbante. My mom would tell me the tragic story of the poor little boy who lived there.

One fine afternoon the sky went dark. Cold and heavy rain started to fall from the black clouds. Some members of that family sought shelter in their house and hovered around the fireplace to dry off, to stay warm. Without warning a massive lightning bolt struck the exterior chimney and made its way down to the fireplace, blowing two people off their chairs and slamming them against a wall, seriously injuring them. A small child that was sitting near the two individuals was hit and died instantly! My mom told me that my grandma worried often about her son, Angelo, when lightning and thunder rang in the sky and there was no sight of her little special boy, as he probably took refuge under a tree.

When we immigrated to America, my mom worried about her frail mom, Genoveffa, and how she was going to take care of *Zio* Angelo. After Genoveffa died, three of her brothers, *Zio* Salvatore, *Zio* Michele, and *Zio* Giovanni divided the duties and their time in taking care of him. Whenever we went back to Villa San Michele, the first thing he would say was, "*Sorma, Marialci comeh shtà?*" (*Mia sorella, Maria Lucia come sta?* He wanted to know how his sister, Maria Lucia, was doing.) And he was so happy when we would hand him a new flannel shirt, a hat, and a brand new knife. He would quickly fetch a piece of wood to try out his new prized possession.

When *Zio* Angelo died, my mom was very sad but also relieved that he was now with his mom and dad and some of his brothers in Heaven. His happy smile could be seen as he was entombed next to his family at the village's small cemetery.

Zio Angelo, 1990

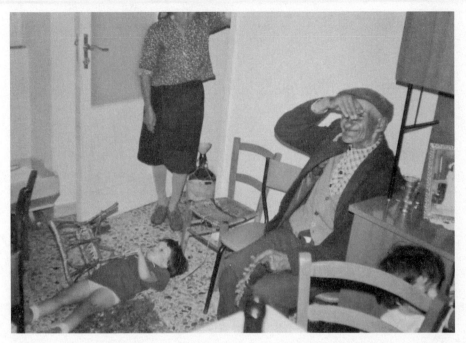

Zio Angelo around the fireplace, always with a smile on his face, 1990

Three of my mother's brothers with the hats, from left: Zio Michele, Zio Cosimo and Zio Angelo, 1975

Chapter XXIV

Il Cimitero · The Cemetery

If one were to ask all the kids and many adults what the most frightening location of Villa San Michele was and is, the obvious answer I am sure would be the town's cemetery, a stone's throw north of our tiny railroad station. The dirt path leading to the cemetery was the least traveled for the children of the village. But there were times when it could not be avoided, or it was forced on some of us.

My sister, Maria, recalls the day when she was with my brother, Ezio, working a piece of land called *Le Fratte*, northeast of town, a short kilometer past the cemetery. As the sun began its descent over the mountain, my sister insisted that they start gathering the cows and the donkey for the journey home, but my brother told her to be quiet and to keep grazing the animals while he finished cutting down the rest of the fresh hay. Maria kept nagging him and finally Ezio agreed to go home, but as punishment for her continual complaining, he sent her home by herself by way of the cemetery. This petrified her because darkness was approaching. Normally she followed the cows from a distance down the trail, but this time she put herself in-between them for protection from the cemetery, from its occupants. She tried to force the animals to run by hitting them with a stick and yelling at the top of her lungs. But they would have nothing of it and walked lazily by the cemetery as they were accustomed. She cried with fear but made it home safely. And my brother would feel the sting of my father's palm on his face again for his continual tardiness.

I dreaded going to that cemetery, as many times I was forced to go when there was a burial. I seemed to be the elected altar boy for those services, as I am sure the rest of the boys of the town felt the same as I. After the church services we would have a procession to the cemetery. The priest and the altar boys walked behind the casket being carried by the pallbearers, a job I would never want to have. The pallbearers had to trek through town and up a steep, rocky hill to the cemetery with the casket on their shoulders. The immediate family followed the priest, with relatives and most of the villagers, young and old, making up the rest of the grief-stricken group. The sound of people crying muffled the slow clanging of the church's distinct funeral bells.

I became even more anxious as we neared the cemetery, as we turned from the path to the big iron gates. I couldn't help but stare at the stairs leading to *l'ossaio*, the bone depository. I was sure that I could hear a commotion below that I interpreted as a collection of bones wandering around! And then as the pallbearers passed through the cemetery gates, all hell would break lose. A lot of the villagers would scatter to their loved ones' tombs and cry at the top of their lungs. The priest, the altar boys, the family, and some of the villagers were left near the casket and the scary hole in the ground. This infuriated the priest but he patiently waited as the mourners made their way back to the freshly dug hole, so

The old cemetery, outside of the walled area, 1975

he could proceed with the burial ceremony. But there would always be some mourners who would not, could not leave their loved ones' grave. The priest had to raise his voice to drown their cries.

When my wife and I went back to Italy in July of 1975 for our honeymoon, the very first event that my twenty-one-year-old bride experienced in my hometown was a burial!

In the early 1960s my father landed a part-time job with the *Ferrovia Statale*, the government owned rail system, working on the local rail line. In the summer of 1963 at the age of ten, I was expected to help out as much as possible because we were shorthanded. My father's new job and Ezio's departure for work in Switzerland had left us undermanned for the impending summer chores. Every day after school during that late spring, I would meet my father at different locations where he had been working the land, while the cows and donkey grazed nearby.

One particular afternoon I was to meet him at a pasture we had leased from Cornello Vigilante, who I think had emigrated to Canada. I seem to remember my father telling me that the land belonged to *Contessa Adelaide Genoino*, a countess who was a direct descendant of the original feudal landlords of the area.

Of all the lands we worked, this was my least favorite. Although close to town and easily accessible, I hated to go there because it bordered the north wall of our cemetery. To my young eyes that wall looked enormous and menacing, though it was only about six feet tall.

The cemetery wall and the adjoining pasture. I could still envision our cows resting near that wall when I took this photo in 2014.

After accompanying me to that plot of land, my dad mounted our donkey and began the long ride alongside the railroad tracks to meet up with the work crew that was replacing worn railroad ties west of the village. He assured me that he would come back to get me and our two cows just before sundown. Keeping an eye on the cemetery wall, I found a spot as far away from there as possible, under a shade tree on the north end of the property. A somewhat flat rock nearby was the perfect spot to do my homework. I made sure the cows were in my sight as they grazed right under the cemetery's wall. I hoped and prayed that they would eventually make their way towards my location, away from the cemetery so I would not have to contend with what lurked on the other side of that stone barrier. I tried to distract myself from the wall and what was on the other side of it by concentrating on my homework and taking breaks from time to time to pick wild berries. I prayed for the sun to stay above the mountains until my father came back to get me. Not only were my prayers not answered, but the sun seemed to descend even quicker than usual that afternoon.

I knew I was in trouble when other *contadini*, farmers, in the area began their trek home. As they walked by the cemetery's dirt road they would warn me, "*Mo tse fa notte, va alla casa*", *ora si fa notte, vai a casa*, they were reminding me that it was going to get dark soon and I should go home. But my father clearly told me to wait for him, and so I reluctantly waited and waited. To make matters worse, the two cows decided to lie down right under the cemetery wall. As crickets started rubbing their wings, making that certain sound to call for mates as nightfall approached, and as the last passenger train left the tiny rail station nearby, I realized that soon I would be all alone in the dark with the two cows — next to the cemetery.

I climbed a tree to look up the railroad track for a sign of my father, but he was nowhere in sight. All I could see were some lights that were already on in the village in the valley below.

In a panic I made the decision to walk up to the cemetery wall where the cows were resting peacefully, to get them up and guide them onto the road for the almost hour long journey back to their barn in Luigi. As I neared the wall I suddenly started to hear some faint noises coming from the other side of the wall, and as I forced myself to look up I saw an image, a ghost! It was sitting there and waving for me to come closer. Chills ran down my spine, but I forced myself to focus on that shadowy shape on top of the wall. I noticed the familiarity of his face and suddenly it hit me that it was that of a middle-aged man who had died and was buried days earlier. While riding his horse to one of his wheat fields nearby, he died, probably of a massive heart attack. At that moment tears filled my eyes and I started to cry quietly, but quickly I began to cry loudly as my cries were drowned out by the dead man and other ghosts that had joined him on top of that dreaded stone wall, calling out my name, *"Tonino, Tonino, vieni qui,"* Tonino, Tonino, come here.

The chanting got louder and louder, and as extreme panic set in I did not realize that I was beating the cows repeatedly with my stick. Surprised and hurting, the cows decided to get up and amble to the dirt path for home. Unfortunately for me, that path went right in front of the cemetery. And as I reluctantly neared its front gates, I thought I saw the iron gate of the cemetery entrance slowly open, and the ghosts that had been sitting on top of the wall were now struggling out of the cemetery, lumbering towards me. If that wasn't enough hell for me, I suddenly heard a noise; that familiar noise of shifting rusty steel. The noise was clearly coming from *l'ossaio*, the bone depository.

The cemetery was very small, so to make room for new burials the oldest graves would be dug up and the bones that had not decayed were stored in a chamber below the cemetery. When my Uncle Alduino went back to Villa San Michele from Argentina for a visit, he had the body of my grandmother, Bambina, exhumed from the old cemetery where she had been buried for over fifty years, and moved to the newer walled part of the cemetery and into a family crypt. When they unearthed her remains, all that was left of her were some bones, a shriveled-up pair of stockings, and her favored hair comb that was obviously made of some non-decaying material.

The new resting spot for my grandmother, Bambina Lombardi

The gate to the *ossaio* was opening, not by any sort of remote control but by the bony hands of the skeletons from the crypt below, as they commenced their creaky march towards me. I thought of *Zio* Michele, the old man whom my friends and I had upset by taking his *bastone*, cane. He cussed at us and warned us that he would get back at us someday. My father had gotten back at me already by giving me a few *schiaffi in faccia*, slaps to the face, after hearing about our disrespect of the patriarch of Luigi.

But now my legs felt rubbery and weak and I screamed in fear as a hand was just about to grab me. As I focused on the ghosts behind me, I suddenly crashed into a ghost who had somehow gotten in front of me. This strong apparition put its hands around me and would not let go. As I tried to wiggle out of the ghost's firm hold in the darkness, all I could do was cry out for my parents, "*Mamma, Papà, Mamma, Papà,*" and as the ghost held on to me I thought I heard my father saying, "*N'avè paura, Toni Papà,*" Don't be scared, my son.

The custom in Italy was for a parent to often include their own *Mamma* or *Papà* with their child's name (*Tonino Mamma* or *Tonino Papà*, something similar to Mama's Tony or Papa's Tony) as an expression of endearment. In the darkness, as the fireflies swirled above, the ghost kissed me while holding me tight, and that's when I noticed that the strong arms and the kiss could only be those of my father. He was on his way to get me and I ran into him as I was looking back at all the skeletal ghosts that had crawled out of their graves and were planning to catch me and take me within the cemetery walls and do God-knows-what with me.

Part of the interior of the cemetery with Monte la Penna in the background, 2003

My father had to work late to finish laying some damaged tracks, and the head of the crew would not let him go. On our way home he told me that I should not be afraid of the dead because they would never hurt me. He did not tell me that there were no ghosts, just that they would not hurt me! I do not recall my father ever assuring me that the events of that evening were a figment of my imagination. Of course not, the whole town surely believed in ghosts and other goblins.

Tales about *il fantasma*, *reh spirit*, what we called a ghost, were ever-present in our remote, backward village. Supernatural beings seemed to be amongst us and not just around the cemeteries but also in other locations. I have forgotten most of the places where a ghost had appeared, where it had taken up residence, but there were many. Most people, including adults, were apprehensive whenever they came close to those locations. Somewhere near my mom's birthplace of Trebbante there was such a place, near the source of a river.

In the late 1800s when bandits roamed the countryside, a government official nicknamed *Spaccone*, roughly meaning a braggart, a Johnny Satellite, was tracking a leader of such bandits. *Spaccone* had chased the bandit into a small, dense forest, but it was a trap and *Spaccone* was murdered. Because of the gruesome homicide, the small, dense, wooded area with a spring became known as *la fonde der spirit, la fontana dei fantasmi*, the fountain of ghosts.

Whenever a traveler, for whatever reason, was forced to go close to that location late in the evening or worse yet, in the dark of the night, without a doubt the ghost would magically appear. Of course these witnesses would swear on their mothers that the ghost had in fact made itself very visible. Whenever we went to Trebbante, my mom made sure that we started back towards Luigi early enough so that we would not be near those woods late in the day. Of course we were leery of that area even during the light of day. *Mamma* and other adults certainly preached about ghosts not hurting you, but they did not seem to believe what they preached! My mom's excuse was that she just did not want to see them.

One evening, as was usual, my brother was running late and by the time he, my sister, and I started on our way back home from *le fratte* — that dreaded fertile land near the cemetery — darkness had engulfed the area. Thanks to the light of the moon we could see the fork in the road, one way leading to Villa San Michele and the other leading to Cerreto, the nearby town. This area was also known to be a popular lurking spot for numerous ghosts. We stayed away from that intersection, preferring to choose the path near the cemetery.

As we carefully surveyed our surroundings, we made our way past the cemetery. We had one eye on the road and one on the burial ground. We safely made our way towards the small rail station and started our descent towards town. A few minutes later we were cautiously walking down the hill. To the east of the path was a cornfield. It was late summer and the corn stalks were tall, dry, and ready to be harvested. It was dark, but we could see the few street lights of our town. Aware of the many ghost sightings, I stayed close to my brother as did my sister, while inspecting everything around us, looking for any movement, listening for any sound, any evidence of a ghost.

Suddenly we heard something coming from the cornfield. My hairs stood straight up on the back of my neck, even if none were there! My brother did not seem to be bothered by the noise, which sounded like a horse or donkey strolling through the cornfield. "*Chi sa di chi è chell'asina,*" Ezio wondered to whom the donkey belonged. He either asked the question so as not to scare me and my sister, or to convince himself that it was just a donkey on the loose and nothing else. But no sooner had he asked the question, when we saw a figure under the moonlight, a white-clad figure that was following the supposed donkey. The figure seemed to disappear for a moment and then reappear. Even my brother stepped up his pace and looked back as we hightailed down that hill and home, where we reenacted the story to my mom. "*Oh Mamma, eva neh spirit.*" *Era un fantasma.* She did not attempt to convince us that it was just our imaginations; she just nonchalantly confirmed that indeed it was probably just a ghost.

If it wasn't freezing cold outside, the usual activity during the evenings was for all the boys of the town to gather and play a game of war or hide-and-seek. Sometimes we would wrestle to see who was the toughest. I remember one night I was having the best of a boy about a year older than me, as the older teenagers who were the enticers, looked on. Suddenly an older boy, a cousin of the boy I was wrestling, hurled the boy's younger brother on top of me and they proceeded to rough me up pretty good. When I was back in the village a couple of years ago, I saw Peppino and as we exchanged pleasantries, I asked him if he remembered that night. He gave me a smile and a nod, but I am sure he did not remember and probably wondered why, of all things, I would recall that silly event!

During those warm evenings we also played a game called *zomba a caviagl, saltare a cavalli,* jump on horses. A boy would lean against a wall and bend down, with his back parallel to the top of the wall and his legs straight. Then another boy lined up behind him, resting his hands on his back area and bending the same way. This was repeated until half of the boys participating made up what looked like a long horse. The remaining boys, the other team, would take turns and with a running start, they jumped on top and as far as possible onto the boys' backs as they held on tight.

Many times someone would misjudge his jump and smash into the wall, causing scratches and bruises and at times a gash on the head. Normally another boy leaned against the wall and in front of the horses, but usually we played the game without the "safety net!" The game continued into the night as one team attempted to pile as many of its participants as possible on the other team, which tried to be strong and not buckle under the weight of all those boys on top of them. The game was won or lost when the horse collapsed.

*Zomba a caviagl, saltare a cavalli,
our game of jumping on horses*

After we got tired and bruised we would gather on the stoop of the bar. Its proprietor was Adelio Lombardi, my sister-in-law Bambina's father. The adults played card games of *scopa*, *tresette*, and *briscola* and enjoyed a glass or more of wine. The drinking game that they played was called *la passatella*. The winners of the card games usually drank the wine while the losers paid for the wine, as the game of cards included *il padrone e sotto*, the boss/owner (of the bottle of wine) and his subordinate. Basically the *padrone* decided who would be allowed to drink a glass of wine. But the *sotto* would have to agree, and sometimes if no agreement was reached, *il padrone* would drink all the wine because as the boss of the game, he was entitled. The wine was paid for by the losers of the card games.

On the stoop by the bar door the older teenagers usually had their own fun with the younger boys. Girls were not allowed and stayed home with their mothers. The older boys would start telling stories about ghosts: where, when, and how a ghost was sighted. We would gather closer as the moon and stars, with the help of the fireflies, sort of lit up the town.

One particular summer night we were led to believe that a ghost was seen roaming the streets of the town. It appeared around one corner and then instantly was seen peeking around another corner up the road. Presently an older kid pointed to a house and informed the frightened audience that he thought he saw a figure, and sure enough as we all turned to look, a white-clad figure peeked out and then disappeared. Another older kid then yelled out that he thought he saw the figure up the street. Of course all of our attention shifted to that location and again we all saw a white figure peek out from the corner of a house. Back-and-forth the ghost went as we all inched closer to the bar's door in case it came after us. The older kids, in a show of toughness, all ran to the corner house where the ghost last appeared and chased the figure away from the area.

By the end of the night I was too afraid to walk past that house on the way to mine. So I waited for an adult to come out of the bar and then walked slightly behind him as he went to his house on the same street as mine. Of course every time I walked past those corner houses I looked closely, hoping and not hoping to catch sight of the ghost.

Years later on my honeymoon, as I retold the story to a group of kids, my cousin, Peppino, informed me that he also played the same game on younger kids. The trick was passed down. Two teenagers covered themselves with two white sheets and jumped out at the appropriate time from the opposite corner houses, as the panic-stricken young audience looked on.

Sometimes those older teenagers were put to the test. Some thought they were so tough that nothing could scare them. One night, one such tough young man was dared to walk to the cemetery by himself and drape his jacket over a headstone. He immediately accepted the challenge. A group of boys escorted him to the last of the row of houses, to the path leading to the cemetery. We waited on the steps of the bar but the fearless young man never came back. The next day someone reported that the courageous boy was spotted walking back from the cemetery as white as a ghost, with the jacket on his back!

Witches also wandered our streets at night. After they recited the Rosary, the women in our town sat around the fireplace during those cold nights and invariably, their conversations would move to witchcraft. They would lament the poor souls that by no fault of their own were born on Christmas Eve, a sure sign that they were doomed to become witches or warlocks. I remember such a person, his name was Giovanni. I don't know if the adults treated him the same, but the kids of the town were afraid of this man. He was just a normal, decent human being, but because he was born on Christmas Eve, we always wondered what he was up to during the night.

Aside from casting evil spells on people, the witches' favorite activity was to torment babies. These witches were capable of transforming themselves into various forms, manifesting themselves as gusts of wind, peculiar noises, shiny objects, and assorted animals. The witches would come in the darkness of night when everyone in the house was in a deep sleep, and snatch the babies from their cradles. The infants would be taken to a clandestine location, where they were put through severe mental distress and starved.

So if a baby cried constantly, witches were to blame. Unfortunately, the baby was probably actually suffering from some health issue or was wet or just hungry. In those days, medical services were nonexistent and the poor, young, uneducated mothers fell for those folklores.

My mother, aunt, and other women of our village would describe in detail how mothers united to battle the witches. If a strange cat was seen nearby or a bird made a strange sound or if chickens became agitated (probably because a fox was rambling around the henhouse) and started to cluck, or thunder sounded (probably because a storm was moving in), those were alarms for the women that a witch was near. They would arm themselves with sticks, fireplace tools, and other household belongings, ready to do battle when the witch showed up to take the baby. In a group, they would hover over the cradle of the spellbound baby. Of course the witch never showed, thanks to the bravery of the women, armed with their artillery. For that night the baby was safe.

I always envisioned la strega, the witch, as being an old hunchback with a cane.

Old women who were malnourished, shabby, and usually living all alone were occasionally associated with witchcraft. These poor, unfortunate women were looked at as being evil and treacherous and everyone stayed away from them, causing them to live out the remainder of their lives in solitude. Many times my sister and I would walk a wide path around a house in which some innocent old woman lived, because people labeled her a witch. The old woman was forced to stay holed up in her house all alone in her own suffering and hardship.

Surely there were people in our village who strongly disputed these myths as untrue and outrageous, but they were outnumbered by the credulous majority. Even if my mom assured me that *la povera vecchiarella*, the poor little old lady, was harmless, in the back of my mind there would always be that possibility that she could grab me and take me away to her wicked hideout to torment me. As cruel as this might seem, at least we did not burn those little old women at the stake, as was done in Salem, Massachusetts in 1692 when a whole community was caught in a frenzy of witchcraft accusations, a practice which was prevalent throughout other politically and religiously unstable parts of Europe in the seventeenth and eighteenth centuries.

Those stories of the supernatural came with us to America. Second and third generation Italian-Americans were told those same stories by their immigrant relatives. *Zia* Bonina Lombardi, who had lived in Denver since 1927, retold these tales to her family and whoever would listen. I recall one such night at her house, where my mom and dad frequently visited her on 38th Avenue, just west of Potenza Lodge. Bonina and her husband, Salvatore, were worthy mentors for the new immigrants from our village. As she easily captured our attention, she recounted the story about a kind and quiet young man of our village who was bitten by a dog. About a month after the bite the poor young man became extremely agitated, and as a full-moon night approached, he went on a rampage and destroyed a lot of the village's meager but cherished possessions. He was very saddened and frightened by his actions because he did not understand any of it.

At the next full moon, the same thing happened to him. Before the next full moon he begged to be restrained because he was afraid that the same thing would happen to him again and he did not want to be responsible for any harm done to anyone or anything. No one wanted to restrain him because his previous reputation was one of a gentle and kind person, but eventually they agreed to put him in a room and secure it so he could not get out. That night, howling was heard throughout the town. The next morning when his family went to check on him and let him out of his incarceration, they found that the tormented young man had hung himself from the rafters.

To this day I have anxiety when I have to spend the night by myself, even in my own house. Those goblins of long ago seem to invade my mind and play games with my manhood. I definitely feel uncomfortable at Mount Olivet cemetery, especially when I am there alone. One early Sunday morning, I went to this cemetery to visit my parents' grave in the Saint Anthony's Mausoleum, where they rest side by side in those outside drawers. There was not a soul in sight. Not a comfortable feeling for me. I almost turned to leave, but realizing how silly that would be, I toughed it out and stayed for a while.

As I stood there thinking about my parents and how much I missed them, I suddenly heard a voice coming from the other side of the mausoleum. Not again! Memories of my childhood experiences came rushing in. Someone was carrying on a conversation but I could not make out any of it. Is he calling for me to come over to the other side? I stepped away from my parents' vault to look in the parking lot for any other vehicles, but my car was the only one there. As I was walking back to my parents' final resting stop, I saw a figure darting past the columns; an old, thin man with long, gray hair and a long beard. Was Buffalo Bill buried here?

I forced myself to investigate and as I peeked around the corner, I saw the ghost getting on his bike, weighed down with all his possessions. And as he rode away, he was still mumbling to himself. I was impressed with the old, frail man for having the courage to have possibly spent the night in the cemetery. I definitely could never do it! At times I feel silly for those events in my childhood that still influence me somewhat as an adult. Cemeteries, ghosts, and goblins I can almost come to peace with, but not flour mills!

Entrance of cemetery, 2012

*My mother ordered a new stone for her parents; the inscription on the bottom says
'Memory of their daughter in America.' 1990*

Chapter XXV

Il Mulino · The Flour Mill

For me, second on the list of the most interesting and the scariest places in our village was the flour mill. Whenever we were close to running out of flour, an important and daily staple of our diet, we would go to our storage room where our wheat was stored in a large wood container. My mom would fill two burlap sacks with wheat, load them onto the saddle of our donkey, tie them down with ropes, and head to the flour mill. She inspected the container closely to make sure that we had enough wheat to last us until the next wheat harvest. *Mamma* pulled the donkey by its leash down the hillside with me in tow, or if I complained of being very tired, my mom would throw me on the donkey's saddle for the journey towards that last structure in the valley. This was where the town's flour mill was located. It needed to be in that location because the river Vandra flowed nearby and the water flow was needed for the mill's operation.

Watermills have been in existence for at least 2,000 years. Water is usually diverted from a stream or lake near the mill, into a holding pond where the water is harnessed. When the water is released, the rushing water hits the paddles of the large wheel that is attached by a vertical axle to the upper millstone, causing it to turn and grind against a stationary lower millstone. All around our streams there were remnants of old mills. The mill still in operation was owned by one of the Melaragno families. It was renovated by a group of young men from the nearby town of Vastogirardi. Thankfully it survived the bombings of the German forces and the Allies during Germany's retreat through Italy in World War II.

We made frequent trips to the flour mill because we did not grind large amounts of grain. This was mainly because stoneground flour would oxidize quickly and thereby go rancid; so we would frequently make our way to the mill. Although the mill scared me, I always went with my mom, enjoying the walk down in the valley, seeing many people on the way and even catching a glimpse of the intimidating breeding *toro*, bull in the pasture, near the hamlet of Zirr.

As we crossed the old wood bridge over the river Vandra, the mill came into sight and its distinctive noise faintly rang in my ears. The huge waterwheel reminded me of the frightening process that lay ahead. The path to the mill was small and it followed the little stream that had been created by the water diversion from the river. Violets and other flowers adorned its banks, and *rondinelle*, swallows, and other birds sang their songs in the trees. This peaceful, serene surrounding would abruptly change in a few minutes as we reached the mill.

The flour mill's proprietors were Teresa and Nicola Amicone. He was a transplant from Vastogirardi. They were a very quiet, gentle couple, but I was afraid of them whenever I would see them around town, including church, because I associated them with the scary flour mill.

After exchanges of pleasantries, the miller unloaded the sacks of grain and emptied them into a chute, where they would go through the grinding process. Nicola walked towards the lever that released the water. That is when I would grab onto Mom's skirt as tightly as possible. As Nicola pulled up the lever, the loud noise of the rushing water engulfed the building, and then all the other different sounds would engulf the room. The huge wheel started turning and it would set all the other pieces in motion, each making its own clicking and clacking sounds.

Il mulino, the mill

I could not stand the noise and prayed for it to be over soon. It seemed to take forever but in reality the rushing water lasted only minutes, and eventually all the other scary noises would stop. Then my mother and I would walk over to the room below the mill where *Trsina*, Teresa, was waiting. With her black dress splotched with flour and her face also coated with it, she reminded me of *un fantasma*, a ghost. This is where the ground wheat was *setacciato*, sieved, separating the bran from the white flour. Eventually we would load the donkey with two sacks, one of flour and one of bran, the latter to be used to make *viverone*, a mixture that was fed to the pigs. And the flour would be used to make bread.

Ruota d'acqua, the waterwheel

When money was available my mom would pay *il molinaro*, the miller for his services, but usually he either took a portion of the wheat or other food products as barter or simply entered the charges into a book for payment, to be hopefully collected in the not-so-far future.

One of the oldest prepared foods since humans of the Old World moved from caves to huts, bread has been a subsistence food in Italy for centuries. Certainly in our village it was the most important staple. In our house its preparation was a weekly ritual. My mother would mix the flour with water in a square, wood container. She added the homemade yeast, *lievito*, a living organism that extracts oxygen from the sugars in flour to produce carbon dioxide and alcohol when it comes into contact with water. The resulting gas bubbles make the dough rise. How much it would rise depended on temperature and the amount of kneading.

My mother seemed to know exactly what to do. Adding a bit of salt as she mixed the dough, sprinkling flour as she worked the dough until smooth and silky, pinching with her fingers to make sure the rising process had begun. She then placed the huge ball of dough in a container and covered it with a cloth, usually leaving it overnight to rise. My father helped with the bread-making process. Early in the morning he would knead the dough again and then my mom would cut it to make individual loaves, cover them again, and leave them to rise some more. *Ammassare il pane, impastare il pane*, kneading the bread, was a familiar phrase, and every family in our village performed that task.

Ammassare il pane, impastare il pane, kneading the bread

On the morning of the bread baking, my parents placed dried wood in the brick oven that was next to our fireplace in our tiny kitchen, and for hours it would burn until the proper heating temperature was achieved. In the wintertime it was a welcomed activity, for it warmed the whole house, but in the summer it made the house brutally hot and we would stay outdoors until the temperature in the house was again bearable.

Placing the round loaves of dough into the oven with a wooden paddle was the last step of the bread baking regimen. My mother knew what dough to put in first and where, because of the different temperatures in the oven. She hardly ever had one burned or underbaked loaf of bread.

Il forno, the oven with wood storage below, 2014

Mamma would always bake something special for her kids. She would add an egg and sugar to a piece of dough and shape it differently every time, and that would be our sweet treat. At Christmas, Easter, and for other special days, she baked all sorts of different sweetbreads.

That cracked, smoke-stained oven with missing plaster was the most unsightly part of our kitchen, but it was the most used and the most essential to our subsistence. All of us were expected to gather the fuel that was needed to fire it up, from small twigs to large trunks. Wood was essential and we made sure we had it, legally procuring it and sometimes illegally gathering it away from the ever-watchful eye of the forest ranger.

Chapter *XXVI*

IL GUARDA BOSCO · THE FOREST RANGER

He seemed enormous in stature with his big German shepherd dog at his side. He had a huge two-barrel *fucile*, rifle, strapped on his shoulder, the barrels extending way over his head, seeming to want to reach for the sky. Whenever I saw him walking towards me, I did not dare to make eye contact, I would just look down and quickly run the other way, afraid that he might either shoot me or unleash the dog on me. His name was Luigi Lombardi. I always thought our little hamlet was named after him and that he was a very important man, but the name given to our small neighborhood was of a distant relative of long ago. This big man was, in reality, barely over five feet tall and was the area's *guarda bosco*, forest ranger. We called him *reh varianeh, il guardiano*.

He and his wife, Vincenza, lived near the fountain, in the same row of houses where our barn and *fondaco*, storage room, were located. He seemed to be everywhere; at least my brother must have thought that, because Luigi caught Ezio many times trying to sneak our animals onto government land for a grazing or trying to cut firewood wood from its trees. And for that reason there was no love lost between the two of them. My brother taught me to fear and to dislike this authority figure, who was also a relative and neighbor. So I grew up fearing this guy and what he represented. Luigi's second wife was always extra nice to me. His first wife died young, leaving behind two young sons. He later remarried and they had a daughter.

Luigi's grandsons, Luigi and Domenico, were my playmates until they emigrated to America in 1958. Luigi's other son, Camillo, was a priest!

*Il guardiano, Luigi Lombardi, with second wife,
Vincenza, circa 1960s*

How could this ranger be so feared and yet have a son in the priesthood? The forest ranger's first son, Nicola, had left his young family and emigrated to Philadelphia to seek a better life for them. His wife, Ida, and their two sons remained in Pagliarone and lived with Luigi and Vincenza. After Ida and her sons left for America, Luigi and his wife were alone. Their son, Camillo, was the pastor in Alfedena, a town north of Pagliarone. He had been in the same church before World War II. Camillo would come to visit his parents regularly, but they seemed to miss their two grandsons greatly. Vincenza must have seen her distant grandsons in me because she always treated me well, although at times scolding me if I was doing something wrong. But *il guardiano*, Luigi, and his companions, the dog and the herculean rifle, always seemed to scare the crap out of me. It wasn't as bad when I saw him out of his uniform, dressed in work clothes, doing normal work like the other men of Luigi.

My assessment of the ranger, Luigi, changed drastically one day when my cow, Paunella, gave birth to a calf and Luigi was my savior. In the meantime my brother and I kept our distance, usually trying not to cause any confrontations. On the other hand, my older brother also seemed to enjoy confrontations, inviting the consequences they would surely bring.

Il guardiano had a beautiful, tall cherry tree in *la padula*, the fertile grounds just south of our little hamlet of Luigi. This tree was full of big, red cherries during that summer of the early 1960s. Luigi seemed to keep a close watch on that bountiful tree. We would see him there as my mom and dad cultivated their small patch of vegetable garden next to his. My brother must have been keeping a keen eye on the cherries and on the forest ranger. One day Luigi left our little enclave, perched on the side of that small mountain. He was going to be gone for a couple of days for a work-related meeting in Campobasso, the provincial capital of Molise. Talk around town was that maybe there were discussions of some changes in some laws that would allow more freedom on government lands. There was a severe shortage of firewood, the town's only source for heat and energy. The townspeople waited anxiously for Luigi to come back with some good news. Ezio was ready to start chopping down trees!

While the forest ranger was away on business, my brother took the opportunity to plan a feast of some delicious cherries. Of course he needed an accomplice, and what better one than his little brother. I remember at first resisting the temptation. Someone would see us and broadcast it around town. Eventually the forest ranger would find out, and we would be in big trouble with him and also our father. But my brother assured me that no one would see us, so reluctantly I joined in and climbed the cherry tree where Ezio was already eating the red, ripe cherries. I ate so many cherries that my stomach felt like it was going to jump out of my body. My brother was calmly enjoying more cherries.

Full and bored, I opened one of the cherries and a big, white worm began to crawl out, scaring me, making me lose my footing. As I was falling to the rocky ground below, my brother grabbed me and asked me what the excitement was about. I told him to open a cherry and again a worm appeared. We opened a bunch more with the same result, a white worm in every cherry that looked like a maggot. We got even more nauseated with the thought of the little creatures starting a colony in our stomachs. We quickly climbed down the tree and ran home with our hands on our tummies.

Not knowing that the acid in my stomach would kill the creatures, I wondered for days what problem the worms were causing, envisioning them starting to crawl out of my mouth and butt. Days later we watched Luigi, his wife, and *Antonio la fonde* pick the rest of the cherries. Should we tell them about the worms? The decision was a unanimous no! *Il guardiano* would either shoot us dead with his rifle or unleash his German shepherd on us to tear us to pieces. Cherries are still one my favorite fruits, but now I always open the first one, making sure I don't see any slimy larvae.

When I went back to Villa San Michele on our honeymoon, I was somewhat startled that I towered over old Luigi. I was just as amazed when I noticed that I was taller than my uncles, who, I thought, were giants when I was a child. As a matter of fact, I was one of the tall men around town back in July of 1975! Our little village had its share of little people. Odd that presently the inhabitants are much taller; nothing has changed except a better, bigger diet. In my mind I had created this enormous man with the rifle and the big dog, but in reality he was just a short, simple man. He came over to my aunt's house to invite my wife and me over for dinner. He asked questions about his son, Nicola, and daughter-in-law, Ida, and his grandsons, Louie and Domenic, who lived in Denver. With tears flowing down his sunken, sun-beaten, wrinkled cheeks, he handed me a letter for his son, asking if I would be so courteous to deliver it to him when we returned home to Denver.

Chapter XXVII

GLI UCCELLI E LE API
THE BIRDS AND THE BEES

La padula, the marshy land that was just minutes from our house in Luigi was where we had our *orto*, vegetable garden. This was a fertile piece of ground on a sloping hill, divided in equal sections for all the residents of Luigi to use. Many fruit trees surrounded it, such as cherry, apple, plum, and my favorite, fig trees. There were also walnut and hazelnut trees. That location always held a special place in my heart. This is where my mom found me. She told me many times that one day she saw a large squash, she pulled it away from the vine and took it home. She complained that it was so heavy. What could be inside this enormous squash, *la cucoccia*? *La zucca*. When she carefully cut it open, there I was, a beautiful, big baby boy. She always said that I weighed a lot, like a sack of potatoes!

In our village and in other remote villages of Italy, children grew up a lot faster than their urban counterparts. We had to. At an early age the kids of our village were introduced to the nature of conception and reproduction. Some of my least favorite journeys were the times when I accompanied my dad to take one of our cows to the Pasquale hamlet in the valley below Luigi, to visit the dreaded bull. Men would guide our poor cow into a stall and then they would go get the bull, *reh tuavar, il toro*. It took two or more men to control the beast and guide him behind the cow, where he would repeatedly jump on top of her. And my poor cow would try to get away from the lunging bull but she was trapped. And the men made sure that the bull performed his task. After what seemed many hours, my father headed back to Luigi with the traumatized cow and son in tow. My father attempted to explain to me in his simple way that the bull would help the cow become pregnant and that in approximately nine months we would have a brand new baby calf in our barn.

I witnessed the same process with the rest of our animals. It became second nature to watch these animals mate, but I was always confused when two dogs became attached to each other, why the ladies of the village would frantically hit them with a broom in hopes that they would separate! The older kids told us what was happening, but younger children didn't quite understand the situation. Eventually I figured out that I did not come from the belly of a squash, but from my mother's belly.

The song by the Four Seasons, "December, 1963 (Oh, What a Night)," always brings back memories of a night back in 1963 in Villa San Michele. It wasn't late December, but late July. All of the boys of the village were having an intense war game, la guerra. It was taking place around le baracche, the temporary housing of our village. A group of us were jousting for positions and trying to sneak up on the other team. The leader of our group, an older kid by a couple years or so, suddenly stopped in front of a window. The lights were on. Windows in those temporary buildings were low enough that one could peak in, especially a kid. As the older kid looked into the room, he suddenly turned and placed his index finger in front of his nose, hitting it gently. It was a sign for us to keep very quiet, a sign he had made numerous times during our war games. We looked around expecting to see some of our opponents lurking, but he frantically motioned for us to come by the window.

Some of us younger boys were confused by what was taking place, but the older guys knew exactly what was going on. The other younger kids in the group and I were pushed away by the older ones, not necessarily to protect us from what was transpiring but to get the best view. I was able to see enough to recognize the naked woman in that bedroom. Thankfully that was all some of us witnessed. The older kids talked about what happened that night for months. The young woman lived in the baracca alone because her husband was in a country in northern Europe, working. He had returned home for the summer, and this was the first night with his young bride in almost a year.

That night a group of kids ranging in ages witnessed a husband and wife making love. Those older boys definitely made a bad choice to intrude on the couple's privacy on that hot and sweltering night, and surely if any adult found out about it there would be hell to pay. For me it was the first time I laid my eyes on the naked body of the opposite sex. That night I also realized that even though plans were underway for me to go away to a Franciscan monastery, where the monks would prepare me for a life of celibacy, a monk's life was never going to happen for me. Even at that tender age, I began to hope that someday I would marry a beautiful young woman like the one in the window. We did not dare tell the leaders of the war games, the fourteen- to sixteen-year-olds about our adventure that night back in '63; partly because they would not believe us, but mostly because we feared that they would spread the news.

Whenever I saw the husband in the streets of the village, I would start to sweat and panic, wondering if one of the kids broke our pact to secrecy. Maybe he was aware of what we saw that night and would now come after me to beat me senseless. And whenever I saw the young bride around the village, a feeling of envy came over me as I smiled at her, envy towards her husband for being married to her. In those moments I temporarily wished to be her husband.

That same summer on a hot afternoon after we were finished with our chores, the same group of kids met on top of the *Colle dei Noci,* the hill separating Pagliarone, the old town, from Campanello/Villa San Michele, the new town. Our mission was to locate *nidi di rondinelle,* nests of swallows. We would then remember the location and wait until the eggs hatched. At the right time, we planned to take the little birds to keep as pets. As we sneaked around a huge rock to follow the path of a bird, we stumbled upon a young couple sitting in a meadow.

Deja vu! The older kids gave us the sign to keep quiet, again! We sat there and watched the young couple caress each other and roll around in the green grass. Eventually we sneaked away and for the next few days we lived in fear. Surely the young couple would find out and the young man, whom we looked up to and feared, would beat us senseless. Although the young couple was probably just making out, in the following days we imagined the young lady's belly growing, she was pregnant! And we imagined a bit later that she had the baby, but she kept it inside her house in a secret room until the baby was old enough to walk outside! Maybe it was best that soon I would be going away to school. Fortunately we were all able to keep our secret, and of course when we saw the couple around town, visions of the activity in the meadow on *Colle dei Noci* filled our minds.

Colle dei Noci (hill separating old and new town) Pietrantonio Lombardi, old Pagliarone below, 1975

From the top of Colle dei Noci, Jackie and cousin Adelia with old Pagliarone below, 1975

During that summer of 1963, a small group of ten-year-old kids received their share of sexual education. Some days, bored and with no plans, we would be persuaded to sneak into some barn, where we would take part in a sex education class given by the older kids, who gave us lessons and instructions. At puberty and adolescence, life was accelerated back then — probably out of need. We were expected to grow up fast, to get married and have kids, to get on with life. At least with boys, nature took its course. Presently our society tends to want to delay that natural process as long as possible. That first date, that first taste of wine, that marriage, that first child, that plastic surgery. God forbid if I offer my small grandsons a taste of wine, I would be reprimanded by my family and probably prosecuted by society.

The Puritans were the religious fanatics of their day, arriving in America in 1620. As the first enduring European settlers of America, their attitudes still pervade our broad American culture. This influence makes American culture, with its basically European origins, different from European culture (even though European teens today seem to also pick up a lot of bad ideas from our teens).

Puritans classified alcohol as something sinful. Drinking is still seen by American culture as something naughty, to be hidden and kept from children — so much so that the youth, especially, indulge in it excessively as a rebellion rather than as just a glass of something to have with dinner.

Talked my grandsons into stop playing a war game on their iPad and come out to the backyard to play a game of war like we used to play as kids in Pagliarone.

The Puritan distrust of sensuality and their no-hanky-panky attitudes about sex also still pervade our broad cultural morality. American television shows of the 1950s such as *I Love Lucy* or *The Dick Van Dyke Show* still depicted Puritan influenced censorship, in that married couples had to have twin beds. And even if a married couple was shown sitting on one bed together, three of their four feet had to be touching the ground. Those censorship rules were greatly relaxed during the 1970s and, like a teenager who has just broken away from too-strict parents, producers of entertainment today rebel against those old boundaries. Sometimes the sex and violence are pretty irrelevant to the plot, but we want to break the rules just for the sake of breaking them.

American kids today probably also grow up too fast, but in a less earthy way than we did. Kids nowadays get a peek at raunchy porn on late-night TV while at a slumber party or something, and sex is pushed at them from TV, movies, and music videos.

It was another story with the girls. If fathers had had access to chastity belts, they surely would have fitted every daughter with one. Pregnant out of wedlock! Those boys did not have enough money to buy one cigarette much less a condom. *"Quattro figli! Auguri!"* Four sons! Congratulations! *"Quattro figlie! Povero te."* Four daughters! Poor you. Maybe some things never really change.

What has really changed everything is cheap, sure, widely available contraception. The whole morality of no sex before marriage started off in the Neolithic period (about 6,000 BC). At this point we became small-time farmers who stayed put, moving into huts. We were now living in permanent settlements as opposed to living the nomandic life of hunters and gatherers. The nomadic clans lived as an extended family, and babies could be cared for by the mother and whoever else was around. But in a permanent settlement, families became more divided in their own huts. If she had sex with him, and he left, she was left to take care of that baby all by herself. And society could see the wrongness of that, not to mention being annoyed by the burden it placed on the rest of them. Her fellow city-dwellers proceeded to whip or worse all the unwed mothers for two thousand years.

The morality that evolved was that if he's going to have sex with her, then he should have to make a commitment to stick around and help raise the baby. Marriage is a Neolithic human invention. Almost all "religious" rules started by people being able to see the wrongness of a situation, of a woman having to raise a child with no support, and God just could not be pleased with that wrongness. That idea continues until mid-1973! The birth control pill changed the wrongness of having sex outside of marriage, because she is not going to get pregnant (well, if she's smart). The rule had been around for 8,000 years, and it's been only 40 years since the arrival of the pill. So there is still some transition in thought going on. Europe has embraced it fully. Americans, with their Puritan roots, still wrestle with it in broad culture. People in the Middle East within their Age of Faith broad culture are still appalled by the transition. But culture is always changing.

I recall a heated discussion in one of the barns by the older kids about why we have hair in certain areas of our bodies. As I think back, I must admit that some of it made some sense. A boy named Nicolino informed us that the hair was to keep our bodies warm. Another kid disagreed; it was to hide our privates. Another swore that it was a signal that you were now a man and ready to marry and father a baby. I don't remember anyone mentioning that it might be for health reasons.

We didn't have television, organized sports, or computers and the internet in that tiny village. All we had was nature and what it offered. I don't believe that some of those customs and practices damaged us in any way. I did not become an alcoholic by having a sip of wine at a young age. Because it isn't taboo to us, I think Italians learn to drink in moderation. And I am not promoting replacing milk with wine!

During one of those lazy summer days, my friend, Pasqualino, my cousin, Terenzio, and I decided to walk all the way down to the Zirr area of Pagliarone, an easy walk downhill. It was the southernmost part of the town. We joined other kids from the village who were swimming in a pool of water under a state road bridge over the river Vandra. Most, if not all of us, could not swim and the pooled water was deep at some places. Some of the older boys knew, or thought they knew, how to swim but I recall many of us struggling to the river banks as panic of drowning set in.

After our swim we spent the rest of the afternoon wandering around the valley, as we often did when there was a break from our chores. We walked the shores of the river Vandra. As young boys go, we were scared of the rushing waters of the river but attracted to it at the same time. We got wet, we drank some of the water, and we ate a lot of wild berries and hazelnuts. In the afternoon we got tired and bored and decided to start heading back up towards our homes in Luigi.

We were halfway home when suddenly I became weak, shaky, feverish, and nauseated. I fell down on the ground and cried. I felt sweaty, hot, and cold. As everything around me started to spin, I tried to stand up and I became even dizzier. What in the world was happening to me? My friends tried to help me up, to take me home. I felt like I was going to die. Maybe that would be okay if it meant putting me out of my misery. Whenever I asked *Mamma* what happened to people who died, she would say that they went to *il paradiso*, Heaven. Up there you did not have to work or go to school, you just played all day and night, because you did not need sleep. But I just wanted to make it home before I died.

In my mind I was very close to dying... fainting because I started to quiver, heave, gag, and then vomit everything that was gyrating in my stomach. The two other boys just watched me from a safe distance, wondering if this was how people behaved when they were about to die. When there was nothing else in me to throw up, my small convulsing body started to relax a bit and except for the foul smell in me, around me, I started to feel a little better. The other boys also had a sign of relief on their faces, but still kept a safe distance from me. I lifted myself up from the dirt and rock pavement and struggled towards my friends and we resumed our walk back towards Luigi.

As we left the Pasquale hamlet behind, we came upon Pietro, another small hamlet. From there my house was very close. Just a short trek, up a steep hill and we would be there. At the bottom of the hill of our houses was Pasquale's house; it was the last in Pietro's enclave. Pasquale lived there with his wife and two sons. His house was a bit different from the rest of the houses of the village. It was fenced in, surrounded by trees, bushes, and flowers. Pasquale was also a bit different: astute, reserved, a bit eccentric, and usually kept to himself. As boys, we always wondered what that fence guarded. I don't know if I was still delirious from my bout with near-death, but I told my friends that I was going to go through his gate and once and for all see what those bushes and trees concealed. We could at least help ourselves to some of his grapes and other fruits from his orchard.

My illness also must have given me temporary amnesia, because I totally forgot that Pasquale was also a beekeeper. My mom was the recipient of some of his honey, given to her by Pasquale's wife, Lucia. As I made my way through the small walkway and deep into the property, I heard a buzzing sound and before I knew it, a swarm of bees was hovering above my head. I turned quickly and ran towards the gate, where my friends were waiting. I was no match for the bees; they were around me in an instant. I felt them buzzing around my head as the three of us ran as fast as we could towards our houses. Suddenly I began to feel stinging on my neck. The two other boys were also not immune to the attack. We battled those bees for what seemed an eternity. We were all crying with pain as we tried to swat the bees while running up the hill. Thankfully the remaining honey bees that had not left their stingers in us and died, decided to leave their prey. The buzzing stopped and we all fell to the ground, exhausted and in misery.

My friend, Pasqualino, however, began rolling around on the ground, flailing at his pants, then pulling them down to his ankles and kicking them off. There was redness and swelling on his legs, on his privates. Agitated and in pain, we made it to the top of the hill. Hearing our wailing, my mom and sister came outside into the hot afternoon sun. As soon as I saw *Mamma* clasping her hands together, lifting them over her head, and waving them back-and-forth, chanting, "*Figl mieh!*" (*Figlio mio!* My son!), I realized that I was in a bad predicament.

Whenever she behaved like that it meant that something was very wrong. She grabbed me and carried me up the stairs and into our house. My friend and my cousin were already running towards their homes nearby. Once in our kitchen, *Mamma* began to pull the stingers out. She applied a wet cloth to my neck and then mixed up a concoction of vinegar, flour, and God knows what else, and applied the remedy to my red, swelling, itching bee stings. As I lay there in agony, she undressed me and there were more bites and more stingers to pull out.

That night *Mamma* stayed awake all night to watch over me as I slept between her and *Papà*. She was very worried because I moaned and was restless all night long. I don't know if that was because of the numerous bee stings or the fainting and vomiting episode. I did not tell my mom or anyone else about the near-death episode, and to this day I wonder what happened to me on that summer day long ago.

Luckily I survived the bee stings. Thank God I was not allergic to their venom, because surely the numerous stings would have probably killed me. I never set foot inside Pasquale's gate again. Whenever I walked by his house, I always listened for that familiar buzzing over my head, as I quickly straddled the farthest part of that footpath of the mysterious house. Hopefully we would soon move to the new town and I would not have to deal with it much.

Recounting the bee story to my brother, Ezio, Jackie, and brother-in-law, Vittorio, as we stand next to Pasquale's house, 2015

Chapter *XXVIII*

LE CASE NUOVE · THE NEW HOUSES

As a young child, I always wondered why our family still lived in Luigi and not in a new house in Campanello, why our hamlet was left behind. We had the *la baracca*, the barracks, but it was even smaller than our old Luigi house. The new houses had *il bagno!* a bathroom!, with a sink and a bathtub! That meant that my mom would not have to boil water a couple of times a year and put it into a big pot to wash us. Yes, we washed our whole bodies only a few times a year. It would always surprise me to know that my feet were actually white and not a dark gray from the caked on dirt. A homemade bar of soap was the only cleansing ingredient we used to clean our bodies, our clothes. No toothpaste or toothbrush, no perfumes or deodorants. I am sure we probably all smelled with body odor but I suppose that if we all smelled, nobody noticed.

Our family and the rest of the families from Luigi had never experienced the luxury of indoor plumbing, of a bathroom. We only dreamed of not having to go fetch water at the outside fountain, not having to use a chamber pot, and not having to walk to the barn and use a smooth rock or green leaves to clean ourselves when not even newspaper or any other paper was readily available.

From our old house, we made the long walk to school, to church, to the train, all of which were close to the new houses. At times we felt inferior and the other kids seemed to feed off of it. Geography in that tiny part of the world was part of the game played in the social structure. We were of the same color, same culture, same class, same religion, and mostly

245

of the same surname, but for some reason there was definite evidence of social classes. Some people had more clout and went through great measures to assure that their family received a new house. Talk of bribes and lies could be heard around many hearths of most homes. Some people intentionally tore stones out of walls and broke chunks of plaster from interior walls to show the authorities that indeed their house was a casualty of the numerous landslides. When we were given the temporary barracks to live in until the new house was ready, my parents were very excited and relieved. But the completion dates for the new houses were constantly being pushed back, and so we waited and waited.

Our village of Campanello with newly built barracks, minus the houses running parallel to the railroad tracks, where our new house would be built, circa 1959

When we finally got our new house, I did not have a chance to enjoy it long because soon after I was sent away to school at the monastery. Hearing the water filling the toilet tank above the toilet was like a magical wonder. I would climb up on a chair just to see it fill up and then pull the chain to see it drain into the toilet. But the water did not always flow through those water pipes.

Although there was plenty of water all around our village, unfortunately water was usually missing from the homes. There was no pumping system to fill the water reservoir and when it got low, it took some time to fill naturally. We did not know when this would occur and many times when we used the toilet and flushed, we were met with the unpleasant surprise of no water. With a bucket in hand we would rush to the town's fountain, where water flowed continually. We filled the bucket and ran back home to fill the toilet tank. After a few of those accidents we learned to peek in the toilet tank before we used it.

Fast-forward ten years when I was back in Villa San Michele for our honeymoon. The water issue still existed but a solution to the problem was in place. Water was turned off during the day to allow the water reservoir to fill. On a warm Sunday morning in early July of 1975 while Jackie and I were enjoying our honeymoon, we prepared for a trip to the sanctuary of Sant'Amico in the nearby forest of San Pietro Avellana.

The town's main fountain, where water was always flowing. Jackie had to have her fill of the fresh, cold water whenever we returned to the village. 2012

Jackie made a last trip to the bathroom. She wanted to wash her hands. She put the stopper in the drain to save water, as she had been taught by *Zia* Leontina. But when she turned the faucet on, no water! It had already been turned off. And off we went on our fun day trip with relatives, spending the whole day at the holy grounds and enjoying a picnic.

Sant'Amico sanctuary in a forest near San Pietro Avellana, 1975

Amico was a Benedictine monk who was born around the year 920. He is said to roam the Apennine Mountains of the *Abruzzi e Molise* region, helping the poor and needy of the area. Legend has it that when a big bad wolf killed a working donkey, the beast was cursed. The wolf was forced to serve Amico as a working donkey, carrying chopped wood from *il bosco*, the forest, to the monastery. When friar Amico's body was discovered in a forest near the town of San Pietro Avellana, a sanctuary was erected in his honor. It is said that he lived to be 120 years old. He was eventually venerated as a saint by the Catholic Church. As a child, when we made countless pilgrimages to the sanctuary, I was always confused by the huge painting of a monk leading a wolf by a rope, loaded down with chopped wood.

Sant'Amico leading wolf loaded with firewood

That afternoon of our excursion to the sanctuary of Sant'Amico, we drove the short distance back home to Villa San Michele. As we pulled up to my aunt's house that late afternoon, my cousin, Peppino, noticed water seeping through the bottom of the front door of the house. He quickly opened the door and saw water cascading down the marble stairs from the second floor, from the bathroom! Jackie had forgotten to turn the waterless faucet off in the morning and when the water was turned back on that afternoon, it filled the sink and flooded the house! Thank God for the stone, cement, and marble floor houses of Italy, no wood! There was no damage, and of course my young bride had to be reassured continually by my Aunt Leontina and Uncle Flavio.

Jackie and I sitting with the first friend we saw, Armando Lombardi, on the train on our honeymoon in 1975. My aunt's store and home door to the left, where water was flowing out; post office to the right

Jackie loved playing clerk in my aunt's tiny store on our honeymoon in 1975.
From left, Zia Leontina, Jackie, Zio Flavio, and their granddaughter, Esmeralda

Our new house had white marble floors, marble stairs, and marble half walls throughout the two-story house, all beautiful even if very cold during those winter nights. I was glad that my mother was finally able to live in a comfortable home. It had a larger kitchen with a propane stove, a fireplace, a bathroom, and a *salotto*, a room that could be a dining room, a family room, etc. Upstairs there were two spacious bedrooms and even an attic, although the attic was more like a loft which some families turned into a third bedroom.

Our new government house, the white one in the center with the balcony, 2014

These houses were essentially the Italian version of public housing; they did not belong to the people, but were property of the Italian government. The villagers either did not fully comprehend that or just conveniently made them theirs. They made major changes and some actually sold them, as we did when we immigrated to America. Many years later, someone in the Italian government discerned this fact and demanded that the existing residents either pay for the houses or be evicted. They all had to pay in the neighborhood of 25,000 euros to buy those homes, which many people had long assumed were their rightful property.

Fond memories of that beautiful house fill my mind, but one memory makes me cringe, as I feel the empty space in my mouth where a tooth once was. Every few months our kitchen was used by a dentist from the nearby town of Agnone. He would come to town and set up shop right in the middle of our kitchen and offer his services to the townspeople. His services, I think, were pulling painful, decaying teeth! I don't think filling cavities and making crowns were part of his services. I had such a tooth, which caused me to sometimes cry with pain.

One summer morning my father instructed his friend, the dentist, to pull my tooth. I quickly became agitated. I had watched grown men moan and cringe as they had a tooth pulled. And as a young boy, the mere sight of his shiny, silver pliers scared me to death. My father coaxed me into sitting in the intimidating chair so the dentist could take a look at my tooth. When I heard the dentist mention that the tooth needed to be pulled, I panicked. I jumped from the chair and eyed the front door to run, to escape, but before I knew it, my father had a firm grip of me and he promptly sat me back down on the chair. I refused to open my mouth. As I cried and clenched my teeth together as tight as possible, my father enlisted my brother to help him hold me down. My father then grabbed my mouth and forced it open and as I screamed, the dentist forced the pliers into my mouth. The dentist took hold of the tooth. He pulled hard while wiggling the pliers, sending shooting pains all over my body. Finally after a considerable struggle from the tooth and from me, he extracted the rotten tooth and held it up for all to see. I cried for the rest of the day as my mother consoled me, while the hole in my mouth throbbed and bled! The dentist either did not have anesthesia or decided not to use it on me. I suspect the former.

A few weeks after that ordeal, my mother needed to go to Agnone to see a doctor. The dentist, who also lived in Agnone, insisted that we join him and his family for *pranzo*, lunch. Part of the abundant meal included *bistecca*, steak. Never in my young life had I seen or eaten that big piece of meat. I chewed and chewed and chewed and as I tried to swallow it, I gagged, so I kept chewing while putting more pieces of meat in my mouth until I had a nice ball of chewed meat occupying one side of my mouth. Suddenly I was not hungry anymore, as I did not know what to do with the ball of meat in my mouth. So I refused all other food including a delicious looking *torta*, cake. My mom kept urging me to eat but I nodded no. When we finally left, my mother admonished me for making the dentist and his wife feel bad by not eating all that they offered. Before she was finished giving me a lesson on being a good guest, I opened my mouth and pulled out the ball of chewed steak!

A few years later we would say goodbye to that kitchen, to that home, as the decision was made to emigrate to *l'America*.

My son, Dominic, and his then girlfriend and now wife, Michaela, in front of our house in Villa San Michele, 2001

Mamma loved those marble stairs in our new home. Sitting on them in 1975

Chapter XXIX

LA FESTA DI SANT'ANTONIO
SAINT ANTHONY'S FEAST

Cerreto, the nearby village, was smaller but much like Villa San Michele. In the mid 1700's some families of Pagliarone moved into the area just east of town, and with other settlers who were already there, they continued the task of deforesting the heavily wooded area to cultivate the land. The residents of the enclave had close ties to their neighbors in Pagliarone to the west and in Trebbante, a little more than two kilometers to the south. They experienced the same issues and struggles as did the people of Pagliarone, but when a railroad line was constructed through the village, the future became a bit brighter.

Every year in May the town celebrated their patron saint, San Felice da Cantalice (1515-1587), with a feast in his honor. Saint Felice was born in Cantalice in the province of Rieti, of the Lazio region. He was an ordained Cappuchin monk with roots as a *contadino*, dirt farmer, in his previous life, as were all of the residents of Cerreto. It is said that he spent his time begging for the poor and giving spiritual advice to humble people around Rome. He would only sleep a couple of hours a night, devoting the rest of his time to prayer.

A small hamlet above Cerreto emerged and was named San Felice, in honor of the saint. I went there many Sundays with our priest, Don Felice, as his altar boy. Usually after he celebrated Holy Mass in our village, we would get onto his Vespa and make the five-minute or so ride to the church in San Felice.

The church of San Felice in Cerreto

I have a lasting memory of one of those feasts. I walked to Cerreto with a group of boys, a brisk half-hour walk. There was a peculiar contraption right in the middle of the street, one we had never seen before. Buckets were hanging on a circular rope that went high and right over a bridge. It was a carnival ride. I don't recall how much it was to ride it, but I had some coins in my pocket and decided to give it a try. I went once and it was fun. Although I felt a bit dizzy, I decided to try it one more time.

After that last go-around, I began to feel dizzier; the world around me started to spin out of control. My stomach did not like what I had done, and I ran under the bridge and threw up everything that was churning in it. After that episode I could not even look at a ride that went around in circles. To this day I am not able to get on a similar ride without thinking of Cerreto, as my stomach begins to quiver. It's sad that I relate that quaint little village with vomit.

The people in Cerreto were always friendly and accommodating. My parents had many friends and relatives who resided there, including my mother's two brothers: *Zio* Giuseppe and *Zio* Domenicantonio. The latter emigrated to Canada in the late 1950s with his wife, Bambina, to join their two sons, Gino and Fiore. *Zizi* Peppino (Giuseppe) lived in Cerreto for the rest of his life. His wife, Raffaela Ciotola, died young, leaving him with six young kids to raise on his own. The feast of San Felice was nice, but the big one for our small world was the feast that took place every June in our town.

Cerreto, as seen from Villa San Michele, 1975

That most important feast day in our village occurred in June to honor *Sant'Antonio di Padova*, Saint Anthony of Padova. Saint Anthony was born Fernando Martins de Bulhoes in 1195 to a wealthy family in Lisbon, Portugal. To the opposition of his family, Fernando entered the Community of the Canon Regulars, an order of priests in the Abbey of Saint Vincent on the outskirts of Lisbon. The Canons were famous for their dedication to scholarly pursuits. There he chose to study theology and Latin. He was ordained a priest by order of the Augustinian Canons. He was assigned to an abbey in a nearby Portuguese town, and there he came into contact with five Franciscan friars who were on their way to Morocco to preach the Gospel to Muslims. He became strongly attracted to the very simple, evangelical lifestyle of those friars. News came a year later that the five friars had been killed in Morocco.

Fernando meditated on the heroism of those men and longed for that same lifestyle of martyrdom. With permission from the Augustinians, he left the priesthood and joined the new Franciscan order, where he became a friar. He moved into a religious retreat and began his life as a Franciscan. He adopted the name of Antonio from the name of the abbey in which he was living. He soon left for Morocco to fulfill his vocation.

On his way there he became very ill, and then the ship he was on got caught in a storm that drove it to the eastern coastal city of Messina, Sicily. From there he made his way to the Umbria region of Italy, where the Franciscan order was born. Because of his sickly appearance it was decided to send him to a rural hospice near the town of Forli, in the Emiglia Romagna region. There he was assigned to work in the kitchen.

Purely by accident, when an ordination was to take place at the abbey, there was some confusion as to who would preach at the pulpit. The Dominicans assumed that the Franciscans would do it, but they were unprepared. The director asked Anthony to do the talk. Anthony objected, but was overruled and was basically forced to go to the pulpit. His very strong voice and eloquence captured the attention of the audience. Very impressed by his ability to preach, Anthony was commissioned to preach the Gospel in the northern region of *Lombardia*, Lombardy. His great preaching captured the attention of the founder of the order, Francis of Assisi. Francis was very impressed by Anthony's visions and ability to teach, especially to the young members of the Order, so Francis paid Anthony to use his skills. Anthony held various important positions within the Order and even outside of it at different schools and universities.

He continued to live a very simple life teaching, while ignoring his many health issues. In 1231 he became very ill with edema. With his body swelling with fluids, he went to a retreat near Padua in hopes that he would recover. There he lived in a simple cell built for him under the branches of a walnut tree. On June 13, 1231, while on his way back to Padua, he died. He became one of the most rapidly canonized priests, as not even a year had passed when, on May 30, 1232, Friar Anthony was declared a saint by Pope Gregory IX.

Saint Anthony statue during feast procession in village, 2012

Saint Anthony is venerated all over the world as the Patron Saint of Lost Articles, being credited with miracles involving lost people, lost items, and lost spiritual things. Many times in our family his name has been referenced in appealing to him to help find something lost.

La festa di Sant'Antonio, Saint Anthony's feast, was funded mainly by the auction of *gli agnelli di Sant'Antonio*, Saint Anthony's lambs. The families who owned sheep in our village would designate one newborn lamb to donate in honor of Saint Anthony to help fund the feast. Days before the celebration, these healthy and groomed lambs would be taken to the church's grounds and put into a corral. The townspeople gathered to inspect the lambs and comment on which was the best, the biggest, and the most valuable, singling one out in their minds for the auction that would take place on the afternoon of the feast day.

I recall the lambs being adorned with colorful bows as they were paraded in front of the altar at the end of Mass while the women sang songs. The lambs were paraded back to the corral and the auction would begin. The money realized from the sale of the lambs was used primarily to pay for the huge marching band and the fireworks. Some families also donated a pig that was fed by all the families. On the feast of *San Martino*, Saint Martin, in November, the fattened pig would be butchered, the meat sold, and the money put into the Saint Anthony's feast account.

Another large part of the funding for the feast came from donations by the emigrants of the town who had gone to the United States, Canada, Argentina, and other European countries. Presently in early June, Salvatore Iacovetta, better known as Sam Shoemaker or *Shmecca*, visits most of the immigrant families from Villa San Michele who live in the Denver area and graciously asks for a donation for *La Festa di Sant'Antonio*.

When the Saint was paraded around town in a procession, the men carrying the statue made frequent stops in front of the houses, where people would pin money on the statue of Saint Anthony. I recall most of the money being foreign, as it was sent by their relatives who had emigrated to those foreign lands. Women would sing songs and recite the rosary while the marching band played lively, loud music, as the procession wound its way around the village. Finally it made its way back to the church for more prayers, and afterwards families gathered in their houses for a bountiful meal.

Saint Anthony statue

On that Saint Anthony's Sunday in June, the young and old alike participated in the daylong party that continued well into the night. I particularly remember the marching band. Every family would host a member of the band. A designated member would be our guest, eating that ample dinner feast with us. Our family would get to know him, and of course he would then be our favorite band member during the festivities. The town's population swelled as its inhabitants and people from the neighboring towns gathered at our church's piazza, which had been prepared for the celebration. Carnival workers set up the mini-amusement park, usually consisting of a couple of carousels and a few games of chance. It was the only time that the kids of the town enjoyed a mini-amusement park.

The afternoon's festivities began with a very loud fireworks display. This was done in daylight because unlike fireworks in this country, ours were all about the noise and not the colors. Presently the fireworks display is conducted in the evening.

As nighttime approached, the young men and women of the village would slowly join the married couples as they danced to the band's music. Often you would see women dancing together; it was an accepted practice, but not so if two males engaged in a similar act. The dance was an opportunity to advertise and display yourself to the opposite sex, of course always within sight of the watchful eyes of parents, siblings, and grandparents. Unfortunately the young men of the town seemed to outnumber the attending young women. Some of the available girls were not allowed by their parents to go dancing.

When we settled in Denver, we left behind many traditions such as *la Festa di Sant'Antonio*, but to our surprise, other traditions awaited us. Another feast was introduced to us and of the same name, Saint Anthony's feast. This June feast was sponsored by the Saint Anthony Society of Denver, established by the early immigrants from our village. This social club was a way for all the immigrants to get together once a month for a meeting that included ways to help members and others in need. Usually these gatherings were also not void of heated, lively arguments about anything we could think of. All was followed by a good meal, where differences were usually put to rest. Fundraising dinner dances were planned throughout the year, and a great Christmas party was held, where the children participated in a nativity play. The most memorable Christmas party was when my four-year-old son, Dominic, sang *"Tu scendi dalle stelle,"* a very popular Italian Christmas song. Forever in our minds are his quivering lips as he impressed the crowd with his performance of the song. The society's summer picnic was also a huge hit, with an abundance of food, drink, and games.

Our four-year-old son, Dominic, singing "Tu scendi dalle stelle" at the 1982 annual Saint Anthony Society Christmas party at the Potenza Lodge. Five-year-old daughter, Daniella, played the role of the Virgin Mary. Godson Frankie Lombardi played the role of Baby Jesus. I am to the back of the camera, with Dolorata Lombardi at top right and Dina Lombardi to the left with Marc and Jennifer Lombardi.

Although for the most part similar to the feast in Italy, the activities on Saint Anthony's feast day in Denver were somewhat different. No lambs or pigs were donated here! At Our Lady of Mount Carmel Church, a Mass was celebrated in honor of Saint Anthony. Mount Carmel church was dedicated in 1904 and became the centerpiece of the Italian-American community of Denver. After Mass the attendees gathered in front of the church while the president of the Society, who for many years was Joe Lombardi, would preside over an auction for the honor to carry the statue of Saint Anthony in the procession that followed. The procession was similar, as people walked behind the statue, winding their way around the streets of north Denver singing and praying. Then the group headed back to church, returning the statue to its place behind and above the altar with some final prayers.

On Saturday and Sunday nights the members sponsored a feast, a bazaar. The many raffle stands offered Italian goods, homemade donated cakes, food, and drinks. And there was the game of chance called Chuck-a-Luck, a wheel with dice numbered from one to six, three dice on each slot. The players would put their money down on squares marked with numbers from one to six. If the wheel stopped at their number, that player would win an equal amount that was bet. If the wheel stopped on a slot with two or three of the same number bet, the bettor was paid double or triple the amount bet. I worked that stand for many years and from my experience I can say with confidence that not many players walked away winners! It was just a fun way to donate to the Society. This feast was the most important fundraiser for the non-profit organization.

Chuck-a-Luck wheel

The best event organized by the Saint Anthony Society was the yearly picnic. This was a chance for all the new and old immigrants of our village and other mostly Italian-Americans to get together on a summer Sunday to enjoy food, drinks, and games. My favorite game was the egg toss. Someone would always have an egg splattered all over their body trying to catch it without breaking it. Although Jackie and I came close some years, we never did win the event. I sometimes thought about buying a fake hard egg for the toss and replacing the real one with it right before the toss started, just so we could win! Many other games played were geared towards the younger side of our large group. The older *paesani* would play *bocce* and *morra*. Eventually the guys would gather for the Italian card game of *tresette*, more intense and more difficult than the popular game of *scopa*. They played until nightfall, when they could not see the cards anymore. The wives were waiting and complaining to the husbands to quit playing so they could go home. Home to most of us was northwest Denver, Arvada, Wheat Ridge, Lakewood, and other suburbs of north and west Denver.

I never thought that the feast of Saint Anthony in 1964 would be my last, as I would leave that village to attend middle school in faraway Todi Italy, and then later emigrate to even farther away America.

Villa San Michele, circa 1964

Chapter XXX

CONVENTO DI MONTESANTO
THE MONASTERY OF MONTESANTO

My future godfather, Davide, would always tell my parents that I seemed to be very studious and interested in education and it was imperative that I continue school after the fifth grade. My brother, Ezio, was the total opposite. He would run away from school on a daily basis to be with his animals. My father had to go looking for him when there was no sign of him as nightfall approached. Ezio always had the same excuse: that the cows did not look full and he needed to keep grazing them until they would not feed anymore. Many times this included trespassing on other people's pastures!

Ezio did not shy away from the backbreaking work of *zappare la terra*, tilling the ground, with either *la zappa*, the hoe, or *la perticara*, *l'aratro*, the plow, pulled by oxen. He performed a man's work from a very young age, from cutting hay and wheat to finally getting the chance to slaughter a pig. I would run away when the men — usually my *Zio*, *Zizi* Umberto — got ready to stick the long, sharp knife into the pig's heart, but my brother would be right there wanting to learn the ropes. He seemed to work around the clock, and I don't remember any instances where he was involved in anything recreational.

My sister and I, on the other hand, were sort of the opposite. As a female, my sister was not expected to be out in the fields as much as my brother and I, but she was expected to help out with all household chores. I suppose being the youngest my mother cut me a lot of slack. My father cut me a little slack, but I was definitely expected to lend a helping hand. It was very difficult for me to go out and help after school. There were soccer and marble games, and in the winter snowball fights and skiing and sledding with our homemade devices.

One cold winter day my mother was ill in bed in our temporary housing, with my sister watching over her. My father was in Luigi tending to the animals and my brother was away in Switzerland working as some other family's farmhand. My father told me to come to Luigi right after school to help out with all the chores, while he made preparations to make the weekly batch of bread since my mom was ill. That day it snowed and when we got out of school, many of my schoolmates went sledding and convinced me to join them just for a while. Time got away from me as I was having a lot of fun, even if I did not have the proper clothing and was freezing my butt off. While I was walking back up the hill for another run, my friend pointed his finger towards the dirt path that led to the old town of Pagliarone.

I turned and saw my father walking up the road at a faster pace than usual. The sun was going down, and I realized that I was in trouble. As he got closer I could see him clearly, with his right arm extended, his thumb over his index finger, pointing the hand towards me and then putting the part of his hand between his thumb and index finger in his mouth, biting it and pointing it at me again while biting down on his bottom lip. These gestures gave me the warning that I was in big trouble and to run home or face a beating in front of all my friends. And so I ran the short distance to the *baracca* with my father in pursuit. I sought refuge in my mom's arms, but she wasn't much help as she clutched her hands, concerned because my hands and other parts of my body seemed to be frozen. My frozen body did not keep my father from giving me a good spanking.

Imitating my father. These gestures from my father meant that
I was in big trouble, and surely a spanking would follow.

 &

That and other incidents convinced my father that I was not cut out for the life of a *contadino*, a dirt farmer. I seemed to excel more in sports, recreation, and academics. This encouraged him to make the decision to send me away to school at the Franciscan monastery that his godson and my future godfather, Davide Carmosino, had strongly suggested to him. Preparations were made during the summer of 1964 for my departure.

I had seen Franciscan brothers before; their sandals, their brown habits with the white rope wrapped around their waists. They came from the *Convento Cappuccino* in Venafro, a town near Isernia. They would help with *l'asta*, the auction, of the lambs donated for the feast of *Sant'Antonio*. I pictured Saint Francis whenever I saw one of those friars, expecting to see a bird in their hands.

San Francesco di Assisi was born in Assisi in 1181 as *Giovanni Francesco di Pietro di Bernardone* to wealthy clothing merchants. His mother was French, which could be why his father started to call him Francesco instead of Giovanni. As a young man, Francesco started showing sympathy for the poor. He would give beggars money, even when working for his clothing merchant father, Pietro, at Assisi's market. His father scolded him for this. As a young man he joined Assisi's army and was captured when fighting against Perugia, a town a few kilometers west of Assisi. He was imprisoned for a year, which led to a great increase in his spirituality. He eventually left behind his affluent life and turned his full attention to helping the poor. His father tried to persuade Francesco to leave the life of poverty, but instead Francesco renounced his father and his patrimony.

While preaching in and around Assisi, Francesco started to attract his first followers. He did not want to be ordained as a priest. Instead he and eleven of his followers went to Rome to ask Pope Innocent III to found a new religious order. In 1210, the order of the *Frati Minori*, Lesser Friars, was founded. The Franciscans took a vow of poverty and continued their preaching in the streets. The order grew quickly with new followers. Eventually it grew rapidly throughout Italy and then Europe. With the Crusaders, Francesco and his followers even made it to the Middle East, hoping to convert the Sultan of Egypt.

A young woman, Chiara Offreduccio (1194-1253), *Chiara di Assisi*, Clare of Assisi, was deeply touched by one of Francesco's messages and joined the group. Francesco then established The Order of Poor Ladies, later referred to with the now more familiar Poor Clares. This new order was for women, with a religious habit similar to the simple destitute-looking clothing of the men. The women lived a life of poverty and chastity, as did the brothers. Clare subsequently was canonized as Saint Clare of Assisi.

Francesco is said to have received the stigmata in 1224 while on a mountaintop, where he was praying during a forty-day fast. Stigmata are body sores that correspond to the crucifixion wounds of Jesus Christ. The term originates from a letter written by Saint Paul to the Galatians, a people of what is now central Turkey. He told them that he bore the marks of Jesus on his body. The word 'stigmata' is plural from the Greek word 'stigma,' meaning a mark, brand, or tattoo. Stigmata are primarily associated with Roman Catholics. Although Saint Paul wrote about the marks of Jesus on his body, Saint Francis had the first record of stigmata in history.

There are many stories about Francesco's love for animals. Birds surrounded him as he sang to them, making peace between people and menacing wolves. On October 3, 1226, lying on his simple bed in a simple hut dying, he thanked his donkey for all his help. Francesco was pronounced a saint in 1228 by Pope Gregory IX. A great Basilica was built in his honor and millions of people journey to Assisi, Umbria to give praise to the man who lived the life of Joyful Beggar under Brother Sun and Sister Moon.

Depiction of Saint Francis receiving the stigmata

On any summer evening before my departure for the monastery, you would have found my mother sitting on a chair outside our house with a basket filled with all of my clothes, as we played soccer on the cobblestone street nearby. On every piece of apparel that I was to bring with me to the monastery, she was asked by the Franciscans to stitch the number 71 in an inconspicuous but easy-to-find location because that would be my identification number at the monastery. I would come to dislike number 71, and to this day when I see 71, I think of all the *mutande*, underwear, *calze*, socks, and *canottiere*, undershirts, and all my other belongings with that little red number 71 crudely embroidered on them. In reality the monks were not trying to label us with a number, but it was a way to identify my clothing, and I would have hated to end up with other students' underwear when the nuns washed them and graciously placed them on our beds.

That summer of 1964 seemed to end before it even started, with the Franciscan monastery always at the back of my mind. Finally the day came in early September, very early in the morning, when my father and I boarded the train that would take us on an all-day trip to Todi, Umbria. My mother and sister cried loudly and steadily the night before my departure in our new kitchen in our new house. They resumed crying even more on the morning of my departure. I was in a mild state of shock and hoped that someone would save me from that impending voyage. But all the relatives and friends who stopped by were there to say goodbye and to wish me well.

How lucky I was to leave that life in that village that led to nowhere and to go up north for the opportunity of a great education and a better future. Didn't my father tell these people that I was admitted to this school only through misinformation that I expressed a desire to become a Franciscan monk? Or did my parents hope that I would pursue a religious vocation? My sister and brother forced me to play the part of a priest in those crudely organized plays that the girls of Luigi seemed to enjoy. I did not want to be a priest then and surely I did not want to be, of all things, a Franciscan monk now.

Nobody saved me, so my dad, carrying a small suitcase in one hand and holding mine with the other, headed for the short walk to the little train station of Villa San Michele, with my mom and sister holding on to my other hand. My mom and sister cried while hugging me, not wanting to let me go, and I the same. Eventually the conductor put an end to that scene, motioning the engineer to get moving. And at the age of eleven, I embarked on a journey that would take me past the familiar surroundings of Villa San Michele to that foreign and faraway town of Todi. It might as well have been at the end of the world because that's where it felt like they were sending me.

We passed San Pietro Avellana, then Castel di Sangro, places I had visited many times, only a few kilometers away. Then we soon reached Roccaraso, a famed ski town. I had been there once before with my mom to visit my sister, who was working in one of the lodges to learn the resort business. My sister was only fourteen years old at the time. As the train lumbered uphill, I was introduced to places I had never seen before. This journey was taking me into the unknown.

My father somehow navigated through all the train changes, Sulmona and L'Aquila, the capital of the region of *Abruzzi e Molise*. At Rieti, he recognized the name and said that some relatives had moved to this town. I wondered why they would move so far away from their village, a hundred miles or so away. A young man from Rieti *aveva avuto il posto*, had landed, a job with the government working the rail line that ran past our village. Years later in Arvada, Colorado, I would find out exactly who these people were and why they had moved to Rieti. Marlene and Patty Jo Bakarich, daughters of Giustina (Chris) Lombardi and Joe Bakarich, were related and told me they knew of the man from Rieti who worked on the railroad. He had met a young woman from Villa San Michele, married her, and they eventually moved back to Rieti. Marlene and Patty Jo presently keep in touch with those relatives from Rieti.

We finally reached the Umbrian city of Terni. Here we would leave the State railway system to find the privately run train service that would take us to Todi. My father purchased the tickets and proceeded to *il binario*, the track, to board the train to Todi. It was a small, blue and white, old rusting train. It was both shorter and slower than the State-owned trains. It looked different than the trains we were used to. Was this an indication of the foreign place where I would spend the next couple of years of my life? The train slowly staggered towards our destination. Although only about fifty kilometers separated the towns, it seemed to take forever in my young and worried mind. My eyes were fixed ahead to get a glimpse of my new home.

After a couple of hours we reached our final destination. Todi's train station was smaller than the other stops we had made, not as hectic, not as crowded. As we got off the train, we received some gazes from people. Did we look different, or did we give away the fact that we felt nervous, disoriented, and distressed. My dad asked an older man sitting on a bench how far *il Convento di Montesanto* was. The man pointed to the hillside and then to the auto-pullman, the small bus parked behind the station. It was too far to walk; we would have to take that bus. Looking around I only saw a few houses. My father realized that we needed to take the bus up the hill and beyond, where the town of Todi was and hopefully, nearby, the Franciscan monastery.

As the small bus lumbered up the hillside, more houses could be seen in the valley below. All was green and those tall trees were everywhere. We did not have those trees in Villa San Michele, the beautiful cypress trees. As the bus wound its way towards Todi we came to a fork in the road. A beautiful structure came into view, *Santa Maria della Consolazione*, a church, a temple. Later I would learn more and visit this site frequently. What I remember most about the place is that it was thought that Galileo Galilei tested his flying machine from the top of *il campanile*, the bell tower of that church.

"*Devi scendere qui,*" You need to get off here, an older gentleman announced to my dad. The other passengers stared at us — at me in particular. My sorrowful appearance must have been a dead giveaway as to where I was headed. *Convento di Montesanto* came into view as the old man pointed to a hilltop on the western horizon. A wall seemed to encircle it with vineyards and olive groves all around the sloping hillside below the structure. Tired and anxious, my dad and I walked down the road towards the monastery. After a half-hour journey we reached the small roadway with the blue sign that read 'Convento *di Montesanto*,' Convent of the Holy Mountain.

Convento di Montesanto. Vineyard and the grassless soccer field to the left, 1975

In ancient times the area was known as "*Monte Mascarano*" meaning Mountain of Spirits. Perched on a hilltop, surrounded by a wall and tall structures, it almost looked like a prison. Its buildings seemed to have been built to keep its inhabitants inside. The Early Middle Ages were a time of raiding and warfare. Those monasteries were built on hilltops to keep away from the skirmishes, and built like fortresses to keep that stuff out.

At the time of the Etruscans who came before Roman rule, the hill was a sacred place, a necropolis with temples and shrines dedicated to various deities. Archaeological remains of Etruscans and Romans have been found throughout the centuries in and around the hill. The Christian history of that hilltop began in 1235 when a convent for the Order of Poor Ladies (Clarisse nuns, today the Order of Saint Clare) was erected. The poor nuns were there until 1367 when the nearby town of Todi was reconquered by the Papal States and the convent was turned into a fortress.

The fortress endured years of conquests and was of strategic importance to many conquerors. Another fortress was built on the hilltop of Todi and eventually the old fortress of Montesanto was abandoned. In 1448 the Lesser Friars of Saint Francis purchased the site and built a monastery incorporating some of the walls of the fortress that were still standing. In 1866 the friars were driven out by the government of King Vittorio Emanuele II and the monastery became property of the Kingdom. In 1895 the Franciscan monks who had turned a nearby farmhouse into their monastery, purchased Montesanto and moved back in. From 1916 to 1970, the building housed the Seraphic College, a residence for about a hundred boys who were aspiring to the Franciscan life.

Sixth grade class of 1964. I am the only one in a tie.

As my father and I walked up the hill, we were introduced to the 14 Stations of the Cross, *la Via Dolorosa*, on the right side of the road. We stared at each station as we made our way up to the fortress. I thought

At the monastery we had to take a foreign language class, we were given the choice of English, German or French. The English and German was taught by an older rotund spectacled gentleman with rosy cheeks and a slow duck like walk. The French class was taught by the young blonde teacher pictured with 1965 soccer team, majority of us chose French! Pietrantonio Lombardi, top right.

I was happy to be going home for my sister's wedding, although the monk in the center would accompany me because he was from the near town of Carovilli and wanted to see his family, but I think the director wanted to make sure that I came back to the monastery, I am second on the left, 1965.

that maybe this was to be my long, last walk of my life as I knew it. We made it to the top and the roadway, as it opened into a small parking area surrounded by tall trees, one tree being very big and old. Later I found out that it was a historic tree; it had been there for centuries. The parking area was encircled by a stone wall. To the left were stairs leading up to a door that was certainly a church. Just to the right of the church we saw a huge door with an arched top that seemed to invite us to walk up to it. My father tried to open it but it was locked.

Jackie and I posing in front of one the Stations of the Cross on one of our visits back to the monastery, 2003.

My dad hesitantly knocked and a short time later the door opened into a dark hallway. A monk appeared, dressed in a brown robe with a white rope belt and simple brown sandals, his clasped hands hanging in front of his stomach. Unclasping his hands, he motioned us to come in.

After introductions, he invited us to follow him through a dark corridor and we ended up in a courtyard. It was a square area with a well right in the center and arches on all four sides of the courtyard. Suddenly a bunch of kids appeared, running and then stopping to look at my dad and me. Some looked to be my age, others looked older. Panic set in to see all those strangers, along with the cold hard fact that my dad would leave me and go back to Villa San Michele the next day.

Il Direttore, the school director, came out to introduce himself. I have forgotten his name, and actually, I don't think I ever knew his name or those of the other monks. We always referred to them as *Maestro, Don Direttore, Don frate, signor frate*, etc. *Il Direttore* was short and slight. He had small, beady eyes and wavy, light-brown hair with a natural *corona*, crown, a shaved head, which monks of the past displayed as a way to denounce vanity and to show a commitment to the simpler, monastic life. What I remember most about him is the fact that he was a terrible singer. He always screwed up during High Mass,

Jackie and I posing at the dark hallway leading into the courtyard, 2012

Jackie posing in front of the well in the courtyard, 1975

evoking giggles from most of us in the choir, in turn invoking *Maestro's* stare, surely to be followed up later with some punishment for our misconduct.

My dad and I met a couple of younger monks and as they welcomed us, another friar approached. I immediately noticed that the smile the others had on their faces was missing from one friar. He was stout, with a round, rose-colored face. His nose was much smaller than the Roman nose of the director. Also, his hair was receding, with a slight comb over in an attempt to hide it. He walked more quickly, more erectly, more urgently, and kept his stare directly at us. I sensed my father tensing up. I remember the stern monk extending one hand to my dad and resting the other hand on my shoulder. I cringed. I am sure he said his

Me posing with a monk in the courtyard with my daughter, Daniella, and son, Dominic, 1990

name, but I didn't hear it. All I remember is him saying that I could call him *Maestro*, teacher, the drill sergeant.

I was already shaking in my shoes as he led us up some stairs and through a hallway, which opened into a large room full of small twin beds: the dormitory. We walked down five steps to a lower level and *Maestro* pointed to a bed in the corner of the room. It had a metal frame, a simple metal headboard, and a single mattress. That would be my bed for two years of my life.

I was number 71 of about 100 boys. My father and I put the bedding on my bed and the rest of my stuff in one of many small lockers that lined a wall in the dormitory. That night my father and I ate dinner by ourselves in a separate guest dining room. A young, shy nun brought us dinner. We could hear the kids outside the door, walking into a dining hall next door. They were talking, laughing softly, and then there was complete and total silence. An occasional spoon banging against a dish was all that we heard through the rest of the dinner.

After dinner a young Franciscan monk led my father and me upstairs to a guest bedroom, where he invited my father to spend the night. Then he led me to my new bed where the rest of the kids were filing in from the restroom and shower area with their pajamas on. They stood next to their beds and then knelt. *Maestro* led them through some prayers and then they all piled into bed. A much taller, younger monk than *Maestro* came by my bed and asked me to follow him with my pajamas and toothbrush. My mom had purchased one for me because it was on the list of things that were required by the monastery. I had never used a toothbrush before. The monk led me into the large, white marbled bath/shower room and told me to brush my teeth and then go back to my bed, change into my pajamas (my first pair) and go to sleep.

I had practiced brushing my teeth with my sister, days before my departure, but still had trouble with the brush and the toothpaste. As I brushed, my hands began to shake and tears filled my eyes as I thought of *Mamma*, my sister, and my brother, of my safe and familiar surroundings back home. I did not want to stay in that place with all those other strange kids and monks. My stomach was in a huge knot as I walked back towards my little bed, the other kids' eyes fixed on my every move. I made it to my bed, hesitantly took my pants and shirt off and quickly put the strange pajamas on, laid my clothes on the foot of the bed and crawled under the covers. A monk blew a whistle as he walked down the center aisle of the dormitory, and as he left the room he turned the lights off. The room was suddenly quiet and very dark. Scared, lonely and confused, I slowly, quietly, cried myself to sleep.

A loud clapping of hands roused me from my sleep. The director was walking up and down the aisles of the dormitory yelling, "*Buon giorno, svegliatevi, andiamo ragazzi,*" Good morning, wake up, let's go boys. Kids hurriedly jumped out of bed, got dressed and rushed to the bathrooms with toothbrush in hand. I hesitantly put my slippers on as the other kids had done and followed them through a door. The large shower area was full of boys washing their faces and brushing their teeth. I waited in line as numerous kids went through their morning ritual. I received various stares, some asked questions, most wanted to know my name and where I was from.

As they finished washing up, the boys went back to the dormitory to dress and make their beds. I did the same. When everyone was finished and standing next to their beds, two friars started walking up and down the aisles inspecting all the kids and their beds, instructing some to adjust a sheet or rearrange a pillow. After a few kids remade their beds to the satisfaction of the friars, we lined up and went out of the dormitory and into the chapel on the same second level of the monastery. After morning prayers in the small chapel, we filed down the stairs to the dining room below. My father was waiting at the bottom of the steps and *Maestro* motioned for me to go to him. My father had a sad, concerned look on his face, probably questioning whether or not he had made the right decision to bring me so far away. How would his boy fare with these serious-looking monks? I hugged him and held onto his hand, hoping that he would say that he changed his mind and we were going back home.

We followed one of the monks as he led us into the same dining room where we were the night before. We sat at the table and a nun came in with some breakfast which consisted of *caffè e latte*, coffee and milk, for my dad and *latte e caffè*, hot milk with a bit of coffee, for me. My throat was completely closed, my eyes were ready to spew out the most tears ever and my voice seemed to have left me. I just sat there numb, anticipating my *Papà* leaving me in that ancient, cold place. "*Meh Toni Papà, magna qualcosa*" *Dai Toni, mangia qualcosa*, Come on Tony, my son, eat something.

My father always ended an endearing comment with '*Papà*.' '*Toni Papà*' was roughly equivalent to his calling me Papa's Tony. I always knew whether or not I was in trouble, because if he just said '*Tonino*' or '*Toni*' it either meant that he was not very happy with me or that the situation was serious. But if he followed '*Tonino*' with '*Papà*' then I knew that I was not going to face any major dilemmas, he was just going to give me some advice, direction, or praise. The same with my mother; I will always remember those words coming out of her sweet lips, '*Toni Mamma*.' Almost always, '*Toni*' was followed by '*Mamma*' with my mother, but with my father the '*papa*' was missing most times when he called out my name.

That morning, '*Toni Papà*' came out of my dad's mouth more than ever. But the love that he was showing towards me did not help; it actually made it much worse. I suppose that if he was cold and in a hurry, it would have made it a bit easier for me to walk away. Of course there was no way he was going to do that. He was about to leave his young son with a bunch of strangers. He hardly touched his continental breakfast: biscuits, sliced bread, *Nutella* (a chocolate and hazelnut spread) and marmalade. He sipped on the *caffelatte*. I wanted so much to ask my father to take me back to Villa San Michele with him, but the words would not come out of my mouth. My throat had completely closed and my stomach felt like a rock.

In what seemed like no time at all, the door opened and *Maestro* appeared. "*Un frate ti accompagna alla stazione*," They offered my father a ride to the train station. By now my stomach was in a tight knot and my throat closed up more, if that was even possible. My poor dad seemed confused and apprehensive. This simple man had lived a very difficult life but what he was about to do was going to be one of the toughest acts of his life. Sensing the anxiety in us, *Maestro* invited us to go outside. We followed him as he walked under the columns of the courtyard. He was headed towards the dark tunnel leading to the exit. When we neared the hallway, the director appeared and extended his hand to my dad, "*Non ti preoccupare, noi prenderemo cura di Pietrantonio.*"

I actually did not hear a word he said, but as my dad and I recounted that fateful morning, he told me that the monks kept reassuring him not to worry, that they would take good care of me. The monks were giving my father last-minute information: They would write, I would write, and they encouraged him to write. That moment of saying goodbye came quickly and suddenly, and I lost it, crying uncontrollably while wrapping my arms tightly around my father's waist. My father's eyes were now flowing with tears. The monks tried to pull me away from my dad but I was holding onto his pants. As tears fell down his cheeks, my father pushed my hands away from his legs and he quickly turned towards the door, looking back at me, waving a trembling hand as I cried out, "*Papà! Papà!*"

Maybe if I broke away from the monk's grasp I could just run out the door and my dad would grab me and take me home with him. As the big door squeaked, the loud noise drowned out my cries. It swung slowly until a loud clunk locked out my father on the other side. Just like a puff of smoke, my dad was gone, leaving hysterical me behind. *Maestro* put his hand on my shoulder and turned towards the hallway that led to the place that would be my home for a couple of years of my young life.

I cried myself to sleep that night and woke up a few times during the night, but all I had left were small heaves, no more tears in me to shed. For more than a month, I quietly cried in my bed and in any other private areas of that far and unfamiliar place where they ate unsalted bread and prayed morning, noon, and night. I was scared and anxious most days. I missed my mom, my dad, my sister, my brother, and everybody else and everything else that was my village. My mother told me many times that she also cried, not only in bed but also with every swinging of the hoe and every bunch of wheat that she cut. My sister would join her many times, both crying, praying, and hoping that I was safe, happy, and in good health.

I witnessed other boys going through the same sad goodbyes during those late summer days. Slowly I bonded with some of the kids in my class, sixth grade. We were the youngest of the group. We were the new arrivals from all over Italy, although there were no others from my region of Molise. The older kids were deadly good in *calcio*, soccer, and *bigliardino*, foosball. We were no match for them and they seemed to enjoy beating the shit out of us. Although yet anxious and scared I decided to work my butt off to get better at soccer and foosball, the only games we played every day. I excelled in the classroom, where some kids seemed to struggle. I felt sorry for them because they were lost, and I wondered if some had even had any schooling. Later I found out that some did not go to school much at home, just so they could help their family put a meal on the table.

I began to receive letters. The monks would give them to us at recess while we were playing *calcio* on our soccer field, which, by the way, had hardly any grass on it, just dirt and sand. The monks would read all the letters first and then hand them to us. We noticed them at times putting some letters in the depths of their brown robes. Surely they did not want the recipient to read them. Once I received a letter from my grandfather, Pietrantonio, who was in America. *Maestro* gave me the letter and I remember that the envelope was different than the others; it had blue and red stripes on it. The stamp was different and it would be a great addition to my stamp collection. *Maestro* also showed me a green paper. I recall seeing the number 20 on it, and it was the same money I saw pinned to the statue of Saint Anthony. He informed me that my grandfather had sent me some money. The money also disappeared into his robe.

Money, as with most other material things, was strictly forbidden to be in our possession. The friars used the money to purchase items that I needed: toothpaste, soap, haircuts, etc. My parents would also send some money; not much, but surely the friars continually asked for a donation. The money was used for incidentals. I remember a time when barbers were summoned to give all of us a buzz haircut when it was discovered that some of the kids had lice. The barbers were paid with some of that money. Everything else was provided by the Franciscan Order. All they wanted in return was a commitment from me to study very hard and to absorb their teachings that would someday lead me to be an ordained Franciscan monk.

Eventually I forgave my parents for sending me to that place that resembled a prison, with those high, massive stone walls. We learned, prayed, and played soccer and foosball. Because of my slight build, I was quicker and faster than a lot of the other kids. I also had a passion and love for the game of *calcio*. I improved daily with dribbling and passing skills. The coach, a young, tall, and strong monk noticed my ambition and adoration for the game. He worked with me constantly and I never relented with my eagerness to improve. The day came when he gave me a spot on the traveling soccer team. What a gift! Now I wasn't so upset with God for putting me in that monastery. I would get to travel all over north-central Italy to play teams from other monasteries and seminaries.

I learned a lot about soccer at the monastery. No shin guards, hardly any grass! 1965

In my first game I was put in at right wing, replacing a kid much older than I — by a couple of years! He was the only foreign student; he was from Greece. He was also maybe the only boy in that monastery who seemed to be truly devoted to becoming a monk. He was a leader and a role model for the rest of us. I was anxious and scared that I was substituted for him.

We were winning and the game almost over. Our center forward made a hard shot on goal and the goalie seemed to bobble the ball as he made the save. Eager to please my coach and my team, I sprinted towards the goalie and attempted to kick the ball into the back of the net. Everything happened so fast, I completely missed the ball but made perfect contact with the goalie's head, knocking him out of the game. I was ejected from the game and I was out as quickly as I came in. With my head down, I headed towards the sideline. I panicked as the coach approached me, "*Buona grinta e energia,*" Nice grit and energy, he quietly mumbled. I was surprised, excited with his comment. I eventually won a starting role as the school's right winger. By the age of thirteen, the coach wanted to send me to another monastery near Perugia to play on an elite team made up of aspiring Franciscans. But that was not to be, as another surprise came my way suddenly and with no warning.

For the two years at the school, I went back home to Villa San Michele only twice: once for my Confirmation and the other for my sister's wedding. During the summer when school was out, the students who were promoted to the next grade were treated to many field trips to other parts of Italy. The other kids stayed at the monastery to study. No one was allowed to go back home. We went on many scavenger hunts, camping trips, and many sightseeing tours. I saw parts of Italy that I would have never had the opportunity to see if I was back at home. Nevertheless, I missed my family tremendously and would occasionally cry at night in bed.

Some nights in the beginning I was so distraught that I would wet the bed. I would cover the embarrassing spot with my towel. After the friars walked by for their inspection, I would remove the towel and make the bed with sheets wet with urine and stick my wet pajamas in my nightstand drawer. Unfortunately (or fortunately), other kids experienced the same issue. One student from the southern region of Calabria, for some reason, could not control his bowels and would occasionally mess in his pajamas and sheets. He was very embarrassed and irritated by the experience. He went from an outgoing, cheerful kid to a disconsolate recluse. Most of us did not dare to make fun of him because we did not want to face the wrath of *Maestro*. But some kids just could not resist the temptation. At recess a few boys sort of teased him by just mentioning it. Ever-present *Maestro* got wind of it and punished the boys by swatting their hands with his always handy round, hard wooden stick. No mention was ever made again of that boy's issue.

Most of the kids at the monastery were from central and southern Italy, not because kids from that area aspired to be monks more than the kids from the north, but because of necessity. The Franciscans "recruited" kids from those parts because parents were usually eager to send their boys to a monastery, where education was guaranteed and it was free. That was the only way for their boys to get an education. The mostly very poor families could not afford to send their sons to school, and without education their sons would be doomed to the same meager life of a *contadino*, a dirt farmer.

There were a few boys from the northern part of Italy and they actually seemed to be more inclined to the life of a Franciscan. They actually wanted to be at the monastery, whereas most of us from the south were forced by lack of another choice to be there. Most of us were from small villages, a few were from bigger towns. These urban kids did not do well when it came time to work the land. We continually searched the forest below the monastery for wild asparagus, truffles, and dandelions, all of which made a great salad, and we also gathered moss for the monastery's state of the art *presepio*, manger. We picked olives and grapes, and we took turns in helping the gardener and the friars do handiwork around the grounds of the monastery, in addition to the rest of the many cleaning chores in and around the complex.

One boy was from Todi, the town that was a few minutes' walk from the monastery. His mom attended Sunday Mass at our church. She would visit with her son but he was not allowed to go home, just like the rest of us. One churchgoer we all looked forward to seeing on Sundays was the young girl who lived in a house on the road below our monastery.

There was a *negozio*, a convenience store, right on the road leading up to the monastery. When the monks allowed us, we would browse in the store as we waited for the bus to take us on some trip. We did not buy anything, we were not allowed, and even if we were, we did not have any money. But we enjoyed looking at all the candy, *gelato*, stamps, and most of all, the daughter of the proprietors, who surely were annoyed by our presence. On our bus rides we would all boast that the very cute, long-haired girl looked at one of us more so than the others. At church every Sunday we anticipated her arrival. She had a cute, simple smile. Her gaze sometimes seemed to express anguish for us, for our confinement in the monastery. For me, she reminded me of a girl from our village who I thought would surely be my wife someday.

My cousin, Adelia, was my informant on my village love. Adelia's job was to keep me informed of a cute girl's love life, and also to relay to her that I wanted to be her boyfriend! All the boys of the village at one time or another wanted a girlfriend, and the girlfriends seemed to change daily. The cute girl's name was Carmela Melaragno; we called her *Carmelina*. Surely she did not want anything to do with me or any of the other boys who desired her and the other girls' attention, and besides, our parents would always remind us that we were related! There were other "girlfriends" but for some reason they remained only in my mind. The irony of it all is that I would eventually marry a girl from Denver who was a distant cousin of my childhood girlfriend. Her name: Jackie Meloragno (Melaragno)!

I thought about my girlfriends in Pagliarone and the beautiful girl of Todi for a long time, especially later in Denver as the American girls stared at me, giggled at me, made fun of me. As time passed I thought about them less and less, until one day I could not conjure up an image of most of them; that part of my life was gone. Regretfully I cannot remember any of my monastery friends; I can't put a name to a face anymore. The only clear and immediate vision is the one of *il Maestro* and *il Direttore* and *il mio allenatore*, my coach.

On a sunny Umbrian Sunday morning, not long after my arrival at the monastery, we were waiting for the bus to take us to the nearby town of Orvieto. I was excited about the trip. From our monastery, on clear days we could see the famous Roman town perched on a hilltop, with *il Tevere*, the Tiber River, flowing below. As we were waiting by the curbside, we noticed a young couple walking towards us, towards the monastery. As they got closer, I recognized them. It was my father's godson, Davide, accompanied by his beautiful bride, Adelina. They were on their honeymoon and came to visit me at the monastery. I should have been delighted and pleased to see familiar faces from the village, but instead I went into a panic and became visibly disturbed by the approaching couple.

I quickly moved to the back of the group of boys and hid. Suddenly all heads turned as they moved to make way for me to greet my visitors, but I froze and became emotional. I was very embarrassed to see them; I did not want them to see me. Maybe I was upset at Davide for imploring my parents to send me to that walled compound. As the young couple made their way towards me, I began to tremble and cry. *Comare* Adelina gave me a hug and tears were flowing down her cheeks. "*Come stai?*" How are you? my future godfather asked. I was able to quietly whisper, "*Bene*," Okay. They had a letter and a small package for me, which a monk promptly accepted. I tried to talk, but fear that I would start to cry uncontrollably prevented my mouth from moving, even though the young couple gallantly tried to get me to open up.

As the autobus approached, *il Direttore* thanked the couple for the brief visit and invited them to tour the monastery after he learned that Davide had also attended school there. I hoped that he did not tell them that he was very close to becoming a priest and suddenly quit! As the kids began to board the bus, I stood next to my visitors, speechless and nervous. The conditioning of the conversion to Franciscan life was taking hold! I worked up enough vivacity to wave to my visitors as they stood by the roadside. On the bus I was upset with myself for being so reserved. Why didn't I ask them to take me back home, to tell my parents that I missed them, my siblings, my friends, the simple life of the village, and for my parents to come and get me, take me back to my world.

Back home, my mom was in constant agony about her little boy, questioning the decision to send me so far away. She cried daily. I received a letter from my mom in the summer of 1965. By now I was fully immersed in education, in the correct Italian language. The letter was written by a woman with only a third grade education. I worried that the monk reading her letter would think of her as an illiterate. I was sort of embarrassed by those letters, but at the same time I wished that the friar would give me one every day. In that particular letter my mom wrote that "*ti vengo a trovà*," she was coming to visit me.

I was drowned in a myriad of emotions. Elated that I would soon see my mother again, I also became worried that she would somehow degrade me with her unpolished behavior. I had seen other parents come through the monastery, dressed shabbily, loud, disheveled, and not able to speak the proper Italian. Their sons would have a distressed look on their faces. I was annoyed with myself to presume that my dear *Mamma* was going to somehow embarrass me. I kept reminding myself that I did not care what the kids, the monks, or the nuns thought of my mom. I counted the days. As fate would have it, something happened before her arrival.

Although we were kept in close check with our movements by the monks, as eleven-, twelve-, and thirteen-year-olds we managed to be mischievous whenever we had the opportunity. We took pleasure in trying to always outsmart our superiors. At mealtime, we were allowed to take as much food as we wanted with one strict edict: that everything on our plates had to be consumed. Many of us who had taken too much would sit at the table forcing that last piece of bread down our throats, gagging, while the other kids were at recess. We were well aware of the rule, but as young, hungry boys, we went through the line with our eyes bigger than our stomachs.

Dining hall still remains in 2015.

Someone came up with a way to get rid of the uneaten food. Under each long, heavy, wood dining table there was a ledge, wide enough to hold pieces of bread and other food. A group of us secretly put a plan in place. We would discretely, carefully place the unconsumed food on the ledge under the table and one of us would sneak back into the lunchroom through an unlocked window and toss the food out the same window, where cats and dogs were waiting to feast on it. We were very cautious, watching every move of the friars and of the other kids, especially those we suspected of being moles.

We all took turns at being altar boys during Mass, alternating between that and the choir. The closest thing to a cookie at our convent was the Host, the thin, baked Communion wafer. The nuns baked thousands of them. They were stored in the sacristy. A few of us would sneak back there and feast on them — before they were blessed, of course!

One night after the monks had made the final walk through the dormitory and retired to their chambers another boy and I decided to sneak out into the darkness and go pick some of the beautiful, ripe grapes in our vineyard. Others had done it without any problems! We made it out of the building and climbed the stone wall. We could barely make out the dark clumps of grapes hanging from the vines. We quickly began to jam as many grapes in our mouths as possible, enjoying the sweet taste.

The little light from the moon revealed the soccer field below the vineyard. The noise from a hundred kids gone, it was quiet… too quiet. For the first time I saw the lights of Todi in the distance and heard the faint noise of the occasional passing car on the road below. I was truly enjoying the peaceful, calm night outside of those stone walls of our dormitory.

Suddenly in the distance, we heard a loud voice, "Hey!" The very loud, heavy scream could not be mistaken. It was that of the gardener-handyman of the monastery, a grouchy middle-aged man who lived at the monastery. Years later in America I watched the movie *The Name of the Rose*, and the mentally challenged custodian seemed to be a dead ringer of our custodian. I never saw anyone visit him and he hardly ever left the grounds. I choked on the grapes in my mouth, spitting them out and sprinting towards the wall with my friend in tow. With a running start, I jumped off the wall, expecting to hit the pathway below. Instead I impaled myself on something, bounced off of it and slammed myself on the ground. My friend was looking at me with an anguished look. And then a hand grabbed him. The handyman was yelling at him. I was lying on the ground in pain, my neck feeling as if it was on fire.

Soon lights came on and some friars came out to see what the commotion was all about. I knew something was very wrong when *Maestro* had a concerned, alarmed look on his face. I was scared, crying, my hands bloodied as I put them to my throat. Even the mean gardener seemed upset at the sight of blood all around my neck. By now I was crying uncontrollably and started to scream for my mom, "*Mamma, Mamma!*"

I kept moaning as the monks, the handyman, and the nuns carried me inside. They took me to a room in an area that I had never seen before. It was the nun's residence, the convent. They laid me down and frantically wiped away the blood from my neck, face, and hands. They had no idea what could have happened to me. They eventually wiped away enough blood to notice a cut across my neck. Did someone try to cut my throat? Did the gardener hurt me?

They decided to bring in my friend to get some answers. My problem had begun as we tried to get away from the screaming gardener. I ran to the top of the wall and jumped. In my terror-stricken state, I forgot that at the bottom of that wall there were wires stretched all along that side of the embankment. These were the same rows of wires where the nuns hung out laundry to dry. I impaled myself on the clothesline! The monks were discussing whether or not to rush me to the hospital in Todi, but as a nun medicated my wounds it was decided that I was not in danger. I had calmed down a bit, my throat throbbing with pain, but my concern shifted to what punishment awaited me. I was taken to the dormitory with my neck wrapped in a white bandage. I must have looked much like the Italian composer, Antonio Salieri, in the movie *Amadeus*, when he tried to hang himself.

All eyes were on me as *Maestro* put me to bed. That was one of the longest nights of my young life. I cried with pain and with panic. That next morning I was taken back to the nuns' quarters and the nuns removed the bandage to inspect and medicate my wounds. A new white cotton bandage was wrapped around my neck and I was escorted to the office of *il Direttore* by one of the monks. Not a good sign. Most kids who were taken to his office went there because they were in trouble. I was scared shitless as I sat in front of *il Direttore* and *il Maestro*. The other kid had told them the whole story, informing them that it was my idea to go steal the grapes, the very grapes from which wine would be made for use during Mass, and also served to us on special occasions. Yes, we drank a small amount of wine on holidays!

I admitted that, yes, stealing the grapes was my idea. I had committed a careless, selfish act and for that I was given one week with no recess or any other entertainment, such as playing foosball or watching soccer games on television. And for good measure, I got only water and bread for a few days. The worst consequence of my injured neck was that I would not be able to play *calcio* for a couple of weeks.

A doctor came by the monastery a few days later and examined my wound. He shook his head when I told him what happened. He informed me that I was very lucky and that there would be no scar because the steel wire sort of scraped across my neck. And there was no sign of infection.

My mom came to visit me that next week. I was a mess that whole Sunday, worried about my mom coming such a long way all by herself, concerned about how she would handle herself, and most importantly how she would react to the huge scab around my neck. For years my mom recounted to me many times about how *il Direttore*, the director himself, met her in the courtyard and said, "*Non ti allarmare quando vedi Pietrantonio, ha avuto un piccolo infortunio,*" Don't be alarmed when you see Pietrantonio, he had a minor accident, and then further explained how it happened.

When my mom saw me she began to cry and caress me continuously as the monks looked on. She kept looking at my scab, crying "*Povero figlio mio,*" My poor son, over and over. She made every effort to speak the proper Italian while at the monastery and I was pleasantly surprised at how well she did. But when we were alone she reverted back to our dialect and was definitely more at ease with that language.

The monks also studied the rather large suitcase she was toting when she came to the monastery. I took her on a tour of the monastery as the rest of the kids caught glimpses of her. I showed her my locker and my bed. She grabbed the suitcase that she had stored next to my bed and put it on top of the bed. She couldn't wait to open it. The luggage was full of goodies: *biscotti*, her homemade biscuits, *caramelle*, candy, and also some wool socks that she had knitted and other undergarments, all with the red number 71 stitched on them. We stuffed the suitcase into my locker and went downstairs for dinner.

We ate alone in the same dining room where I had eaten with my father when he brought me there. Alone in the small dining room, I told my mom that I did not like it there and that I wanted to go back home with her, that I could just take the train every day and go to school in nearby Carovilli or somewhere else, anywhere but here. I cried. "*Eh Toni Mamma neh fa a cushy,*" *Toni, non fare così*. She begged me not to say that, not to make things more difficult on her than they already were. She also cried.

We both ate a little and then she took a 1,000 *lire* note and handed it to me, telling me that my brother, Ezio, had sent it to me, "*se le vadagniata alla Svizzera,*" *l'ha guadagnato in Svizzera*, money he had earned while working on a farm in Switzerland. I reminded her that I was not allowed to have money, any money, much less a huge amount like that. "*Annascunreh,*" *Nascodila*, She quietly suggested that I hide it from the monks. It was the equivalent of about a dollar, but with much more buying power. With that money I could buy many things, if only I could somehow manage it without the monks noticing.

One thousand lire

A nun came by and invited my mom to go with her, and the nun would show her the bedroom where she could rest for the night. The

next morning my mom hugged me and kissed me continuously, as she said goodbye with a very sad face with huge tears flowing down her cheeks. I did the same, again hoping that she would take me back home with her. But as *Maestro* stood by, I knew it wasn't going to happen. Forever in my mind is the sight of my thin, sun-beaten mom crying, with her arms extended to hold me one more time in that dark hallway of the monastery's exit.

Later that day I went upstairs to the dormitory to hide my money. *Maestro* was already standing by my locker, inspecting it. He grabbed the suitcase and took it with him to his quarters. I became very upset and my annoyance towards him amplified a bit more. I went over to my locker to see what was left of my goodies. Gone, only my new undergarments remained. I swore that there was no way that he would take my 1,000 *lire*. I noticed my little black tie hanging in the back of the locker. I pictured my brother wearing that same tie. I used to fiddle with it when I wore it, sticking my finger through the bottom of it. It suddenly dawned on me! God finally decided to help me. I looked around to make sure no one was watching and I took my rolled up 1,000 *lire* and stuck it inside the tie.

That night after dinner, the kids feasted on cookies and candies, "*Cortesia della Signora Lombardi, la Mamma di Pietrantonio,*" A gift from Pietrantonio's mom, *Maestro* announced from his dining table to all the salivating boys.

I would have to confess to God that I did not like *Maestro* and sometimes I had bad thoughts about him. But he was our protector, our guardian. When we ventured out of the monastery, walking in a perfect straight line to the center of town in Todi, other kids would follow us and make fun of us. *Maestro* would get in their faces and just with his stare he inflicted the fear of God in them and they would take off running.

We were required to go to confession once a week. At night we would take turns going to the chapel. *Maestro*, sitting on a chair, would invite us to kneel in front of him and he would listen to our confession as he rested his hand on top of our heads. I wonder now if there were any kids in that school stupid enough to confess any sins to *Maestro*, the same man who continually disciplined us for any small infraction; the man who put the fear of God in all of us. I never did, but he always invited me to recite ten *Ave Maria*, Hail Marys, and ten *Padre Nostro*, Our Fathers. I always wondered how many prayers had to be recited by those who actually confessed to having sinned!

I recall one afternoon in study hall, the kid sitting next to me wanted to make a trade for one of his stamps. He had a beautiful triangular one from Ethiopia that I finally convinced him to trade for a couple of stamps from *gli Stati Uniti*, the United States of America. The stamps I was trading were on the envelope of a letter I had received from my grandpa, Pietrantonio. We both looked at *Maestro*, who seemed to be immersed in reading one of his many religious books. He was sitting at his desk, perched on top of a stage where he could easily survey the whole room. We were still in negotiations on the trade. I was trying to convince my friend to give me one more of his stamps, since he was getting two American stamps to the single Ethiopian.

I was focused on making that trade, unaware of anything going on around me. My friend was ignoring my requests. Instead, his alarming gaze was fixed on something on the left side of me. I looked up and standing there was *Maestro*. In an instant I was on the ground seeing stars in my eyes. He had smacked me on the side of my face, knocking me to the ground. My coveted stamp was gone and my left cheek hurt for days. How could I confess anything to a friar of whom I was horrified? Never mind that as a twelve-year-old living in a monastery perched on top of an Umbrian hilltop, rarely leaving its walled confines, I didn't know just what sins we could possibly commit — except for stealing some grapes or communion hosts. The former I had to confess, but the latter was going to go unconfessed. I took my chances with going to the deepest crevasses of hell rather than dealing with the wrath of *Maestro*.

Funny that even though I never confessed to any sins, I was given the numerous prayers for penance in order to have my sins forgiven. I was actually willing to say the prayers, hoping that even if I did not confess to *Maestro* that I ate the communion hosts and that I sneaked into the lunchroom to discard uneaten food, that hopefully all would be forgiven.

Some of us actually decided to skip confession sometimes, and thanks to a mole we got in trouble. We had a few kids who would do anything to gain favoritism with the monks. We thought we knew who those kids were, but were not sure of some. The monks did not invite other kids to tattle and did not entertain the possibility of moles getting on their good side. There was no good side for anyone. We were all equal and the monks seemed to be annoyed with gossiping boys. Most of us did not even try to squeal on a fellow student.

I have been asked numerous times about the Franciscan monks and their treatment of students at the monastery. They had the enforcer in *Maestro* who gave out the majority of punishments, hitting us with open hands, sticks, and at times a swift kick in the butt. He put the fear of God in us, but a monster he was not. He played soccer with us, and even with his brown habit and sandals he would usually defeat us. He played foosball against us and normally won. He raced against us and always won. We got out of line and he literally beat us. He made us walk in a neat, straight line when outside the confines of the monastery, not allowing us to look at people, especially members of the opposite sex. With one monk in front, one in back, and one on each side of us, we did not dare to look around. We were a chain gang without the chains. At least members of a chain gang can look around.

But we were not taken somewhere to do heavy work. Instead we were taken to theaters, museums, and many other educational and fun events. The rest of the friars were for the most part gentle, nurturing souls who educated and enlightened us in many aspects of our lives. At the time, I hated being at that monastery, but I received a wealth of knowledge. I was taught so many of life's good values. The monks made me a stronger better human being — something that would come in handy when I came to America, where those values were tested many times.

I can also say without hesitation that at no time was I or any of the other boys, ever a victim of any sexual abuse; although physical and mental abuse, maybe. And this was not necessarily because the monks were cruel; rather they professed that it made us better human beings, admirable Franciscan brothers. When friends talk about the hell they went through in basic training when they decided to become soldiers, I am quick to point out that I endured almost two years of basic training in a monastery!

My time at the monastery enabled me to meet and see many people and places that the rest of the boys from my village could only dream of. Those boys could only see these in some worn out school book, or on a small black-and-white television.

One hot day while at some abbey in Tuscany on our summer tour, a monk came to a group of us while we were playing chess and asked us to go to the soccer field and help some missionaries from Africa, who were trying to learn how to ride a bike. As we reached the field we noticed the four young men, about eighteen years old, struggling to keep their bikes upright. I think that some of us were surprised to see that the young men were black. It was the first time I had ever laid eyes on a black person. I noticed their bright, white teeth as their laughter blared, and they spoke a very strange, loud language while attempting to ride the bikes. I was startled, a little afraid of them. I had only seen black people in books, and those were depicted mainly as primitive, spear wielding savages. But these men were very nice, and thankful for our help. We would hold the back of the bike seat as they rode around the track. They did not seem to mind as they continually fell off the bikes, turning their black robes gray with the summer dust. Their big, bright eyes lit up when they were able to ride by themselves for a bit on those old bikes.

For the next few days while we played soccer, the young African missionaries would be on the track riding the bikes, laughing and having fun, and then one day they were gone. We did not have any feeling of discrimination or prejudice towards them. We missed their genuine, gregarious attitude, their loud smiles, and how happy and thankful they were with the simplest gifts of life. Of course we realized that they looked different but we did not have any idea that some deemed them inferior. I did not even know what discrimination was. I would eventually learn it all too well in America, where I became a victim of it.

Back at the village, one spring in the early 1960's we watched *il Giro d'Italia* bike race on television at the church of Villa San Michele. In the cobblestone streets, all the older kids would ride old, beat-up racing bikes and they would all call out as they pedaled as hard as they could, *"Taccone! Taccone!"* They wanted to be and they thought they were, just like him. He was Vito Taccone, the professional bike rider from our region of *Abruzzi e Molise*. His nickname was *"il camoscio d'Abruzzo,"* the chamois of Abruzzo, for his abilities as a climber on his bike. The nickname was also for his sometimes fierce and sometimes out-of-control nature. As we watched him on that small black-and-white television, I never in my wildest dreams ever considered that someday I could and would watch him ride in the *Giro d'Italia*, second only to the Tour de France, the worlds' most popular and coveted bike race.

The news that the three-week race included a stage that would come near Todi, on a roadway near our monastery, was a constant conversation amongst all of the boys. The friars had allowed us to watch one of the previous stages that Saturday night in May of 1965. The next morning after Mass, much to our surprise, *Maestro* announced that a bus would be picking us up to take us to a road very close to our monastery where we could watch the race. There was excitement all around because bike racing was only second to soccer in Italy in sporting popularity. I remember walking up a road already full of onlookers. It took some time, but finally we found a space on a curve to accommodate all of us. We took our positions and waited and waited.

Suddenly a roar could be heard down the hill and around the curve. Cars, motorcycles, and police with sirens started coming around the corner. There were more cars coming with racing bikes of different colors and different styles attached to their roofs. In what seemed an instant, the bicyclists appeared in a tight group, weaving and jockeying for positions. I tried to look for Taccone. Finally he appeared in the middle of the pack and before I could take it all in, the swarm of bees was gone, over the hill, and out of sight. We tried running up the hill to follow them, but *Maestro* put his hand up and we all froze. The event was over so quickly, so swiftly that it was sort of anticlimactic.

Lagging close behind were other amateur bike riders and a few minutes later we saw beautiful sports cars, led by a shiny red one, *la Ferrari*, as we heard others call it. We gazed as the cars slowly drove by, as *Maestro* waved for us to head towards the waiting bus. As we walked back he said that we, the Franciscans, would never sit in one of those *macchine*, machines, much less own one! When I went back home, one of the first things I bragged to my friends about was that I saw the *Giro d'Italia*, saw Taccone, our Abruzzese hero, and the red Ferraris. I don't think I even mentioned the fact that later that summer we also went to see a monk, who one day would be proclaimed a saint.

I had never before heard the name of the monk and future saint, Padre Pio. The Franciscans scheduled *una gita*, a trip, to San Giovanni Rotondo in the region of Puglia. All the students were taken on a pilgrimage to see the Capuchin monk who had the stigmata. Whatever that was or the meaning of it all did not matter much to me or to the other students. We were going on a long trip, that's all that really mattered. For a moment I dreamed of running away as we got close to my world. The bus would be going through *Abruzzo e Molise*, my region, and not far from my village. Maybe when we stopped at an *Autogrill*, the Italian version of a rest stop/restaurant/convenience store on the highway, I could just find my way home. But it would remain only an impossible dream.

The bus ride seemed to take forever. Finally we reached the monastery that late afternoon. We spent the night there and attended Holy Mass celebrated by this famous monk, Padre Pio. To my young eyes, the little monk seemed very old. He was short and sort of chubby, with a long gray beard and thick eyebrows. His gaze as he walked up to the altar was contemplative. All eyes were transfixed on the celebrant in that packed church and Mass was like all the other hundreds I had attended, until Padre Pio raised his hands to the sky in prayer.

There for all to see were his wounded hands. They revealed two dark spots on his palms resembling dried blood. A low murmuring engulfed the church and people were making the sign of the cross. At the sight of his blackened hands I became alarmed, and as I looked around our group I noticed the agitation amongst my friends. For the rest of Holy Mass I had my eyes fixed on his hands and tried to comprehend the reason for those sores.

Padre Pio, like Saint Francis and our entire monastery, was a member of the Lesser Friars Capuchin Order. Padre Pio lived with his stigmata for over fifty years. Many doctors and scientists studied his hands and for the most part came away with something unexplainable. They were perplexed that the wounds never became infected. Presently eighty percent of reported stigmata marks are on women.

Later in the afternoon we had a private audience with Padre Pio and what I will never forget is the pat on our heads with his hand, which was now covered by a black glove. Padre Pio was proclaimed a saint on June 16, 2002. The ceremonies were presided over by John Paul II in Saint Peter's Square. Hundreds of thousands of pilgrims were present. I suppose I will always have questions about Padre Pio's stigmata, such as were they real or concocted? As the subject of stigmata is occasionally raised, I always have the distant memory of Padre Pio's gloved hand on my head.

Padre Pio

One of my favorite memories of my life in the monastery was its famous *presepio*, manger. It took up a whole room of the monastery. It had many moving parts to it, including a small river. Many times we were sent down to the forest below our monastery to search for moss, rocks, and other natural materials needed to improve *il presepio*. At Christmastime people would come from all over Umbria and Italy to view the spectacle of our monastery's Nativity scene. During that special holiday season the friars would take us to visit other mangers. My favorite was the live representations throughout Umbria and surrounding regions. Many towns would assemble elaborate mangers and the people of the town would play the roles of the Nativity. Farmers gladly lent their cows, donkeys, and sheep for the display.

il presepio, the manger, 2012

It was a cold, rainy, early spring day after soccer practice when a friar, who was also our soccer coach, informed me that plans were being made to transfer me to another monastery near Perugia. That monastery had a more advanced soccer team made up of boys thirteen years old and older. He told me that the curriculum was also more advanced and it would fit me better. I was heartbroken by this news. I did not want to leave my friends, my safe haven. The only move I was willing to make was home. I did not understand why they wanted to get rid of me. I was one of the better students, although granted, mischievous at times.

One early afternoon in late March of 1966, I was summoned by a monk to the director's office. I was mildly shocked to see my father sitting with *il Direttore*. I surmised that he was there to take me to the new monastery, but to my great surprise he announced to the director that he was there to take me home. We were emigrating to America and we were to return to my village immediately to begin the process. My father recalled that the friar was not very brotherly when he heard the news, he was moderately upset. Nevertheless, the monks provided him with dinner and lodging. As we gathered all of my belongings, the other kids looked on, puzzled by the sudden turn of events for me, wondering if my father was there for my transfer to the other monastery. News eventually circulated that I was going home and then to America. Some of my closer friends, my teammates on the soccer team, were very sad and I was somewhat saddened that I would have to say goodbye to my hundred friends.

I remember the following morning when my father and I headed for the archway that led to the exit tunnel of the monastery. All the students, the monks, and nuns were there to say *arrivederci*, goodbye. The *Direttore* and *Maestro* were waiting by the door that led to the outside world. They both hugged me and wished us *buona fortuna*, good luck, in America. The director's last words to me and my father were, "È *meglio così, perchè non credo che Pietrantonio avrebbe fatto un buon frate*," It is better this way, because I don't think Pietrantonio would have made a good friar. With that last parting shot, we headed out the door and down the hill to wait for the bus to take us to the train station. Surely they were upset that their two-year investment in me was lost. To this day I wonder how many of those boys became friars, living the simple spiritual life in some monastery, perched on some hilltop of Italy or in other parts of the world.

The view of the old tree and Todi as you came out of the monastery's tunnel, 2012

*I returned to visit the monastery many times when in Italy and
met all the resident Franciscan monks. 1990*

*The soccer field seems to have been frozen in time;
the same dirt, the same goal, an older player! 2003*

Chapter *XXXI*

PREPARAZIONE PER L'EMIGRAZIONE
PREPARATION FOR THE EMIGRATION

I was happy to be back at home with my family. I definitely needed to go through some reconditioning. I felt awkward around the village, and my friends were aloof and indifferent towards me. When my friend, Pasqualino, came over one morning and asked me, begged me to come out and play soccer in front of the church, I was reluctant but both my mom and sister persuaded me to go out. I don't know if I felt I was now too good for my old friends or vice-versa. Definitely the mood was different, there was some sort of distance between my lifelong friends, and that distance seemed to increase when I played soccer with them in front of the church. Some of the kids that could run circles around me two years before were no longer able to do so. My soccer skills had improved considerably. But as the days passed we eventually were able to reconnect.

Upon my return home I was sad to find out that my *Zio* Umberto, his wife, Ida, and my cousin, Terenzio, had already left for America just days before I returned home. I wondered why they had not waited for us. It would have made the trip easier for all involved, as we could have given support to each other. The reason for the need to get to America first was unknown to my parents when I asked them. We were perplexed as to why.

On March 31, 1966 we went to *Napoli*, Naples, for the mandatory physical and mental examinations at the American Consulate. A family from the southern region of Calabria had gone through the same examinations and was sitting near us in a waiting area after all the various exams. They had family in America, *Pizziburgo*, Pittsburgh. They were called into a room and after a while they came out, the wife crying uncontrollably. They were told that they did not pass the exams. We watched them as they left the building, their dream broken. We sat there on the wooden bench speechless, anxious, wondering if we would be given the same fate.

Finally a man came out and called out, "Lombardi." My parents were visibly nervous. The examiner must have noticed it and quickly congratulated us on the fact that we were being allowed to immigrate to the United States of America. My father eventually asked the examiner why the other family was not allowed to go to America and the American officer told him that the three boys had failed the exams because they were illiterate. They would not be allowed entry into the United States of America, even with the relaxed rules of the new immigration law.

On October 3, 1965, President Lyndon Johnson traveled to New York to the site of the Statue of Liberty, where he signed the Immigration and Nationality Act of 1965. The law before the 1965 Act excluded Asians and Africans, and preferred northern and western Europeans over southern (Italy) and eastern Europeans. The prior law was passed so the United States would be made up primarily of northern and western European people. During the civil rights movement of the 1960s this law was seen as an embarrassment to the U.S., especially to President John Kennedy who called the quota system nearly intolerable. In nearly all the homes of Italians who immigrated to America after 1965, there is a picture of President Kennedy hanging somewhere in their homes, not because he was the first Catholic American president, although that helped, but because he was instrumental in reopening immigration for them.

The new 1965 Act proposed by Representative Emanuel Celler of New York, co-sponsored by Senator Philip Hart of Michigan, and heavily supported by Senator Ted Kennedy of Massachusetts, marked a radical break from the prejudiced immigration policies of the past. It replaced them with a preference system that focused on immigrants' skills and family relationships with U.S. citizens and U.S. residents.

Quotas were set at 170,000 immigrants per year, per country. In 1965 only about 25,000 Italians immigrated to America. Around the same

FORM FS-398 3-17-58	**FOREIGN SERVICE** **UNITED STATES OF AMERICA** **MEDICAL EXAMINATION OF VISA APPLICANTS**	PLACE American Consulate General
		DATE OF EXAMINATION March. 31. 1966
At the request of the American Consul at	CITY Naples	COUNTRY Italy

| *I certify that on the above date I examined* | NAME LOMBARDI Pietrantonio | AGE 12 | SEX M |

I examined specifically for evidence of any of the following conditions:

CLASS A:

TUBERCULOSIS (in any form)

LEPROSY (Hansen's Disease)

DANGEROUS CONTAGIOUS DISEASES:

Actinomycosis	Granuloma Inguinale	Ringworm of scalp
Amebiasis	Keratoconjunctivitis infections	Schistosomiasis
Blastomycosis	Leishmaniasis	Syphilis, infectious stage
Chancroid	Lymphogranuloma Venereum	Trachoma
Favus	Mycetoma	Trypanosomiasis
Filariasis	Paragonimiasis	Yaws
Gonorrhea		

MENTAL CONDITIONS:

Feeble-mindedness	Previous occurrence of one or more	Mental defect
(mental deficiency)	attacks of insanity	Narcotic drug addiction
Insanity	Psychopathic personality	Chronic alcoholism
	Epilepsy (Idiopathic)	(See proviso, sec. 34.7, USPHS Regs.)

CLASS B:

Physical Defect, Disease, or Disability Serious in Degree or Permanent in Nature Amounting to a Substantial Departure from Normal Physical Well-Being.

CLASS C:

Minor Conditions.

(Check number (1) below or complete number (2))

My examination, including the X-ray and other reports below, revealed:

(1) *No defect, disease, or disability* ☑

(2) *Defect, disease, or disability, or previous occurrence of one or more attacks of insanity, as follows (give class—A, B, or C—diagnosis, and pertinent details*):*

Chest X-ray report ___ Negative ___

_____ from Dr. ___ Hathcock ___

Blood serological report ___ Under Age ___ from Dr. ___

Urinalysis report ___
Step 1 o. k.

_____ from Dr. ___

| SIGNATURE OF MEDICAL TECHNICAL ADVISOR
Franco Ermenegildo, Medical Officer, USPHS | TITLE
Thomas A. Hathcock, Medical Director, USPHS | DATE OF FINAL NOTIFICATION |

My medical examination document

number of Italians immigrated to the U.S. each year until the early 1970s. In the following years, the numbers started to decline steadily, as Italy's post-World War II economic recovery was finally starting to improve the lot of the Italian people. Our village's population, nevertheless, steadily began to decrease as families left for jobs throughout Italy. Many moved to the coastal town of Termoli, where they sought employment in a Fiat automobile parts factory. Some opted to make the daily drive to the Molisan Adriatic town about a hundred kilometers west. They did not want to leave the serene life of their village for the hustle and bustle of the bigger town, so they commuted to avoid paying rent or purchasing a house. Many made the permanent move to those industrial towns and many live there now in retirement.

As my parents hashed and rehashed the decision to start a new life in America, my father's past would revisit him in the form of a letter from the Regional Office. The American immigration authorities had found an arrest warrant and a conviction on my father's records. In 1957 while *alla fiera*, at the market, in Forli del Sannio called *La fiera di San Biagio*, my father was accused of stealing a pair of boys' shoes. I very vaguely remember looking out of our kitchen window as the *Carabinieri*, the State Police, handcuffed my father and led him away, as family and friends tried to stop them. My mother, with her hands up in the air, was crying and tugging at the *Carabinieri*, with my sister, brother, and me crying uncontrollably.

My brother remembered more. *Papà* was accused of theft but he was actually protecting a nephew who wanted to buy the shoes for his young child. Supposedly there was an ensuing disagreement about the price of the shoes after the money had already changed hands. Frustrated and tired from the long day at the market, where my father had sold and bought some livestock, he put the shoes under his armpit and instructed his nephew to walk away and begin the long walk home before it got dark. The shoe vendor screamed at them as they hurried away.

The next day the *Carabinieri* showed up in our small hamlet of Luigi and arrested my father. He was taken to jail in Forli del Sannio and on March 2, 1957, he was convicted of simple theft and given a fifteen-day sentence, plus a fine of 2,400 *lire*, the equivalent of a couple of dollars. The sentence was suspended and he was given five years of probation. My father was so upset over the ordeal that he became ill with one of his intermittent bouts of depression.

An even more serious problem, and something that could definitely block our entry into the United States, was the records that were discovered of my father's military life during Benito Mussolini's Fascist reign. Research of my father's military service did not turn up anything relating to the issue. Someone had made an accusation that my father was a member of the Fascist Party and that he had been sent to Spain to fight in the civil war there. Mussolini had promised General Francisco Franco arms and men. Mussolini initially failed to keep his promise, but eventually sent arms and troops to Spain to fight with Franco's right-wing nationalists. The men who were sent to Spain were called volunteers, so as not to upset the League of Nations treaty.

There was no evidence that my father was a member of Mussolini's Black Shirts, *Camicie Nere*. It is very unlikely that my father was a member of Mussolini's elite militia because the Black Shirts were mainly made up of former army officers, intellectuals, and landowners; my father was none of those. For a young man who did not know how to tell time until in the military, a young man who did not even know how to ride a bike (he would never learn) my father was not a likely candidate for Mussolini's Black Shirts. But he did learn how to administer a penicillin shot, how to be a medic.

My father never talked about Mussolini much except to say that he met him (saw him). He recalls Mussolini on his beautiful white horse, inspecting his base. The only thing my father remembered of the inspection was Mussolini's brief speech, in which he reminded the troops that they were descendants of the ancient Romans and that they should fight like those Roman warriors. I am surprised that Mussolini did not wear the same uniform worn by Julius Caesar!

Although my father seemed to be holding something back when talking about the war, I don't think that he was ever a member of the Fascist Party. As a matter of fact, the only documented membership on my father's record was of his becoming a member of the Christian Democratic Party in 1958. So it was highly unlikely that he fought in the Spanish Civil War. The immigration authorities must have concluded the same, because neither the legal issue nor the military issue kept us from emigrating to America.

During the emigration process my father had to find and file many documents that the United States Immigration Service required. No stone was left unturned to make sure that we were good candidates for immigration to America. On the other side of the ocean, my grandfather was also busy providing a myriad of documents for the United States immigration authorities. He sought help from attorney, Albert Carmosino, a fellow Pagliaronese. He also had to find someone who was willing to sponsor us. That individual would have to be willing and able to receive, maintain, and support us when we arrived in America. An assurance would have to be given in the form of a bond to the United States Immigration and Naturalization Services that we would not become a burden on the United States government and would not seek any public assistance.

My grandfather implored a prominent member of a *Pagliaronese* immigrant family for help. His name was George Lombardi, owner of Lombardi Brothers Meat Packers. George's father, Celeste, was an early immigrant from our village. George signed an Affidavit of Support promising to hire my father in his meat processing plant when we arrived, although my dad never did work for Lombardi Meat.

In order to raise the money needed for the three of us to travel to faraway America, my father began the process of selling most of our possessions. I was very sad to see our cows being led away by their new owners. Our donkey was sold to a man from the nearby town of Carovilli. Most of our lands were sold or merely dedicated to various friends and relatives. Our house was sold to my sister's in-laws, Giovanni and Carmela Ienco. My mom and I made a last walk down the street to *il sartore*, the tailor, Giovanni Lombardi. I remember him always dressed in nice clothes.

Giovanni, with help from his wife, Cleonita, was making a nice gray, checkered suit for me with some wool fabric that he conveniently had on hand. My mom instructed him to make it a couple of sizes bigger so I would grow into it! Days before our departure, my mom helped me fill a small suitcase with my best clothes and other items I wanted to take with me. To this day I think of my prized stamp collection. I clearly recall putting it in the suitcase, but mysteriously it went missing during our journey, never to be found again. I believe that a customs agent must have seen my stamps and confiscated them for *his* collection!

The night before our departure my mother cooked her last dinner in our kitchen, as friends and family congregated to say their last goodbyes. Tears flowed continually and I don't know how many times I heard "*Ma cheh vuo fà, queshta è la vita*," our dialect version of "What can you do, this is life." The mood was sort of festive, but it turned melancholy in an instant as people said their last goodbyes. Some of my friends stayed up

UNITED STATES DEPARTMENT OF JUSTICE
Immigration and Naturalization Service

Form approved
Budget Bureau No. 43-R425

AFFIDAVIT OF SUPPORT

(Fill in with typewriter or print in block letters in ink)

(b)(6)

I, ___George Lombardi___ Residing at _____
(Name)

_____   **USA**
(Street and number)   (Country)

being duly sworn depose and say:

1. I was born on _____ so, answer either a, b or c, as appropriate.
(Date)   (City)   (Country)

   (a) If a United States citizen through naturalization, give number of certificate of naturalization _____

   (b) If a United States citizen through parent(s) or marriage, give number of own certificate of citizenship _____

   If none obtained, attach statement explaining how citizenship derived.

   (c) If an alien lawfully admitted to the United States for permanent residence, give 'A' number _____

2. That I am __49__ years of age and have resided in the United States since ___Birth___

3. That this affidavit is executed in behalf of the following person(s) at present residing at ___Villa San Michele,___ Campobasso, Italy

NAME	SEX	AGE	COUNTRY OF BIRTH	MARRIED OR SINGLE	RELATIONSHIP TO DEPONENT
Vittorio Lombardi	M	47	Italy	Married	Cousin
Maria Lucia Lombardi	F	44	Italy	Married	Cousin
Ezio Lombardi	M	19			Cousin
Maria Lombardi	F	17			Cousin
Pietrantonio	M	14	Italy	Single	Cousin

4. (a) That I am employed as, or engaged in the business of _____

   at _____ and derive a net annual income of $ _____ (b) That I have on deposit in savings
   (Address)

   banks in this country $ _____) That I have other personal property, the reasonable value of which is $ _____
   (d) That I have stocks and bonds in the amount of $ ___---___ , market value, as indicated on attached list
   certify to be true and correct to the best of my knowledge and belief. (e) That I own real estate at _____
   _____ with mortgages or other encumbrances thereon amounting to $ _____
   (f) That I have life insurance in the sum of $ _____ , cash surrender value of $ _____ . (g) That if self-
   employed, I attach a copy of my last income tax return or report of commercial rating concern which I certify to be
   true and correct to the best of my knowledge and belief.

   (b)(6)
   (See reverse side for nature of evidence of net worth to be submitted)

Form I-134 (Rev 5-1-64)

60

Document filed by George Lombardi, personal information whited out / page 1

with me for the entire night, until my mom begged me to go to sleep because we would have to wake up before dawn for our journey by bus to Napoli, where a ship waited.

5. That the following persons are dependent upon me for support:

NAME OF PERSON WHOLLY DEPENDENT	NAME OF PERSON PARTIALLY DEPENDENT	AGE	RELATIONSHIP TO ME
Mable E. Lombardi		45	Wife

6. (To be filled in, if appropriate.) That I have previously submitted affidavit(s) of support for the following person(s):

Name	Date submitted
John Iacovetta	1960
Antonio Lombardi	1965
Dominick Iacovetta	1965
Emilio DiRienzo and Family	1965

7. (To be filled in, if appropriate.) That I have submitted visa petition(s) to the Immigration and Naturalization Service, on behalf of the following person(s):

Name	Relationship	Date submitted

8. That I am willing and able to receive, maintain, and support the persons listed in item 3 above. That I am ready and willing to deposit a bond, if necessary, with the Immigration and Naturalization Service to guarantee that such persons will not become public charges during their stay in the United States.

9. That this affidavit is made by me for the purpose of assuring the Immigration and Naturalization Service that the above-named persons will not become public charges in the United States.

10. That my reasons for signing this affidavit are: Vittorio Lombardi and his family would like to be re-united with the other members of their family who now reside in these United States. I have employment for him in my meat processing plant at Union scale.

Execution of affidavit. You must sign the affidavit in your full, true, and correct name and affirm or make it under oath.
In the United States the affidavit may be sworn to or affirmed before an immigration officer without the payment of fee, or before a notary public or other officer authorized to administer oaths for general purposes, in which case the official seal or certificate of authority to administer oaths must be affixed.

Outside the United States the affidavit must be sworn to or affirmed before a United States consular officer.

SUBSCRIBED AND SWORN TO BEFORE ME THIS

10th day of November A.D. 19 65

at Denver, Colorado

(Signature of officer)

Signature of person preparing form, if other than deponent. I declare that this document was prepared by me at the request of the deponent and is based on all information of which I have any knowledge.

SIGNATURE

Address: | Date:

(Signature of deponent)

(Title of officer)

Nature of Evidence of Net Worth To Be Submitted.—The deponent must submit in duplicate evidence of net worth as follows:
1. Statement from an officer of the bank, postal or other financial institution in which you have deposits giving the following details regarding your bank account: (1) Date account opened, (2) total amount deposited for past year, (3) Present balance.
2. Statement of employer, preferably on his business stationery, showing: (1) Date and nature of employment, (2) Salary paid, (3) Whether position temporary or permanent.
3. If self-employed: (1) Copy of last income tax return filed or (2) report of commercial rating concern.
4. List containing serial number and denomination of bonds and name of purchaser.

61

Document filed by George Lombardi / page 2

State of **Colorado**

County of **Denver** ss.

PETITIONER'S DECLARATION OF INTENT

I, **Antonio Lombard:** born on **Sept. 12, 1896**

at **Pagliarone, Italy** declare that I am

still (an American citizen) (a legal resident of the United

States) and that I still desire to have my (~~brother~~ ~~sister~~)

(son) ~~(daughter)~~ **Vitorio Lombard:**

born on **September 1, 1918** at **Pagliarone, Italy**

enter the United States for permanent residence and, therefore,

desire that the visa petition which I filed in (his) (her)

behalf be considered revalidated.

(signed) *Antonio Lombard*

Subscribed and sworn before me this **21st** day

of **March**, 196 **6** .

My commission expires April 22, 1967

Mary E Mulloy
Notary Public

One last document filed by my grandfather in 1966 to insure our permanent immigration process. The document also shows that he had permanently abandoned his birth name of Pietrantonio and adopted the shorter version of Antonio.

My mom's and my visa pictures. I can see the start of the infamous uni-brow. 1965

My mother cooking her last pasta on our fireplace. She cut her long hair that she always had in a bun and fixed it to look more American. May 1966

I don't understand why I was dressed in a shirt and tie before our departure, or why someone had decided that I needed glasses. May 1966

Form. FS-510 10
ROME: ITALIAN/ENGLISH 11-65

DEPARTMENT OF STATE FOREIGN SERVICE OF THE UNITED STATES OF AMERICA

Form Approved
Budget Bureau No. 47-R150.2.

DOMANDA DI VISTO D'IMMIGRAZIONE E DI REGISTRAZIONE QUALE STRANIERO

APPLICATION FOR IMMIGRANT VISA AND ALIEN REGISTRATION

(b)(6)

ISTRUZIONI: Il presente modulo dev'essere riempito in DUPLICE COPIA a macchina o, se a mano, in stampatello leggibile. Si deve rispondere a TUTTE le domande pertinenti. Alle domande non pertinenti rispondere: « non pertinente ». Se lo spazio sul modulo è insufficiente, rispondere su fogli separati, in duplice copia, usando gli stessi numeri che contrassegnano le domande. NON FIRMARE questo modulo fino a quando il Funzionario Consolare non lo richiederà. Il diritto consolare per la presentazione di questa domanda di visto d'immigrazione ammonta a $5,00. Tale diritto dovrà essere pagato in dollari USA o in valuta locale per un ammontare equivalente, oppure mediante assegno circolare quando Lei si presenterà al Funzionario Consolare.

AVVERTENZA: Qualsiasi dichiarazione falsa od occultamento di fatti materiali può essere motivo per la Sua esclusione permanente dagli Stati Uniti. Anche se Lei fosse ammesso negli Stati Uniti, l'ingresso fraudolento potrà essere motivo di procedimento penale e/o espulsione.

[INSTRUCTIONS: This form must be filled out in DUPLICATE by typewriter, or if by hand in legible block letters. All questions must be answered, if applicable. Questions which are not applicable should be so marked. If there is insufficient room on the form, answer on separate sheets, in duplicate using the same numbers as appear on the form. Attach the sheets to the forms. DO NOT SIGN this form until instructed to do so by the consular officer. The fee for filing this application for an immigrant visa is $5.00. The fee should be paid in United States dollars or local currency equivalent or by bank draft, when you appear before the consular officer.

WARNING: Any false statement or concealment of a material fact may result in your permanent exclusion from the United States. Even though you should be admitted to the United States, a fraudulent entry could be ground for your prosecution and/or deportation.]

Io sottoscritt..... faccio domanda di visto d'immigrazione e di registrazione quale stranier..... presso il........................... degli Stati Uniti di...........................

e dichiaro quanto segue: [I hereby apply for an immigrant visa and alien registration at the United States........................... at........................... and state the following facts:]

1. Cognome [My family name is] CARMOSINO *Lombardi*	Nome [My first name is] Maria	Secondo nome [My middle name is] Lucia

2. Nome completo nei caratteri della lingua d'origine (se diversi dall'alfabeto latino) [My full name in native alphabet (if other than Roman letters are used) is
CARMOSINO Mria Lucia

3. Altri nomi da me usati o con i quali sono stat.. conosciut.. (Le donne sposate indichino il cognome da nubile) [Other names I have used or by which I have been]. known are (If married woman give maiden name)]
Lombardi -Carmosino Maria Lucia

4. Data di nascita [The date of my birth is] Giorno [Day] Mese [Month] Anno [Year] 15 luglio 1921	5. Luogo di nascita [My place of birth is] (Città o località) [City or town] Vastogirardi	(Provincia) [Province] (Campobasso-)	(Stato) [Country] italiano

6. Età [My age is] anni 44	7. Professione od occupazione attuale [My present calling or occupation is] agricoltrice ~ *Farmer*

8. Indirizzo attuale [My present address is] Lombardi Carmosino Maria Lucia -
Frazione Villa San Michele di Vastogirardi (Campobasso)

9. Sesso [My sex is] ☐ Maschio [Male] ☒ Femmina [Female]	10. Stato civile [My marital status is] ☐ Celibe o nubile [Single (never married)] ☒ Coniugat [Married] ☐ Vedov [Widowed] ☐ Divorziat [Divorced] ☐ Separat [Separated] Compreso il mio matrimonio attuale, sono stat... coniugat... .... volte. [including my present marriage, I have been married .... times]

11. Nazionalità [My nationality is] Italiana

12. Connotati [My personal description is]

(a) Capelli [Color of hair] castani
(c) Statura [Height] m. 1,64 piedi [feet] pollici [inches]

(b) Occhi [Color of eyes] castani
(d) Colorito [Complexion] naturale

14. Scopo del mio viaggio negli Stati Uniti [My purpose in going to the United States is] a scopo di lavoro - per raggiungere mio suocero Lombardi Pietrantonio- *with husband*

15. Intendo rimanere definitivamente negli Stati Uniti (In caso contrario indicare la durata del soggiorno) [I intend to remain in the United States permanently or (Give length of time)] SI	16. Intendo entrare negli Stati Uniti dal porto di [I intend to enter the United States at the port of] New Jork.

17. Ho (non ho) il biglietto di viaggio fino alla mia destinazione finale [I (Do) (Do not) have a ticket to my final destination]
Si

19. Il mio indirizzo definitivo negli Stati Uniti è [My final address in the United States is]
2915 w 25 ave st Dever Colorato - U. S. A.

20. La mia situazione finanziaria è la seguente [My personal financial resources are]

(a) Contanti [Cash] 200,000
(c) Beni immobili (valore) [Real estate (value)]
(b) Depositi bancari [Bank deposits]
(d) Vari [Other]

IL PRESENTE MODULO SI PUÒ OTTENERE GRATIS PRESSO TUTTI GLI UFFICI CONSOLARI DEGLI STATI UNITI D'AMERICA
[THIS FORM MAY BE OBTAINED GRATIS AT CONSULAR OFFICES OF THE UNITED STATES OF AMERICA]

27

My mother's application for immigration visa

Form Approved
Budget Bureau No. 47-R150.2.

FSH 11-65 DEPARTMENT OF STATE FOREIGN. SERVICE OF THE UNITED STATES OF AMERICA

DOMANDA DI VISTO D'IMMIGRAZIONE E DI REGISTRAZIONE QUALE STRANIERO

APPLICATION FOR IMMIGRANT VISA AND ALIEN REGISTRATION

Il presente modulo dev'essere riempito in DUPLICE COPIA a macchina o, se a mano, in stampatello leggibile. Si deve rispondere a TUTTE le domande. Alle domande non pertinenti rispondere: « non pertinente ». Se lo spazio sul modulo è insufficiente, rispondere su fogli separati, in duplice copia, usando i numeri che contrassegnano le domande. Allegare tali fogli ai moduli. NON FIRMARE questo modulo fino a quando il Funzionario Consolare non lo richiederà. Consolare per la presentazione di questa domanda di visto d'Immigrazione ammonta a $5.00. Tale diritto dovrà essere pagato in dollari USA o in valuta locale equivalente, oppure mediante assegno circolare quando Lei si presenterà al Funzionario Consolare.

AVVERTENZA: Qualsiasi dichiarazione falsa od occultamento di fatti materiali può essere motivo per la Sua esclusione permanente dagli Stati Uniti. Anche se Lei fosse ammesso negli Stati Uniti, l'ingresso fraudolento potrà essere motivo di procedimento penale e/o espulsione.

INSTRUCTIONS: This form must be filled out in DUPLICATE by typewriter, or if by hand in legible block letters. All questions must be answered, if applicable. Questions which are not applicable should be so marked. If there is insufficient room on the form, answer on separate sheets, in duplicate using the same numbers as appear on the form. Attach the sheets to the forms. DO NOT SIGN this form until instructed to do so by the consular officer. The fee for filing this application for an immigrant visa is $5.00. The fee should be paid in United States dollars or currency equivalent or by bank draft, when you appear before the consular officer.

WARNING: Any false statement or concealment of a material fact may result in your permanent exclusion from the United States. Even though you should be admitted to the United States, a fraudulent entry could be ground for your prosecution and/or deportation.]

Io sottoscritt___ faccio domanda di visto d'immigrazione e di registrazione quale stranier___ presso il _____ degli Stati Uniti di _____ at _____ and state the following facts: [I hereby apply for an immigrant visa and alien registration at the United States ___ at ___ and state the following facts:]

1. Cognome [My family name is]	Nome [My first name is]	Secondo nome [My middle name is]
Lombardi	Pietrantonio	

2. Nome completo nei caratteri della lingua d'origine (se diversi dall'alfabeto latino) [My full name in native alphabet (if other than Roman letters are used) is]
Lombardi   Pietrantonio

3. Altri nomi da me usati o con i quali sono stat.. conosciut.. (Le donne sposate indichino il cognome da nubile) [Other names I have used or by which I have been known are (If married woman give maiden name)]

4. Data di nascita [The date of my birth is] Giorno [Day] Mese [Month] Anno [Year]	5. Luogo di nascita [My place of birth is] (Città o località) [City or town]	(Provincia) [Province]	(Stato) [Country]
10/I/1953	Vastogirardi	Campobasso)	italiano

6. Età [My age is]	7. Professione od occupazione attuale [My present calling or occupation is]
anni 13	scolaro

8. Indirizzo attuale [My present address is]
Lombardi   Pietrantonio - Frazione   Villa San Michele   di Vastogirardi (Campobasso)

9. Sesso [My sex is]	10. Stato civile [My marital status is]
☒ Maschio [Male] ☐ Femmina [Female]	☒ Celibe o nubile [Single (never married)] ☐ Coniugat [Married] ☐ Vedov [Widowed] ☐ Divorziat [Divorced] ☐ Separat [Separated]

Compreso il mio matrimonio attuale, sono stat.. coniugat.. .... volte. [including my present marriage, I have been married .... times]

11. Nazionalità [My nationality is]
Italiana

12. Connotati [My personal description is]

(a) Capelli [Color of hair]	(c) Statura [Height] m. 1,48
castani	........piedi [feet] ....pollici [inches]
(b) Occhi [Color of eyes]	(d) Colorito [Complexion]
castani	roseo

14. Scopo del mio viaggio negli Stati Uniti [My purpose in going to the United States is]
per raggiungere mio nonno Lombardi   Pietrantonio- e per apprendere la lingua

15. Intendo rimanere definitivamente negli Stati Uniti (In caso contrario indicare la durata del soggiorno) [I intend to remain in the United States permanently or (Give length of time)]	16. Intendo entrare negli Stati Uniti dal porto di [I intend to enter the United States at the port of]
SI	New Jork.

17. Ho (non ho) il biglietto di viaggio fino alla mia destinazione finale [I (Do) (Do not) have a ticket to my final destination]
si

18. (a) Vado negli Stati Uniti a raggiungere la seguente persona (Indicare nome, indirizzo ed eventuale parentela) [I am going to the United States to join the following person (Give name and address and relationship, if any)]	18. (b) Sono stato richiamato dalla seguente persona e/o organizzazione (indicare l'indirizzo se diverso da quello dato in (a)) [I am sponsored by the following person and/or organization (Give address if different from (a)]
Lombardi Pietrantonio- 2915w 25 ave st.- DEVER COLORATO	LOMBARDI Pietrantonio -2915w.25ave st. DEVER COLORATO

19. Il mio indirizzo definitivo negli Stati Uniti è [My final address in the United States is]
2915 W25ave st. DEVER COLORATO;

20. La mia situazione finanziaria è la seguente [My personal financial resources are]

(a) Contanti [Cash]	(c) Beni immobili (valore) [Real estate (value)]
(b) Depositi bancari [Bank deposits]	(d) Vari [Other]

IL PRESENTE MODULO SI PUÒ OTTENERE GRATIS PRESSO TUTTI GLI UFFICI CONSOLARI DEGLI STATI UNITI D'AMERICA
[THIS FORM MAY BE OBTAINED GRATIS AT CONSULAR OFFICES OF THE UNITED STATES OF AMERICA]

"my application for immigration visa" my reason for immigration stated is "to reunite with my grandfather Pietrantonio and to learn the language"

COMUNE DI **VASTOGIRARDI** ●

RROVINCIA DI **CAMPOBASSO**

Li 21 marzo 1966

Al PROCURATORE della REPUBBLICA

presso il Tribunale di

I S E R N I A

OGGETTO: **RICHIESTA CERTIFICATO PENALE.**
(IN CARTA ESENTE DA BOLLO)

Si richiede il certificato penale al nome di CARMOSINO Maria Lucia

nat^a a Vastogirardi

(Campobasso -------) il 15 luglio 1921 per uso di emigrazio=

ne a scopo di lavoro.

IL SINDACO.

CASELLARIO GIUDIZIALE
Certificato

Procura della Repubblica presso il Tribunale di

Al nome di

NULLA

nato il   in   (o

Stato)   ISERNIA 22 MAR.1966   sulla richiesta di

IL SEGRETARIO

che in questo casellario giudiziale risulta
(De Toma Ivan)

EDIZIONI A. B. C. - RIMINI

33

Even my Mamma had to provide a criminal record certificate.
Stamp with NULLA means that NOTHING or no criminal past was found.

COMUNE DI VASTOGIRARDI

PROVINCIA DI CAMPOBASSO

CERTIFICATO DI MATRIMONIO

Il sottoscritto Ufficiale dello Stato Civile
CERTIFICA

Che LOMBARDI Vittorio ------------------

nato a Vastogirardi ----------- il I settembre 1918

E

CARMOSINO Maria Lucia --------------------

nata a Vastogirardi ----------- il 15 luglio 1921

Contrassero matrimonio in Vastogirardi ------------------

il giorno ventotto -------- del mese di gennaio ---------

dell'anno millenovecentoquarahtadue -----------------

Cosí risulta dal registro degli atti di matrimonio di questo Comune dell'an-

no 1942 ----- al N. uno   P. II   S. A

A richiesta di Lombardi Vittorio ----

si rilascia il presente in carta libera per uso di emigrazione a

scopo di lavoro.

Dalla residenza Municipale 21 marzo 1966

L'impiegato del ramo   L'Ufficiale dello stato civile

tip. fagnani - pescopennataro

47

My parents had to prove that they were indeed a married couple. / page 1

Stato: REPUBBLICA ITALIANA
Etat:
Staat:
Stade:
Estado:
Staat:
Devlet:

Comune di: VASTOGIRARDI
Commune de:
Gemeinde: (ISERNIA)
Municipality:
Municipio de:
Gemeente:
Köy veya mahâlle:

ATTO N. 1 - P.2^ - S.A - ANNO 1942 (2° UFF.)

Estratto dai registri degli atti di matrimonio
Extrait des registres de l'état civil concernant un mariage
Auszug aus dem Eheregister
Extract of the register of marriages
Extracto del registro de matrimonios
Uittreksel uit de registers van de burgerlijke stand omtrent een huwelijk
Evlenme kayit hûlâsasi sureti

a) **Luogo di celebrazione del matrimonio** — lieu du mariage — Ort der Eheschliessung — place of marriage — lugar del matrimonio — plaats van huwelijksvoltrekking — evlenme yeri

VASTOGIRARDI

b) **Data della celebrazione** — date du mariage — Datum der Eheschliessung — date of marriage — fecha del matrimonio — datum van het huwelijk — evlenme tarihi

28/01/1942

c) **Cognome del marito** — nom de famille du mari — Familiennname des Ehemannes — surname of husband — apellido del marido — familienaam van de man — kocanin soyadi

LOMBARDI

d) **Prenome del marito** — prénoms du mari — Vornamen des Ehemannes — christian names of husband — nombres de pila del marido — voornamen van de man — kocanin adi

VITTORIO

e) **Data di nascita o età del marito** — date de naissance ou âge du mari — Geburtsdatum oder Lebensalter de Ehemannes — date of birth or age of husband — fecha de nacimiento o edad del marido — geboortedatum of leeftijd van de man — dogum tarihi; yas

01/09/1918

f) **Luogo di nascita del marito** — lieu de naissance du mari — Geburtsort des Ehemannes — place of birth of husband — lugar de nacimiento del marido — geboorteplaats van de man — kocanin dogum yeri

VASTOGIRARDI

g) **Cognome della moglie prima del matrimonio** — nom de famille de la femme — Familiennname der Ehefrau — Surname of wife — apellido de la mujer — familienaam van de vrouw — karinin soyadi

CARMOSINO

h) **Prenome della moglie** — prénoms de la femme — Vornamen der Ehefrau — christian names of wife — nombres de pila de la mujer — voornamen van de vrouw — karinin adi

MARIA LUCIA

i) **Data di nascita o età della moglie** — date de naissance ou âge de la femme — Geburtsdatum oder Lebensalter der Ehefrau — date of birth or age of wife — fecha de nacimiento o edad de la mujer — geboortedatum of leeftijd van de vrouw — dogum tarihi veya yasi

15/07/1921

j) **Luogo di nascita della moglie** — lieu de naissance de la femme — Geburtsort der Ehefrau — place of birth of wife — lugar de nacimiento de la mujer — geboorteplaats van de vrouw — karinin dogum yeri

VASTOGIRARDI

k) **Scioglimento o annullamento** — dissolution ou annulation — Auflösung oder Nichtigerklärung — dissolution or nullification disolución o anulacion — ontbinding of nietigverklaring — zeval veya butlan

= = = =

Data in cui è rilasciato l'estratto con firma e bollo dell'ufficio — date de délivrance, signature et sceau du dépositaire — Ausstellungsdatum, Unterschrift und Dienstsiegel des Registerführers — date of issue, signature and seal of keeper — fecha de expedición firma y sello del depositario — datum van afgifte, ondertekening en Dienstzegel van de bewaarder — verildigi tarih, nüfus (ahvali sahsiye) memurunum imzasi ve mührü

VASTOGIRARDI li - 4 LUG. 2002

L'Ufficiale dello Stato Civile

My parents had to prove that they were indeed a married couple. / page 2

The night before our departure the two friends from the town of Cerreto that would take us to Naples make a toast for a safe journey. Orlando Appolonio, a family friend and owner of a grocery store in Cerreto, he would always hand me a handful of candies! Pietrantonio Lombardi, Vittorio Lombardi, Maria Lucia Carmosino Lombardi, Emilio Di Rienzo (our driver)

Chapter *XXXII*

LA NAVE · THE SHIP

The Michelangelo and the Raffaello were two Italian ocean liners put into service in 1965. These beautiful ships were the most modern of the time, examples of fine Italian design and imagination. We purchased tickets to immigrate to America on the Raffaello, named after the great Renaissance painter and architect, Raffaello Sanzio da Urbino, who was born in 1483 in the town of Urbino, in the Marche region of Italy. The Michelangelo was named after another great painter, sculptor, poet, and engineer, Michelangelo di Lodovico Buonarroti. He was born in 1475 in Caprese, a small town near Arezzo in the Toscana region of Italy. Michelangelo, Raffaello, and the other great Italian painter, Leonardo da Vinci, formed the trinity of great masters of *il Rinascimento*, the Renaissance.

The Renaissance was the great cultural rebirth that began in the 14th century and lasted to the 16th century. Italians of north-central Italy were instrumental in that great reawakening of the arts in Europe. Eventually, the movement that would take Europe out of the Middle Ages and into the start of the Modern Age spread throughout the continent, including France. Perhaps a more fitting universal referral to that great period of growth in all components of society might be *il Rinascimento.* This is the Italian for Renaissance.

The Raffaello, a liner with first, second, and third class cabins, traveled primarily across the north Atlantic. Our cabin was at third class, the lowest steerage of the ship; although it was nothing like what we usually envision as steerage for the immigrants of the past. We had our own comfortable, windowless cabin, with our own bathroom — a far cry from the overcrowded quarters that the earlier immigrants endured. For me this was an adventure never to be forgotten.

The Raffaello. Unfortunately, in 1976 the ocean liner was taken out of service with the increasing competition from air traffic. It was sold to the Shah of Iran and was used as floating barracks. In 1979 it was heavily damaged and looted during the Islamic revolution. In 1983 it was partially sunk during the Iran-Iraq War. The ship is presently partially submerged in the port of Bushehr, Iran, but not visible.

I remember the early morning of May 14, 1966. Most of the town's residents had gathered in and outside our house in Villa San Michele. My parents and I walked to my uncle's house to say goodbye to my grandmother. My *Zio* Angelo was already sitting by the fireplace and started calling out my mother's name as we walked in, "*Marialci!*" My mom walked over to hug him, crying and shaking her head. My 87-year-old *mammuccia, nonna*, grandma, was still in bed, and as we walked into the room my mother let out a loud, "*Mamma mea!*" She knew — we knew — that this would be the last time she would set her eyes on her elderly mother. *Mammuccia* Genoveffa would die three months after we got to America. *Mamma* held onto her tightly, calling her name, "*Mamma, Mamma, Mamma mea bona*," Mom, Mom, my dear good Mother, not letting go until my aunts pried her away. It seemed like an eternity until we finally left that house, with my *nonna* sobbing and my poor *Zio* Angelo confused and calling out my mother's name, "*Marialcia mea*." As we walked towards our house, people were coming out of theirs, crying goodbyes. It seemed that the whole town had gathered outside our house. It reminded me of the gatherings on funeral days.

I wished and hoped that my dad at that moment would realize the grave mistake I thought he was about to make and announce that we would not go. That moment never came, just more crying and more goodbyes. My mother would not let go of my sister, Maria, who had married on February 20, 1966 and would not be coming with us. And my brother, an adult son at twenty-one years old, did not qualify with our grandfather Pietrantonio's immigration papers and could not go to America with us. Ezio would have to wait for my parents to file the proper documents for him to join us when we reached America. My mother had to be literally pried away from all her loved ones. I was witnessing one of our family's saddest moments and was confused about it all. We were going to a better place to live a better life, hopefully, but yet we all cried and tightly held onto each other until Emilio, the bus driver from Cerreto who was hired by my dad to take us to Napoli, honked his horn and announced that if we did not get going we would miss the ship.

A thought came to my mind at that moment: I should just run away and not get on that bus. But suddenly I felt someone's hand grab me and lead me to the door and onto *la corriera*, the bus. Thank God my sister, her husband Vittorio, my brother, and most of my aunts and uncles were coming to Naples with us, because otherwise I think it would have been hell getting my mom on that bus. Emilio was finally able to get all of us seated and as he closed the door, I felt as though I was being put into a coffin alive and wanted to yell, but couldn't. I was frozen and could not move or talk.

The morning of our journey, relatives and friends waking up very early to say goodbye to us. Foreground my pensive brother Ezio, my father smoking a cigarette to calm his nerves! Me in my brand new plaid suit watching my mom and sister hug. May 14, 1966

My father still holding his cigarette as he tries to keep everyone calm.
My sister Maria and me crying. May 14, 1966

I vividly remember that soon after we left, as the sun had barely risen over the eastern horizon, we were near the bordering town of Carovilli. We noticed a man pulling a donkey down the road. As we pulled up next to him my mother let out a yell and began to sob again. The man was pulling our trusted and reliable donkey that he had purchased from us. The donkey, frightened by the noise of the vehicle, perked up her ears and looked up and stared at us as we drove by. It seemed that our poor donkey was upset that we sold her, that we were leaving her behind.

By mid-morning we finally reached the port of Naples. Napoli was a large, congested port city in the Campania region of Italy and it seemed as though it took Emilio forever to reach the docks, where the ocean liner, *la Raffaello*, was anchored and waiting for her passengers. I first noticed a huge banner hanging from the gigantic ship, *Benvenuti a bordo*, Welcome aboard. At that time, family and friends were allowed to go on board and tour the ship. All of our relatives joined us on board and helped us to our cabin. It was the first time for many of us to take an elevator. We were hesitant to get into this box to go deep into the hull of the ship, but we did it and hung on as it started its descent.

My *Zio* Flavio seemed to be fascinated with the ship and went out on his own to explore it. We found him later on the top deck. He informed us that he had gotten lost, as he explained, "*Sopra e sotto, sotto e sopra, con quel cazzo di ascenzore e non potevo trovare il piano della vostra cabina, tutta questa mattina sopra e sotto, sopra e sotto!*" Up and down, down and up with that damn elevator and I could not find the right floor of your cabin, so all morning I have been going up and down, up and down! The way he explained it with his hand gestures and voice made us all laugh uncontrollably on that very sad morning. My uncle Flavio was one of the funniest people I knew, and he and his sister, my *Zia* Ida, were good storytellers.

The time finally came for the guests to leave the ship in preparation for the imminent departure. I privately prayed that my dad would change his mind and we would go back home with our family. As my mom clutched my sister, crying uncontrollably, I knew that this day would be one of the saddest of my young life.

As the ship started to slowly pull away from the dock, people cheered and the passengers tossed streamers down from over the railings. With my parents by my side, we waved goodbye to our family, tears flowing down our cheeks.

As the streamers broke away, we were on our way to America (Michelangelo-Raffaello.com). 1966

For the next five days I made the most of what the Raffaello had to offer. I made friends with a couple of thirteen-year-old boys who were also immigrating to America. We played endless games of foosball and ping pong. We went to the theatre to watch movies. We watched one that, as thirteen-year-olds, we probably should have not been watching. We wandered around the enormous ship with no one monitoring us. My father spent most of the days smoking, drinking espressos with other immigrants, discussing what might await them in the new world. *Mamma* liked to wander around the ship aimlessly when she wasn't sea sick. The other boys and I always tried to sneak up to the first class section of the ship, but the watchful eyes of the ship's crew usually prevented our entry. We did manage it a few times. We were amazed when we stumbled upon a pair of brand new sports cars on display on one of the upper decks.

Many years later I read *Michelangelo e Raffaello, La Fine Di Un'Epoca*, a book about the two twin ocean liners and how they were the end of an era in ocean liners. In the book I discovered that those sports cars were the first to be brought to New York by the Italian car maker, Alfa Romeo, for a car show. I also learned that some of the ship's passengers were celebrities. Throughout the Raffaello's voyages, many of the passengers were movie stars, princes, princesses, kings, presidents of countries, and other famous celebrities.

The Raffaello's first stop from Naples was Gibraltar. I had only dreamed of ever setting eyes on that rock as I read about it in my geography classes. We did not get off the ship. I am not sure that we, the immigrants, were even allowed to get off the ship, so we watched from a lower deck as peddlers on small boats tried to sell us trinkets. The same could be said of *le Azzorre*, the Azores, islands surrounded by the waters of the Atlantic Ocean. I remember green, rolling hills with a scattering of white rocks and some mountains in the distance. A day after that, the

Alfa Romeo 1600 Spider sports cars on board (Michelangelo-Raffaello.com), 1966

Raffaello stopped in the middle of the ocean and another ship pulled up next to it. It was the *Michelangelo*, its sister ship, on its way back to Italy from America.

On the fourth day of our journey, even though the sea looked calm, a lot of people were getting sea sick. We were told that the waters were calm on the surface, but the lower depths of the water were in an uproar. My poor mom lay in our cabin in pain, nauseated, vomiting continually, and lamenting, "*O Mamma mea, o Mamma mea, che song capitate,*" O Mamma mia, o Mamma mia, che cosa mi è successo, wondering what in God's name had happened to her.

I recall running down a corridor near our cabin, seeing people with agonized looks on their faces. I did not notice anything on the shiny floor, and by the time I did, it was too late. I slipped and went sliding down the corridor on something slick and slimy. Struggling up to my feet, I noticed that my pants and shirt were saturated with what I quickly realized to be vomit — not mine, but someone else's. Suddenly I felt queasy as I wobbled my way down the long corridor, people staring at me as I got even more ill at the sight and the smell of the vomit on my clothes. My mom could hardly move, but managed to help me get out of the foul smelling pants and shirt. Even my *canottiera*, the traditional Italian sleeveless undershirt, was soaked. We stayed in our cabin for the rest of the day. The thought of going to dinner was absolutely out of the question.

The next morning the ocean was calm. My mom, feeling a bit better, decided to take her usual walk around the ship with her permanent long face, as she thought about her relatives that she left behind. She later recounted that she became disoriented and got lost. My dad and I could not find her anywhere, going back-and-forth to our cabin, around the various decks of the ship, and back to our cabin in hopes that she was there. No sign of her. The concerned look on my father's face made me nervous. Looking down the dark waters of the Atlantic, I panicked, as the thought of her falling overboard crowded my mind. We asked a ship attendant for help. He reassured us that my mom was somewhere on the huge ship.

The ship's crew finally found my mom. We saw her coming down a hallway accompanied by a crew member, who turned out to be the captain of the ship, *Comandante* Salvatore Schiano. My mom did get lost and somehow strayed to the bridge deck. The captain happened to be there and actually took my mom on a tour of the ship's navigational area.

On the clear and warm morning of May 19, 1966 there was a commotion throughout the ship. People were running down the corridors, excited. Land had been sighted! Leaving our packed bags in the cabin, we made our way to the upper deck to have a look. It was difficult to find a place for a good view, but I squeezed my way to a railing and was joined by my parents. The first thing we saw was a shape in the distance that looked like a bridge. As the ship inched closer we saw the long, towering bridge that spanned across the horizon, behind it an endless array of very tall buildings. It had to be *la Città di Nuova York*, New York City.

As the Raffaello slowly got closer to the city we noticed a huge statue of a woman holding up a torch. The ship passed very close to that statue and around it. The statue was not part of the huge city, but on its own island. The Raffaello slowly navigated towards a dock but we hardly noticed the docking, we were too captivated by the sights of the enormous city. An announcement was made in Italian and in some other language that I assumed was English, but it sounded Greek to me! They gave us instructions to prepare for disembarkation, so we made our way back to our cabin to get our belongings and prepare for the next portion of our journey.

After going through all the lines and after all our credentials were checked, we were finally allowed to find our luggage. A member of the Raffaello crew helped with all the proceedings. We followed him outside. How thankful my father must have been for his help, for we were overwhelmed with the pandemonium all around. The crewman eventually directed us towards one of the many big, long, yellow cars. He said something to the taxi driver and also handed him some sort of coupon. The Raffaello official also gave my mother a brown paper bag and as we were invited to get into the taxi, he said *"Arrivederci e buona fortuna,"* Goodbye and good luck. And just like that we were riding in that huge, yellow car through streets filled with numerous other large vehicles.

UNITED STATES OF AMERICA
IMMIGRANT VISA AND ALIEN REGISTRATION

OF: (Family name)   (First name)   (Middle name)

LOMBARDI   Pietrantonio   —

I- 2336702
I-2336702

ACTION OF SPECIAL INQUIRY OFFICER

POINT OF

I certify that the immigrant named herein arrived in the United States at this port on

T/n RAFFAELLO
(Name of vessel or flight No. of aircraft)
and was inspected by me and

IMM. & NATZ. SERVICE
NEW YORK CITY 197
ADMITTED

MAY 19 1966

CLASS.
TO

detained for further inquiry by special officer under
Symbol
Section .... of the Immigration and
Nationality Act

_____
Immigrant Inspector.

The immigrant herein was (admitted) (excluded)
and { no appeal taken / appeal taken } under

Symbol ....

Section .... of the Immigration and
Nationality Act.

Special Inquiry Officer

ACTION ON APPEAL

ADMITTED

EXCLUDED

DATE

This visa is issued under Section 221 of the Immigration and Nationality Act, and upon the basis of the facts stated in the application.

AMERICAN Consulate General

AT Naples, Italy

Norman D. Leach
Vice Consul   of the United States of America.

IMMIGRANT CLASSIFICATION

NONQUOTA (Symbol)   QUOTA (Symbol)
P4-3

VISA PETITION NO., IF ANY
VP. s. in behalf of father

IMMIGRANT VISA NO.   QUOTA
12316   Italian

ISSUED ON   (Day)   (Month)   (Year)
31   Mar   1966

THE VALIDITY OF THIS VISA EXPIRES MIDNIGHT AT THE END OF
(Day)   (Month)   (Year)
30   Jul   1969

NATIONALITY (If stateless, so state, and give previous nationality)

Italian

PASSPORT

NO.
4773667/P

OR OTHER TRAVEL DOCUMENTS (Describe)

ISSUED
TO   LOMBARDI Maria Lucia CARMOSINO
incl. son: Pietrantonio LOMBARDI
BY   Police Auth. Campobasso, Italy
ON   March 3, 1966
EXPIRES
March 2, 1969

Service No. ....
Tariff Item No. ....
Fee Paid $20
Local Cy equiv. ....
Sec. 212 (a)(14)-cert. attached
Sec. 212
Sec. 212 (e)(1)-not applicable

FORM FS-511
5-61

16—74687-2   U.S. GOVERNMENT PRINTING OFFICE

IL PRESENTE MODULO SI PUÒ OTTENERE GRATIS PRESSO TUTTI GLI UFFICI CONSOLARI DEGLI STATI UNITI D'AMERICA
[THIS FORM MAY BE OBTAINED GRATIS AT CONSULAR OFFICES OF THE UNITED STATES OF AMERICA]

24

Debarkation documents

Debarkation documents

Ship manifest

Looking up we could not even see the sky, as the tall buildings seemed to come together. People, cars, buildings, noise everywhere. We were in awe, curious, scared, and confused. None of us said one word while riding through New York City, we were numb. Where we were headed we did not know. The driver could have taken us anywhere, maybe to some forced labor camp like some of the immigrants of long ago. After riding through that maze of buildings, people, vehicles, and all the different noises, the car finally pulled up to the curb in front of a white building, reminding me a bit of some of the buildings in Italy.

The driver dropped us off in front, said something that we did not understand, pointed to a door, and left the three of us standing there as people were glaring at us, upset with us for being in their way as they hurried around us. Remembering those tense, scary moments with the three of us just standing there lost in New York, I wondered if maybe it would have been better to be like our counterparts of years ago, who, when they disembarked on those same docks, were put on barges and taken to Ellis Island. At least they were not alone in not knowing what to do next.

Slowly we made our way inside Grand Central train station where it was a chaotic scene, to say the least. We found a tiny empty space to put our luggage down and just stood there, not knowing what to do next. It was then I first realized that there were many different types and colors of people in America; either that or maybe we went to the wrong country. It crossed my mind, could we be in Africa? I was very surprised to see so many black people in one place, mixed in with many other different shades of skin colors.

I could tell that my parents were extremely anxious, as was I. How I wished I had chosen English as my foreign language at the monastery instead of French. It would have been very useful to us now. Not knowing one word of the language imprisoned the three of us in that small corner of the train station. With some paper in hand my father ventured out into the crowd to attempt to find help, in hopes of getting us on the right track and the right train to Denver. After a while he made his way back to us and informed us that he could not find anyone to listen. As we were contemplating what to do and where to go next, we noticed another family that had been on board the Raffaello with us. I had played with those kids on the ship.

They were going to Detroit. "*Aspetta*," wait, we are going there too, my dad uttered. "*Datroite, no Denverr*." The Detroit bound family seemed to be having the same problem as we, but then what we hoped was a train station clerk came by and motioned for them to follow him. My father stuck a piece of paper in front of his face, making sure that he saw it and would hopefully help us. The official put his hand up and said something; hopefully he said to wait there and he would be back to help us. As the minutes went by, my parents lamented that maybe he was not going to come back and that we should get moving and try to find the train to Denver.

Finally the clerk came back and motioned for us to follow him with our luggage to a window. The attendant behind the window printed our tickets and we were then escorted down some stairs, as we struggled with our luggage. Another clerk, a middle-aged African-American, must have noticed the problem we were having with our luggage — which included a very heavy trunk — and approached us with a cart. He loaded the luggage onto the cart and motioned for us to follow him. We walked through mazes, down inclines, down elevators and escalators, finally making it to the train tracks, where we boarded a train that was hopefully headed to Denver.

We settled into our seats and the anxious look on my parents' faces was still very evident. Were they thinking the same as I? What in the hell in God's name were we doing here in this faraway land, on this different, unfamiliar train headed to God knows where? How I wished I were back in Villa San Michele with my brother, my sister and her husband, safe and happy. A lump was in my throat and I could not even speak; I could not, or surely I would begin to cry and that would make matters worse. My parents would feel even more guilt for bringing me this far, and for what? It's not like we lived on a dirt floor in a stone hut with no windows, as previous immigrants did. We had a nice house with marble floors, and a fireplace with a propane stove. We owned animals and my father had a part-time job with the *Ferrovie Statale*, the government railroad. There had better be streets paved with gold and money trees in Denver, or we were going to be very disappointed.

The train eventually started moving, and off we were for Denver, Colorado. As the hours passed and darkness approached, we wondered how much longer it would be before we reached Denver. Other immigrants who came back home from Denver warned my father that they recalled taking many hours on a train to reach their destination. A train employee, a nice, slightly older black man, would periodically come up and down the aisles and people would buy coffee and doughnuts. We watched and did the same. My father inconspicuously took the money bag that my mom had sewn from a piece of cloth, from around his neck and under his jacket, shirt, and undershirt and carefully pulled out some money. He had exchanged the *lire* to dollars in Italy; I believe we had $1,700.

The *panini* sandwiches that were in the brown paper bag given to us by the ship official, were consumed earlier in the day. We had hoped to reach our destination before nightfall, but darkness came and went and we woke up from our very restless sleep to a landscape of endless wheat and cornfields. As we reached towns, we noticed areas full of old, rusted out cars and other machines. Their cemeteries resembled Italy's, although ours had stone walls and theirs, a variety of fencing materials. The farmhouses in Italy were made of stone, but in America's countryside we saw mostly white, wooden structures. The country seemed to never end. We stared out the window in amazement, wondering just how big this America was.

Fortunately the black gentleman came down the aisle again, stopping next to our seats. As always, he said something, looking for a response, but none came; my father would just sort of nod. I am sure he thought we were deaf and mute and so he pushed the cart down the aisle shaking his head a bit. Other passengers would do the same as they left their seats and went somewhere for extended periods. We hardly moved from our seats except for the bathroom in the back of the car and to stretch a bit. We suddenly realized that we had been on the train for almost twenty-four hours. My mother eventually started to put doubt in our minds. Had we missed Denver as we slept?

The coffee man came by again. He was sort of surprised to hear my dad say, "Denver." The man babbled on and on, at the same time making a circular motion with his hand. Did he say that arrival at our destination of Denver would be the next day? That could not be, we had not eaten anything since midday the day before. We were hungry, tired, anxious, worried, and upset. We accepted some very black hot coffee and some unfamiliar sweets and returned to quietly staring out the window at the endless, empty landscape. The longest trip of my young life previously was to the monastery in Todi, an eternity away, but actually only about 175 miles from our village. All of Italy is only about 1,000 miles long from north to south, and New York to Denver is a distance of about 1,800 miles. We were in for the longest adventure of our lives.

The day passed slowly. Other passengers were leaving their seats, but we did not dare. As the train made its stops we hoped that the long trip was over, straining our eyes to look for any signage that resembled 'Denver.' A sign of Denver was nowhere to be found. Again we quietly wondered just where this place was. Another nightfall approached as the sun hid behind the endless cornfields. People seemed to want to talk to us, maybe to help us; probably to tell us that there was a restaurant car where we could go to eat a meal! Surely the coffee man also tried to tell us that, as he pointed towards the back of the train. We had spent two days and two nights on that train with no real meal, just coffee, milk, and doughnuts.

The next morning the May sun came up, shining its rays on something on the western skyline. As we got closer we noticed a mountain range that spanned the whole western horizon. Those peaks did not mean anything to us. We did not have any idea that we were very close to our final destination.

Chapter XXXIII

DENVER

On Thursday morning of May 21, 1966 the train pulled up to the rail station in lower downtown Denver. Weary eyed, we struggled out of the train and my father immediately saw a welcome familiar face. My Uncle Umberto was standing on the platform with another man, a stranger to me, but my father mumbled to my mom, "è *Volindo*," it was Olindo, a friend who had immigrated to Denver many years earlier, better known as Bill Lombardi, son of Antonio (Sperry) and Giovannina (Jenny) Lombardi who owned a bar called The Columbus Inn. After the hugging and the kissing and "*Comè eet reh viayeh?*" (*Come è andato il viaggio?* How was the trip?) we gathered our luggage and then followed the two men to a parking lot where a huge black car was parked. Dazed, mentally and physically drained, we struggled into the large car and headed towards our final destination of that new strange world.

I took in the enormity of it all — streets that were wider than some of our expressways; concrete, asphalt and trees everywhere, cars that seemed bigger than our buses, and all the *semafori*, traffic lights. I felt as if we had reached a land as far away from Villa San Michele as possible. It was nothing close to resembling the land we had left seemingly so long ago, but in actuality was only seven days earlier. As we pulled up to a row of houses, Bill honked his horn and out came my cousin, Terenzio, followed by his mom, Ida. Next, a short sort of rotund figure wearing an apron emerged with a little girl in tow. "*Papà*," my dad murmured in a low sort of trembling voice.

Denver's Union Station, circa 1960s

Standing there squinting his smallish eyes to get a good look at us was a short man. I noticed his bowed legs that were sporting black cowboy boots. He had a smile on his face that almost seemed forced, but he was probably just nervous. A little girl was latched onto his leg and she was not about to let it go anytime soon. There he was, *Papà* Pietrantonio, the man after whom I was named, my grandfather. Under normal circumstances I suppose I should have opened that car door and run as fast as possible to him to give him a long, huge hug. Instead I just sat there next to my father, who was fixing his eyes on his father for the first time in some thirty-five years.

As I turned towards my dad, I noticed tears flowing down his cheeks as he was fumbling, trying to open the car door. He wasn't having much luck but my uncle got out of the front seat and came back and opened it, allowing my dad to get out and walk the few steps towards his father. My dad's head was shaking slightly and his arms extended as he hugged his father for the first time in a long time. Being away from my family for a couple of years at the monastery was very difficult for me. I can't imagine what thirty-five years was like, but I assume that it must have been immensely painful for my father. My mother filed behind my dad to meet her father-in-law for the first time, and I followed behind her. I don't remember if I kissed him or hugged him as he, now also crying, said something to me, to us. All I recall is the anxiety, tension, fear, and the awkwardness of the moment.

Eventually we were led through a door of the seemingly large house. We were expecting some sort of living quarters but we were introduced to a workshop instead. It was a shoe repair shop with various tools and that distinctive, familiar smell of leather and other materials that I had smelled in shoe shops in Italy. We were then led to a doorway

Papà Pietrantonio holding unknown child, circa 1960s

draped with a fabric enclosure and into the living quarters of the house: a living room, kitchen, a bath and three small bedrooms, and *la cantina*, a wine cellar, in the back of the house. That dwelling would now house three families, totaling eight occupants. Nothing in that house resembled what we had left behind: the marble floors, fireplace, and marble stairs leading to porcelain floored bedrooms upstairs. These floors were covered with a material that felt spongy as you walked on it... carpeting! The bedrooms had small closets where clothes were stored replacing the tall, fine wood dressers that we were used to in our house in Italy — the home and its surroundings that I was already missing considerably.

Initially this house seemed enormous and nice, but as we visited relatives and friends in the following days and weeks, as they welcomed us to Denver with nice dinners, I began to notice that my grandfather's house was tiny and old compared to those bigger and usually newer homes of our friends and relatives. As thirteen-year-olds sometimes do, I complained about our living situation but my parents were quick to squash it, reminding me that we were going to give our new world a chance.

Denver circa 1966

Chapter XXXIV

SCUOLA MEDIA · LAKE JUNIOR HIGH SCHOOL

On May 25, 1966, five days after we reached Denver, I started school at Lake Junior High School in what would become the most difficult two weeks of my young life. My mother insisted on dressing me in that oversized gray checkered suit, with the white shirt and the black bow tie. The shiny black Italian dress shoes were replaced by the colorful cowboy boots that my grandfather had made especially for me as a welcome-to-America gift. With my *borsa*, bag, containing my school records, my grandfather along with my dad drove me to this gigantic building by a lake, my new school. My concern, my worrying and disappointment had begun the day before when I learned that I would not be going to the same school as my cousin, Terenzio. He was two years younger and attended a grade school on 23rd and Federal Boulevard – appropriately named Boulevard Elementary – just a couple of blocks away from where we lived!

As soon as we walked in I knew that my time here would be very difficult. I was more than scared; I was in a daze, in a fog. Nothing seemed real and familiar as we walked through the enormous hallway. We were guided to the office and there began the lengthy process of getting me enrolled in school. My father took out my school records, telling my grandpa to tell the woman that those number tens on the records were my grades, the highest possible. He would proudly mention this more than once. She seemed uninterested and confused by all the back-and-forth discussions between my grandfather and father. Finally I was enrolled and to my shock, my security blankets, my grandfather and my father, left me there with these strangers. I had a huge lump in my throat as they walked down the long hallway.

Lake Junior High School, circa 1966

A woman came in and talked to me, and not being aware that I did not understand a word she was saying, she seemed annoyed by the lack of acknowledgement from me. Another woman came around the counter and they talked, and I got this look from both of them as if to say, "What the hell are we going to do with this Italian kid?" She motioned for me to follow her down the hallway. We came to a door and she opened it and that's when my nightmare began.

Even now as I think about that day, I sense the complete and utter panic that I felt on that morning of May 1966. As I followed the woman into that classroom, my protected world came to an end. Instantly there was pointing and laughing in my direction. The female teacher said something in a loud voice to the students and there was a short silence, but as the office woman walked me towards an empty desk in the back of the class, the snickering began again. I forced myself to sit down at that desk as my heart pounded, feeling as if it was going to jump right out of my chest.

For some reason I went deaf. I stopped hearing the noises of the room. I kept my head down avoiding any eye contact. I could still sense every eye in the room fixed on me but for some reason my brain went into a defensive mode, where it did not allow the sounds to affect me. Suddenly I began to hear the sounds, but they were garbled and in very slow motion. I thought I was going to die and assumed that this is what happened just before it happened. But just before I took my last breath, a loud bell rang and as all the students rushed through the door, I sat alone in that classroom, not knowing what to do.

The female teacher walked over to my desk and picked up the paper that I was given in the office. She studied it for a moment and then motioned for me to get up and to follow her. As we walked out of the classroom, a crowd had gathered in the hallway. They all wanted to take a look at the freak alien with the plaid suit, bow tie, and cowboy boots who was sporting a businessman's black leather bag as he walked out into the hallway. As the teacher looked back towards me, I rushed to hide behind her as we started to walk down the hallway. She looked at my paper and pointed to another room.

We walked in and I could see that this must be some sort of art class. The elderly female teacher took the paper from the first teacher, who then left after a short conversation. I stood there and again felt all eyes on me. I was still numb. All I could think of was God and all the prayers that I said to Him at the monastery. And then I thought, is this what you gave me in return? Could He maybe make *Maestro* appear in that classroom and protect me, give those students his stare and maybe slap a few of the bullies around and make them leave me alone? At least, please God, send my grandfather and my father back inside this school and take me away from this hell. Instead I felt the hand of the elderly woman as she pulled me towards a desk, and again I forced myself to sit down.

The art teacher yelled out something and as the room became quiet, she picked up a book and began to read. And one by one the students said something back to her as they raised their hands. After a short pause, she started to talk again and all the students turned towards me as she spoke. I can only guess that she was informing the class of a new student as she struggled mightily, attempting to say my name, Pietrantonio Lombardi. The students were now giggling and probably wondering from what planet I came. All the while I was thinking what a strange planet my parents had brought me to. As the class moved forward, I again sat there, not knowing what to do. A black kid said something to me, but of course I did not understand him. He eventually got up from his desk and directed me to the art supplies on a table. Noticing that the rest of the students were involved in drawing and painting projects, I attempted to at least draw something on the art paper. As I picked up the pencil I noticed that my hand was trembling, and again the movements and sounds of the room went into slow motion.

And then the unimaginable happened. My eyes welled up and I started to cry. Putting my head down into my arms on the desk, I attempted to hide that pathetic scene from the students, but to no avail. I felt a tap on my shoulder but ignored it, choosing to keep my head down in my only secure world of my arms. Another tap, this time harder, and reluctantly I raised my head. Of course all eyes were on me, but through the blur I noticed that not all the students were giggling, some had a look of compassion and pity.

The teacher motioned for me to get up, as she said something to me. With my head down I followed her out of the classroom. Thank God there wasn't an audience waiting for me in the hallway. I followed her down the enormous hall and into the office, where the nightmare had started. I sat there clutching the only thing familiar to me, my school bag, wiping my eyes and trying to regain control of my emotions. Discussions were taking place as more people joined in the meeting.

A young woman walked into the office and after a brief meeting with the other teachers, she walked towards me and gave me a caring look and began to talk. All I could decipher from what she was saying was the word Mappelli. But as she continued to try to communicate with me I noticed that some words were beginning to sound familiar. I heard her say the words Italiani and Abruzzo and *famiglia*. Miss Mappelli was able to have a calming effect on me and I finally regained my composure. I later learned that she was trying to communicate with me in Spanish because, although her family was originally from the Abruzzo region of Italy, she did not speak Italian but had learned Spanish in college.

She was assigned to me for the rest of the day, accompanying me to the lunchroom where I refused to take out my lunch because the whole lunchroom was staring at me. Miss Mappelli went to the lunch line and brought me back a small carton that she opened, and while handing it to me I heard a word sounding like *cioccolato*, chocolate. It was chocolate milk, my first ever, and the start of a love affair with the drink. We walked out of the lunchroom and made our way outside and I immediately realized that this was recess.

I fell in love with chocolate milk.

A gleam of excitement came over me. This would be my opportunity to show these American kids my soccer skills. I looked down at my feet and noticed the pointy cowboy boots, but it couldn't be any worse than playing barefoot which I had done many times before. I viewed the playground, hoping to see a soccer game taking place. To my surprise there were no soccer balls to be seen. Some boys were throwing a brown, oblong ball to each other, like the ball that Peppino's grandpa had sent him from America. Others were trying to hit a small, white ball with a stick, and others played *palla a canestro*, basketball, the only game that was familiar to me. Why weren't they playing soccer? I asked Miss Mappelli, "*Calcio?*" as I made the kicking motion. She did not seem to understand what I was trying to say. So we stood there watching the boys and girls play all these games that I had never seen before.

The rest of the school day was a serving of more staring and giggling from the other students, and finally the agonizing trip into hell was over. Miss Mappelli escorted me out of the school and when I saw my father with *Papà* Pietrantonio, I became emotional again, with tears filling my eyes as I ran over to them. My father immediately saw the anguish on my face and gave me a much needed hug. On the way home I recounted my hellish experience. I asked my grandfather why they did not have soccer at recess and he informed me that Americans did not play soccer.

Just when things could not get any worse in my life, they got worse. I somehow dealt with all the challenges presented to me in this new world, but not being able to play the game I loved, the game I played every single day back in Italy, the game that I had worked hard to excel in at the monastery, the game that in Italy might have given me the opportunity to improve my life — there was no way I was just going to give that up. My parents did not understand or sympathize with me. To them it was just a game and not essential to my life. They had never had the opportunity to play or watch the game I loved. So when I begged them to take me back home because I missed playing soccer, they ignored me. But they did consider all the other difficulties that we encountered. Life was not going to be a pot of gold in America as we had hoped, dreamed.

I endured two long weeks at Lake Junior High School. The teasing, taunting, and bullying continued, and at times I was very concerned not only about my mental well-being but also for my safety. Down the street from my grandfather's house lived a family who was friends with my grandfather. They had four kids and one of them was in seventh grade. He walked with me to and from school. I did not realize it at the time but he was not a popular kid, and he had also experienced bullying from other students. The bullies would take advantage of the convenience to taunt two of us at the same time. That boy, Dan Quinones, helped me in so many ways, teaching me English words as we walked home, helping me learn and understand a little about this new, curious culture that was thrown at me. He also introduced me to his mother's Mexican food, for which I learned to acquire a taste, welcoming every chance to eat it at his house.

I noticed that at school, Dan was a loner and shy, his head usually down to avoid eye contact. He might have felt that I made matters worse for him and I would not have blamed him if he avoided me, but he never did. Although he was not able to offer any help, he never left me when the bullies — some older and bigger — taunted us as we walked home. Some egged us on to fight by pushing us, but we both refused. One day a small group including some girls surrounded us, and a man stopped his car and came to our rescue. He yelled and pointed at them as they ran down the street.

My cousin, Terenzio, and I spent a lot time at Dan's house that summer, watching endless American television, eating their food, riding their bikes, and always trying to befriend his two older sisters! Years later I learned that those kids all died at middle age from alcoholism and other ailments.

I missed my old life very much. As difficult as it was at the monastery, I would have even agreed to go back there, although the monks probably would have refused to take me back. As I watched my parents also struggle mightily with the present and what the future might bring, I hesitated to complain so much. At times you could cut the tension with a knife. They could not find work, and they did not speak English! The living arrangement was not very appealing and my grandfather, along with his daughter, was showing signs of annoyance with the substantial addition of residents in their home.

Chapter *XXXV*

La Mela Rossa · The Red Apple

The school year ended, and the last two weeks of it were my hell that had finally ended. I had not learned much English. I didn't want to learn English, I wanted to go back home. I became more and more withdrawn. My parents were concerned. My grandfather told them that it was very important for me to learn to speak English so I could begin to interact with the other kids of the neighborhood. I was not as outgoing as my cousin, Terenzio. The monks had taught me to be more reserved. *Papà* Pietrantonio usually said that his grandson, Terenzio, would be a lawyer and I would be a doctor, because of our different personalities. He must have asked all of his friends if there was a place I could go to learn to speak English.

One day my grandfather was talking to a man outside the corner liquor store just east of his shoe shop. They both looked at me as they spoke, and I realized that I was the subject of their conversation. Not understanding a word they were saying, I only could guess as to what they were talking about, "My grandson, *he no can speaka*." A woman who seemed to have had too much to drink was back at the liquor store for more. She started to chime in on the conversation and eventually slurred out some information. Evidently she knew of a school where I could go to learn how to speak English.

And so the next day, in my adopted school uniform of my gray checkered suit and cowboy boots, *Papà* Pietrantonio, accompanied by my father, drove me the short distance to this huge building, North High

School. Walking up those stairs I already began to feel overwhelmed by the sheer size of the school. Once inside, we walked through a huge hallway and into an office: more discussions and more staring. After my father signed some papers we sat at a bench and waited. Presently, two young women walked in and after more conversations, my grandfather told me that they were going to take me to the classroom. Things were looking up. The two girls were beautiful, with short skirts and nice black boots; nothing like my multi-colored cowboy boots. My grandfather and father waved goodbye, telling me that they would pick me up after a few hours, and walked down the long corridor towards the exit doors and to the parking lot.

The two girls, with a tight grip on my hands, led me up some stairs, talking to each other and staring at me. As we walked down the hallway I could hear a commotion coming from a doorway down the corridor. As we reached the room the noise got very loud. I was scared, nervous. The girls led me into a room full of out-of-control and screaming kids. Some of the kids seemed to be about my age, some younger, and some much older. When they noticed me, a few came running up to me, gesturing uncontrollably, grabbing me, grabbing one another. It was an absolutely chaotic scene, nothing like what I was used to at the monastery. The two young teachers led me to a desk, sat me down, and quickly attempted to restore order, but were not having much success. I imagined how different that situation would be if the Franciscans were in control; these students would be shaking in their shoes for sure.

Finally, some sort of order was restored. Some of the students had wandered over to my desk and began to touch and hug me. Again I was shocked by the way the school system operated in America. Back at the monastery I could not even touch myself, much less someone else. The teachers tried earnestly to teach — at least that's what I gathered, since I did not understand a word they were saying. I thought the class would never end; all I kept thinking about was home. I became frightened when my eyes filled with tears. Surely I would be teased by the students, but no one seemed to notice.

It seemed like an eternity but after a few hours, parents came by to pick up their sons and daughters and I noticed that the parents did not have much luck in controlling the kids, either. What sort of country was this America, where kids ran wild like that? My grandfather and my dad finally showed up to pick me up in my grandpa's maroon 1964 Ford Falcon. The two beautiful girls waved at me as I quickly walked to my father. As I looked back they were still talking, while watching me with a puzzled look. I thought I noticed them shake their heads. I wondered why, because I had been quiet and had not moved from my seat once, even when I should have tried to escape from some of the students as I was scared to death of the whole situation. I had attempted to learn by sounding out what the other students were loudly sounding out, over and over again.

"*Come è ita la scola?*" *Com'è andata la scuola?* How did school go? my grandpa asked me in his Pagliarone dialect. "*Un casino.*" I basically told him that it was a chaotic scene. I also informed my dad and grandpa that these kids at least did not stare at me and laugh, but they touched me and tried to hug me all day long. *Papà* Pietrantonio wondered why the other students would do that, and I wondered why the two young, pretty teachers did not hug me. I certainly would have welcomed that.

My grandpa asked me if at least I learned any English and I told him that with all the confusion I managed to learn only how to say *mela*, apple, in English. He asked, "*E come si dice mela,*" How do you say apple? I told him, "aaaaapplllllhhh." "*Ma che dici?*" What are you saying? "*Si dice,* 'apple'," although thinking back, his pronunciation of apple actually sounded more like "*appllah!*" My father also asked, "*E com'è cushì longa kaella parola?*" (*Perchè è così lunga quella parola?* Why is that word so long?) I suggested to my grandpa that he was wrong, because we practiced it most of the day and every time the students would say it the same way, "aaaaapplllllhhh."

After repeatedly telling my grandpa that apple was the only word I learned and that the other students were out of control and did not seem to want to learn anything, my father suggested maybe it would be appropriate to have a talk with the young teachers. My grandfather blew it off and said to stick with it and not to complain so much. I needed to learn English and this was the only school that was available. After a few days of the same, the young teachers did more staring at me and had more discussions about me. I was still insisting that I wasn't learning anything and suspected that neither were the other kids and that these kids were different. And I began to wonder why these kids could not speak English and just where in the heck were they from? I could not understand why we worked on the same words every day.

Finally, after my numerous pleas not to take me back to that disorganized mess, my grandpa and my dad drove me over to North High School and this time they got out of the car and walked over to the two young teachers who were waiting outside for their students. The conversation was intense. The teachers pointed to me and then to the other students. My grandfather was shaking his head while one of the women put her hand up to her mouth, signifying the international gesture of disbelief. He shook the two young women's hands and walked over to us, telling us to go to the car.

I was relieved that I was going back home with them but wondered why I was not staying. Maybe the teachers were not happy with my participation in class. I was confused. My father and I wondered what happened out loud and *papà* Pietrantonio said, *"Kaella scola n'è peh te,"* *Quella scuola non è per te*, That school is not for you. He was a bit embarrassed, and reluctantly he told us that he had enrolled me in a speech therapy class for mentally challenged kids who had difficulty speaking.

My mom was sorry to have put me through that experience and I began to notice that she also questioned the decision that she and my dad had made to come to America. I actually had started to like some of the bubbly, happy kids in that class and thought about them often. Later when I was in high school at the same North High School, I was walking down the hallway and suddenly a girl came up to me, and with the biggest smile on her face, hugged me tightly. It was one of the mentally challenged girls in that class of three years ago. She recognized me, and she was very happy to see me again. Maybe she was the only normal student in the hallway that day.

That summer in 1966 I learned how to speak a little English on the streets. My cousin, Terenzio, and I hung around the neighborhood with other kids, and along with learning all the bad words we also managed to learn the most basic of the English language. The American kids seemed to want to learn Italian — Italian bad words. All the while my parents and I tried to adapt and learn to live with two other families in a tiny house, in a strange and faraway land. And the vision of a young woman holding up a red apple will be forever etched in my memory.

Chapter XXXVI

Nuove Feste · New Holidays

With the advent of television in our small village, we were introduced to many American television programs and movies. We particularly loved the cowboy and Indian movies. As kids we did not realize that those scenes were from years gone by, or we just did not want to accept that what we saw was mostly fantasy and not reality. We would all be very disappointed when we saw the words 'The End' appear on the screen. We did not know what they meant, other than when those words appeared, we eventually figured out that it meant that the movie ended, *la fine!* We did not want it to end. A look of disappointment on our faces, and it was back to reality!

I could not wait to watch the weekly program called *Bonanza*. I did not know what to expect when I came to Denver, but what I hoped to see most was an assemblage of cowboys on their horses, toting guns or bows and arrows. After all, this was the American West. I was disappointed that the characters of *Bonanza* on these televisions spoke English!

Ernesto Falasco was a Denver fireman, who came from our village when he was a small boy. He took a strong interest in us and other recent immigrants, helping in many ways as we coped with our new world. He would assemble all the newcomers and take us on many road trips to points of interest all around Colorado. One day in early July he organized a short trip into the foothills to the Mother Cabrini Shrine, the Buffalo Bill grave, and then we completed the day with a picnic in a nearby park. He would patiently explain in basic terms the meaning of all the historical sites.

Ernesto also explained to us that that day was a very important holiday in America, the fourth of July, when people go to the mountains, beaches, and have picnics or backyard barbecues with family and friends. Then at night there were fireworks in celebration of the day when America declared its independence from England. Before then, July 4 had been just another day for us. Our special summer day in Italy was August 15, *Ferragosto*, Assumption Day, with the same events. In Denver we stopped celebrating that day; it was just another day here in America.

Celebrating Ferragosto with family and friends in Villa San Michele,
at a picnic area called la crocetta, 1990

As we visited Buffalo Bill's grave and museum, I asked Ernesto if I would ever see any Indians and cowboys, and if they were still fighting each other. He gave me a smile and said that those conflicts were long over and that they never really slaughtered each other like we saw in those movies. As a matter of fact, he told us that when the first immigrants, the pilgrims, came to this land, the Indians helped them to survive, teaching them to fish and hunt, and introducing them to new vegetables to eat. He continued to explain in elementary fashion that even though the Indians were usually depicted as the bad guys, we were not so innocent because the white men took their land.

Ernesto told us about another very important holiday in America, Thanksgiving. On that fourth Thursday in November, he went on to tell us we celebrate by giving thanks to the Almighty God for all that we have. Along with many other foods, turkey is the main dish and it goes back to when the Indians helped the pilgrims hunt the wild birds. That fourth Thursday of November back in Italy was just another day!

As we embraced these new holidays, we also gave up many public and religious holidays of Italy, many of which we cherished and anticipated. Of course as a child, my favorites were *la Befana*, the Epiphany, and *la Pasquetta*, Easter Monday. On April 25 we had *la Festa della Liberazione*, Liberation Day, the day in 1945 that Allied forces finally liberated Italy from the Nazis and Mussolini's troops. In particular, this day honors all the fallen partisan resistance fighters who fought Nazi and Fascist soldiers. Other Italian holidays were May 1, *Festa del Lavoro*, the equivalent of Labor day; June 2, *Festa della Repubblica*, the birth of the Italian Republic in 1946; November 1, *Tutti I Santi*, All Saints Day; December 8, *Immacolata Concezione*, the Immaculate Conception; and December 26, *Santo Stefano*, Saint Stephen's Day. We missed celebrating those holidays as we adjusted to American public holidays. In those early years we would think about them, but eventually they just slowly faded away from our lives.

Ferragosto 2014, brother Ezio, zio Flavio Carmosino, me, zia Leontina Lombardi Carmosino

Chapter XXXVII

CASA AFFOLLATA · CROWDED HOME

My grandfather had lived by himself for many years. He and his young daughter, Coco, had a system, a lifestyle that suddenly had been interrupted by two families moving into their small house, which also doubled as his shoe repair business. My father finally found work at St. Anthony Hospital with the help of a nurse who was a distant relative. I only recall her last name, Milano. His nursing skills from World War II landed him the job as a nurse's assistant. He endured that for a couple of months, but finally the problem of not being able to speak and understand English caught up with him.

My father would come home and complain to us about the problems that he faced on a daily basis, actually on a nightly basis; he worked nights. He was having problems adjusting to the schedule. Back home he was with his animals very early in the morning, but this night work was different. He obviously was given the undesirable tasks of changing diapers, giving baths, and shaving the male patients. He did not mind that, but he was also qualified to perform many of the same functions as the other nurses. But a huge obstacle prevented him from that; he could not understand, read, or write English. We could see the frustration in his face. Patients would become angry and yell at him when he could not figure out what they needed. After a couple of months he could not take it anymore, so he quit his first job in this country. He felt demoralized and unworthy. He became depressed. He had never quit a job before. The small house was overcrowded and people were getting on each other's nerves.

After much contemplation, the decision was made to go back home; home where we could understand and speak to people, home where my sister and brother were. Surely they were missing us as much, if not more, than we were missing them. Whatever little money my parents were able to save was used to buy train and ship passes for the trip back to Italy. All our belongings were shipped ahead of time by train, to New York. A couple of nights before our departure, relatives and friends started to come over the house to say their goodbyes and wish us well. Each and every one of those people tried to convince my father to stay a little longer, to give it a chance. Over and over again, he was told that he was making a huge mistake, "Your son will have a better life if you stay."

Immigration papers allowing my brother to join us, arrived a few days before our departure. And our *paesani* strongly suggested to my dad that my brother should also be given a chance at a better life here. Domenico Capobianco, a compatriot from our village, even promised my father that he would get him a job at the Rocky Mountain News, working with him as a janitor. Domenico was a master stone mason back in Italy, but here in America he settled for any job that brought money to his family. All night long those people pleaded with my mom and dad to stay.

On the last night before our trip back home to Italy, our friends and relatives were able to convince my father to stay a little longer, to wait at least until my brother, Ezio, arrived. Maybe conditions would begin to improve. I clearly recall Nicola and Gilda Lombardi saying, *"Ma che cia i a fà all'Italia,"* *Ma che cosa farai in Italia,* implying that there would be nothing to do back in Italy. Arrangements were made for our belongings to be sent back to Denver from New York. Any money saved was lost and we were back to zero, financially.

My father was hired by the Rocky Mountain News as a janitor, a far cry from the medical field or the farming life that he was familiar with in Italy. But we were thankful that the head of our family was going to be able to support us without anyone else's help, public or private, although the immigrants from our small village would surely help in any way. The earlier immigrants from our area were a tight-knit group. They helped each other in any way and were obviously there for us. In Denver, my mother had an aunt by the name of Cosima, her mother's sister. Cosima had immigrated here in the early 1900s. Her children helped us tremendously, especially Pasquale (Pasky) Lombardi. My mother's cousin, Tony Lombardi, and his family — who owned Tony's Place, a bar on 35ᵗʰ and Tennyson — also helped us with adjusting to America.

Pasky owned a motel and bar in Federal Heights, on 88th and Federal Boulevard. My father and I would go there every Monday and Tuesday, my father's days off, to clean, paint, cut the grass, and perform any other handyman work. My father did not shy away from any work, no matter how menial or how dirty. The very first time Pasky took us there, we passed a huge cowboy statue on the way, on Federal Boulevard, and I thought that we were now in real cowboy country. I kept looking for the Indians on their horses, with their bow and arrows. We also did yard work at their house on 42nd and Grove Street. Pasky had a motorized machine and he showed us how to walk behind it and to just go back-and-forth. Why wouldn't they just have cows or sheep eat the grass?

My mother's cousins, from left top to bottom: Pasky Lombardi with wife Josephine, Joe Gust with wife Stella Lombardi, father Ray Labate with Zia Cosima, Ralph Bruno with wife Lucy Lombardi, John Labate with wife Carolina, Jimmy Digiacomo with wife Eva. Deceased at the time of this photo, circa 1960, were Zia Cosima's other daughters, Pierina Lombardi and Annie Lombardi.

We also decided to find a place of our own, with hopefully a bit more elbow room. There was an elderly Italian woman with living quarters in the basement of her home at 2601 West 39th Avenue. It was in a neighborhood where many friends and relatives lived. The two-bedroom

Tony and Giuseppa Lombardi, circa 1966

dungeon was dark and musty, but very cheap and she would pay all utilities, we were informed, wondering exactly what they were. The landlady was very nice and my mom and dad helped her out with all sorts of chores. But every night my mother would cry and lament about our bright and sunny marbled floors in our home back in Villa San Michele. We felt as though we lived in a cave and we only lasted a couple of months before we decided to move out, in fear of the three of us getting sick in the dark, musty home below ground.

My mom and dad befriended a family that lived at 3844 Clay Street. My parents met them while walking around the neighborhood hoping to meet somebody, maybe someone who was from Italy. And one day we got very lucky. Their names were Ralph and Louise Giardino. She was from Rome and he from Grimaldi in Calabria, the toe of Italy. They had a beautiful daughter, Mary Lou. When I looked at Mary Lou I wished I were about five years older. The nice couple took an interest in us and our well-being. They talked their neighbors into renting their duplex apartment at 3826 Clay Street to us, even though they only wanted two people as tenants since it was only a small one-bedroom. Mary Lou remembers her mother casually informing her dad that they needed to buy a new refrigerator, and he remarked that the one they had was in perfect condition, so why buy a new one? She agreed but told him that Vittorio and Maria did not have one in their new apartment, so Louise gave them the refrigerator.

The owners of the apartment were Floradeal and Thelma Kephart (and our names were odd?). They were a mother and her spinster daughter, who lived in the downstairs apartment, which added to their weirdness. Our apartment was very small, but my mother was happier because at least it was above ground. Things were a bit better for us, but not much. We still missed our family, our home, our village, our former life. Even though we were closer to many of our compatriots, everything about America was different: the food (even the Italian was a bit different), the people, the culture.

We missed the simple things of our former life: our fireplace, our chickens, our cows, and our donkey. We were rural people from deep in the mountains of Italy, thrown into an urban bustle of a western American city. I forgot what a piece of my mom's bread tasted like. I could not get used to the bread that would stick to the roof of my mouth. It was too soft, too mushy. I was slowly getting used to and enjoying some of the new food and drinks, like Pepsi, Coke, and Dr. Pepper. But our favorite, and probably cheaper drink, was Kool-Aid. The considerable use of ice in drinks was also new to us and it took a while to get accustomed to the ice-cold drinks.

When we first arrived in Denver, *Zia* Ida could not wait to show us the huge *negozio*, grocery store, "*Si chiama Sefuaè*," It is called Safeway, she excitedly told us as we walked the short distance to 26th and Federal. We could not believe the enormity of the store, aisle after aisle of food, most of it unknown to us. There was no *gelato*, Italian ice cream, *nutella*, a dark chocolate and hazelnut spread, *mortadella*, Italian cured sausage, *fichi*, figs, or *cachi*, persimmon, some of my most favorite foods.

And about the way they washed their clothes! My grandfather had a contraption that washed clothes for you, *la washamachina*. As I found out later, our washer was an older model, yet we were very impressed. It washed and rinsed the clothes and then you would just have to put the wet items through two rollers and the water would be wrung out. Although clothes dryers were available, *Papà* Pietrantonio did not have one. That part of the process was similar to that of our village. Weather permitting, my mom would hang clothes on a clothesline and in cold whether they were hung on chairs and other things close to the fireplace. My mom was sort of apprehensive about *la washamachina*, as my Aunt Ida showed her how to use it. Although these convenient appliances have come a long way since the 1960s, my wife will hang clothes outside at every opportunity, claiming that they feel and look better when dried by the sun!

Three women washing clothes in a stream in Pagliarone, circa 1934
(Lillian Lombardi Bertollt collection)

Washing clothes in an outdoor fountain was a vast improvement over washing them in a stream. Villa San Michele's main fountain, where women washed their clothes daily, sometimes waiting in line for their turn, 1975

When in Rome... My wife washing clothes in the village's fountain. The women gave her a hard time for wearing gloves! 1990

In America, my mom experienced an enormous leap in progress by washing clothes with the washing machine.

Zia Ida and my cousin, Terenzio, could not wait to show us the small boxes lined up on a shelf at Safeway. We bought some and when we got home my aunt opened one of the boxes, poured the powder in warm water, mixed it, turning the water red, and then she put it in the *frigorifero*, refrigerator. After an hour or so she took it out. The red water had hardened. She invited us to touch the congealed substance. It wasn't hard, it felt soft and it rebounded as you pushed down on it. It trembled as we looked in amazement and then we scooped some of it with a spoon and carefully put the wiggling red creation in our mouths. I had never tasted anything like it. The concoction was sweet and it squeezed between my teeth as I tried to chew it. Our refrigerator always had a bowl of this new dish after that first experience with Jell-O. The different flavors of Jell-O and Kool-Aid made for cheap and varied treats.

The best thing about our Clay Street apartment was that it was across the street from Luban's Drug store. Whenever I had some money I would go there to buy candies and sometimes a drink from their soda bar. The owner was MaryAnn Kearn, very tall and very loud, but generally amiable. Also down the street there was another huge store called Miller Super. My mom and I would get lost in there looking at all the different, strange food. We did not have the money or the knowledge to buy what was for sale, so we settled for the bare minimum.

My *Zio* Umberto and his family had also decided to move out of *Papà* Pietrantonio's house, and luckily they rented a house a block away, also on Clay Street. It was the house that *Zia* Cosima, my mother's aunt, had lived in for many years until her death.

The first basement apartment we rented, 2015

Our one-bedroom apartment on Clay Street, 2015

Chapter *XXXVIII*

Scuola Media
Skinner Junior High School

With our new home on Clay Street I would have to go to a new school. I was heartbroken that I could not go back to Lake Junior High school. Not! I had nothing but very bad memories from that school that haunted me that whole summer and maybe beyond. I was glad that I would be going to a new school, but not very excited about dealing with another unknown. Unfortunately my cousin, Terenzio, would be going to Columbian Grade School on 40th and Federal. At least we could have supported each other. My mom went with me to enroll, but she wasn't much help. Four months in America and she had learned very little English, if any at all. With my limited knowledge of English, we managed to enroll at Skinner Junior High School in Northwest Denver. I was given a schedule of the classes that I would be attending. It was very confusing but I finally sort of figured it out with help from some friends.

My reputation must have preceded me because from the very first day of school, I was picked out as the different one and the one who could be easily picked on. After a couple days of school I was called into the office and someone pointed out and asked why I was not going to physical education class, my last class of the day. That next afternoon I did not have a clue where I was supposed to go for that gym class. I wandered around for a while and finally decided to ask some boys, some of whom had poked fun at me the previous days. I did not have a choice. So with my very broken English

I walked up to them and pointed to the class I was looking for. They spoke amongst themselves for a few seconds and then told me to follow them. They pointed to some stairs going down and told me that my class was through the doors at the bottom of the stairs.

As I walked down those stairs, the group of boys stayed at the top, watching me. I opened the doors and walked in. Soon there were screams coming from inside, girls running around in various stages of dress, covering themselves up with towels. A female teacher grabbed me by my hand, yelling, jerking me towards the door. As the door opened, the boys were up the stairs laughing uncontrollably. The teacher dragged me up the stairs and to the office. She told a secretary what I had done and they both looked at me with mild disgust. It took me a while to explain as best I could that some boys told me to go through those doors for the physical education class. I had seen boys going down those stairs before, but the stairs to the boys' locker room were actually on the opposite side of the corridor. The only difference was the 'Girls' sign above the door.

Skinner Junior High School, I wished they had the same banner on the wall when I enrolled. (Did you say hello to the new kid?) 2015

Unfortunately, that experience was the beginning of another difficult school year. The way the girls sneered at me, I knew I did not have a chance in hell of befriending any of them. When I finally became familiar with the school and my classes, I tried to do well in each one. The gym class was a struggle, starting with lining up for the attendance check. Either the gym teacher was not able to even come close to pronouncing my name, or I suspected that he intentionally butchered it. He seemed to enjoy saying "Pie? Pee?" a few times, until I just raised my hand and shyly said, "Call me Tony." For some reason that teacher, a tall blond Anglo-Saxon looking man with wavy hair and glasses, treated me almost as badly as most of the students. Not knowing what to do, I was a non-participant for most of the class and nobody was stepping forward to help me. I recall struggling immensely with dribbling and shooting a basketball, the rest of the kids imitating my awkward shot and laughing. If I could only get them on a soccer field... but soccer balls were nowhere to be found, just like at Lake Junior High.

Things got much worse in that gym class. One day after I showered and was drying off in front of my shower, the leading class clown snuck up behind me, and with a swift motion hit my buttocks with a wet towel, sending shooting pain down my leg, invoking laughter and jeers from other students. Fighting back tears as the pain subsided I peaked at my butt and noticed a large, red welt. With a slight limp I struggled through the rest of the day. Skinner was going to be as bad, if not worse, than Lake Junior High. I decided not to mention a word about my struggles to my parents. They felt guilt and anxiety about our predicament and I did not want to burden them with more problems. I endured the almost daily slap of the wet towel from the blond-headed boy. He was slightly taller and heavier than I. He was not one of the popular boys. He tried hard to fit in with the in-crowd but he was not at that level. I suppose he hoped that slapping the ass of the dorky Italian immigrant, who was at the very bottom of the popularity hierarchy, might get him there.

I endured as best as I could all the pranks and mischiefs directed at me, but it was wearing on me. In social studies class I was sitting at my desk minding my own business, when the boy in front of me pointed to something on the ground, making a disgusted, nauseated face. I looked down and saw something that immediately brought me back to the ship that brought us to this unforgiving land. It was vomit. I scrambled to my feet, careful not to step on it, calling it to the teacher's attention. I waved my finger back-and-forth and informed the class that it wasn't my vomit. Simultaneously the whole class broke out in laughter, including the teacher. The kid who had warned me about the mess walked over and picked up the plastic prop.

In that same class during a World War II discussion, the teacher asked me if we studied it in Italy. Of course we did. I also mentioned that my father had fought in the war in Africa, a big mistake on my part. Now I was an enemy of the State. While staring at me, the teacher spent the rest of the class telling us how two American soldiers with one machine gun were able to capture hundreds of Italian soldiers.

Luckily, a kid named Leonard Zaragosa befriended me. I was so thankful that someone was willing to be my friend. I think he was intrigued by my situation, my accent. Leonard took it upon himself to teach me more English and encouraged me not to be intimidated by the bullies. He waited for me in the mornings on 40th and Federal and then waited for me with a couple of his friends outside the school for the walk home.

At home, things were getting better. My dad was getting used to cleaning other people's messes for a living. And my mom, with the help of Bambina Iannacito, a delightful caring soul who was one of the earlier immigrants from our village, landed a job at a laundry at 4100 Federal, called Colorado Cleaners. I would walk by that laundry every day and watch *Mamma* press clothing in a hot and sweaty small room. I wondered if that work was harder on her than cutting wheat on a hot summer day in the countryside of Pagliarone. Bambina would usually hand me a dime and with a sweet smile, told me to buy a candy at Luban's Drug.

In the meantime, my brother had written a letter informing us that he was finalizing plans to join us in America in December of that unforgettable year of 1966. I was beginning to feel mad at myself for not having the same drive to excel in school and in life in general, as I had done back home in Italy. There was nothing for me to work hard for. I was not happy to be in America, I wanted to go back home. I was going through the motions of life without any direction. I was confused about everything that was happening to me. I did not know how much more of the daily bullying and ridiculing I could take.

I loved sports, athletics, but the thought of going to gym class made me very anxious and distressed. I lacked skills in most of the exercises that we were put through. I had never seen the apparatus used for those drills. I was forced to get on a trampoline, feeling scared and apprehensive.

I had difficulty jumping up-and-down and the other boys seemed to enjoy my failures.

I will always remember the day that life changed for me in America. It was just another difficult day at school. On this late fall day we went outside where a running track had been prepared. With my skinny, wiry body and endless soccer games, I could run. I ran faster, longer. I won a race. I beat the boy who slapped me with his towel. He was upset, others were upset, and some were impressed. I now worried that some of the bullies would come after me for beating them at the age-old sport of running. The positives outweighed the negatives and overall I was happy and energized.

Standing in front of my locker changing into my clothes, I felt someone behind me and some of the boys started gathering around. As I turned I saw the blond-headed boy, holding his towel with both hands, suddenly snapping it towards my butt. I noticed his smirk as I felt the sting. I also felt an enormous amount of anger flow through my body. I tightened up, recoiled, and with adrenaline flowing in my veins, I clenched my fists tightly, I turned, and with all the power I could muster, I punched the boy in the face, striking his left eye. He went sprawling to the ground, dazed and in pain. I also felt tremendous pain in my hand.

Almost all the boys had gathered, summoning the gym teacher. The teacher instantly started yelling at me as he helped the boy up. Were those tears I saw? Mr. Tough Guy was crying in pain, in embarrassment. The teacher barked at all the other students to go back to their lockers. "Why did you punch him?" he snapped. I told him he hit me with his wet towel, and I turned to show him my red behind. "Come with me, you're going to the principal's office." And pointing to the injured boy he said, "And you go to the nurse."

I hardly understood what he was screaming about, but the story was recounted to me by another boy the following school year when my English had improved. At the time I explained as best as I could about the continual bullying from that boy and many others. I believe I was scolded for fighting because that is not allowed in American schools. But bullying was okay? Something was said about being expelled, records, and if I do it again I will be kicked out, and so on. I was finally allowed to go back to my class.

Then at recess something very odd happened. A Hispanic boy actually came up to me and asked if I wanted to play baseball with them. He caught me by surprise but I accepted the invite. A couple of problems prevented my full participation: I had never played baseball in my life and my right hand was swollen, so I could hardly grip the bat. But they did not laugh at me. Instead, they tried to teach me how to play baseball. Things were changing; they were beginning to accept me, sort of.

I did not see the towel snapper for the rest of that day. I was told that he was sent home. The next day I saw him, everyone saw him, and I could not believe my eyes. His eye was closed shut and it had a red and purple ring around it. My hand was swollen and it hurt, but I think he got the worst of it. The bully never touched me again. I suspect he was told by someone with authority not to bother me anymore. As the school year went along he actually became a friend and the other kids backed off a little, but not completely. My accent and demeanor were too enticing not to be picked on.

As December approached, I was getting excited because soon my older brother, Ezio, would be coming to Denver. He was coming with another family, Ninetta Lombardi and her three kids, Salvatore, Fernando, and Elsa. They would travel to Denver on an airplane. We were officially the last of the families from Villa San Michele to immigrate to the United States by ship.

I also was getting a good grasp of the English language, and my parents even bought me some new clothes from a huge store called K-Mart. I was starting to assimilate into the great melting pot of the United States of America.

On December 12, 1966 we, along with the rest of the close-knit immigrant families of Pagliarone, went to the airport to greet my brother and the other family. We were loud. We wore our emotions on our sleeves as we crowded around the exit tunnel. TWA Airline agents asked, demanded that we move back, but we looked at them like we did not understand what in the hell they were saying... and some of us didn't! We just ignored them. As the new immigrants walked out of the tunnel, they were mobbed by the throng of a screaming, cheering Italian welcome wagon. *Mamma* was crying, arms up in the air as her eldest son, confused and tired, appeared. "*Maria mea come shta,*" asking him how her daughter, Maria, was doing, and then her crying got louder as she mourned the death of her mom. The questions were endless. It would be many years before my mom would see her family in Italy again, and some she would never see again. *Com'è brutta la lontananza*, How awful it is to live so far away from your family, was a constant complaint.

We were happy to have Ezio with us. I felt a bit of comfort in knowing that now I could call on him if I got in trouble. But then I thought of Italy when I would get into fights with other kids and my brother was nowhere to be found. He was working the land and tending to our animals. Things would be the same in America. A few days after his arrival, when the Christmas and New Year holidays had gone, my brother wanted to find work. He was willing to do anything "*peh vadagnià la yurnuata,*" *per guadagnare la giornata*, to earn a day's work. My dad's friend, Michele Carmosino, known or referred to as *Michele di Linzitto*, a family name reference, was nice enough to convince his employer to hire Ezio at the large bakery on 27th Avenue, near Decatur Street.

Michele's wife, Giuseppina, was instrumental in helping my mom with a woman's adjustments to this country. They had been childhood friends from their little hamlet of Trebbante. They renewed their friendship and became very close, and "*semme pure parente,*" *siamo anche parenti*, we are even related, they would always say to whoever would listen.

Michele Carmosino and Giuseppina Carmosino with their 3 sons Robert, Joseph and little Vince, circa 1957

I remember my brother waking up very early in the morning, waiting for Michele to pick him up to go to work. He slept on a single bed in our small living room, I on a sofa, and my mom and dad in the only bedroom of the tiny duplex. Every little noise we made, we got yelled at by the mother and daughter owners who lived below us. They were not very happy when they learned that my brother had moved in with us. Every once in a while they would go on a screaming rampage, fueled by the whiskey in their system.

A few months passed and my brother wanted to get a car and a driver's license. He could not read, write, or understand English. How could he possibly pass the driving test? I recall an Italian-American man who worked at the driver's license office on 6th Avenue, near Denver General Hospital. My father gave the licensing clerk a brown paper sack with a gallon of wine and also handed him something else, a tip, for his help! The clerk assisted my brother with the test and soon after, we walked out of there with a driver's license in my brother's name. It was another step towards assimilation and freedom for our family.

Salvatore (Sam) Lombardi and his wife, Bonina, took us back to our apartment and promised to help us look for a used car. One of the very nicest early immigrant couples, Sam and Bonina lived on 38th Avenue, east of Tejon Street. Whenever I drive by there, their image comes to mind. They had two sons, Victor and Sam, and a daughter, Lucille. Sam and Bonina were very helpful to us and to the rest of the later immigrants. Sam would be there for us again to take my father and me to the driver's license office to help me with my driving test.

Salvatore and Bonina Lombardi, circa 1960s

My brother got a car, but even I realized that maybe he should not be driving until he could at least read road signs! Ezio was now able to go to work by himself. One morning he overslept. I remember him jumping out of bed, dressing quickly, cussing, and dashing out the door. When he came home he complained about the supervisor yelling at him, throwing stuff around, and probably saying that he had given the immigrant a chance. *"Ma kaer si ditt?"* *Che cosa gli hai detto?* And what did you tell him? We all wanted to know. He realized that the boss was very upset that he was a couple of hours late for work, but Ezio just did not know how to say that he overslept. Suddenly, as he looked down in shame, he saw his watch. Pointing to it frantically, Ezio kept saying "no drrrrr, no drrrrr, no drrrrr." That was the best he could do to let the supervisor know that the alarm clock did not go off.

My brother's arrival pretty much made our journey to America permanent. He was willing to work, to do whatever he could to make our new life in America fruitful. My parents became good friends with John and Anna Lombardi. We were related. Of course all the Lombardi, Carmosino, Iacovetta (Yacovetta), Iannacito (Cito), Melaragno (Meloragno), Onorato, Rotolo (Rotola), Capobianco, Ciotola, Falasco, Mazzocco (Matz), and Milano families who lived in the Denver area were in some way related. Their families had come to Pagliarone from Forli di Sanno, Roccasicura, and other neighboring towns. And many would be on the move again, this time not across the valley but across the ocean to America: the United States, Canada, Argentina, and other parts of Europe. They left their tiny village that was nestled in a remote valley of the Apennine Mountains of south central Italy for new and hopefully better lives abroad.

John's father, Carmine, knew the bartender at the Marigold, a bar on 40th and Tejon Street. The bartender's name was Nick Fiorella. Nick's family had owned the bar but had sold it to a man named Jim Tunstead, whose mother was an Italian-American. I've always found that Italian-Americans with non-Italian last names are those who will advertise and work hard at holding onto our traditions more than Italian-Americans with Italian last names. Even if some have a very small percentage of Italian lineage, they want the world to know that they are part Italian.

Mr. Tunstead gladly hired us and treated us very nicely. He continually wanted to know about Italy and its people. He also brought my brother and me to watch midget car races at Lakeside Race Track, where he raced his own midget car that he kept in a garage behind the bar. At about midnight every night, my father and brother would go to the bar and stay all night. Many nights I accompanied them, cleaning the place until 7:00 a.m. when Nick would come in and let us out. I would try to sleep on a booth seat but usually was up all night, buzzing from overdosing on a variety of cold soft drinks, candy, and gum!

My brother would take me directly from the bar to school where I struggled to stay awake. Eventually I would dose off at my desk, another reason to be made fun of. Finally my homeroom teacher in typing class asked me to bring one of my parents to school to talk about my sleeping issues. I kept making excuses and they kept asking why I could not keep my eyes open. My parents never went to Skinner, and I never told anyone at school that at the age of fourteen I was a night janitor at a bar. I am sure if I informed my parents that I occasionally fell asleep in class, they would have barred me from accompanying my brother at our night cleaning job. They wanted me to get an education.

We endured the nagging landlords as best we could. They were not happy that four people were living in a small one-bedroom apartment. They would continually bang on the ceiling every time we made a little noise. My parents performed many menial jobs for them in hopes of deflecting the continual harassment. But finally we had had enough and began looking for a new place to live. In Italy we had lived in the same house for many years, a house where my father was born and where his father was born. And now in America, in less than a year we had lived in three different places.

My brother, Ezio, reconnected with some of his childhood friends: Tony Carmosino (son of Nicola and Elia Carmosino) and Robert and Joe Carmosino (sons of Michele and Giuseppina Carmosino). His friends helped him get acclimated to life in America. I recall those guys picking him up and taking him out on the town. And I struggled on with the pursuit of fitting in. I had a few friends but usually hung around with my cousin, Terenzio, and brothers Salvatore and Fernando Lombardi, also new immigrants. Later, Antonio and Carlo Lombardi di Nicola (Nicola's sons) and Sandro Lombardi would join our close-knit group.

As I attempted to fit in, another curve was suddenly thrown my way. There was a TV series in the 1960s called *The Addams Family*, a sitcom about an eccentric, wealthy family with a bizarre and creepy lifestyle. The cast included a tall butler named Lurch, dressed in a dark suit with a white shirt and a black bow tie. Lurch's blond hair was combed forward and a dark unibrow adorned his Frankenstein-like face without the scars. He hardly spoke and when he did it was sort of inaudible. A picture of me sat on my mom's dresser for years. I avoided looking at it because it brought back painful memories. In the picture I have on a dark blue jacket with a white shirt and a black bow tie. My hair is blond, combed forward, and my eyebrows are dark and thick, a dead ringer of a Lurch mini-me!

A girl, who was also an immigrant, noticed my resemblance and as kids often do, started to refer to me as Lurch. I wished she would have kept that to herself because it spread like wildfire and girls and boys alike started pointing at me and calling me Lurch. I did not have any idea what they were talking about. From that day on some kids did not refer to me by Tony or even the difficult Pietrantonio, they called me Lurch! I eventually saw an episode of *The Addams Family*. I was heartbroken that now people thought of me as this homely, dumb butler. I had to endure that label for a couple of years, even though I started to comb my hair differently and plucked the center of my unibrow to have two, though still thick, eyebrows.

As I write this in June of 2012, I am watching a news report of some middle school boys bullying an elderly woman who was working as a

A young Lurch? 1967

monitor on their school bus. These boys made fun of her weight and looks. They were relentless in their abuse. I thought about those boys. Were they that vicious or just caught up in a moment of disdain?

Young teenagers can be very vulgar in some situations, but they are not necessarily that way in their everyday lives at home. The girl who pinned that name on me was generally nice, and later she probably regretted giving me that Lurch label. I must admit that I was upset at her for doing that to me but eventually I forgave her. She was just being a teenager, looking for attention, wanting to fit in. She is a friend to this day, although when I see her I immediately think of Lurch!

My parents were unaware of all my struggles. I did not want them to know. And if they knew, it probably would not have mattered much. They certainly would not think of coming to school to complain to school officials.

One day, I was coming in from outside during gym class. While running across the basketball court I grabbed a ball that a student was shooting layups with and shot it at the basket across the way, as I kept running towards the locker room. Suddenly I was on the floor, dazed. The kid who was shooting the layups came up behind me and punched me in the right temple. I got up and tried to fight back, but was disoriented. Some kids came to my rescue. I noticed that the bigger, taller kid seemed sorry that he punched me, but he probably would not have punched anyone else in the class. I had disrupted a layup contest and that was reason enough to punch the little wop[8].

---

[8] *One of the derogatory slang terms for Italians was 'wop.' It was an acronym for 'without papers.' The term came into use in the 1920s at the height of Italian immigration, as many Italians came to the U.S. illegally and undocumented.*

Participation in class discussions became almost non-existent for me. I usually knew the answers to questions and could have contributed to discussions posed by the teachers, but became very hesitant to raise my hand because of the other phenomenon that had developed at Skinner, the mocking of my accent. Even the teachers chuckled at the way I sometime pronounced words. I just could not deal with the laughing by my classmates as I spoke. I just made the decision not to talk anymore. At times the jokesters would force me to say a word just so they could laugh at me. Instead of 'three' I would say, "tree," "I am" instead of 'I have,' "where" instead of 'were,' or I would write 'butt' instead of 'but,' and so on.

Despite the myriad of obstacles, I managed to keep up with schoolwork – not the straight A's (10's) I was accustomed to in Italy, but acceptable for the Denver Public School system. The consequences for not studying and working hard here were much more relaxed than those which I was familiar with in an Italian monastery. There, if you did not learn what was expected in a grade, then you repeated that grade. Not so, here. Oral exams were almost nonexistent, where in Italy they were compulsory. But armed with the education I had received in Italy, I held my own. My parents surely thought that I excelled in school, as I did in Italy. They had no idea and I concealed from them most of my struggles at school and other social settings in America. I had not touched a soccer ball for months and no one seemed to care.

Celebrating my brother's 23rd birthday with family and friends. Ezio and I are standing, while Elsa Lombardi is sitting next to my mom and dad. June 1967

Chapter XXXIX

Calcio · Soccer

During recess at Skinner I would just watch as other kids played basketball, football, and baseball. Girls kept hitting a ball tied to a rope around a pole or jumped from one square to another. All were games I had never seen before and had no idea of their rules and purpose, but worst of all I had no idea how to play them. The two games I excelled in, *calcio*, soccer, and *bigliardino*, foosball, were missing here.

Bored, with nothing to do at recess one fall day, I saw a football on the ground and started to kick it around. Then I started to kick it up in the air, each time higher, trapping it with the bottom of my foot when it came down. Most kids did not seem impressed and were busy with their own sport games — except for one kid, whom I had seen in school but did not know his name. He wandered near and asked me if I knew how to play soccer. I had never heard that word soccer before or if I did, I probably had forgotten it. *Calcio* I understood as football, the only word that I knew for the sport I loved. Later I would understand that here the term football referred to the American gridiron sport of football. The word soccer came from England. The word was derived from 'soc' from the official name of the sport "association football", the suffix '-er' added to it. Adding the '-er' to various words created slang words that were prevalent at Oxford University starting in 1875, soc-er. The word gained popularity in the United States to distinguish the sport from American football. Apparently the English did away with term because it had become too "American".

The kid at school was a German-American boy whose name was Walter Pressnitz. (Unfortunately, he died on a soccer field many years later of a massive heart attack; he was only in his late thirties.) Walter suddenly showed interest in me and mentioned that he played soccer on a team and that I should come to a practice. I informed him as best I could that I did not have a way to get there since my parents did not drive and if they did, they would not know where to go. And even if they knew where to go, they would not take me anyway! The boy did not give up. He kept asking me to come to a practice. After continual begging on my part, my parents eventually agreed to let me go. One afternoon after school, a team parent picked me up at home. I have no idea where we went, but when we got there I was ecstatic to see soccer balls everywhere. Two men came and introduced themselves, John Ziel and John Wittek. They were the coaches. I was a little rusty but after a few practices I was ready to play.

I played right wing for the Denver Kickers, a club made up of mostly German-American boys. Members of that team treated me like a king, picking me up for practices and games. They would take me to a club, the Denver Turnverein, on 16th and Clarkson, and feed me and let me play as much foosball as I wanted. They became my second family. I made new friends. They did not make fun of my accent or my culture. The coaches were serious but nice. The parents of the other players, mostly German-Americans, were also very nice to me. I am sure they wondered why my parents were never at any of the games but many of them, being immigrants themselves, probably understood the arrangement of priorities of recent immigrants.

Both my mother and father worked on Saturdays. And if they didn't work, I doubt they would have come to watch me. They basically thought of soccer as a waste of time. My mom worried about the likelihood of me injuring myself. My brother was immersed in working as hard and as long as possible. His thrill came

The original junior team, 1966 (courtesy of John Ziel)

from getting a bigger paycheck. My thrill came from making a great pass or scoring a goal! I loved soccer and he loved working.

Playing soccer with the Kickers was the only fun for me. After a championship game in the fall of 1967 — which we tied but then lost in the tiebreaker that gave the win to the team with the most corner kicks — the coach, John Ziel, singled me out as having a promising future in soccer. He said my endless energy, grit, and great feel for the game were refreshing. I will never, ever forget those comments because they came at a time in my young life when I was often ridiculed in school and on the streets, and those positive comments helped me keep my pride, my confidence above water, if just barely.

On April 13, 1968, the day before Easter, my soccer life would change forever. We were playing on a field at the military installation of Fort Logan in southwest Denver. I was the right winger and exploiting the other team's left fullback, a Hispanic boy, much bigger than I, a bit overweight, and not very agile. He was probably new to the game. I was moving the ball down the right flank. The fullback came up on me and as I dribbled past him, he attempted to kick the ball away from me. I made a move with the ball to go past him and as I pulled the ball back I felt the pain, I heard the snap; everybody on and off the field heard the loud snap. Roland Lux, our goalie, and Gabe Weissbeck and Bob Ohle, our fullbacks, mentioned that they heard it all the way at the other end of the field. It sounded like a tree limb being snapped in half.

The injury happened as I dribbled the ball away with my right foot, placing my foot where the ball had been. All the opposing player could attempt to do was kick the ball away. With a running start, he swung his leg and his shoe met my leg directly, snapping and breaking both my fibula and tibia, halfway between my knee and my ankle.

I lay on the field in great pain, crying — loudly crying! I knew that my leg was in bad shape when I looked down. The coaches tried to help me, but I could see my leg was lying sideways. "It's broken," was repeated by all. Eventually I was taken to St. Anthony Hospital. Before anything could be done, my parents needed to sign the consent form to treat my injury. My German caretakers called and went to pick them up from my house at 4520 Wyandot Street. By then the whole team had made their way to the hospital. They probably couldn't wait for my parents to get there so my mood would improve.

I was in pain and scared, not only about what had happened to my leg, but about what my parents, my dad in particular, would do to me. As they walked in, my dad was many paces ahead of my mom. I immediately knew I was in for a lashing when he brought his hand to his mouth and bit it. I knew the gesture. It meant I was in big, big trouble. I prayed that he would not embarrass me too much. He began yelling at me, at the coaches, at the parents, at the other players. He kept reminding me of how many times he had told me not to play that stupid game. The Germans, young and old, were surprised and confused by my father's reaction. He became even more upset when he was told that both bones in my right leg, the fibula and tibia, had snapped in half. If only I had been wearing shin guards, but what were they? They existed, but I never saw any and surely they were not required by rule, as they presently are.

I would need a full leg cast and would be on crutches for at least three months. I could not go to school and did schoolwork from home. I also could not help out with our night cleaning job. Some of the parents on the soccer team picked me up to take me to the doctor appointments and were generally very accommodating and concerned. If I had to take a taxi to the appointments or if my family encountered charges for any medical need, the German club paid for it. But unfortunately, either the doctor did not care or he did not realize that I was growing rapidly. He should have changed the full leg cast a few times to allow my right leg to grow.

My cast came off in June and a couple of days later my mother and I boarded a plane for Toronto, Canada to visit my sister, Maria, and her young family. The trip had been planned and my mother counted the days until she could see her daughter and her first baby granddaughter. With one crutch in hand I boarded a United Airlines plane. It would be the first time for both of us on a plane. In Chicago we had to change planes and had to hustle to the gate. Hobbling through Chicago O'Hare airport, we finally made it to the gate. I sat down in a chair and suddenly became ill. I began to sweat and shake, feeling like I was going to vomit. I panicked, my mom panicked. An airline representative saw my mom with that look of concern that only a mother can have. The representative came over to assist, while another one brought me some water. After a while I began to feel better and was allowed to board the plane. My right leg was sore and weak and not well enough to travel.

Later that year when I was experiencing back and hip problems, it was discovered that my right leg was more than one-half inch shorter than my left and was still visibly smaller than my left leg. A shoe lift seemed to alleviate the problem, but that problem would hound me for the rest of my life. The doctor had also failed to inform me about rehabilitating my leg with therapy and exercises. With a slight limp I tried to play on my team that fall. Of course my parents were livid with me but I begged and begged and they finally gave in to my pleas, but warned me not to get hurt again. I was much slower and more hesitant, with less power. Actually I was scared to death to make any type of contact, worrying about getting injured again, worrying about what my dad would do to me if I hurt myself. I kept reminding myself that with time I would be my old self again. I kept going to practice and the coaches hoped that I would eventually return to my old form.

In the meantime, I had introduced my cousin, Terenzio, and other immigrant friends, Salvatore, Fernando, and Sandro Lombardi to the team. One afternoon Salvatore, Fernando, and I were going to soccer practice at 26th and Clay Street in northwest Denver. The three of us got on my bike, with me pedaling, Fernando on the handlebars, and Salvatore on the seat. We took turns pedaling. It was a struggle but we were close to our destination. As we coasted down Clay Street on 33rd Avenue my vision was obstructed by Fernando on the handlebars. I did not see the red and white '57 Chevy coasting down the street and then stopping. We picked up speed going down the incline as Fernando warned me to brake. But it was too late. I slammed into the back of the car. Fernando ended up on the trunk of the car, Salvatore somehow fell on the ground by the bike, and I went airborne and flew over the car, slamming my face on the asphalt.

The driver got out of the car in a panic. I recognized the young man, who had some sort of physical handicap. He lived in the neighborhood. He was visually upset and when he took a look at me, he started to scream and convulse. My bloodied face must have scared the hell out of him, as it did Fernando and Salvatore. I could not see my face but from the reaction of the bystanders I knew it was bad, it felt bad. One side of my face was raw and bloodied. I did not even feel the pain in my badly scraped leg. Scared and in pain, the three of us limped back to our homes before the police or ambulance showed up. I endured the look of utter panic and concern on my mom's face and the yelling from my dad as he treated my badly scraped face. I sported a huge scab on my face for weeks, fueling more staring and bullying.

I reluctantly decided to stop playing soccer after a game during which an opposing player slide tackled me, sending shooting pains up that right leg. My parents would surely kill me if I broke it again. Sadly, I walked away from the sport that I loved so much and did not play organized soccer again until college. My coaches and teammates were as upset and disappointed as I was. Not only was I walking away from soccer, but also from many great friends who had made it easier for me to accept some of the miseries that America had tossed my way. I can truly say that if I had not hooked up with that German-American club, I would have surely convinced my parents to go back to our Italy.

There is always a discussion with my friends about the sport of soccer and its lack of popularity in the United States. Why did a country with so many immigrants not embrace the game? The early immigrants, mostly poor and from small remote villages, probably never saw a soccer ball, much less played the game. As soon as they were able, they were put to work in the fields or to look after farm animals.

Although some form of the game of soccer was evident during the Renaissance (1300-1600), the modern version was introduced to Italy by English sailors in the northern port city of Genoa in the late 1800s. By the early 1900s the game was being played in northern Italy, and clubs were established such as Juventus, Milan, etc. It was nonexistent in the south, especially in the remote towns. The only sports the early Italian immigrants knew and played were those that they were introduced to in America: baseball, football, and basketball.

As *calcio*, literally meaning 'kick' in Italian, became more popular — especially with the introduction of television — the rest of Italy became familiar with it and the young children began to play it. The sport's popularity soared and spread throughout Italy and Europe like wildfire.

Only some of the immigrants of the 1940s and later had played soccer when they arrived in the United States. And although there were some soccer leagues in America, the game was confined and eventually immigrants steered towards the more popular American games. Soccer did not have a chance with sports like baseball and football, in which Italian-Americans participated and some excelled. My sport heroes in

Italy were athletes like Sandro Mazzola, Gianni Rivera, and Giacinto Facchetti — very famous in Italy but virtual unknowns in America. The heroes of Italian-Americans were Joe DiMaggio, Yogi Berra, and Vince Lombardi, all foreign to me and most Italians.

In 1972 I met Joe Asciutto. He was the accountant for Arnie Lombardi, my boss and mentor, and the owner of Cosmopolitan Upholstery Company. Mr. Asciutto was also the president of the Sons of Italy Lodge in Denver. When I mentioned to him that I wished there were Italian-Americans who played soccer, he invited me and some of my friends to be his guests at a Sons of Italy monthly meeting at Potenza Lodge on 38th and Shoshone. We met many Italian-Americans at the meeting, including three of the club's members: Luciano Busnardo, Mario Del Piccolo, and Gianfranco Marcantonio, who were avid soccer players. They wanted to put together a Sons of Italy soccer team.

Not only did we forge new friendships, we enjoyed many years of organized club soccer. As years went by and we got older, new younger players joined the team and kept the OSIA (Order Sons of Italy in America) Eagles going in the top amateur league in Colorado. But we wanted to keep playing at some level, so we organized a new team and played in the Mile High Soccer League. That team was sponsored by the Saint Anthony Society of Denver. We played for Saint Anthony's teams for many seasons and competed for and won the league championship many times. But it was always a challenge to keep the team together. There were some hotheads on the team and subsequently this issue caused the team to break up. Soon after, a new team was formed and it was sponsored by Joe Shutto's Miller Super grocery stores. My best memories of that team are that I was able to recruit players who had never played soccer before. Most notable were Louie Lombardi and Angelo Capobianco.

In the 1980s and 90s my soccer life also included coaching, helping other coaches, and taxiing kids, including my own children, to and from soccer games. I was elated when my son's competitive soccer team became part of the Denver Kickers' youth soccer program. Unfortunately the memory that comes to mind when I drive by the beautiful Kickers' club in Golden on a daily basis, is the tragic soccer game in which a sixteen-year-old went up for a header during a game, fell to the ground, and never stood up again. An undetected heart ailment took the young life of Jason Santorno on that

Many guys played for Saint Anthony Society soccer and we won many league championships.
From top left: John Lombardi, Michele Vitale, Marc Moscoso, ?, Antonio Lombardi, Ray ?, ?
Moe ?, Brian Moscoso. Bottom left: ?, Angelo Capobianco, Chad Knudson, Anthony Lombardi,
Walter Weryk, Andrezej Strzeszewski. Circa 1985
Longtime players missing from picture but members of team: Sandro Lombardi, George Lombardi,
Fred Lombardi, Raffaele Vitale, John Vitale, Mario Del Picccolo, Luciano Busnardo, Lou
Busnardo, Gianfranco Marcantonio, Louie Lombardi, Benito and Armando Sarlo, Terry Lombardi

Celebrating one of the many league championship trophies with Louie Lombardi and our team manager, Arnie Lombardi, circa 1980

spring morning of 1995. A couple of weeks later his mom, Carla, attended one of the Kickers' games. As I tried to console her about the loss of her son, she said that she wished she had just one more day, just one more day. She wanted to hold him, to tell him so many things. "All I want is just one more day," she kept repeating as she cried.

While playing indoor soccer I broke my toe, again! Of course my grandsons wanted to know all about it. They are questioning machines!

I recounted some of my soccer injuries, of which I have had many. I

Holy Family grade school soccer team, 1982. From top left: 19 Leaf Igo, 32 Andy Lindahl, 18 Bobby?
Livingston, 22 John Belfiore, Assistant Coach Mr. Livingston, 21 Nat Green, 36 Daryl Berg, goalie
Karl Politzki, 39 Brian Rasmussen, 33 Joey Hein, Coach Anthony Lombardi. Bottom left: 11 Marco
Carmosino, 24 Cain Politzki, 20 Carlos ?, 3 Adelio Lombardi, 2 Bobby Widhelm, 5 Jason Hart

1994 Denver Kickers under-16 A team. Top left: Anthony Lombardi, ?, Caine, Jeff Miller, Ryan Cook,
Bubba Davis, Nick Singleton, Jason Santorno, Mark Wolf, coach Pete Ramirez. Bottom row, from left: Pete
Ramirez, Matt Christensen, Mike Gonzales, Dominic Lombardi, Brad Palik, Paul Wehde, Maurice Yang

thought about all the broken bones, sprained ankles, and torn muscles. Twice I broke my nose: once from an elbow as I climbed over an opponent's back for a header and once from a head-butt as I got into an opponent's face. Both were the result of, from my wife's point of view, my over-aggression!

Two of those numerous injuries come to mind that are sort of funny now, but weren't so funny then, especially for my wife, Jackie. When our son was delivered by a Cesarean section, the doctor, Mario Coringrato, came into the room and congratulated us on our beautiful, healthy baby boy. He also informed us that we were extremely fortunate to have this baby because his mother's uterus was paper thin and could have ruptured, putting mother and baby at risk. He was blunt and informed us that both mother and baby could have died. He also made it clear to us that another pregnancy was absolutely out of the question and steps needed to be taken to avoid it.

I noticed my wife in bed, fresh out of a Cesarean delivery, with tears in her eyes. I certainly did not want her to go through any other procedure that the doctor might present to us. I immediately told the doctor that I would have a vasectomy. He quickly told me that that was not an option. He went on to bluntly give us scenarios as to why, including the event of a divorce! The only option was a tubal ligation procedure. He then informed us that since St. Anthony Hospital was a Catholic institution, the procedure was not allowed! He instructed us that when able, my wife should have the procedure done at Lutheran Hospital in Wheat Ridge.

On the Friday of Memorial Day weekend of 1979, my wife had her tubes tied and hopes of another child were gone forever. That Saturday I took my eighteen-month-old daughter and three-month-old son to my parents' house because my team was playing in a soccer tournament. My wife was told to rest in bed for at least a couple of days. At the soccer tournament I was kicked in my leg just below the knee, causing a bruise and swelling that sent me to the emergency room! There was a broken blood vessel and to relieve pain and pressure, I was prescribed bed rest and to keep my leg elevated above my heart. The look on my wife's face when I limped into our bedroom and hesitantly informed her to move over because I needed to keep my leg elevated for a couple of days, was one for the ages!

One hot, dry, fall Sunday afternoon, while playing soccer and going for a slide tackle, a 200 and something-pound opposing player slammed on top of me causing excruciating pain in my right shoulder. After a few minutes when the pain seemed to subside a little, we wrapped the shoulder and I went back out on the field. When I went up for a header and when my feet hit the ground, I felt an even more extreme pain in my shoulder. Emergency room! Prognosis: broken and separated shoulder. Treatment: wear a sling for six weeks! I had started my own upholstery business with employees totaling one – me! Six weeks of not being able to use my right hand meant disaster.

I had carpooled with friends, fellow coaches, and soccer players Pete Ramirez and Mark Wehde. On the way home I knew I was in deep crap because I was supposed to get home to attend my daughter's first piano recital that afternoon. Instead I spent that time in an emergency room. When we got home I begged my two friends to come in for a beer, hoping to minimize the wrath from my wife. When she opened the door and noticed the shoulder sling — and already upset with me for missing the recital — she shouted, "If you don't quit playing that f***ing game, I am going to divorce you." My friends in unison said that they would pass on the beer! My wife hasn't divorced me and I haven't quit playing the game. After one week of trying to use my right hand while wearing the sling, I removed it and toughed it out.

Of all the injuries that I suffered, that my teammates experienced, and opponents endured, one comes to mind as being the most dreadful. It did not happen to a player but to a young spectator. On a warm, spring Sunday afternoon, members of our team, along with wives and kids, were waiting for another soccer game to end. We mingled with other spectators. We had played soccer against the same teams for many spring and fall seasons, so we sort of became acquaintances with most players and their families.

That particular day some members of our soccer team were lying around trying to catch up on their sleep, as we pulled an all-nighter of poker and *tresette* card games. We normally played the addicting games on Saturday nights during the summer and winter, but foolishly we had played the night before a soccer game. At five that morning, one of us was making a run to 7-Eleven, not for coffee to help us stay awake but for another pack of cigarettes!

We were all pretty exhausted and weary of hearing some of the guys exaggerate their winnings or losses from the card games! As game time neared, a truck pulled into the parking lot and a familiar player from the opposing team got out with his constant friend, a German shepherd dog. As usual he tied the dog to a tree, behind but fairly near all the spectators, and prepared himself for the game.

We had seen a young mother with her two-year-old son numerous times before, as she usually watched her husband play goalie while keeping an eye on her wondering young son at the same time. The little boy inched closer to the dog and we all heard the mother ask its owner if the dog was good with kids. The owner answered that the dog was kid friendly.

The first soccer game was about to end, but was very intense and all eyes were on the game. We suddenly heard a muffled bark that was followed by a scream. I will never forget the little boy's cheek and one eye barely hanging from his face. All of our shrieks were drowned out by a scream that only a mother could make as she ran to her wailing baby. The father raced from the goalie box to the aid of his family and without hesitation, grabbed his little boy and raced as fast as his legs would allow across the street to a Denver firehouse to seek help.

The dog's owner seemed to be in shock. Some people consoled him, while others yelled at him for having his dog at the game. My wife and I ran to our four-year-old son and five-year-old daughter as they played with other children not far from the incident. Thankfully they did not witness the dog biting the little boy's face, but unfortunately Adelio our 9 year old nephew witnessed the tragedy.

As we reluctantly went back to playing our game, we saw an ambulance taking the young family away to a hospital. And at that next Sunday's game, we learned that doctors were able to save the little boy's eye and stitch his cheek back to his face. My wife had been bitten by a dog as a young girl and was scared of them. That unfortunate incident made her even more terrified of most dogs.

Presently I get my soccer fix playing indoors with old and new friends, and playing outdoors on Sundays in an over-60 league. As I limp around and move gingerly with my sixty-plus-year-old body, my wife suggests that maybe I should give up the sport; that I retire from the sport that she claims I sometimes play as if I am getting paid. I use the "it's great for cardio" excuse. She mentions that I should stick with the games that people my age play, like *morra* and *bocce*! But I have decided that as long as I can compete I will keep playing, keep enjoying the sport I love, even at the risk of injuries.

While playing at the beautiful Kickers' field in Golden, Colorado with the over-60 team, John Ziel, Gabe Weissbeck, and

Anthony Lombardi, Gabe Weissbeck, John Ziel, Rolund Lux, 2015

Rolund Lux relived some of the memories of some fifty years earlier. John reminded me that he gave me the nickname, "The Blond Italian," as some people assumed that I was a German immigrant!

Some fifty years later I rejoined the Kickers on their inaugural over–60 soccer league team. From top left: Ata Katebini, John Malcut, Mansour Rasi, Erich Dietrich, Abbas Poursadigh, Sal McNally, Klaus Degler, Steve Davis, Greg Letham, Phil Griffin, Hossein Kazemi, Craig Robb. Bottom left: Jerry O'Grady, David Frankland, Arlie Rinehart, Jorge Nasta, Phil Coffman, Don Pillar, Don Bove, Anthony Lombardi, Scott Byker, and John McGee

My wife and I have given up whatever Saturdays might have had in store for us to spend most of our time watching our grandchildren play and learn the game. On any given Saturday we see many of our friends cheering for their own grandchildren. Some of us are reliving our soccer past through them. And some of us wish, hope, and dream that maybe someday some of them, even one of them will play at a high level; and we all pray that hopefully we are around to watch them achieve those and all other goals in their lives.

Chapter XL

MORRA

During one of the trips we made with my mom's cousin, Pasky Lombardi, when he would come and get my father and me to go do some sort of work at his motel in Federal Heights, I recall him telling my dad about a *morra* group that played weekends in some north Denver bar. He asked my father if he played in Italy and if my dad wanted to go play with him. If I could read my father's mind, he was most likely thinking about whether or not he had made a mistake by coming to America, and playing *morra* was the last thing on his mind.

There wasn't an organized club but we did play *morra* in our village. Usually an impromptu game would take place in the cantina or in some *piazzetta*, small piazza. As young kids we would watch, learn, and play. I was a bit surprised that the game was alive and well here amongst the Italian-American community, whereas in our village it was losing popularity. I found that many other traditions were being held onto in America, where in Italy we were trying to forget them, lose them, which was also true of the many Italian dialects. There are so many immigrant traditions that were passed down to second and third generation Americans. Whenever we go back to our many Old Countries, we find that the modern residents have left the tradition, the folk song, or the game behind and have no idea what we're talking about!

For many years, Pagliarone immigrants organized yearly Fourth of July and Saint Anthony Society picnics, and invariably a *morra* game would emerge. As the men yelled at the top of their lungs, other park goers, startled by the screaming, would get a look of concern on their faces, probably thinking that a shouting match was taking place and surely fisticuffs would soon follow. Those Italian men seemed to be very angry, but it was just mock anger. Those men were playing *morra*.

The hand game dates back centuries. In the Bible it may have been referred to as "casting of lots." The game was evident in the Greek and Roman Empires. The Romans called it *micatio*, and playing it was referred to as *micare digitis*, literally meaning 'flashing of fingers.' Eventually the game came to be called *morra*, derived from the verb *micare*.

The game can be played by two or more players. Two players face each other with one arm above their head, their hand in a tight fist making sure that the opposing player does not get any early indication of how many fingers he will expose. They then simultaneously thrust that arm forward in front of them, opening their fist to expose from one to five fingers. At the same moment, both shout out a number from two to ten. If one of the players guesses the sum of the fingers exposed, that player is awarded a point. For example: One player shows or exposes two fingers and the other shows five fingers. One says *otto*, Italian for eight and the other says *sette*, Italian for seven. The player that barked out *sette* wins because two plus five equals seven. If both would have called out *sette*, then the game would go on until only one player predicted the correct sum. Games normally go up to fifteen points but it varies depending on the number of players.

The *Morra* Society of Denver is over seventy years old. Its fifty or so members meet every Friday night between November and May to play the game they grew up with, the game they love. They presently meet at Hyland Hills Golf Club in Ciancio's restaurant on 96th and Sheridan Boulevard. Usually ten teams made up of five players on each team play for various honors at season's end. The men all want to play well, want to win, but the night is about being together with friends. For me, lifelong friendships have been forged during the time I have been a member. The guys share a meal and refreshments together, pray for the sick and departed, and play *morra*! Many times a hat is passed around to collect money for some needy cause.

While the game is still played in many parts of Italy and variations of the game are played all around the world, it is losing the following it once had. Today, if you were to ask some young people in Italy if they know the

Members of the Denver Morra Society at their 2015 morra banquet (MorraSociety.com)

game of *morra*, they might just answer, "*Non lo so*," they would have no idea what you are talking about. And I suspect that if the young people of our Italian-American community don't embrace the game, it will eventually vanish. Some days I contemplate going around to all the elementary schools in the area and teaching the children how to play *morra*. It would teach them strategy, quick thinking and decision-making, composure, and of course addition to ten — in Italian!

Playing morra with my grandson Anthony, 2015

Here I am playing with my grandson Gianni, 2016

Chapter XLI

Bocce

Bocce is a fun game played for the most part on lawns or courts, although I have seen it played on a variety of fairly level surfaces. It's played on many different venues: beaches, baseball infields, gravel roads, dirt patches, carpets, and while on a Caribbean cruise it is played on the deck of a ship on a rubberized surface! It is played by both genders, by old and young.

Anywhere from two to eight players can play this fairly simple game. It requires a small ball, about one to two inches in diameter and usually white or yellow in color, called *il pallino*, literally meaning 'the small ball.' The *pallino* is thrown by a player from one team, followed up by the same player throwing a bigger ball of a different color, a *boccia* ball, about three to four inches in diameter, in an attempt to get the *boccia* ball as close to the *pallino* as possible. A member of the opposing team then throws his ball of a different color (*bocce* balls are usually, but not exclusively, green and red) in an attempt to land it closer to the *pallino* than his opponent's ball. Whichever team's ball lays closest to the *pallino* waits, while a player from the other team throws a *boccia* ball in an attempt to land it closer

bocce balls

to the *pallino*. If successful, the team originally closest can throw their remaining balls to earn back the position of the closest. This continues until all four balls from each team have been thrown. One to four points can be scored per frame, and there is one point for each ball closer to the *pallino* than the closest ball of the opposing team.

Normally a player can roll, lob, bounce, or bank a ball. An opponent's ball can also be hit to take away an opponent's point or points, or to make it easier for a teammate to get closer with his throw. Visual or mechanical measurements are made to determine which balls are closer. The team that reaches a predetermined point total, usually between twelve and twenty-one, wins the game. The game is also sometimes played under a time system.

Humans have been throwing objects at targets from the beginning of time. The Egyptians played a form of the game thousands of years ago. The Romans borrowed the game from the Greeks and eagerly began to play it. While on their numerous conquests, the legionaries played *bocce* with whatever they had that was somewhat round, such as coconuts, melons, or an orb of carved wood. As the Roman Empire faded, so did *bocce*, coming back through a revival after the Dark Ages.

The game's players would face many obstacles in the ensuing centuries. The Vatican condemned the game, claiming that it led to degenerate gambling. Many rulers followed suit, claiming that playing *bocce* had become too much of a distraction, that the working class was not being very productive because of the excessive time spent playing *bocce*. Only the nobility were allowed to play the popular game!

Fast-forward to the 1970s when the game was really starting to catch on worldwide, especially in America. Presently this leisurely, sometimes rowdy game is played in parks and backyards all over the world. Although it is called by many different names, the Italian name *bocce* is the most recognized.

World-famous people made *bocce* their favorite pastime: Hippocrates, Roman Emperor Augustus, Galileo, Leonardo da Vinci, Henry VIII, Queen Elizabeth I, and Giuseppe Garibaldi, to name a few. George Washington reportedly

Evidence of the game dates back to 5200 BC.

built a *bocce* court at his home in Mount Vernon in the 1780s. It is said that he was equally at home on the *bocce* court as he was on the battlefield!

During an interview, author John Grisham was asked what his Sundays were like. He responded that after church and brunch, he and his wife spent the afternoon playing *bocce* in their backyard.

The Pelè-Babe Ruth-Michael Jordan-Vince Lombardi of *bocce* was Italian Umberto Granaglia. He was named Player of the 20th Century. He won forty-six Italian and thirteen World *Bocce* Championships.

Pope John Paul II playing bocce, circa 1990s

As a kid growing up in Italy I did not play *bocce* much, since there were no *bocce* balls and no court. In July of 1975, a court was built in the village on the very spot where we played marbles as children. Looking out my kitchen window today I see the *bocce* court in my backyard. Surely some neighbors might think of it as a bit odd, and to others it might even seem bizarre!

Townspeople building the first bocce court in our village, 1975

One summer day a married couple who owned the lot next to ours was staring at our court and yard. The wife knocked on our door and initially asked about what we thought of the area and were we okay with the very Santa Fe-style home they were planning on building next door! Eventually the questions shifted to our backyard: What was the meaning of the statue of a monk (Saint Francis), the lions and the other statuaries, and also what was the rectangular, red gravel structure used for? Her probing questions were annoying me and I mumbled, "Và fà in culo," then I thought of giving her a bizarre answer like, "Have you ever heard of Opus Dei? Well, we are members of an even more controversial Catholic Order called Opus *Bocce*. At the end of each month, on the last Sabbath, after sunset, huge candles are lit and lined along the rectangular structure, the altar, and all the members disrobe and then throw heavy plastic balls at each

other as we confess the past month's sins away! And then we end the rite by cutting off the heads of a few chickens and drinking the blood, as the headless chickens stumble around the altar!" That's what I wanted to tell her, but of course I went on to describe our beloved game!

Villa San Michele's bocce court, photo taken 2015

Bocce for us is a game we love, a tradition that we cherish. It's who we are, what we do. For years a group gathered on the grounds of Columbian Grade School and later at Skinner Junior High School to play *bocce* and the Italian card game of *tresette*. Presently some of the same guys play on the *bocce* courts of Lombardi's Roman Gardens in Westminster Co. which is the present home of the declining Saint Anthony Society.

A few summers ago a group of friends decided to have what has come to be known as "The Summer *Bocce* Tour." Every other Friday night during the summer we gather at a member's house for refreshments, an exquisite pot luck dinner, and games of *bocce*, followed by some excellent desserts and more refreshments. The host couple also invites other couples to complete the fun evening. *Bocce* leagues have formed and games are played at various sites, including the two indoor courts at Mickey's Top Sirloin restaurant near 70th and Broadway in Denver.

In those first early years after our arrival in America, the games we played — those we brought over from Italy — were the last thing on our minds, especially the adults' minds. The adults' minds were set on finding jobs, feeding their families and providing them with an honorable place in which to live, a place called home. And over time, as we have become established and comfortable, we have taken pride in the traditional entertainments of our homeland.

Summer bocce group 2015 from left, back to front: Michael and Geralyn Pomponio, Michael and Myra Marranzino, Ernest and Anette Marranzino, Anthony and Jackie Lombardi, Jack and Linda Caruso, Frank and Judy Vessa, Philipp and Nikki Rossi, Doris Bieber and Patrick Mariano.

Our bocce court in Golden, Colorado, 2015

*Our bocce court in Arvada house, from left: Dominic Lombardi,
Terry (Terenzio) Lombardi, uncle Bill Lombardi, Salvatore Lombardi, Nick Mariani
(his back to us) and Antonio (little Tony) Lombardi. Notice regulation soccer goal to the
left! Circa 1995*

Chapter XLII

CASA NUOVA · BRAND NEW HOME

In 1966, Oreste and Claudina Lombardi came to Denver with their three children: Mario, Erminia, and Alberto by way of Buenos Aires, Argentina. They had immigrated there in the 1950s. They then immigrated to the United States to be closer to Claudina's sister, Gilda, and other family and friends from the village. They were also in search of a better life than that which Argentina had to offer. They came to Denver and would be our next-door neighbors for a few years.

My father heard about some new houses being built on 45th and Wyandot and that an Italian-American builder, Palmer Homes, was building these houses *fatte tutte di mattoni*, fully built with bricks. Italians were not used to siding or wood houses. They did not need anything extravagant in a house, just as long as it was built out of bricks or stones! The new houses had three bedrooms with an unfinished basement, no garage, for $15,300.

In the summer of 1967 my parents bought their first house at 4520 Wyandot Street, and Oreste and his family bought the house next door. I will never forget the monthly payment on our new home because I would have to take my dad to First Federal Savings Bank on 38th Avenue on the first of every month to make the $153 house payment. Actually it would just be deducted from his savings account, with an entry in his little blue savings book that my father would continually have me check to make sure that the amount in that savings account was what it should be. We lived in that house for a few years until we purchased a duplex on 44th and Perry Street in northwest Denver in 1971, where my parents lived for the rest of their lives.

Our family's first house purchase, 4520 Wyandot Street, Vittorio and
Maria Lucia Lombardi very proud to own a piece of l'America. 1967

My parents loved their duplex. Since they did not drive, it was convenient to be within walking distance of a grocery store (Safeway), a general store (TG&Y), Holy Family Catholic Church, Lakeside Mall, and their doctor's office on 43rd and Lowell. My mom especially loved walking to Safeway. All the employees knew her and vice-versa. She went there daily, to get out and to get in on any daily deals — and the produce manager would make her great deals on fruits and vegetables. That store that she loved to go to almost cost her life one late afternoon.

It was the summer of 1985. My 74-year-old mom made her familiar walk to Safeway. After paying for her groceries she headed out the door, with her purse securely strapped around her shoulder and her hands firmly on the shopping cart, pushing it out the door for the couple of blocks' journey back home. As she slowly, carefully pushed away from the store she heard screaming, laughing, and then suddenly she was jolted from the cart and dragged by a car. She then found herself on the pavement of the parking lot. Witnesses later told me that a car full of young boys and girls drove up behind her, one grabbed her purse, and the car sped away. But my mom did not let go of her purse, she could not, it was strapped around her shoulder. Luckily the strap snapped and the thieves drove away with the purse as they looked back yelling and laughing.

With her purse gone, my mom did not have any identification on her. She lay on the asphalt, injured but conscious. Someone called the police and an ambulance. Thankfully our distant relatives, Sam (Sabatino) and Rosa Ciotola, had a daughter, Cindy, who worked at Safeway. Upon hearing the commotion, Cindy ran out to see what was going on and she saw my mother lying on the ground, crying. She quickly ran to my brother's house and told my sister-in-law, Bambina, about the accident. *Mamma* was taken to Lutheran Hospital and was admitted with a broken shoulder and other bumps and bruises, but miraculously without any life-threatening injuries, reaffirming just how tough this lady was.

That afternoon I went looking for an older, rusting, brown Buick vehicle, a description given to me by a man who chased the car for a while on his bike. I did not find the car but I am confident that if I had found it and its occupants, I would not be here today because I would have fought them until they were dead. That day was the only day in my life that I wanted to kill somebody, the somebodies who robbed an elderly, helpless woman. The next day a man brought us my mom's purse, which he had found in a dumpster near a housing project, near 44th and Lipan Street. Her fifty or so dollars were gone.

On another afternoon in the early 1980s, my kids and I were having lunch at the duplex under the patio when suddenly a young man bolted through the gate and sprinted past our table and out the other side. Soon after, two police officers ran through the same gate and asked us which direction the young man went. It happened so quickly that we did not have a chance to panic. The kid was being chased by Denver police for robbing a store somewhere on Tennyson Street.

We became concerned about my parents' safety, so a decision was made to move them out of their duplex. They purchased a house on the same cul-de-sac where we lived in Arvada, but it turned out to be a mistake. Even though they were happy to be close to us, they felt trapped because they were away from all the conveniences they had enjoyed in north Denver. After a couple of years they sold the house and moved back to their beloved duplex, which had been rented out. In the 1990s their neighborhood went through a transformation. Young, friendly families were again moving into the area and we felt better about the neighborhood. Also, my brother and his family were still living up the street.

In their north Denver neighborhood, my parents must have sometimes thought they were still living in their tiny village in Italy, because they would often leave their doors unlocked. We always reminded them to lock their doors, even in the daytime. But it did not seem to sink in. One morning while my mother was in the front yard watering their flowers (about the only job my father allowed her to do in the yard) and my father was downstairs shaving, someone walked in through their unlocked back door and stole my mother's purse that was sitting on the kitchen table. Luckily that was the last of the dangerous episodes for my elderly parents that took place at their modest and inviting home.

Mamma and Papà in their duplex kitchen, 2000

Fruits of their hard labor were exhibited by our relatives and friends through ownership of real property. All of the immigrants from our village owned at least one house. Renting was avoided at all costs. After all, they had left a place where ownership was hard to obtain if you were a dirt farmer. They did not mind working long, hard hours to achieve the goal of putting a roof over their loved ones' heads. And although they expected all family members to earn an income as soon as legally able, our parents also insisted that their children go to school. They did not mind paying for their education as long as it guaranteed an admirable and profitable career for them.

I sometimes thought about just quitting school, but knowing that my parents would be disappointed, I stuck it out, just barely. In Italy I had been a hardworking, focused student, but somehow I had become fed up with school in Denver. I did not feel like doing the work required to excel. I wanted to give up, maybe just get a job and run from all the hurdles that that part of my young life put in front of me. I could not muster enough courage to communicate to my parents the turmoil inside me that was caused by the environment of these American schools. I was embarrassed and ashamed by some of my grades. I was disgusted with myself for losing the drive to excel. And as the end of junior high school came, I was already panicking with the idea of going to a high school, a much bigger school with perhaps more possibilities of harassment.

Chapter *XLIII*

LICEO
NORTH HIGH SCHOOL

In the fall of 1969 I enrolled at North High School for my next educational endeavor. The good thing about the new school was that I would be with some of my friends and relatives: Louie Lombardi, Dominic Lombardi, Alfredo (Sandro) Lombardi, Salvatore Lombardi, Fernando Lombardi, Mario Lombardi, Frank Lombardi, Edilia Lombardi, and a year later my future wife, Jackie Meloragno. Other friends and relatives would come to North a year or two later, like Terry Lombardi and Vince Carmosino.

I met Jackie while staying with my cousin, Terry, who lived around the corner of 40th and Clay, where Jackie lived with her mom, dad, and two sisters, Cynthia (the oldest) and Angela (the youngest). I had to work extra hard to win her over, like pulling up to her house with my pink car or a friend's car and blasting the radio until she came out on her porch. At that point we would peel out, go around the block and do it all over again. I was a real lady's man! Old man John Bucci and other residents of the area thought I was a pain in the ass! Also, a lifelong relationship was forged at North with Jackie, me, and Louie Lombardi's future wife, Elaine Yatckoske, a Lutheran with German and Norwegian ancestry. After she married Louie, Elaine embraced the Italian culture, converted to Catholicism, and is now more knowledgeable and a better participant of Catholic and Italian traditions than many people born to it.

Going into high school I was somewhat relieved that I had friends and we could support and protect each other from whatever this new encounter would throw our way. Of course I would have to go through the nerve-racking first day of school with roll call. By now people knew me as Tony, but on the school records my name was Pietrantonio. As soon as the teacher reached the last names that began with the letter L, I would start to get nervous. Some teachers would just stop and take a breath and then attempt to pronounce my name. I would try to anticipate when my name was coming up and raise my hand and tell them to just call me Tony, to change the name of the records to Tony. Most of them obliged and were thankful that they did not have to butcher my name. However, some took the opportunity to make light of it and deliberately kept mispronouncing it, even though I would raise my hand to get their attention. One such teacher even went as far as to suggest that with a name like that I must be involved with all the *mafia* types working up the street at Hover Ford car sales. The same teacher also suggested that my name should be Pie, a good all-American pie.

I endured it all. By now I was immune to all the fun poked at my name and at me. Thankfully I had my close friends to support me, protect me. One such friend was Louie Lombardi. Our paternal grandfathers (his was the forest ranger, Luigi) were first cousins. It did not seem long ago that I was playing with him in our little hamlet of Luigi before he left for Philadelphia with his brother, Dominic, and mother, Ida, to meet up with their dad and her husband, Nicola. Louie was the popular Lombardi at North, due to his good looks and the fact that he played on the football team until a bad knee injury ended his career. He was also a year or so older than the rest of us and more mature. He did not need to be my close friend, he had many popular students who were his friends, but he did not leave us behind. Riding on his shirttails, I moved a bit away from the nerd crowd and to the average section of the student body.

That new stature suffered a setback due to the suggestion by Louie to join the ROTC (Reserve Officer Training Corps). He talked me into enrolling in that program that was being offered at North High. The main reason we joined the ROTC was because Louie guaranteed me that we would get to shoot rifles at some firing range. I had never shot a rifle or handgun before so it seemed like an intriguing idea. We never did get to shoot a rifle. The closest we got to it was at sort of a shooting range in the basement of the school. We would point a plastic rifle and another ROTC cadet would make a mark on a target a few feet away.

I do remember the colonel in charge of the program giving us a pep talk when the training program started. His name was Walter Ramsay, a big-boned man with a wide, square face pitted by acne. He was tall and scary looking. He told us that the ROTC program would, among many other opportunities, arm us with leadership skills, help develop logical thinking prowess, teach us how to communicate effectively, and build good mental management skills. We would also learn the history, purpose, and structure of the military service, and most importantly we would develop skills necessary to work effectively as members of a team. The cadet program would teach us the fundamentals of leadership in the U.S. Army, where we would be appointed as officers. All excellent reasons for sticking with that program. But since we would not be shooting real guns, Louie and I made the decision to leave the program after that semester. We had each been issued a uniform and when we opted out we were asked to return them. We kept ignoring the requests to return the uniforms; we wanted to keep them.

One day we each received a letter from the FBI stating that if the uniforms were not returned promptly we would be arrested. The next day we gave the uniforms back to Colonel Ramsey and he took the opportunity to belittle us for not returning them on time, for chickening out of the program, and to tell us that we had made a big mistake. And although he did not say it, I sensed that he was thinking that Italians were soft and did not make good soldiers! In retrospect, we did make a mistake. We should have taken that opportunity to improve our chances for an admirable career. A missed opportunity. We gave in to peer pressure. We were made fun of as we went through our exercises on school grounds, laughed at when we wore our uniforms. This was 1969, at the height of the Vietnam War, and the military drew a lot of criticism. My mother was not very happy either. She thought that I was being prepared and groomed so they could send me to Vietnam to fight a war, and she had bad memories of a war.

I was grinding my way through high school while holding down a job at Rockmont Envelope Company, working the eight-hour swing shift as a machine operator and then a machine adjuster. Things were going pretty well. Now I always had some money, and I had a 1963 Chevy

Super Sport convertible and a girlfriend. One fateful night, bored, my supervisor and I wanted to use a table saw to cut some wood to make a tool box. We fashioned a rope to use as a belt to run the saw. The serpentine rubber belt had been removed from the table saw as a safety precaution. When we were finished cutting the boards I turned off the machine, and as it was winding down I reached for the extra rope that was on top of the table to get rid of the evidence. As I dragged it across the table, the blade caught the rope and pulled my hand towards the spinning, sharp cutting tool. I suddenly felt pain in my hand and when I pulled it back I noticed that part of my middle finger on my left hand was barely hanging by a piece of skin. My supervisor screamed in horror and I just held my bloody left hand with my right, surely in shock.

My sister-in-law and other employees had gathered and they took me to the lunchroom to wait for an ambulance that had been summoned, and also to advise my dad and brother who were there cleaning the offices, lunchroom, and bathrooms. We had a contract with Satriano Brothers Cleaning Company to clean that building at night. We had befriended the supervisor and he eventually hired me and Ezio's wife, Bambina. When my brother saw my bloodied hand he let out a scream, turned white and almost passed out. My dad, although in a panic, cleaned my hand of the blood to see the extent of the injury. I was taken to Rose Medical Center hospital with my father at my side, trying his best to keep me calm. They reattached my finger and stitched up the other injured index finger. The doctor mentioned that if the saw had not been turned off and winding down, I would have lost my arm in the saw at its maximum power.

My career as a machine adjuster at Rockmont abruptly came to an end. My sister-in-law, Bambina, and her cousin and my childhood friend, Salvatore Lombardi, worked there for many years. In addition to our cleaning contract at Rockmont, we also cleaned Hover Ford and the Denver Catholic Register. I was still working at night, which was always part of my high school days.

During those long days and nights I wondered what my life would have been like back in Italy. I daydreamed of playing soccer for some team, maybe my favorite team, Juventus. The prospect of my staying at the monastery and my vocation as a Franciscan monk was also a possibility. Instead I was cleaning other people's messes in Denver, Colorado, in faraway America.

Back to reality, I had to push myself to learn. In Italy it was so easy for me. The environment at North High School made it difficult to learn, to excel. I remember being in a class where the elderly social studies teacher had dozed off and I was asked to pass a marijuana joint to a student that another student was selling him. If a student did not have a bit of drive, he or she could have easily fallen through the cracks, as many did.

But I want to express a note of thanks to some teachers who saw potential in me. There were those who took an interest in me and took a liking to me: Mr. Jim Schrant, Mr. Theodore Speros, Miss Martha Epp, my counselor Mr. Rex Stuck, and others who wanted to see me learn and succeed, regardless of my background or popularity. But there were some teachers who seemed to be indifferent or apathetic. In defense of those teachers who did not seem to like me, it was in some instances of my own doing.

Ms. Pomponio would give me a frown every time she saw me in the hallways. She was the Italian language teacher at North. Looking for an easy A and with most of my friends already enrolled, I decided to take her beginning Italian course. The first day of class she warned the students, who were mostly of Italian heritage, that this was a class to learn proper Italian. The dialects that most of us learned from our parents and grandparents were not proper Italian, and she would not allow dialects to be spoken in her classroom. After a few days of her class, I just could not take it anymore. I realized that I was wasting my time and the only positive was that I was helping a lot of the other students in the class.

One day at the end of class I walked up to Ms. Pomponio and informed her that I wanted to drop her class and enroll in the French course. She asked me why, and I bluntly told her that I could teach her more Italian than she could teach me. She became infuriated and started to blabber about my dialect and so on. She never forgave me for my honest answer. One day she singled me out and reprimanded me for being too close to my girlfriend in the hallway. She continued to harass me and I often wondered why I was so dumb as to piss her off, when I could have been more diplomatic and just said that I wanted to learn more French.

Reflecting on my time at North, I think that it did not totally prepare me for higher education, nor did I totally appreciate my stint there; rather I simply just survived it. One morning, as I parked my pinkish Ford Falcon in a school lot I was faced with a question of survival. As my girlfriend and I were walking towards school from the parking lot, a group of boys were in the process of stealing another student's car; it was Anthony Tacito's nice black Chevy. Annoyed by our presence, they practically threatened to kill me as they pushed me around and called me names, while my girlfriend watched in fear. I had seen those troublemakers in school but not very often, more than likely they had been expelled. I later found out that they were current and former students involved in some Chicano gang. Without sounding bitter, it was what it was.

Maybe I should have been more enterprising and taken better advantage of what was offered. Some teachers made suggestions to join various clubs and I just chose not to, maybe out of antipathy towards the numerous bullies. Or I was just angry that no one seemed to want to do anything about the bullies' constant epithets of '*dago*,' '*wop*,' and other derogatory names. I don't know how many times bullies would ask me what sound a cow's poop makes when it hits the ground or what sound a flat tire makes as it rotates. Why were Italian immigrants the ones tagged with those names? Didn't other nationalities come over without official papers? But the real reason I wasn't involved in high school activities was that after working all night long cleaning buildings, I was just too tired and uninspired.

❖❖❖❖❖❖❖

LIST OF GRADUATES

Girls, 311; Boys, 330; Total, 641

Chleborad, John	Felix, Ronald Lionel	Lange, Marie Jose
Cirbo, Karen Faye	Fenner, Robert Alan	Lange, Patrick G.
Clark, Phillip Andrew	Ferguson, Carol Roseann	Larche, Lorraine
Clark, Robert David	Ferguson, Linda Lea	Larson, Christopher B.
Clem, Roy James	Fernandez, Juanita S.	Larson, Gail Lynn
Clow, Patti Anne	Fetterolf, Felix Lockwood	Larson, Patricia Marie
Clymer, Janine Diane	Finkenbinder, Stephen Haley	Laso, John Edward
Cody, Carla Patrice	Fisk, Dale Bernard	Laureta, Frances Elizabeth
Cohen, Tuvia Jechiel	Flores, Betty Jean	Lazuk, Terry Ann
Conner, Robert Leroy	Foster, Cheryl Lynn	Leberer, Gary Olin
Connor, Timothy John	Foster, Stephen Michael	Leiker, Daniel Lynn
Cook, Karla Kay	Fowler, Bonnie Lee	Lewis, Paul John
Cook, Richard Keith	French, Stan	Liberman, Michael
Coombs, Glenn Leroy	Fuchs, Rochelle Rahela	Lidke, Paul Kenneth
Coover, Russell Louis	Fuller, Curtis Richard	Lindstrom, Eric Leonard
Corbitt, Jay Junior	Galbaugh, Glenn Gerald	Livingston, David Mark
Corbitt, Justin Ray	Gallegos, Martin	Lochric, Judy Ann
Cordova, Edward Larry	Gallegos, Sharon Loretta	Lombardi, Alfredo
Correa, Joseph	Gallegos, Tobias Eleuterio	Lombardi, Dominic Joseph
Correa, Mary	Gallo, Paulette Ester	Lombardi, Frank Angelo
Correa, Rebecca Ann	Games, Lisa Kay	Lombardi, Louis Anthony
Craver, Louis James	Garcia, Christopher Jerome	Lombardi, Pietrantonio
Cuneo, Daniel Herbert	Gargaro, Daniel Paul	(Tony)
Currence, Daniel Benjamin	Gargaro, Gloria Jean	Lombardi, Salvatore
Cvitanovich, Anita Kay	Geist, Janel Maxine	Loostrom, Pete Bruce
Daniel, Paul Michael	Geppert, Borys	Lopez, Richard Daniel
Danner, Gerald Lee	Gerk, Mary Lynn	Lowe, Donald Paul
Danz, Rebecca Marie	Gillespie, Robert Scott	Loya, Renee
Dardano, Kenneth Paul	Girard, Janet Lee	Lucero, Anita L.
Dardano, Phyllis Lucille	Gomez, Daniel Philip	Lucero, Geraldine Elaine
Davey, Michael Angelo	Gonzales, Joseph T.	Lucero, Mary Antoinette
Davis, Rebecca Lea	Gonzales, Mary Valvina	Lucero, Peggy Diane
Davis, Steven Scot	Gonzales, Norma Jean	Lucero, Rovan Anna
Debber, Randee	Gonzales, Rita Catherina	Luevano, Yolanda Marie
DeCrescentis, Paula Lee	Gonzales, Ruth A.	Luff, Donald
Deffert, Viktor	Goodall, Charlene	Lujan, Benjamin A.
DeHerrera, David Willie	Goodman, Theresa Mary	Lujan, Charles Anthony
De La Cruz, Darlene Loretta	Goodnight, Rose Marie	Luna, Jaquelyn Dena
DeLange, Jeffrey David	Goodrich, Douglas Lee	Lyles, Kathryn
		Macias, Dora Jean
		Maciuk, Paul
		Madrid, Steven Jonathan
		Madrid, Veronica
		Maes, Robert
		Maestas, Nancy Louise
		Makelky, Rosemarie

A small cropping taken from North High School's 1971 Graduation Program.
The graduation list of 641 students reflects a strong showing of Lombardi's

I did manage to find time to be involved in some stupid, immature childish escapades. I feel like punching myself in the face when I think back on the senseless stuff I was involved in during my high school years. Most of the incidents I just choose to put out of my mind forever, but some linger.

One night, driving around with some friends and low on gas, we tried siphoning gas out of vans of a janitorial service, where friend and fellow immigrant, Tony Lonardo, worked. Tony swallowed some of the gasoline and became sick and started screaming and vomiting, alarming neighbors who called the police, and we almost got caught.

On another night at a pool hall on 50th and Federal, none of us had money so we stuffed shirts in the goals of a foosball table so the balls would not fall through and we would not have to pay for more balls. A kid, a regular there, told management and we were warned with a lifetime ban if we did that again. We harassed the kid and kept threatening him with physical harm until he had had enough. Suddenly he pulled a gun out of his waistband and stuck it in my face. All I remember is his finger on the trigger and his hand shaking. I thought I was going to have my face blown off. I was scared shitless and speechless. My friends apologized to him profusely, until he pulled the gun back from my face and walked away. Like idiots we waited for him outside to get a piece of him, but he never showed.

Speaking of guns in your face, while working at Cosmopolitan Upholstery in the early seventies, a young man wearing black gloves stormed through the back door of the business and ran in one of the back furniture storage rooms. Seconds after, a man wielding a gun appeared through the same door, pointing the gun at me, screaming, "Where is he? Where is that son of a bitch?" He was a Denver fireman, whose name escapes me. He had walked in on two burglars at his mom's north Denver home. One ran away and the fireman was determined to catch him. The burglar was later found by Denver police, hiding amongst our old furniture in the back room, scared to death, still wearing the black gloves. The gloves would not leave fingerprints while they burglarized other people's homes.

For a brief time at North, my cousin, Dominic Lombardi, and I decided to become part of a group of students who dressed in cutoff jean jackets with chains hanging out of various parts of the jackets. We thought we were cool! That got us in trouble with school officials and we were also jeered by the school's jocks. One day we decided to ditch school and go to Jefferson High School in Edgewater so Dominic Lombardi could see his new girlfriend, Rita Lonardo, who was a student there. We entered the school dressed in our jean jackets and then proceeded to open every classroom door to find Rita. The school's principal was warned and then the security staff. We were detained and the officials were about to call the Edgewater police, but we begged them not to and promised to never set foot on that school's grounds again.

The three of us (I don't remember the other guy's name, but he was the one who got us to wear the ridiculous jean jackets) started to walk back to North High school and we decided to hitchhike. When a guy in a truck did not stop, our friend flipped him off. The driver hit his brakes, got out of the truck and ran towards us, and caught our friend. We thought the much bigger driver was going to kill our friend, but another car stopped and the driver let our friend go. That day I decided to shed the jean jacket and to distance myself from that kid. Dominic did the same soon after.

My time at North High School did give me an opportunity to reconnect, to get to know my grandfather a little better. He had reverted back to his previous life with his young daughter, at the same house and business as when we first set eyes on him. He seemed most comfortable with that setting. Even though he visited us, at times bringing us food that he bought from friends who gave him great deals, he seemed most content being alone at his shop, at his house, and with just his young daughter. Many times Louie and I would drive the few blocks from school to join him at his house for lunch. He would prepare extravagant meals for us, from pasta dishes to barbecued steaks, and always with a glass of his homemade wine. We probably attended our afternoon classes a little tipsy but he insisted, claiming that one glass of wine was good for our health and nobody would ever know.

I think that although he enjoyed making me lunch, he wanted to use the time to tell me stories of his life. I am so thankful that I urged him to tell me about his escapades. I learned so much about his life, his dreams, and his missed opportunities. It seemed that whatever new discoveries, new horizons he embarked on, he had good intentions, but they never quite worked out the way he had envisioned. I believe that if his sons would have been with him during those years, they would have supported him and given him the impetus to purchase those pieces of land, those structures that he almost purchased but never did.

One July evening of 1970 while at work at Rockmont Envelopes, I received a phone call from some friends saying they heard that my grandfather was involved in a serious car accident that afternoon, near his house on 26th and Federal. He had attempted to make a left turn into oncoming traffic and was hit by another car. He walked away from the wreck but was then taken to Denver General Hospital. While still in the emergency room, he passed away unexpectedly. Later, the cause of death was determined to have been a result of internal bleeding.

Even the headstone makers made a mistake in writing Pietrantonio correctly!

We were sad, but thankful that we were able to be with our patriarch for four short years. His daughter, Coco, went to live with my uncle's family. My father offered to help, but as we all sat in the office of lawyer Albert Carmosino, my uncle insisted on taking permanent custody and took control of my grandfather's estate. I remember clearly, as my father informed the attorney that he did not want anything from his father's estate. Instead, whatever his father had should be given to Coco, his young daughter. But somehow some quarrels evolved and bad feelings lingered. Life was different in America, but in some ways life and family struggles were exactly the same as back in Italy.

High school graduation, June 1971,
with papà, Jackie and mamma

Chapter *XLIV*

VIETNAM IMMINENTE
VIETNAM LOOMING

During the Vietnam War, all of us were worried about being drafted. I sometimes wondered about it and considered that maybe I should go back to Italy where I would be safe from that awful war. I vividly recall the night of February 2, 1972 when the draft lottery was conducted to determine the order in which men born in 1953 would be called to report for induction into the military. Thirty-six blue plastic capsules had been drawn, and thank God my birthdate of January 10 was not one of them. On the 37th draw my heart almost fell to the floor when January 10 was shown on TV. The belief was that the first 125 dates picked would surely be drafted into the U.S. military.

I, along with my girlfriend, Jackie, and the rest of my family became very anxious. I could hardly sleep that night as thoughts ran through my head... If we had stayed in Italy, I would not have to worry about going to fight in an unpopular war. Maybe I should just go to Canada as many other young Americans had done; I could live with my sister. Many young men did choose to leave the country. Many tried to avoid military service, claiming to be conscientious objectors, refusing to serve in the military based on the grounds of freedom of conscience and/or religion. One of the most famous of these objectors was heavyweight boxer Cassius Clay (Muhammad Ali).

At number 37, for sure I was headed for Vietnam. In early summer of 1972 I received a letter asking me to report to the Federal Courthouse for a physical. I passed it with flying colors, coming in at 5'10" and a whopping 135 pounds. I was informed not to leave town and I would receive a letter with a date of when to report.

Louie Lombardi was drafted as a result of his birthdate being picked in the 11th draw for the year of his birth. On a warm day in October of 1971, I vividly recall taking him to the same place where I had my physical, which was also the place of induction. Louie's brother, Dominic, also accompanied us. We asked the sergeant in charge of the new draftees if it would be okay to tag along as they went through the check-in process. The final stage of the process was for the draftees to recite The Pledge of Allegiance. Two draftees refused to recite the pledge. As we sat in the back of the room with the very nice accommodating sergeant, he informed us that those two recruits would probably be the first soldiers sent to the front lines of Vietnam.

After we hugged Louie, the bus slowly pulled away from the curb and headed to Stapleton Airport, where Louie would depart for basic training in California. Dominic and I stood there with a lump in our throats, wondering what would happen to Louie as he waved back to us from the back of that army bus. Surely his eyes were tearing up even more than ours. While he served in the United States Army, students and other inciters protested the war. Louie did go to Vietnam towards the end of the war, spending three months there in a teaching capacity and was never involved in any fighting in the futile war.

July 1, 1973 was a good day for me and other young men who had been waiting to be drafted, because on that day the draft ended and a voluntary army system was established. On August 15, 1973 the Vietnam War, that awful war, officially ended. Like other wars, the Vietnam War was extremely ugly. The official reason our government gave us for our involvement in Vietnam was to stop the spread of communism, a supposedly classless society with no private ownership of land or business. A communist government would take care of all and all would work as equals with no one profiting from their labor, as the marginal product of labor would be shared equally and everyone would be protected.

When North Vietnam's leader, Ho Chi Minh, with Communist China's backing, moved troops to invade South Vietnam, our government decided to intervene. The French had intervened before us and basically made a mess of the whole thing. In the beginning, 1959, our soldiers were told to fire back only if fired upon, but by 1965 combat units were deployed and an all-out war broke out. By 1969 there were 543,000 American soldiers in Vietnam. A lot of the soldiers, along

1972 RANDOM SELECTION LOTTERY DRAWING CALENDAR

	JAN	FEB	MAR	APR	MAY	JUN	JUL	AUG	SEP	OCT	NOV	DEC
1	150	112	203	012	058	015	039	323	219	215	107	170
2	328	278	322	108	275	360	297	027	017	128	214	090
3	042	054	220	104	166	245	109	003	226	103	232	056
4	028	168	047	280	172	207	092	313	356	079	339	250
5	338	096	266	254	292	230	139	063	354	086	223	031
6	036	271	001	088	337	087	132	208	173	041	211	336
7	111	154	002	163	145	251	285	057	144	129	299	267
8	206	347	153	050	201	282	355	131	097	157	312	210
9	197	136	321	234	276	083	179	007	364	116	151	120
10	037	361	331	272	100	178	089	249	217	342	257	073
11	174	026	239	350	307	064	202	125	334	319	159	082
12	126	195	044	023	115	190	340	198	043	171	066	085
13	298	263	244	169	049	318	306	329	229	269	124	335
14	341	348	117	081	224	095	305	205	353	014	237	038
15	221	308	152	343	165	016	359	241	235	277	176	137
16	309	227	094	119	101	032	074	019	225	059	209	187
17	231	046	363	183	273	091	199	008	189	177	284	294
18	072	011	357	242	098	238	121	113	289	192	160	013
19	303	127	358	158	148	052	332	105	228	167	270	168
20	161	106	262	314	274	077	033	162	141	352	301	149
21	099	316	300	004	310	315	005	030	123	288	287	080
22	259	020	317	264	333	146	286	140	268	191	102	188
23	258	247	022	279	216	212	365	302	296	193	320	252
24	062	261	071	362	246	061	324	138	236	256	180	155
25	243	260	065	255	122	143	035	290	291	009	025	006
26	311	051	024	233	118	345	204	076	029	078	344	351
27	110	186	181	265	293	330	060	034	248	325	135	194
28	304	295	045	055	018	053	185	040	070	327	130	156
29	283	---	021	093	133	075	222	084	196	349	147	175
30	114	---	213	069	048	142	200	182	184	346	134	281
31	240	---	326	---	067	---	253	218	---	010	---	164

In 1972, military draft lottery drawing results for men born in 1953

with a lot of the American public, strongly opposed our involvement. Over 58,000 soldiers lost their lives in Vietnam and at the end we did not stop communism. It can be argued that Vietnam was the first major war the United States lost, the War of 1812 against England being the actual first big loss, although the U.S. considered both wars a draw.

I eventually decided to let destiny take its course. If it was meant for me to go fight in Vietnam for the United States of America and if it was meant for me to live here for the rest of my life, then so be it. Luckily the volunteer army saved me. After reading many letters that I received from Louie, it seemed that military service was not, at least from his experience, so bad after all.

Chapter XLV

La Barca E Il Falco Rosa
The Boat And The Pink Falcon

When my brother arrived from Italy, we realized that we needed to get a form of transportation. Not a mule or a donkey, but *la macchina*, the car. We could not afford to buy a car so relatives came to the rescue. My father had some relatives who lived far away from north Denver, in a place called Commerce City. Their name was Milano. There were families with that last name in Cerreto, the tiny village two kilometers east of Villa San Michele. We had gone to their house in Commerce City with *Papà* Pietrantonio many times. It seemed so far. They lived in a white farmhouse. They gave us a car that had been parked on their property for a long time; it was a red and white 1953 Ford.

The Ford was old and battered but it worked, and my brother was so happy with his first car. One night, while parked in the back of our apartment, someone stole the battery and other parts from it. It would have cost too much to replace all the parts, so my brother and father set out to look for another vehicle. They finally found one that cost more money than we could afford, but somehow we made it work. It was like getting an older but hardworking donkey that would need to be taken care of so it could perform the work. For some reason my father and brother thought that washing the car and cleaning the inside would insure that the car would perform well, because they seemed to be doing that continually. Slowly my brother learned a bit about the inner workings of the car, such as where to put the oil! Angelo Capobianco and Robert and Joe Carmosino were his mentors.

Although my father tried many times to learn how to drive a car, it never worked out for him. Watching him drive that gray monstrosity of a car my brother bought was painful. He never really grasped the difference between the gas pedal and the brake pedal. But the real annoying exercise was when he would turn the wheels and then forget to straighten them out after the turn! And when he realized that he needed to straighten out the wheels, he would overcompensate and go up a curb or over a parking block. We would go around and around in some empty lot, as his grip on the steering wheel got tighter and the sweat dripping from his face more noticeable. Eventually he became upset and disillusioned and finally gave up. But every time I hesitated to agree to take him and my mom somewhere, he complained that he regretted not learning how to drive. I guess it is much more difficult for a fifty-something-year-old person to learn how to drive than a teenager!

The enormous car my brother bought, a 1959 Pontiac Bonneville, was not the easiest to drive because of its size. I know this because in 1968 when my brother left for Italy to find a bride, he parked the car in the backyard of our house, next to the shed that my father built with the help of Dominic Capobianco and Renato Lombardi. Almost every night, with the usual cousins and *paesani*, friends, I would take the keys and sneak the car out of the backyard, carefully maneuvering it out of the small alley. We would drive the car around and even ventured to the Scotchman one night, where the Denver police were very visible. There was one officer there named Buster Snyder, who would eventually give me my first ticket after I got my license, for making an illegal left turn coming out of the Scotchman.

One night while driving the car back to its parking spot in the backyard, I noticed a truck parked in the alley. There was very little space between the truck and the telephone pole. We all determined that there was sufficient room to guide the car past the obstacle. As I drove the car towards the truck, on my left I made damn sure not to scrape the car and the truck, but I totally ignored the telephone pole until I heard the noise of the passenger side of the car scraping the pole. Someone, or all the passengers, yelled to stop but it was too late. In a panic I tried backing up, but my inexperience caused me to dig the car into the pole even more. That dark night I basically destroyed one side of my brother's car. To avoid my father's wrath, I parked the wrecked side of the car very close to the shed.

My father never noticed the damage until my brother came back from Italy. I heard them talking about it as I lay in bed with a cast on my right leg from my soccer injury. My brother also agreed with my parents that I should not play soccer anymore, but he felt bad for me and showered me with gifts from Italy, including delicious Swiss dark chocolate bars like those he brought back for me from his days in Switzerland. He invited me to eat the chocolate but I just could not do it. I made the excuse that my leg hurt too much. In reality, I was sweating the eventual discovery of the wrecked car. As my brother went out the back door and headed for his car, I felt like punching myself in the face, wondering how stupid I was for taking his car all those nights.

I could hear my brother talking to my dad in the back yard. I waited, as they would surely surmise that I was the culprit. When my brother came into the bedroom, to my surprise, he calmly asked what happened. I told him that one night, only that one night, my friends and I decided to start the car and take it for a short drive around the block so the battery would not discharge, and that the idiot neighbor parked his truck in the alley causing the telephone pole to practically take out the whole side of his car. I was surprised; maybe they felt sorry for me lying there with a badly broken leg, but neither my dad nor brother yelled at me. My brother just said that he would buy another car, that that one was old anyway. The real reason for buying another car was that when I looked out the window I was shocked to see the whole passenger side caved in. It didn't look so bad the night of the accident!

Ezio standing next to his first car purchase, 1959 Pontiac Bonneville 1968

As soon as I turned fifteen years and nine months old, my father allowed me to get a driver's permit, not necessarily because he wanted me to have a car but because he needed a chauffeur to take him and my mom to countless destinations. For years, every Saturday and Sunday morning at 5:30 a.m., I would have to take my father to work at the Rocky Mountain News. And when it was my dad's turn to drive, I would have to pick up other coworkers, including Dominic Capobianco, Nicola Lombardi, Renato Lombardi, and Antonio Carmosino, until Antonio decided to move back to his village because he and his wife could not adapt to life in America. But while they were here, I was their ride to work, as their weekday driver had the weekends off. And yes, they all worked at the Rocky Mountain News as janitors.

When one immigrant was lucky enough to find a job somewhere, other fellow immigrants ended up working there soon after. Maybe it was because these people were relentless in asking their bosses to please hire one or more of their relatives and friends, but I like to think that those bosses hired them, knowing that they would be as dependable and hardworking as their existing immigrant employees. Some of the more popular places where immigrants from our village worked were Samsonite Corporation, Gross Taylors, American Beauty, and Burlington Northern Railroad.

My father heard of an elderly Italian-American man who worked at Samsonite, the luggage company, and he had a car for sale, a 1961 Ford Falcon. I was excited just to be getting a car; I did not care what year, make, or model. My brother took us somewhere in south Denver to see it. As we approached the house, I still could not believe that I was going to have a car of my own to drive, despite the fact that I was going to be my parents' personal chauffeur. But when we pulled up to the house, my mouth dropped to the ground at the sight of the small, faded pinkish car. I begged my father not to buy the car, but at $250 he was not going to pass up the deal.

My first car, ready to be driven to Easter Mass, with my mom and Bambina, very pregnant with Vittorio (Vic Lombardi), 1969

Sporting my unibrow, with baby Vittorio, 1969

A few days later, the pink car (it was probably originally beige but it was now sort of a faded pink) was parked in front of our house. I was still excited, but very apprehensive about the fact that for sure I was going to be ridiculed at North High. I recall informing my dad that other kids *"mi pigliano in giro,"* would make fun of me, with that little pink car. He brushed that off, acting as though he did not even hear me. He either did not have a clue as to what I was going through at school, or knew all too well but chose to let me deal with it; to him it was nothing.

Ridicule is not a strong enough word to describe what I went through with that car. After a couple of weeks of that nonstop nonsense, with the help of friend Vince Carmosino, I decided to do something to make the pink car manlier. We decided to paint some stripes and remove the ugly hub caps. With some masking tape and some black paint we found in my basement, we went to work. We painted two black stripes from back to front and then some black and white polka dots on the rims. The car looked... hideous, but hopefully not so... pink. The madness did not stop there. In a moment of sheer insanity I took a small brush and wrote in my ugly cursive, "I love Jackie," on the passenger front fender with the black enamel paint.

What had I done? What would my father and brother do to me for destroying *la macchina.* As we stared at it, panic sat in. I decided to wash the paint off. With a bucket of hot water and soap, we tried in vain to remove the graffiti from the car, but to no avail. I learned that enamel paint will not come off very easily. I was teased so much, that in church I would complain to God and ask Him why he was doing this to me, and then I would beg Him to somehow kill the car. My confidence in God was restored when that following winter, the car died. Did someone tell me that it needed antifreeze? I did not even know that such thing existed.

At that time, we were cleaning Hover Ford offices for Satriano Brothers and my brother and I became friends with Harry Capra, the sales manager at the popular car lot at 29th and Federal. Harry made us a great deal on a 1963 Chevrolet Impala Super Sport convertible! As I drove the car around North High School I took tremendous enjoyment in watching the same people that made fun of my pink Falcon, drool over my boss car. And with the new wheels, I crawled a bit further out of the nerd hole.

My cool car. I drove to Toronto, Canada with my father in tow. I barely knew how to drive around Denver, much less almost 1,500 miles across America. In front of my sister's house on Dufferin Street, Toronto, Canada, 1971

Chapter XLVI

CITTADINANZA · CITIZENSHIP

As soon as our five-year permanent residency permit expired, my father was adamant about becoming an American citizen. I am not really sure why, maybe he still hoped that my sister and her family could join us from Toronto, Canada. He needed to be an American citizen to initiate the proper immigration paperwork for her. Those papers were never filled out, even though my sister would have loved to reunite with us. My brother-in-law might have resisted the idea, probably because his own sister lived in Canada and he had already started to lay roots there. In Toronto, the shock of leaving our Italy was not so terrible because of the numerous Italian immigrants and the many Italian-friendly conveniences of their community.

After five years in America, my parents were beginning to realize that this was going to be our permanent home and that we should embrace it fully. For me it was essential to become an American citizen. If I ever wanted to go back to Italy just for a visit, which I very badly wanted to do, I would have to be an American citizen or else the moment I stepped off the plane I would be drafted into the Italian military for two years, which was compulsory for all Italian men.

In September of 1971 we filled out all the exhausting paperwork. I encountered a big problem because I could not provide my green card. My wallet, along with my green card, had been stolen from my gym locker at North High School and I did not apply for a new one. Finally we filed all the required paperwork and waited for a response. We received a letter notifying us to appear at the Federal Courthouse at 18th and Stout Street in downtown Denver, on October 22, 1971 at 10:00 a.m. Two witnesses, who had known us for the continuous five years that we had resided in the United States, accompanied us: Pasquale Melaragno, who was Jackie's grandfather, and Salvatore Lombardi, husband of Bonina.

My petition for naturalization

I was pretty confident that I would do all right with the looming exam, but for my parents it was another story. I tried to teach them about the basic form of government and basic writing and reading skills in English, but it was a struggle to say the least. The fact that they both had a third grade education made it that much more difficult to teach

My mother's petition for naturalization

them simple English. Their approach was that it was going to be fine, that the government would let them become citizens, regardless. They pointed out that many of their friends were citizens of the United States of America and could hardly speak English. They made a valid point. What they did not know was that those people were over the age of fifty-

My father's petition for naturalization

five and had lived here more than fifteen years, and so they were exempt from most of these requirements.

The exam was a total fiasco. The woman examiner was unfriendly and serious. She flunked my parents with flying colors and suggested not to come back for a second exam until they could demonstrate the ability to read, write, and speak English and have some knowledge of our government. All my mother could say was "*Come eva brutta qaella femmina,*" *Come era brutta quella donna*, pointing out how mean-spirited the woman was. We were given study guides and told to come back no earlier than ninety days.

I had three months to teach my parents basic English and to teach them the fundamental history and form of government of the United States of America. I suspect that most American citizens did not know a lot of the answers to those questions, such as how many amendments our constitution has. This was one of the questions I was asked and the only reason I knew that there were twenty-seven was because it was in the test guide. With my parents, first I would have to try and teach them the reason for the constitution and then who wrote it and what it contained. Impossible! I rescheduled the exam for about six months later, giving me more time to teach my parents. I must admit that I became very agitated around our kitchen table some nights, because my parents just could not absorb most of the exam material.

The day of our second exam was a very anxious day for me and for my parents. We realized that they did not learn much more than they had known for the initial exam. My parents hoped and prayed that we would not get the same examiner. Things were looking up when a tall man came into the exam room and was very pleasant. I was tested first and passed. The examiner quizzed my father next and asked him if he could write in English. I am sure my dad did not even understand the question, but he nodded and said yes. The examiner put a piece of paper in front of him and asked him to write, "I work hard." My father quickly and proudly said, "Rocky Mountain News." And as he turned to me to give me a look of pride that he had answered the question, I quietly told him what the examiner had actually asked. With the examiner sitting directly across from us, my dad sneakily told me that he wasn't sure he could write it. I softly begged him to try his best.

As the examiner looked on and with us squirming in our seats, I told my father again what to write, but to make it clear what to write I told him in

Italian. He picked up the pen and with some hesitation began writing "*Io lav...*" Suddenly I panicked and quickly told him to do it in English. "*Nl saccie,*" *non lo so,* I don't know how, he whispered to me, hoping that the examiner had suddenly fallen asleep and would not hear him. It seemed an eternity but eventually my dad did write something, in what language I don't know! It was not English, nor Italian; it was a combination of the two, with some of our dialect thrown in for good measure. Taken from a copy of our application papers, here is my father's version of "I work hard:" "ai UorK H ard!" Not too bad. The examiner then asked him to write "we live in Denver," and after thinking a long time my father wrote, "UI Liv IN Denver." The examiner looked at the simple writing, nodded, and thanked my father.

Surely we were doomed. But the examiner intervened with a smile and actually started small talk with my dad while looking at the scribbling, wanting to know a little about our background. He then asked him who the governor of Colorado was and, surprisingly, Dad answered correctly, John Love! I breathed a sigh of relief. The examiner next moved to my mother. "God help us," I prayed. The problem with *Mamma* was that if she did not understand a question, she would always nod and say 'yes.' I tried to explain to her that saying nothing might be a better option, but to no avail. All I could do was remind her that it is sort of dangerous to say 'yes' to a stranger's question. Her response to that was, "*Eh, mamma, it'sa okaia.*"

The examiner exchanged pleasantries with her. As my father and I fixed our eyes towards her, we could clearly see her anxiety. If she failed the exam, our quest for naturalization would be denied and we would have to reapply, a costly proposition. *Mamma* managed to give the examiner her soft innocent smile, the same smile that was her definition. Handing her a piece of paper, he asked her to write, "I work in my home," and again I quietly informed her to write it in English. From a copy of her application, here's what she wrote: "ai vuorch in mai HO M E." The examiner gazed at the scribble and then decided to have her write something else. My poor mom was visibly nervous, her hand shaking as she then attempted to write, "I live in Denver." She wrote, "ai levi in Denver," and I was pleasantly surprised as I looked at her handiwork that she actually spelled "in Denver" correctly. Things were looking up, but not by much.

A copy of my father's written test is shown above and my mother's is below, 1972

The examiner scribbled something on the paper and then addressed *Mamma* again, "Mrs. Lombardi, can you tell me the name of the Father of Our Country and the first president of the United States of America?" Of course she turned to me, whispering, "*Che ditt, neh capisce,*" she did not clearly understand what the question was. I whispered back, hoping that the examiner, who was an arm's length from us, would suddenly become blind and deaf. I softly told her the question. She suddenly got kind of excited and said loudly and proudly, "*Neexonne.*" Oh no, we were in deep shit. The examiner thanked her for the answer and reminded her that he was our then current president, and again repeated the question.

My mom kept nodding as if she clearly understood every word. Then her puzzled look confirmed her confusion, and the fact was that she had no idea what he had just asked her, nor who the first American president was. I again whispered, "*Il primo presidente dell'America?*" "*Eh mamma, nl saccie,*" *non lo so,* she did not know, but I could tell that she was thinking hard. In a moment of awkwardness, and facing the realization that we were on the brink of surely failing the exam again, she shouted, "*Bufalo Bille!*" Buffalo Bill!

I cringed while my father kept his gaze on the examiner, a hint of pride on his face for my mom's answer. The examiner suddenly let out a long, loud laugh. We all managed a nervous laugh of our own. As the examiner got up he put his hand out to us and said, "Congratulations, you will soon be citizens of the United States of America."

My parents were not quite sure what the hell was going on and I quickly told them the good news in our dialect "*Semme passat!*" We passed! I don't know how many times my parents thanked the amiable federal official who towered over us. My father, now a bit less nervous, started to ask a bunch of questions. After a while I had to ask him to "*shatatt zitta mo,*" *e ora basta, silenzio.* *Papà* had suddenly turned into his usual outward self and would not stop talking, so I had to tell him to be quiet. Since the examiner's grandparents were also immigrants (from Germany) this might have helped us.

As we were walking out of the Federal Court building, my parents were very relieved, and I noticed a sense of pride on their faces. My mom kept reminding us how nice the tall man was, and that she was going to make him some *pizzelle*, and my father mentioned that a gallon of wine would also be nice. "*Niceh*" and "*thatsa niceh*" were my parents' favorite words in their limited English.

In August of 1972 we went back to the Federal Courthouse to receive our Certificates of Naturalization and to take part in the very nice celebration with other naturalized citizens. Sadly, we had to renounce our Italian citizenship, but for the most part we were happy. We were given American flags, booklets, posters, etc. by nice elderly volunteers. On that day my name was no longer Pietrantonio. After much thought I decided to change my name to Anthony Peter, a reverse of the meaning of my original name Peter Anthony. My father also legally changed his name from Vittorio to Victor, and my mom from Maria Lucia to Mary Lucy. After the ceremony, with a brown paper bag containing my mom's homemade *pizzelle* and a bottle of my dad's homemade wine, I went searching for Mr. A.R. Brassart, our examiner, so my parents could give him the goodies and say thanks once more.

We were now entitled to most benefits, rights, and responsibilities of being an American citizen. By pledging allegiance to the U.S. we gave up any prior allegiances to Italy, thus giving up our Italian citizenship. We were now expected to support and defend the Constitution of the United States of America and to serve the country when required.

THE UNITED STATES OF AMERICA

No. 9594340

CERTIFICATE OF NATURALIZATION

Petition No. 25496

Alien Registration No. A-17 137 685

·ORIGINAL·

Personal description of holder as of date of naturalization: Date of birth January 10, 1953 sex Male complexion Medium color of eyes Brown color of hair Blond height 5 feet 10 inches; weight 140 pounds; visible distinctive marks None

Marital status Single Country of former nationality Italy

I certify that the description above given is true, and that the photograph affixed hereto is a likeness of me.

Anthony Peter Lombardi

(Complete and true signature of holder)

UNITED STATES OF AMERICA
DISTRICT OF COLORADO } ss:

Be it known, that at a term of the U. S. District Court of District of Colorado held pursuant to law at Denver, Colorado on August 25, 1972 the Court having found that Anthony Peter Lombardi then residing at Denver, Colorado intends to reside permanently in the United States (when so required by the Naturalization Laws of the United States), had in all other respects complied with the applicable provisions of such naturalization laws, and was entitled to be admitted to citizenship, thereupon ordered that such person be and (s)he was admitted as a citizen of the United States of America.

In testimony whereof the seal of the court is hereunto affixed this 25th day of August in the year of our Lord nineteen hundred and Seventy-two

Seal

James R Manspeaker

Clerk of the U. S. District Court.

By Deputy Clerk.

IT IS PUNISHABLE BY U. S. LAW TO COPY, PRINT OR PHOTOGRAPH THIS CERTIFICATE.

DEPARTMENT OF JUSTICE

Copies of our citizenship certificates

THE UNITED STATES OF AMERICA

No. 9594339

CERTIFICATE OF NATURALIZATION

Petition No. 25495

Alien Registration No. A-17 137 684

·ORIGINAL·

Personal description of holder as of date of naturalization: Date of birth July 15, 1921 sex Female complexion Medium color of eyes Brown color of hair Brown height 5 feet 6 inches; weight 130 pounds; visible distinctive marks None

Marital status Married Country of former nationality Italy

I certify that the description above given is true, and that the photograph affixed hereto is a likeness of me.

Mary Lucy Lombardi

(Complete and true signature of holder)

UNITED STATES OF AMERICA
DISTRICT OF COLORADO } ss:

Be it known, that at a term of the U. S. District Court of District of Colorado held pursuant to law at Denver, Colorado on August 25, 1972 the Court having found that Mary Lucy Lombardi then residing at Denver, Colorado intends to reside permanently in the United States (when so required by the Naturalization Laws of the United States), had in all other respects complied with the applicable provisions of such naturalization laws, and was entitled to be admitted to citizenship, thereupon ordered that such person be and (s)he was admitted as a citizen of the United States of America.

In testimony whereof the seal of the court is hereunto affixed this 25th day of August in the year of our Lord nineteen hundred and Seventy-two

Seal

James R Manspeaker

Clerk of the U. S. District Court.

By Deputy Clerk.

IT IS PUNISHABLE BY U. S. LAW TO COPY, PRINT OR PHOTOGRAPH THIS CERTIFICATE.

DEPARTMENT OF JUSTICE

One of the obvious benefits was the right to vote. We would also be free to travel abroad without any restrictions and be protected by our government. We could now run for elected offices, except for president (who must be U.S. born) and were eligible for financial aid and full retirement when living abroad. We were expected to honor and respect the freedoms and the opportunities that citizenship gave us — and we would, sometimes more so than American-born citizens. Weeks later we began to receive various letters from government officials and offices, congratulating us for becoming citizens of the United States.

Although it crossed my mind to correct my mom and tell her who the first president really was, I just let it be. If she went to her grave thinking that Buffalo Bill was America's first president, so be it. That answer was most likely the reason that the good-natured examiner granted us citizenship!

City and County of Denver

W. H. McNichols Jr
MAYOR

CITY AND COUNTY BUILDING · DENVER, COLORADO · 80202

AREA CODE 303 297-2721

September 14, 1972

Mr. and Mrs. Victor Lombardi
4520 Wyandot Street
Denver, Colorado 80211

Dear Mr. and Mrs. Lombardi:

Congratulations on being naturalized as a citizen of the
United States.

You are now privileged to take up the varied duties of
citizenship which include the all-important right of voting.

I urge you to register as soon as possible so you will be
able to participate fully in government by voting for the
candidate of your choice and on the issues that appear on
the ballot from time to time.

For your information, the law in Colorado provides that you
must be at least 18 years of age, and a resident of a Denver
precinct for at least 32 days before you have the privilege
of voting.

If you meet these requirements, I urge you to come to the
Election Commission office, Room 150, City and County
Building, 14th Avenue and Bannock Street, and register.

Anyone who is eighteen years of age may register for all
relatives living at the same address.

All employees of the City government join me in congratulating
you on becoming a citizen.

Sincerely,

Bill McNichols

W. H. McNichols, Jr.
M A Y O R

Copies of 'welcome to citizenship' letters

State of Colorado

EXECUTIVE CHAMBERS

DENVER

JOHN A. LOVE
Governor

September 14, 1972

Mr. Anthony Peter Lombardi
4520 Wyandot Street
Denver, Colorado 80211

Dear Mr. Lombardi:

Congratulations upon becoming a citizen of the United States.

Our nation owes much to citizens like you who come to our shores
in search of freedom and opportunity. America's great heritage,
culture and cherished ideals of freedom reflect the contributions of
our foreign neighbors.

I am sure that you, as a new citizen, are aware of the many advantages
there are in this great country of ours, and it is hoped you will take
an active interest in the civic affairs of your state and local government.

Welcome as a United States citizen and as a resident of Colorado. We
hope great success and happiness will be yours.

Sincerely,

John A. Love

John A. Love

JAL/cb

PETER H. DOMINICK
COLORADO

COMMITTEES:
ARMED SERVICES
LABOR AND PUBLIC WELFARE
JOINT COMMITTEE ON ATOMIC ENERGY
SELECT COMMITTEE ON EQUAL
EDUCATIONAL OPPORTUNITY
SELECT COMMITTEE ON
SMALL BUSINESS

United States Senate
WASHINGTON, D.C. 20510

September 21, 1972

Mr. and Mrs. V. Lombardi
Mr. Anthony Lombardi
4520 Wyandot Street
Denver, Colorado 80211

Dear Mr. and Mrs. Lombardi & Mr. Lombardi:

It gives me great pleasure, as your United States Senator,
to welcome you as a new citizen of our great country.

Sharing in the right to select those who will run your Government, from County Commissioner to the President of the United
States, is one of the great privileges which citizenship carries
with it, and I hope that you will always take an active part
in the political activities of your city, state and nation.

I am taking the liberty of adding your name to our mailing list
in order that you may receive our newsletter concerning current
events in Washington. Please feel free to write me concerning
your views on matters of importance to our country and let me
know if I can be of any assistance to you.

With best wishes.

                    Sincerely,

                    Peter H Dominick

                    Peter H. Dominick
                    United States Senator

PHD:ch

427

THE WHITE HOUSE
WASHINGTON

Dear Fellow Citizen:

I extend to you a warm welcome to citizenship of the
United States of America.

George Washington, the first President of the United
States, once said this to his fellow citizens: "The
name of American, which belongs to you in your
national capacity, must always exalt the just pride of
patriotism..." By your free choice you have become
a citizen of this country; the name of American is now
yours.

As an American, you now share not only the rights of
all Americans but the common heritage which has
always called forth the "just pride of patriotism". As
an American, you now have the opportunity to engage in
the most rewarding activity of free men: full participation in the democratic process of a self-governing
people.

Our constitution begins with the words which we all
know: We the People. We, the People, your fellow
citizens, by birth and choice, salute you, because on
this day you have become a most valued citizen of the
United States of America.

Richard Nixon

Chapter XLVII

UNIVERSITÀ E MATRIMONIO
COLLEGE AND MARRIAGE

When many of my classmates — with help from their counselors and parents — were looking at the possibility of attending college at the University of Colorado, Colorado State University, University of Denver, Metro State College and many other in-state and out-of-state colleges, I also made the decision to attend college. My parents probably would have been all right with my getting a job with the railroad, as my brother Ezio had done. That position was an admirable one and much more lucrative than that of a dirt farmer. But the idea of attending a college, a university would be a dream come true for them. After all, I would be the first in my father's and mother's families to achieve the feat. But the predicament as to where the money to pay for a college education would come from was lurking. The only college that was even conceivable was Arapahoe Community College (ACC) in Littleton, Colorado. I decided to attend that school with my cousin, Dominic Lombardi. The only good memory that I have of my short stay there is that I played on the soccer team. It was too far of a drive from north Denver and it just did not feel right. So after one year I transferred to Metropolitan State College in downtown Denver, where the tuition was higher but manageable.

In 1975 I received a Bachelor of Arts degree in Business Management and a minor in history. I was the first in my family to receive a college degree. Many sons and daughters of Pagliarone's later immigrants preceded and followed me in obtaining a college education, making their families proud of their achievements. Most of those students worked full-time jobs while attending school. I worked full-time at my distant cousin Arnie Lombardi's business, Cosmopolitan Upholstery and managed to make the dean's list a few times. And I believe that I received a good education and grew intellectually.

I gained knowledge from the business and real estate courses that served me well when I later embarked on my own real estate investments. My professor, Mark Cohen, was a real estate attorney and broker. He presented me with the opportunity to get a real estate license and work for his firm. I thought about it and decided against it because of my already full schedule.

I did go to some practices for the school's soccer team and played in a couple of games, but there was no time, Arnie needed me at work. Or was there something else going on? Did my heart fail me? Why wasn't my whole heart there, as it was at the monastery? Or was I upset at the game itself, for failing me, for injuring me? It seemed that the game that I loved so much was slowly fading, leaving me... and more opportunities missed. It just wasn't meant to be, or as my mother always reminded me, it wasn't part of my destiny.

On June 1, 1975 at the old Denver Convention Center, family and friends gathered for the graduation commencement. Senator Gary Hart was the keynote speaker. Maybe someday I might have been able to tell my children that the president of the United States spoke at my college graduation ceremony. But it was not to be. In 1984 Hart ran a formidable campaign against the eventual democratic nominee Walter Mondale, and afterwards Hart was a consideration for Mondale's vice president, but Mondale chose Geraldine Ferraro, an Italian-American, as his running mate. They lost by a landslide to the incumbent president, Ronald Reagan. Gary Hart was considered the frontrunner for the Democratic Party in the 1988 presidential race. In 1987 during his campaign for president, he was photographed with Miami model Donna Rice. Ms. Rice was sitting on his lap on the luxury yacht named Monkey Business, which led to his quick demise. The question was raised in the media as to whether marital infidelities had anything to do with a president's ability to govern.

At the end of June 1975 I married my high school sweetheart, Jackie Meloragno. That same year many of my friends from our village also tied the knot. We were all in our early twenties and I am not sure any of us were really ready for marriage, but back then it seemed to be the right time, the right age to marry.

Our wedding party, from top left: Elaine Lombardi, Sandy Lombardi, Angela Meloragno, Cynthia Meloragno, Jackie Meloragno Lombardi, Anthony Lombardi, Terry Lombardi, Vittorio Ienco, Ezio Lombardi. Bottom left: Sharon Veltri, Coco Lombardi, Bambina Lombardi, Maria Lombardi Ienco, Dominic Lombardi, Gary Lombardi, Arnie Lombardi, Vince Carmosino, Louie Lombardi. Flower girls: Carmela Ienco, Lorella Ienco. Ring boy: Vittorio (Vic) Lombardi. June 28, 1975

Excitement was in the air as we prepared for the special occasion for Jackie and me, but the happy event wasn't without its near tragedy. My sister, Maria, came from Toronto with her husband, Vittorio, and their three children, Carmelina, Giovanni, and Lorella to celebrate my wedding. My brother had just finished building a new triplex next to his existing one.

Now he owned a six-unit complex, with a bigger unit for his own growing family. Their second-floor bedroom included a nice balcony.

A couple of days before the wedding, my sister's children, along with my brother's sons, Victor and Adelio, were playing in a sandbox under the new balcony. The kids, who ranged in age from two years to eight years old, had been playing there off and on for most of the day. Ezio had just returned from taking the Canadians on the Coors Brewery tour. My sister was halfway down the street to my parents' house when she decided to turn around and get her three children from the sandbox so they could eat lunch.

My brother was inside the house and heard a crackling sound and walked out to investigate. As he looked around he noticed that the sound was coming from the balcony above the sandbox. The adults all scrambled to get the kids away from the sandbox and suddenly the huge balcony fell to the ground, flattening the sandbox and all its contents like a pancake. They could not believe their eyes when they saw the balcony on top of the sandbox where the five children had been playing. Panic and pandemonium broke out. Everyone there was very agitated, upset, and very annoyed, yet after a while everyone was very thankful. They thought they had just witnessed a miracle; five young lives being saved. If it weren't for the warning crackling sound sent from Above, those five children would have perished.

When the contractor came over to inspect the collapsed balcony, he became visibly shaken and had to be helped to a chair, avoiding the majority of the concern from my brother, as Ezio felt bad for him. The weight of the balcony's concrete floor caused the inadequately installed support joists to collapse.

With a miracle in our pockets we were able to celebrate a beautiful wedding at Mount Carmel Church, where Jackie's parents and grandparents were also married. Some of the wedding traditions that we knew in Italy were gone, and instead new traditions were embraced. That afternoon, relatives and the wedding party enjoyed a lunch at La Bates Italian restaurant near 58th and Broadway. That evening, friends and relatives joined us at the Loretta Heights College reception hall for a night filled with food, drinks, and dancing. Jackie loved to go and hear Frankie Reno, a Denver policeman who performed at various night clubs, singing Frank Sinatra-style songs. I asked him if he could stop by before he went to his weekend gig and he graciously surprised my new wife with a few of her favorite songs. On that following Monday, Jackie and I boarded a plane (her first) for a six-week *viaggio di nozze*, honeymoon, to Italy, to my small village of Villa San Michele where it all began for me.

Presently, college is not merely an option for most descendants of Villa San Michele; rather it is a priority, a goal. Parents and grandparents push their loved ones to pursue higher education, constantly reminding them that it is the only way to success. "*Va a la scola, imparateh qualke cosa,*" *Vai a scuola, impara qualcosa*, Go to school, learn something. These words are now being expressed by every immigrant of the Italian community, joining their predecessors in urging their loved ones to get a college degree.

Our wedding guests enjoyed the popular songs, sung by Frankie Reno, 1975

Ready to board TWA for our honeymoon to Italy, 1975

Across the ocean in a small village of Italy, parents were also urging their children to continue their education, so they could escape the life of a *contadino*.

My wife's father was Dominic Melaragno, the son of Pasquale Melaragno, who came from Pagliarone, the hamlet of Ciacarancio. He immigrated by himself in 1916 when he was sixteen years old. Pasquale's wife was Domenica (Minnie) Lombardi, whose parents also came from Pagliarone. They lived a stone's throw away from our house, in a hamlet named Pietro. Their last name was changed from Melaragno to Meloragno, probably when Pasquale went to work for Union Pacific Railroad.

This is one of four certificates from Italy I presented to prove when I was born and that I had been a resident of my village, all somehow a requirement before our wedding.

As a third generation American, my wife, as with other young American brides of native Italians, was in for a culture shock when she married me. Jackie did her best to assimilate into the extended family. She was not in the same line of thinking with most of the women who came from our village in Italy. These women were very blunt, very dubious in some ways. My wife was very confused when asked a direct personal question. She learned quickly where this culture began when we went back to Pagliarone for our honeymoon.

Jackie's parents and grandparents: Dominic (Babe) Meloragno and Frances Meloragno, and Pasquale Meloragno and Domenica (Minnie) Lombardi Meloragno, on our wedding day, 1975.

On our honeymoon in 1975, the village people pelted both of us with a myriad of questions. Jackie was very confused when an elderly gentleman, when told that we had just gotten married and were on our *viaggio di nozze*, honeymoon, promptly asked Jackie how many kids we had. She did not and could not answer him because she did not understand him, and I ignored the question. She did not know that this old guy thought that, because he was probably told at some time that most American women already had children from previous marriages and then they remarried. She was continually asked by the women of the village if she could leave them what she was wearing because they really liked it, and that she smelled really nice and could they have some of it — meaning all of it. She did leave many of her clothes and other items, as did I. After all, we could just buy more when we went back to America, the land of plenty.

On our honeymoon in 1975, Jackie tries milking a goat!

On our honeymoon in 1975, Jackie contemplating whether or not to ride a workhorse!

Chapter XLVIII

MAMMA, NONNA, NONNINA
MOTHER, GRANDMOTHER, GREAT-GRANDMA

"She was the best mom, grandmother, great-grandmother, sister, aunt," and so on. This statement is heard often, especially during eulogies. Of course most of us think that we have or had the best of these people in our lives. And that's the way it should be. To us there is no better such person on this earth. It's admirable to hear people make such claims. If there were more bests, this world would be a much better place. To me and to our whole family, *Mamma* was simply the best!

Don't let anyone tell you that the father is the boss of the Italian household. It may seem that way at a glance, but deep at the heart of the Italian family unit, it is *la mamma* who rules. She keeps it together, withstanding a variety of obstacles including a demanding and needy husband and sometimes combative and radical children. In my own family, my *mamma* took her share of criticism from my father, most of it unwarranted, usually as a result of my mom's benevolence or just because that is what these men did. Arguing was part of the daily routine. The kids were used to it and we probably thought that something was wrong if the daily banter was missing. The men loved to argue for argument's sake. Arguing about something seemed to give those hardened immigrants energy and determination!

I can honestly say that I don't remember my mom laying a disciplining hand on me very often. I don't think I can make that claim for my brother and sister. I was the baby and somehow seemed to be special to her, from the day she delivered me on that cold January morning of 1953 in front of our fireplace, while my dad, brother, and sister slept. It was just *Mamma* and *Zia* Vincenza, an old midwife. No doctors or nurses or sterile surroundings. She had gone through the same process three times before. Her first child, Bambina, died at the tender age of four months old in 1943. Little Bambina passed away shortly after becoming sick with some unknown illness. My mother had to deal with her baby's birth and sudden death without my father, who was away fighting a war. Imagine the anxiety when my brother was born, worrying that he might fall victim to the same mysterious illness. She worried constantly while all of us were small and did not stop worrying about us, about her grandchildren, and her great-grandchildren, until the very day she died.

Mamma was the best book I ever read, ever heard. I heard that book over and over and never tired of the stories it told. My father was the ruler of our home, but *Mamma* was the glue that held it together. She and the rest of those immigrant mothers put their families before anyone or anything else.

Those little women never backed away from the very hard work, such as hauling everything but the kitchen sink to faraway plots to till those parched lands. Walking home at the end of the day, already carrying a heavy load, they would keep an eye out for any small twig in sight. They would pick it up and bring it home, adding it to the pile of twigs that would be our only source of heat during the cold winter months.

Mamma never rested. The only reason for her existence seemed to be to make sure that her family survived. All the women of our village scraped and clawed to provide for their families. The men, they worked very hard but they seemed to find time to get together at night to have a drink of wine and play cards or *morra* at the local *cantina*. The women, they stayed home, always doing something for the family. Their only social time was at church and on those cold nights around a neighbor's fireplace, knitting, mending, and telling stories, usually to a group of young ones sitting on tiny wooden chairs or on the floor. All the while, the women kept a watchful eye on the children, making sure that the kids did not fall into the fire.

In the darkness and in deep snow, she would carry me and help my brother and sister navigate the long walk on our way home from the hamlet where she was born, where she lived until she married my father. The holes in her shoes did not seem to bother her much. All that mattered was our protection; it was the only thing on her mind, not at all different from most mothers on earth. It pained her to have to put us in our either cold or stifling hot straw beds at night.

I never really thought about it growing up, but when I returned to my village, to our old crumbling house, I noticed the smallness, the simplicity of that special place. As you enter, a tiny kitchen welcomes you with a fireplace and a bread oven, a small cupboard, and a small table with four small rush chairs. A small doorway without a door leads you into an even smaller rectangular room, our bedroom. Another doorway without a door leads into a matching room that was my parents' bedroom. Thankfully I don't remember much about privacy issues. But our mom kept that petite house as neat and clean as the environment allowed.

Jackie and cousin Adelia posing in front of fireplace where I was born, 1975

Mamma never stopped. She couldn't stop, she refused. Every ounce of energy she had, she used to keep her young family as safe as possible. The tiny kitchen was her operating room, and the hearth her operating table. She kept us safe from its flames as we tried to keep warm. She battled the smoke as she hung the black soot-covered pot filled with cold water from the hot, black soot-covered chain hanging over the fire. And while waiting for the water to boil, she would be mending some piece of clothing that at times looked like a patchwork of rags.

Mamma always made sure that her children and her husband were fed, before she even thought about taking a bite — and then it was usually a very small bite. My mother seemed malnourished. She was as thin as a beanpole and looked older than she really was, as did most of the other women of the village. One would have to look very hard to find anyone who was overweight in our village. There is something to be said for that Mediterranean diet of ours, where meat was rare and fruit and vegetables were somewhat plentiful. Add to that our constant movement and you get minimal weight gain. Most, if not all, of the women who came here during the 60s immigration rush eventually gained weight. I would have never thought that my poor *mamma* would have to be warned by her family to taper her eating habits because she was getting fat! Her downfall was her refusal to throw any of God's gifts away. Her solution was to eat all leftovers, avoiding the minor predicament!

Mamma making one of our favorite meals, polenta, in her northwest Denver home, 2004

When my father died, my mother took on many more jobs around the house and surprisingly to all of us she did a darned good job! She even found time to take in what daytime TV had to offer. Many times I had to inform her that some of that stuff just wasn't true, while other things reported were true. She refused to believe what Monica Lewinsky was saying about President Clinton. *"Kaella puttana, dice bia bugie,"* *Quella puttana, dice solo bugie,* Monica was just a liar. And she wanted to know why they were talking so much about her dress and we could not find the proper way to tell a *nonna* what they found on her dress! "*Povere Hillari e Chelsi,*" she felt bad for the president's wife and daughter. She could not keep up with the myriad of new technologies and at times she had a hard time with old ones.

When my nephew, Vic, lived in Austin, Texas, working as a sportscaster at a TV station there, *Nonna* went to spend a month with him. The first few nights, she slept with him in the only bed of the small one-bedroom apartment. But her nightly dreams and nightmares, accompanied with a variety of moans, drove Vic to the couch. On occasions when he came home late at night, he found her sleeping on the sofa and did not wake her. The young bachelor enjoyed her company, her cooking, her stories, but at times things got a bit precarious when he wanted to entertain a friend! The ladies truly loved *Nonna's* company and her cooking, although they were a bit disappointed that they would not be able to spend the night. A few times *Nonna* accompanied Vic on dates and one of the questions *Nonna* would always ask the date was if she was going to marry her nice grandson.

One night while he was at work, *Nonna* called Vic. He had written his phone number down for her, nice and big, in case of an emergency. She asked him if she could call her daughter, Maria, in Canada. Vic told her that Maria's phone number was on the phone on the wall. But pushing those buttons with the huge numbers on that phone was different than the buttons with which she was familiar. When Vic got home *Nonna* seemed somewhat frustrated. She had dialed Maria's number all afternoon and night and always got a busy signal. Vic wondered if she had the wrong number and asked *Nonna* to show him what number she was calling. She promptly went to the phone on the wall and told him that she dialed 1-2-3-4-5-6-7-8-9-0, the numbers on the buttons on the phone and not the number on the list right below the buttons! After the laughing subsided, *Nonna* told Vic that she would go to *H e B* (a store called HEB) in the morning and buy some groceries. The store was a good half mile away so he told her that he would drive her there, to which she replied, "*No itsa okaia, me ve a piglià reh padrone.*" She had already befriended the owners and they had been giving her rides!

While Vic and Terri were living in Phoenix and enjoying their newlywed status, my mom and dad went to spend some time with them —

'some time' to Old World Italians meant about three months! It cost too much for the flight to just stay a week! Surely Terri must have wanted to strangle Vic. My father turned the barren backyard and struggling front yard of Vic's house into an oasis, while my mom was the consummate cook and housekeeper.

One afternoon a coworker of Vic's came into the TV station and notified Vic that his elderly grandparents were in the median of a major thoroughfare, picking oranges from a tree. Vic had noticed the abundance of oranges in the house but did not realize that they came from a tree in the middle of a roadway. Of course when my parents noticed the orange tree full of oranges, they just could not bear the thought of them going to waste.

My mother gained some fame in Phoenix, as a number of billboards invited fans to listen to Vic and *Nonna* on a sports talk radio show. When Vic took a sportscasting position back in Denver, he brought the *Nonna* spots with him. While on the air, he would call her and ask her which team she thought would win, "*Nonna, Arizona o Nebraska?*" Usually she would say "*Che?*" What? wanting Vic to repeat the question. Finally, in her heavy accent she would say, "*I thinka so Arizona.*" We, the family, knew that the team she usually picked was either the one that was easier for her to pronounce, or the one she just remembered better. Vic also mentioned that she would usually pick the team that he revealed last — easier to remember!

In our village, when we moved into our new government-built house in Villa San Michele, my mother was able to experience the pleasures of a propane stove: not as much smoke inhalation, fewer burns on her hands, and, thanks to a better economic situation in our town, plenty of food for her family. Just how much better could life get beyond having a roof over our heads and food on our table? Soon after, we would find out as we gave it all up to begin anew in a foreign land.

I don't know how the immigrants of years before made it in this new land, as the fathers and sons ventured so far, leaving wives and daughters behind. If it weren't for *Mamma* protecting us with everything she had, my father, my brother, and I would have failed. We surely would have run back home to Italy with our tails between our legs. And many of those early travelers did go back home. They did not immigrate; rather they migrated like birds. They worked long and hard and then went back to

Italy to bring the family some hard-earned dollars. With that money, they were able to build a new house or buy another cow. In the coming spring, they would make the long trip back to those timber or mining camps in the Rocky Mountains and to many other back-breaking jobs in the area.

Although my father was the one who made the ultimate decision for us to stay in America, *Mamma* was the one who made it possible for it to be permanent, even though deep inside she missed her village very much.

Italian nonne love their great-grandchildren. With Baby Anthony and Gianni, 2006

She always gave them money so she would not get mice in her house!
With Baby Sofia, Thanksgiving Day of 2007

Mamma wished that Papà was with us on a cruise to the Caribbean,
so they could have reminisced about our journey on that ocean liner of long ago. 2003

Chapter XLIX

PAPÀ, NONNO, NONNINO
FATHER, GRANDFATHER, GREAT-GRANDPA

I get emotional when I think of my parents. We miss them dearly. They brought us into this world, nurtured us, and sacrificed to make our lives better. They gave up their familiar home and ventured out into the unknown to give their children a chance at a good life. They worked day and night, cleaning toilets to save enough money to put a roof over our heads. They used many ways and means to get ahead, some of those a little embarrassing, to earn that almighty dollar. They never did all this for themselves; rather it was always for their children.

My father taught us that hard work brought great rewards. He went a little overboard with my brother, Ezio, creating a workaholic. My dad pushed me to keep going to school. He was instrumental in helping me overcome an introverted demeanor that I had developed while at school at the monastery, making me more outgoing, more confident. My father was also a great salesman. He surely could sell a comb to a bald man at one of his many garage sales.

My dad was able to strike up a conversation with anybody, at any time. Even with his limited grasp of the English language, he talked to people with whom I would never consider striking up a conversation. At the age of forty-eight, he came to a new land and made the most of it after accepting the fact that even with his limited knowledge of the ever important language, it would be best for his kids if we stayed in America.

After some doubt, he realized that the opportunities to improve our lives were much greater here than back in Italy. He always lamented that if only we could have come here when he was younger, how much better he could have made our lives. Maybe, maybe not.

I believe that the reason that we, the immigrants, strive so hard to succeed is because we came from an earlier life of despair, where opportunities to improve were minimal and we were resigned to live as best we could, the way our ancestors had lived before us. Once we realized that we did not have to be ruled by *la signoria*, the privileged ruling class, we went full speed ahead in the quest for a better life. Many of the immigrants before us were happy to have a job and a modest house for their family, with just enough land to grow a few vegetables. They congregated to a certain area and did not venture out much. Italian immigrants often settled in American city neighborhoods called Little Italy. Little Italy, in whichever city, was very much different from the real Italy, because most of those immigrants usually came from small rural villages and were then suddenly thrown into a bustling urban community. The first immigrants from our village tended to live near, if not next to, their fellow immigrants in the Little Italy area of Denver, where they had some semblance of the life they had left behind.

Although some of our Denver neighborhood's *paesani* had ventured into the real estate market, this business did not fully develop for most until the arrival of the later immigrants, their 1960s counterparts. One of the original champions of this movement was my brother, Ezio. It started with a purchase he made with my parents of a duplex on 44th and Perry Street in northwest Denver. Soon after, many *paesani* owned at least one duplex. The allurement of the added income from tenants drove them hard to accumulate more real estate. In their prior lives, they were the ones paying rent to the landowners, be it money or crops, for the use of the land.

Next, my brother eyed a triplex on 43rd and Perry with some adjacent land. He knocked on the owner's door and was told that it wasn't for sale, but Ezio did not give up. Eventually the older fellow decided to sell. It wasn't long after that purchase that my brother built another triplex next-door. Then later, he popped the top of his unit to accommodate his growing flock. He also finished the basement, not because he needed the finished space (it actually served his family better unfinished), but because he somehow needed to stay busy every waking hour of his day. And so my workaholic brother created work for himself.

One night in the summer of 1976, I was helping him glue down a linoleum floor, and I was also installing upholstered pieces for his built-in bar in the almost finished basement. It was very

Papà with grandsons, Dominic and Mario, in his colorful yard. All were happy because they were going to Canada, along with Mamma. 1993

late. His sons, seven-year-old Vittorio and three-year-old Adelio, had been put to sleep by their *nonna* in the second-floor bedroom. As *Mamma* left for home, she reminded us that it was getting late and we should call it a night. My brother's wife, Bambina, was at work on her night shift at Rockmont Envelope Company. I was exhausted and finally informed my brother that I was going home, a block down the street where my wife and I lived in my parents' basement apartment as newlyweds. He of course tried to make me stay. "We are almost finished," he kept saying. No, we were not almost finished, there was a lot more to do, and we could do it the next night or nights. I ignored his pleas and limped home.

I had just gotten into bed when I heard a noise. It sounded like a child screaming, crying. As the screaming got closer, louder, I sprang from my bed and ran upstairs and outside. Panic set in when I saw my mom with her hands clutched above her head, a sure sign of despair. My nephew, Victor, recalls *Nonna* calling out his name, "*Vittr.*" "*Ma che si fatt?*" What happened? Did his dad hit him? Was that the reason he ran to *Nonna*'s so late at night? No, his dad did not hit him, but *Papà* was on fire!

As I looked up the street towards my brother's house, I saw flames shooting out of the basement windows. I probably ran the short distance in record time. When I reached the complex I saw my brother outside, in a daze. He was holding Adelio and crying out "*Mamma mea, mamma mea, che song fatt!* Mamma mia, mamma mia, what have I done. The "Mamma mia" would be replaced by something like "Oh my God," in an American setting. I reminisced with Vic about the fire and asked him what he remembered. He and Adelio were awakened by my brother's screams, and as they ran downstairs their dad was there in a panic. The three of them ran outside and Victor then ran to his grandparents' house for help.

My parents had walked to and from my brother's house thousands of times; that night was the first time they ran. Their screams caused lights to come on in houses up and down Perry Street. My wife, Jackie, followed close behind as she carried seven-year-old Victor. My brother was outside in a panic, crying, wailing. He reminded me so much of my mother, his hands up in the air, "*Che song fatt! Che song fatt!*" What have I done, over and over and no one could calm him down. With the help of Mark Herlocher, a high school friend and a fireman who was renting the house next-door, we extinguished most of the flames with garden hoses.

Soon Denver firefighters showed up and took over. To my surprise, they broke almost every window in the house. To me it seemed that they were making more damage than the fire and smoke had already done, but obviously they knew what they were doing. During those very anxious moments, neighbors gathered as they were awakened by the commotion. Then a car pulled up. It was my sister-in-law's friend dropping Bambina off from her swing shift job at the envelope factory. It was close to midnight.

Bambina scrambled out of the car and her obvious panic added to the bedlam. My brother was taken to St. Anthony Hospital with burns to his hands. He was hospitalized for a couple of days and was treated for shock. The house was a mess, but with the help of family and friends it was eventually put back together. The smell of smoke, however, lingered for months.

Earlier that night after I had left, instead of calling it a night and going to bed as I suggested, my brother chose to linger, to create more work, to probably over-clean some of the tools. He cleaned some tools on the floor in the furnace room, using gasoline as a cleanser! The gas somehow ignited and as he scrambled, perhaps attempting to put the fire out, his hands caught on fire, along with the rest of the gas-soaked rags. Quickly the whole basement was in flames. Thankfully, little Victor woke up and ran to *Nonna*'s. He was scared and he also wanted someone to help his screaming dad.

The idea of a duplex sounded very enticing to those within our group of new immigrants from Pagliarone. Live on one side and rent out the other. The additional income would help with the mortgage payment,

*Perry Street compound.
My brother and his family have
lived in the house on the left for
over fifty years.*

although a lot of the properties were paid for in cash! Almost every dollar earned was put into a savings account and the money was not used to buy a shiny new car, but to purchase real estate. Some of these immigrants became very frugal, spending as little as possible for daily essentials. They became obsessed with saving money to purchase more houses, more duplexes, more land, because after all, they did not make land anymore!

The first generation of immigrants did not engage in any form of entertainment that required spending money. Some of these immigrants had never seen the interior of a theater or a restaurant, nor enjoyed elaborate vacations. Their version of a vacation was to go visit a relative, where paying for a hotel room and meals was avoided. Their entertainment was to keep adding to their savings account at the bank, excited to see the amount steadily grow. They were not slumlords; on the contrary, the yards were manicured, the interiors were cleaned, painted, and maintained with an obsession. Even though they had never seen a mechanical room, these uneducated but intelligent immigrants learned how to do the basics of plumbing, electrical, and other maintenance projects, which meant a higher return on their investment. As landlords, they policed their properties and at times the tenants would become very irritated by the landlord's constant scrutiny and inspections.

My father turned the duplex on 44th and Perry Street from a rundown, neglected property into a beautifully manicured place, with rose and vegetable gardens. The product of his efforts prompted the North Denver Tribune to write articles, with pictures of his rose and tomato plants in the yard, urging and challenging north Denver residents to emulate my father's work. People would constantly stop by to admire his healthy rose and tomato plants.

From the day he was hired, my father worked every weekend at the Rocky Mountain News. On Mondays and Tuesdays, his days off, he would be in his yard at dawn making sure that every blade of grass was straight! Cutting and trimming the grass became an obsession. I don't know how many times he yelled at me for using the whole width of the lawnmower, as it was meant to be used. He insisted on using only half, so the other half would cut over the grass that already had been cut. It needed to be cut twice and it had better be a nice straight line! My son, Dominic, and nephews, Victor, Adelio, and Mario, clearly recall my father following close behind when they helped him, making sure that only half of the cutting blades were used. He would be on his hands and knees, meticulously trimming the grass near the sidewalks. And he would not quit until all of the grass was swept and the walkways and driveway were hosed until squeaky clean. If my father did not have to pay for water, he would probably have watered the concrete surfaces continuously! He often forced me to stand there and water the lawn by hand, because he believed that that was the only sure way to keep every blade of grass looking green and lush.

When Frank Capra, our tenant for many years and a plumber, installed an automatic sprinkling system on the two adjoining duplexes, my father was not very happy. The water running down the sidewalks and the spotty coverage made him very nervous. We would just shake our heads as we watched him sitting in a chair, watering his lawn by hand.

My mother was not allowed to do much yard work. My father would yell at her, "*Tu neh riendeh niendeh deh kaeshte,*" *tu non ti intendi nulla di questo*, that she did not understand anything about yard work. I heard that same comment many times from my father. I would get very upset with him because I knew that my mom knew more than he presumed. When my father passed away, *Mamma* took over the yard work and did an admirable job. I am sure that *Papà* was watching from above with a surprised smirk.

One summer my father and coworker, Renato Lombardi, dug a basement under Renato's duplex, a block east of ours, by hand! On Mondays and Tuesdays, their days off, you would find them hauling dirt out of the basement through a small window. People walked by and shook their heads, yet slowly but surely they dug a basement under one side of that duplex! During the winter months, endless tasks were performed in the interior of those duplexes, some, if not most of them inessential. The men fed off of each other; if one added new paraphernalia to his duplex then the rest would follow.

Many duplexes and other properties were purchased by immigrants of Pagliarone (Villa San Michele) in the area of the Berkeley neighborhood of northwest Denver. My parents and brother, Ezio, bought a duplex at 3950-60 West 44ᵗʰ Avenue in 1971 and other paesani followed: Renato/Gilda Lombardi, Umberto/Ida Lombardi, Nicola/Ida Lombardi, Antonio/Ninetta Lombardi, Oreste/Claudina Lombardi, Michele/Giuseppina Carmosino, Salvatore/Teresa Iacovetta, Joe/Mary Carmosino, Antonio Carmosino, Giovanni/Maria Carmosino, Vince/Diane Carmosino, Louis/Elaine Lombardi, Anthony/Jackie Lombardi.

My dad and my brother, Ezio, became addicted to painting. They would continually paint walls that did not need to be painted. Whenever I was asked to help, I would soon be fired. My taping was unacceptable and I either dipped the brush too deeply or rolled the roller incorrectly and/or my painting strokes were not up to their standards. The constant complaint was that I got more paint on me and the floor than on the walls. I am sure they realized that I was intentionally careless, so I would be banished from the usually unnecessary project. As a teenager I had better things to do.

I tried to tell my parents that there were too many trinkets inside and outside of our house, but they kept finding places to add more. The concrete and plastic statues, ducks, chickens, and God knows what else, were strewn everywhere. The plastic flowers that were stuck into the flower boxes during the winter months were over-the-top. But their comment, "*Ma so nice,*" but they are nice. My parents had found a new source for purchasing these items besides Kmart, *Targetta, Woolco, TGeY, Wulwort, Mangomeriword,* and other Lakeside Mall stores. The store off of 52ⁿᵈ and Pecos, called House of Green, became the principal location to purchase furniture that bordered on gaudy. And then a new venue was discovered, *la flee marketta*, the flea market.

Maybe the flea market reminded them of *la fiera*, the outdoor markets, in Italy. Whatever the reason, my father loved to shop there. He could barter there, "*How mucha?*" "Ten dollars," the seller would reply. My dad would counter with, "*I give you two dollareh.*" I would have to endure the rant from the vendor for being insulted by such a low offer. It did not phase my father one bit; he would offer the seller fifty cents more. On Saturday or Sunday afternoons, I would have to take him and my mom to *la flee marketta*. There, we would usually run into their compatriots and they would exchange information on the best deals of the day. And then I would have to endure the many, "*Hey common, you maka good price.*"

I knew we would be going somewhere when my dad approached, dressed in his nice slacks, his suit jacket, and wearing his aftershave, Aqua Velva. I could smell it from a mile away and once in the car, it was almost unbearable. He must have used a whole bottle of the stuff every time we went somewhere. He seemed to annoy all of us by his insistence on always being the last one out of the house. Usually with everyone in the car and ready to go, he would say, "*Waitta, waitta*," and he'd go back inside to check on God knows what. It became a routine and part of our going-out ritual. He liked to look neat and smell good. He was very particular about his clothes. He would not let my mom wash or iron them; he had his own little setup in the garage where he would do his laundry, to my mom's delight. God knows, she did not want him complaining to her about that; she thought that he did enough grumbling and criticizing about everything else.

I am sure my father loved my mom, but I never heard him say so, nor she to him. I never saw him give her a kiss. I did see a lot of arguing about stuff that did not matter. It was usually my dad accusing my mom of not being *furba*, cunning, enough or not understanding the situation at hand. My parents never called each other by name. *Quatrà*, girl, in our dialect was the only name I ever heard my dad call my mom. And *vagliò*, boy or guy, in our dialect was the name that my mom called my dad. Once in a great while I would hear *Mamma* call my dad *Vittò*, Vittorio, and it seemed kind of strange.

Papà was a short and compact man. Not an ounce of fat on him, he was trim and muscular. He was the toughest man I knew — just as other sons usually think of their father as the toughest person they know — and not just because he accomplished some amazing physical feats, but also because of the countless pains he endured in his life, both physically and mentally. I was amazed at how *Papà* could work so hard for so many hours and never tire. All of those men and women who immigrated from our village seemed to have endless energy. They were just so used to the very hard, backbreaking work they performed every day in the fields around our village, ever since they were children. That hard life had hardened them, prepared them for the obstacles that America was going to hand them.

As a young man, when I helped my father when he was in his fifties and sixties, he outworked me and had more left in his tank when I would finally run out of gas. My brother, on the other hand, hung with him. Ezio had lived the hard life back in Italy for longer than I. I recall one hot summer day when my father decided to pour a concrete driveway in front of our new house. All the *paesani* seemed to have a love affair with cement. They poured concrete in the oddest places around their homes! The week before the pour, my dad and Ezio had worked nonstop at preparing part of the front yard for the concrete driveway. Forms were set and the three of us were waiting for the cement truck to arrive, when my brother was called into work at the Burlington Northern rail yards of Denver.

Ezio never turned down overtime work and he constantly reminded his superiors that he was available for the extra work anytime, holidays included. It seemed as though he spent more time there than at home, with his wife and young son, Victor, who all lived with my parents and me. One night while on a double shift at the railroad yards, Ezio was tired and cold. He went inside a railcar to rest a bit, but soon fell asleep and woke up hours later somewhere in southern Colorado. He was so tired that he did not hear the train pull away from the lower Denver rail yard. Fellow employees poked fun at him for always being available for overtime. They would tell him that Burlington was taking advantage of him and Ezio was confused by their reasons for not working when asked. Some fellow employees must not have liked the idea of my brother being the ultimate employee. One night after a shift, he noticed a note next to his lunchbox saying, "*Dago*, go home."

My father was confident that the three of us could do the concrete driveway job, so he did not bother asking any of his friends to help. When the truck pulled up to our house, the driver looked around for the cement finishers but all he saw was my dad in his blue coveralls and me, a skinny sixteen-year-old, standing next to him. The driver asked me who was going to finish the concrete. I told him that my father and I were going to do it. He shook his head and informed us that we would never finish that driveway, that the heat would dry it before the two of us could even spread it out, much less finish it. I tried to translate to my dad what the driver said, but before I was even finished, my dad, clearly annoyed, motioned to the driver to start pouring the cement out of the chute.

My father hurriedly raked the cement, instructing me to do the same. That was my initiation into the cement finishing craft. I did not have a clue as to what to do and my dad did not seem to know much more than I. The driver kept telling us to find help and my father just ignored him. I could see my dad becoming upset with the truck driver, as the driver held onto the cement chute. As we frantically tried to shovel and rake that gray slime into the formed area, the driver stood by and watched us struggle. Suddenly my father instructed me to go to the other side of the driveway, as he grabbed a long two-by-four board and told me to grab it, too, and as he set it on top of the fast-drying concrete, he asked me to help him pull and push the board back-and-forth to spread out the cement evenly. After a couple of minutes of that, my arms felt like they were going to fall right off my shoulders. The pain was extreme and any strength I had left was zapped by the hot sun of that July day of 1969.

More cement poured out of the chute as more pain poured into my arms. Finally I could not go on anymore. I was just barely hanging onto the board, as my father pulled and pushed the twelve-foot long piece of wood. Suddenly I just let go from the weak grip I had on the homemade leveling tool and got up from my knees to get a drink from the hose behind me. Flashbacks of my life at the convent came roaring back into my head as I saw stars and felt pain on one side of my face. My father had picked up the board and whacked me on the side of my head with it. In a loud, angry voice he asked me why I could chase a stupid soccer ball around all day, but could not pull the board. At the same time, he seemed to be upset at himself for hitting me with the piece of wood. The look on his face was that of regret and sorrow.

While my dad was still holding up the long board, the driver suddenly let go of the chute and grabbed my side of the board and helped my father smooth the cement out. The surprised, frightened look on the driver's face said it all. Surely he thought that this small man was going to beat the shit out of him if he just stood there staring. I decided to bear down and work as hard as my sixteen-year-old body could, or else I was going to get whacked again with God knows what. That truck driver was amazed that we actually worked that concrete until it was smooth and good to go. You just could not tell my father or other men from our village that a job was too difficult to finish. I recall many times when some jobs were just too challenging, but that did not stop them from giving it a try. Our father ingrained in us that no matter how grueling a project was, hard work and perseverance would bring it to fruition.

During the winter months my father must have painted some walls more than once, just to stay busy. Television was only a means to aid him in falling asleep for the night, and not understanding it was only partially the reason for not watching it. My mom would say that the television was watching *him* sleep! I sometimes wondered why a certain room was painted with multiple loud colors, but the question was answered by the fact that the wild-colored paint was on sale at *Mangomeriword*.

One winter season my father, bored and without any projects inside our house, decided to wallpaper the interior of his garage with somebody's discarded, loud, red brick colored wallpaper. He accented the walls by hanging pictures, paintings, and what some outsiders might have thought were other gaudy paraphernalia. I suppose the decorations, amongst the yard tools and the collection of God knows what, made it much more attractive when we celebrated Communions, birthdays, New Year's Eve, and other celebrations in our two-car garage/event center. And of course it became a packing house when a lamb or goat was butchered, or when sausage and *prosciutto* were being prepared inside the wallpapered walls of our garage.

One early-spring season, my nephews, Vic and Adelio, could not wait to get home from Holy Family grade school. They had a new pet, a soft, woolen lamb in their garage. They loved to pet it, to hear it bleat, to feed it just like their father had instructed them to do. As long as they could remember, they had always yearned for a pet, maybe a dog. They begged their parents, they asked Santa Claus, but to no avail. Finally, Victor at the age of ten, and Adelio, at the age of seven, had their first pet. Not a puppy, rather a baby sheep, but they were not going to complain. They showed off their pet to all their friends. The lamb was a big hit with the neighborhood friends and classmates at Holy Family Grade School.

Ezio reminded his boys to feed the lamb the grain from the sack in the garage. A couple of weeks passed and the little lamb was growing, it was nice and fat! One afternoon, when school got out, the boys ran home and straight into the garage to see their fluffy pet and to feed it. When they opened the door, they were surprised to see something hanging from the ceiling. It was the lamb, skinned! Their one and only pet was now food for the family.

As a kid, it was magical for me to see men cut a slit in one of the legs of a recently butchered lamb. They would stick a small, wooden pipe into the opening and then take turns blowing into the flute-like pipe. The lamb would blow up like a balloon, as the skin separated from the body – our way of skinning a lamb. A couple of days later, on Easter Sunday, we gathered at my brother's house for dinner. Part of the elaborate dinner was roasted lamb. Victor and Adelio refused to eat any of it. They envisioned their soft, woolly pet and could not bear the thought to take a bite of it!

In our Perry Street house we had a kitchen on the main level, but for most Italian-Americans, upstairs kitchens were usually just for show. The kitchen in the basement got the bulk of the use. But even two kitchens did not seem to be enough in our house, so my father slowly put together what was starting to look like a third kitchen in the garage. Never enough kitchens in our culture!

My father and his compatriots continually worked in their yards, sometimes overplanting and exaggerating the inclusion of stuff! Every bit of space was used for something, as they spent hours *alla yarda*. It was easy to identify the properties owned by Italian-Americans by the way the yards were adorned. Two lions in concrete, sitting on top of a brick column are sort of pleasant to most, but when an amateur artist decides to paint them a variety of colors, as some of our families did, then it bordered on the ridiculously gaudy. No paint was to be wasted, or was it; no time to be wasted, so they painted.

One late summer afternoon, I answered the phone and my father was on the other end of the line, crying. I panicked and demanded to know what was wrong. I was fearful that something had happened to my mom. They were getting up in age and we worried about their health, their safety. He eventually informed me that he could not cut the grass anymore. I was confused and asked him to explain. He informed me

*Our yard was intertwined with flowers and vegetables amongst
the lawn, no space wasted, nothing left bare.*

that he could no longer keep up with the lawnmower! That was the
beginning of the end for *Papà*. Even though his life had been filled with
many obstacles, the last two years of his life were the most difficult. He
started suffering small strokes that eventually left him immobile and
unable to speak. He died in a facility where, as a family, we swore that no
members would ever end up. But when my mother tried and was unable
to care for him at home, we had to put him into the dreaded nursing
home, where he passed away on April 16, 2002.

*My mom and dad, all smiles with their 3 children at their 50th
wedding anniversary, January 1992*

Chapter L

TRAGEDIA · TRAGEDY

It was just another late August afternoon of 1964 in Villa San Michele. Women were sitting on their stoops sewing, mending, and surely gossiping about some young couple who was seen talking, wondering when an engagement announcement would be made. And more than likely, they were trying to guess which young women the two visiting young *Americani* would pursue while here in the village. The street was void of most males, who were working in the fields, but there were plenty of old men and children sitting in front of their family's houses, enjoying the warm summer afternoon or playing in the streets. More than likely, the elderly men were discussing that year's wheat crop or harvests of years gone by.

That day, for some reason, I was hanging around the main street of town. Maybe my parents were giving me a bit of a vacation before I went away to school. Usually I would be at Luigi, our old farmhouse, helping with the summertime chores, although in late August most of the wheat had already been cut and taken to the area where it would be thrashed. I was playing soccer with some of the boys on the main cobblestone street, as the girls were standing nearby, talking and watching us play. Younger children chased each other, while small babies crawled around near the watchful eyes of grandmothers. Suddenly all of our eyes caught sight of a car that had turned onto the same cobblestone street. We scattered onto the sidewalk and we all set our eyes on the shiny automobile. It eventually stopped right in front of us, where the road ended and the barracks began.

The main street of town where many happy memories transpired, but sadly, a tragic one remains in my mind. 2014

The sparkling new car was a rare sight in our village. Most of the few cars that called Villa San Michele home were relics from years gone by. The two Italian-American tourists who had immigrated to America years earlier, got out of the car and proudly stood next to it. Their cousin from Villa San Michele was also there. Other boys and a few young men, who had come home early from the fields or had just hopped off the train from various destinations, gathered near the American tourists and their car, examining it, admiring it. The cousin jumped in the driver side of the car. He wanted to learn how to drive and maybe show off a bit. Soon that normal afternoon would be altered forever by the impending driving lesson.

One of the *Americani* got into the passenger seat while the other looked on, standing next to the car with the other onlookers. The cousin seemed excited, nervous but eager to learn how to drive a car. After a quick instruction of the car's instruments, the car slowly pulled away from the curb and gently turned around and pointed towards the other end of the street. *Pasqualuccio* (Little Pasquale) Lombardi, a little old man, was seated in his chair in his usual spot in front of his house, taking in the sights and the warm sun. He also took interest in the driving course that was occurring in our quiet, safe cobblestone street. There was a bit of excitement all around, something new for the village people to experience.

Without warning and in an instant, the car gained speed and appeared to be out of control. For a moment we were amused by the demonstration, the rest was a blur. The car jumped the curb. Some of the young onlookers quickly jumped out of the way; some threw themselves on a pile of dried branches and a woodpile, as the car slammed into the wall of a house up the street. There was a moment of total stillness after the crash, followed by the loudest scream I had ever heard, that the whole town heard. I remember women with their hands up in the air, crying, wailing uncontrollably. People were running towards the wrecked vehicle.

The American and his cousin got out of the vehicle and both were shaking, screaming, attempting to pull the car back. I was confused and as we ran up the street and got closer, I saw *Pasqualuccio* pinned between the car and the house. He was motionless. As we got closer I was able to get a glimpse of him, as people in total panic gathered around him, trying to get him to move, to say something. But he only moved when members of his family shook him, urging him to respond. I noticed blood coming out of his ears. As the crying and screaming got louder, I panicked and I ran away from the chaos.

I did not stop running until I reached my safe haven of Luigi. My *mamma* and *Zia* Ida were home and I told them the tragic news. They would not believe me and I remember my aunt warning me not to cry wolf, not to lie, because people would never believe me again. I kept telling them that it was true, that *Pasqualuccio* was hit by *la macchina degli Americani*, the American's car. They wondered how a small kid like me could concoct such a terrible story. They soon learned that I was telling the truth, as the whole village got wind of the terrible inconceivable tragedy. That innocent old man had become the unlikely first and only fatality of a car accident in our village.

A few days later I left for school in Todi, Umbria, and that memory would revisit me during some lonely nights. Fifty years later that memory, ingrained in my mind, would revisit me again, hitting me square in the mouth, harder than ever.

The last time I heard my mother's voice was April 3, 2009. It was the Friday before Palm Sunday. She had already begun her Easter baking. I knew she had done something out of the ordinary when she called me at my shop, laughing that laugh that I had heard many times before, that laugh that said, "Don't be upset, but I've done something that you might not approve of." When the laughing stopped, she informed me that she had baked all day and had about twenty loaves of sweetbread and other Easter pastries, and that Jackie should come and get some because she did not have enough room in her refrigerator or freezer. She already knew that I would scold her, that at almost eighty-eight-years-old she did not have any business working all day, making so many sweetbreads.

Jackie went down that afternoon and picked up various loaves of her Easter goodies. *Mamma* had already walked to my brother's house up the street with bags of the sweetbreads. Jackie recalls my mom holding those loaves of bread proudly in her extended arms. She gave Jackie enough to feed an army. She reminded Jackie to give some to Daniella and to Dominic because they loved to eat them. She thought that we all loved what she made and if we did not then there was something wrong with us. Even if some of her grandkids did not care much for her excellent *polenta*, they would tell her that they liked it and that it tasted great. Of course she would make them more *polenta*, more often; after all they told her that they liked it!

Mamma called me that Saturday morning but I was on the other line with a customer and did not click over; I would call her later. I always hesitated to click over to my mom. I would explain to her that I was talking to someone else on the other line and to hang on, but she would just keep talking and did not understand the process. I would listen for a bit and tell her to wait, but she just kept on talking. Frustrated, I would click back to my other caller and speed up the conversation. As I clicked back to my mom, I would either get complete silence because she had finally hung up the phone, or else she would be on the other line still talking, having no idea that I had been on the other line.

When I called back that afternoon she wasn't home. She was probably at Safeway, looking for deals, or maybe at some other store with my sister-in-law, Bambina, or at Sunflower Market with her neighbor Kathy Lucas. I did not get to talk to her, but Jackie had spoken to her earlier and told her that we would call when we decided which church we would go to on Palm Sunday, to see if she wanted to join us.

Sunday morning, Palm Sunday, we were having breakfast with our very pregnant daughter, Daniella, her husband, Frank, and their young children, Anthony and Avery. I remember looking at the clock and Jackie mentioning that we should call *Nonna* to see if she wanted to go to church with us. At that same moment the phone rang. It was before 9 a.m. Jackie answered and almost immediately became agitated. In a panic, she handed me the phone. My niece, Terri, Vic's wife, was on the phone. She was crying, "Uncle Tony, Ezio got into a terrible car accident. Bambina and *Nonna* were with him. They are trying to resuscitate them." In a panic, I asked what she meant by resuscitating them.

Hearing those words created chaos among everyone in our kitchen. My seven-month pregnant daughter rapidly began pacing the floor, jumping up-and-down, demanding clarification. Crying, Terri told me that they had just loaded Ezio and Bambina into an ambulance and the firemen were still working on *Nonna*. By now we are all in a panic. The three- and four-year-old grandchildren got scared and started crying, along with my wife and daughter. It was very difficult to stay calm.

Shaking uncontrollably, I asked Terri where the accident happened and where they were taking them. They were on 44th and Federal Boulevard and they were taking Ezio and Bambina to Denver Health, and taking *Nonna* to St. Anthony Hospital. Terri did not know their condition, but the firemen were working on *Nonna*. I screamed at Terri to please call Vic and tell the ambulance people to take them all to the same hospital. Terri told us not to go to the accident site, but straight to Saint Anthony's. Vic, Mario, Adelio, and Dana were going to Denver Health.

Why would they separate them? It didn't make sense. I was in a panic. I was mad at the emergency personnel. Why were they being so insensitive by sending injured family members to different locations? Later I was given the explanation. I begged my daughter to stay home with her husband and children, but she insisted on going with us and was in the car before my wife and me.

Suddenly the whole world almost stopped. Everything around me was moving in slow motion: the garage door took minutes to open; the car seemed to slow down instead of accelerating. Every Sunday driver seemed to be out that morning, driving as slow as possible. The traffic lights took forever to change from red to green. People refused to get out of the way. Didn't they know that my mom, brother, and sister-in-law were badly hurt and needed us? I was driving fast and erratically, and as I looked in my rearview mirror, I could see my pregnant daughter sobbing, repeating over and over again for God to please make sure *Nonna*, Ezio, and Bambina were okay. I regained a bit of composure and realized that if I did not slow down, I could cause another tragedy on that Palm Sunday. It seemed to take forever to reach St. Anthony Hospital. We were actually there in less than a half-hour.

I ignored the 'no parking' sign and pulled right up to the emergency entrance. I rushed in with my wife and daughter in tow. I frantically asked the nurse where my mom was. She begged me to calm down and asked for some information. She mentioned that someone matching my mom's description had been brought in and they would need my help in identifying her. We kept asking if she was alive, but the nurse would not give us a definitive answer, pleading with us to calm down. We were asked to wait in a waiting room and someone would help us. The world around me was still moving extremely slow. The nurse's words were not coming out of her mouth fast enough and she was writing down information at a snail's pace. The waiting room was closing in on us. We could not sit; the three of us paced back-and-forth.

Finally, after what seemed an eternity, a door opened and an elderly man in a suit walked in. Instantly I wondered why a doctor would be in a suit and not in a surgery gown. As he got closer, I saw his name tag. I never saw his name; I saw only what was under his name, in letters that seemed to be bigger than his chest: "CHAPLIN."

I immediately realized that my mom had died. We started to cry uncontrollably, demanding to see her. The nice man was trying to calm us down, trying to get us to sit down. There was no way we could sit. We moaned and cried. I worried about my pregnant daughter. She was hysterical, crying out, "*Nonna, Nonna*," over and over. Soon a nurse appeared and led us through a maze and into a small room. "*Mamma, Mamma*," I cried out, as we saw her on a gurney, lifeless with some sort of cord tied around her jaw. I instantly wanted to remove that thing from her mouth. Maybe she would talk to us. She was unconscious, sleeping, anything but dead. I kept saying, "*Mamma, dimmi qualcosa*," talk to me. "*Mamma, apri gl'iuocchieh!*" *apri gli occhi!* open your eyes!

After regaining some composure, I noticed that her beautiful face was intact except for a small cut above her left eye. I lifted the white sheet covering her body and did not notice any trauma on her upper body or her legs. The recurring question asked was, what caused her death? Although her death certificate gave the cause of death as resulting from a blunt trauma, we were not convinced. Bambina recalls my mom saying, *"Mamma mea, ma che è succiess mo,"* *Mamma mia, che cosa è successo,* Mamma mia, what happened?

After the initial impact of the two vehicles, my brother was knocked unconscious and his foot must have pressed the accelerator, causing the car to speed ahead and jump the curb, making impact with a concrete wall. My brother's head split open, blood gushing out while he lay on *Mamma*'s lap. That was just too much for my mom's eighty-eight-year-old heart to take. The pain of seeing her son lying there, bleeding profusely, caused her to suffer a massive heart attack.

At the time, my son, Dominic, was at church with his family. Finally after numerous tries, Jackie was able to reach him, telling him of the accident and that he should come to the hospital. This was one of many difficult calls we would have to make in the coming week. When my son, his wife, Michaela, four-year-old son, Gianni, and two-year-old daughter, Sofia, walked into the emergency room, I ran to embrace him, telling him that *Nonna* was gone.

The next painful phone call was to my nephew, John Ienco, in Toronto, Canada. I felt for him. He would have to go to my sister, Maria, and give her the awful news. I kept thinking about the day we left Toronto, after New Year's Day of 2009. My mom had spent about six months with my sister and her family. Jackie and I went there to celebrate New Year's with them and then brought *Mamma* back home. At the airport, the last words *Mamma* whispered in my sister's ear were, *"Chi sa se zarvedemm,"* *Chi lo sa se ci rivedremo,* Who knows if we'll ever see each other again, hugging and kissing each other as they both cried.

We hurried to Denver Health after signing some papers and all of us, minus the grandkids, said one more painful goodbye to *Nonna*. She would be picked up by the Denver coroner's office for an autopsy. At Denver Health the news was bad, but both Ezio and Bambina were alive. I reluctantly made matters worse by announcing to all my nieces and nephews and other relatives and friends who had gathered, that *Nonna* was dead. The continual weeping was taken to a higher level by all.

My brother lay motionless in an operating room. His skull looked as though it was split in half, but luckily the deep gash had not fractured his skull. The doctors would stitch him up and deal with the other injuries that he suffered. His left ear looked as if it would fall off at anytime. I wondered if the initial impact caused his head to strike the driver's door, knocking him unconscious. None of them were wearing seat belts on the short trip to Mount Carmel Church on that Sunday morning.

My sister-in-law, Bambina, recounted the events before the accident. As usual, Ezio was busy doing some work when she reminded him that it was late. They would have to pick up *Nonna* and then their daughter, Dana, and her fiancé, Victor Quinto, to talk to the priest about their upcoming wedding at Mount Carmel church. My brother was complaining about something, a normal characteristic of his, when they picked up *Nonna*. Bambina gave up the front seat for *Mamma*, as she moved to the back of the minivan.

When Ezio reached 44th and Federal from the west, he moved to the right lane to make a right turn onto southbound Federal Boulevard. While waiting at the intersection, an eastbound car on the left was stopped next to him and Ezio could not see the oncoming southbound traffic on Federal. He inched forward, but went too far. A southbound car clipped him, spinning his van around, but a driver that was following that car later communicated to us that he could have easily avoided my brother's minivan by swerving a bit. The minivan stopped for a few seconds in the middle of the street and then sped out of control through a bus stop shelter and into a concrete wall that separated a house and a commercial building. For a long while, Ezio was told that the accident wasn't his fault. He did not remember any part of the collision. Months later when he was examining the police report, he noticed his careless driving violation.

Bambina went through some rough days recovering because her breathing airway had swelled from the trauma. Gradually she healed and, although with difficulty, she started to talk about the accident. She was aware, she kept asking about *Mamma*. And I kept telling her that *Mamma* was okay and then I stopped verbalizing the rest of the sentence, thinking that *Mamma* was okay now with *Papà* in Heaven. After continually still asking where *Mamma* was, we finally had to tell Bambina that *Mamma* had died from the accident. Bambina immediately started convulsing and wailing. As we tried to calm her, we were wondering if we had made a mistake by telling her of *Mamma's* passing.

My brother was unconscious for a couple of days. When he began talking he asked about his wife, and he would also whisper, "*Mamma*." We told him not to worry about them, they are fine; concentrate on getting well. As he started to open his eyes and look around, he saw me standing there. Out of the blue, he said, "*Tonì, portami a chel dl Lvg, iamicenna,*" *Portami a Luigi, andiamo,* Take me back home to Luigi, let's go. He wanted me to take him back home to our small hamlet of Luigi, Pagliarone, Italy, where it all began for us. I wonder if he was trying to tell me that he wished he had never left Italy, so this tragedy could have been avoided.

One of the most painful things I had to do during those difficult, sad days was to tell my brother that our *mamma* had died in the accident. As I sat with him, we recounted stories of our past, many told here. I only talked about happy, funny stories. I wanted to make him smile a bit. He had just had his gallbladder removed to add to his various injuries, and I avoided his inquiries about *Mamma.* "*Andò shtà Mamma?*" *Dove è mamma,* He kept asking where Mom was and we were having a difficult time with the prospect of informing him that *Mamma*'s body now rested next to *Papà*'s at Mount Olivet Cemetery. While other family members went to get something to eat in a room especially reserved for the numerous daily visitors, I asked him if he remembered our Super Bowl trip. Of course he did and he added that *Mamma* continually pushed us to go, "*Vittr v'aspetta, e ve le merditate,*" *Vittorio vi aspetta e ve lo meritate,* she kept urging us to go, Vic was waiting, go and have some fun, we deserved it. I did not need to hear that at that moment, and as I fought back tears, I recounted our trip to the Super Bowl to my distressed and ailing brother.

It was ten years earlier, while Vic was back home from Phoenix for the Christmas holidays of 1997, that our sports talk turned to the possibility of the Denver Broncos going to Super Bowl XXXII in San Diego. At Christmas dinner at our house, we all wondered how nice it would be to attend a Super Bowl game. We were all jealous that Vic was going as a reporter for his TV station in Phoenix. It was just a dream, just something to talk about at dinner. Suddenly Vic, with his mouth full of food and sounding somewhat excited, said something. It was barely audible, but did he just say something about all of us joining him at the Super Bowl if the Broncos make it? Yeah, right! "You guys fly down to Phoenix and then you can take my SUV and drive to San Diego." Vic was now standing and pleading with us. I casually mentioned that even if we did go to San Diego, how in the heck would we be able to get tickets? "I'll get a press pass!" Vic shouted.

So the plan was to go to the Super Bowl and with one press pass, nine of us would get in! The idea got legs and the boys were starting to imagine the possibility. It was sort of forgotten until Denver beat Pittsburgh on January 11 and would play the Green Bay Packers for the **Lombardi** Trophy. Suddenly the idea of us going to the game was revived. Eventually we made the decision and six of us flew down to Phoenix and spent the night with Vic and Terri.

I asked my brother, now lying in the hospital, if he remembered how he did not let his briefcase out of his sight while we made our Super Bowl trip. We all wondered what he had in it but he would not tell us. On the Friday morning before Sunday's game, Vic, Terri, and my wife, Jackie, flew to San Diego. My brother (clutching his briefcase), his sons, Adelio and Mario, my son, Dominic, and I piled into Vic's SUV and headed for San Diego. We somehow all stayed in one hotel room!

We spent the Saturday before the Super Bowl at the NFL Experience, near the stadium. Adelio, Dominic, and Mario were filmed and made it onto ESPN SportsCenter, as they each wore a foam cheesehead which we had fashioned at our upholstery shop. But these cheeseheads were not yellow, they were blue and orange! It also helped that all of us were wearing blue T-shirts with orange embroidery that said: THIS LOMBARDI IS A BRONCO FAN!

Sunday morning we hopped into a taxi and headed for the stadium, not knowing exactly how we were going to get in. Vic had actually procured two press passes! The decision was made for my brother and me to use the press passes, and Adelio got in as Vic's assistant! Thank God this was pre-9/11! I promised my wife, Dominic, and Mario that I would figure out a way to get them in. In the meantime, they had found some Broncos fans with a generator-powered big screen TV in the parking lot and would watch the game with them.

I was surprised at how easy it was for me and my brother to walk in through the media door. Vic warned us not to cheer as we took our seats in a press box. We needed to look and act like reporters, and media people don't cheer! Vic went down to the field to do his work. My brother, Ezio, his son, Adelio, and I sat there somewhat nervously with a tablet in hand, anxiously awaiting the start of the game. While watching the game I thought of my wife, son, and nephew left outside the stadium, but later my wife informed us that they were having so much fun with all the diehard fans who just made the trip to be close-by, without having had any intentions of getting into the stadium!

When the Broncos scored their first touchdown, the group of people sitting in front of us erupted in a loud cheer. They were media people from southern Colorado. So much for reporters not cheering; and of course we joined them in cheering for our Broncos. When the first half came to a close, I had a plan for the rest of the family to join us in the press box. As I made my way out of my seat, I noticed my brother, serious, with tablet in hand, acting like a reporter! He was writing something. I looked down and noticed that he had written, *"John Elway kick filgol."* But Jason Elam was our kicker!

I saw a friend of Vic's who was a reporter from Austin, Texas, where Vic had been a reporter before Phoenix. I pretty much begged him to lend me his pass, lamenting about our group left outside. Reluctantly he handed me his pass. With my brother's pass and the borrowed one, I made my way outside and found my people. Jackie was jovial, but the boys had sad faces. I wanted Jackie to see the halftime show. Quickly, I put a pass around her neck and another around Dominic's, leaving poor twelve-year-old Mario there, instructing him not to move and I would be back for him. With press passes around our necks, we went in. I then went back outside with a pass in hand, put it around Mario's neck, and that's when I noticed that the pass was hanging almost to his knees! I became a bit anxious, wondering how the young guard at the door would react to such a young reporter, a kid.

I sort of tried to shield Mario as we reached the door. We were just about to walk in and then our luck suddenly ran out. "Hold on, wait a minute, what's this?" The guard pointed to diminutive Mario. "Who are you with?" he barked. I had forgotten the call letters of Vic's TV station. I tried to look at the pass, but nervous and in a panic, I blurted out something that was not even close to the correct letters. My nephew, Mario, to this day, reminds us all of my calm, cool, and collected rendition of the call letters! "K...K... P... PCS and O... Phoenix." The correct letters were KPHO. The guard gave us an "I know what you are up to!" stare and then motioned us to go in. We all sat together in the press box and watched the second half of the Super Bowl game.

People started calling our relatives back home. They were sure that they had seen Adelio, Dominic, and Mario on the field after the Super Bowl!

Armed with our passes, we were able to go onto the field after the game. I was just feet away from where Pat Bowlen lifted the Lombardi trophy and said, "This one is for John!" meaning John Elway. The festivities continued until we got home the following Tuesday, although as we made our way to my van, I realized that I had forgotten the keys in a drawer at the hotel in San Diego!

Super Bowl XXXII, Dominic, Adelio, and Mario Lombardi. 1998

After recounting all that fun to Ezio, as he now lay in the hospital, I was able to get my brother's mood to be a bit more jovial. I asked him if he recalled what he had in the briefcase. He smiled and mumbled that he had $3,000 in cash, just in case we needed to buy tickets!

The next day my brother seemed to be in better spirits. A decision was made to give him the bad news. He kept wondering why *Mamma* was not coming to see him. With the rest of the family, including Bambina in a wheelchair, I told my brother the terrible news as my hands trembled and my voice quivered. Barely able to cry, he kept saying, "*No, no, mamma mea bella, mamma mea,*" *mamma mia,* my beautiful mom. "*Che èglia fa mo!*" *Cosa devo fare adesso!* What am I going to do now! We all cried, we felt so bad for him because we realized that he would have to live with this for the rest of his life. We prayed that God would give him the strength and faith to overcome the guilt.

We had buried my mom while Ezio and Bambina were still hospitalized and unable to attend. The church overflowed with family and friends, saying their last goodbyes to her. As my nephew mentioned in his eulogy, Grandpa would be jealous. She certainly had more friends than he, and he had many. My son, Dominic, and nephew, Vic, did an excellent job in reinforcing what we already knew: that this lady, this simple lady, to our eyes was the most pleasant, generous, funny, and forgiving soul one could ever meet.

It's a common practice to bring fatalities of accidents to the nearest hospital, so that they can be legally pronounced dead. That is why my mother was brought to St. Anthony Hospital, the closest to the scene of the accident.

Although there are many, many more than these, for her funeral the grandchildren composed a top ten list of the most humorous memories we have of *Nonna*:

#10. The time *Nonna* thought Mario's belt lying on the floor was a snake and she sprinted out the back door faster than Carl Lewis on steroids.

#9. The time Mario broke his collarbone. His mom and dad weren't home so he walked over to *Nonna*'s house. He could not explain to *Nonna* about his injury, as he spoke about three words of Italian back then. So to make his collarbone feel better, she gave him a Sprite.

#8. During Christmas vacation one year, while back home from Notre Dame, Vic wanted to surprise *Nonna*. He put on a wig and changed his appearance so she would not recognize him. Adelio told *Nonna* that this guy was a friend who had just been released from jail. Vic suddenly started to open the cabinets and closets, went through the bedrooms, and opened the fridge and started to pull out various items. *Nonna* could not take it anymore and cautiously reached for Vic and said, "*Eh no, no, dats no nice, Adelio dirr ca non si fa cushì,*" urging Adelio to tell his friend that what he was doing wasn't very nice. Then Vic took his mask off and *Nonna*'s face lit up like a Christmas tree.

#7. On one of our many family trips to Glenwood Springs, we somehow got *Nonna* to get on a floatie. She was fine for a while, with her trademark white bonnet on her head and the rest of her body covered to protect her from the hot sun. Somehow she lost her balance and fell into the warm sulfur water. After a few seconds she came up, her arms wailing. She was blowing air and water out at a staggering rate, while crying, "*O mamma meaaa,*" screaming for someone to find her dentures at the bottom of the pool.

#6. There were a countless number of crank calls from her grandsons, trying to sell her something. All she would continue to say was, "*Me no speaka English*" and that was until you threw in the magic word, 'free.' "*Free? Okay, whate free?*" Finally the prankster would identify himself and she would start laughing and say, "*Ma puots-ess,*" Darned you. She loved the 'buy one, get one free' ads from the different stores. She would buy all those items and divide them up with her family, and when we lectured her on the fact that we already had some and she should not buy anymore, she would say, "*Mah buy one eh one freee!*"

#5. *Nonna* was walking around in downtown Denver at the 16th Street Mall. She took the bus there. She heard a girl yelling something that she understood, "Free." The girl was handing out free cigarettes. There were actually four girls handing them out, one on each corner. *Mamma* came home that afternoon on the number 44 bus with about 100 packs of cigarettes. She was very excited because my brother was going back to Italy and they would make great gifts for all the relatives. When asked how she was able to get all those free cigarettes, she said that she went around and around collecting the cigarettes, changing her appearance so she would not be recognized by the girls handing them out. She did this by putting on her scarf, her sunglasses, her coat, and so on. Surely the girls recognized her, but they were probably entertained and/or wanted to get rid of the samples as soon as possible! And how long did it take her to collect the loot? Almost the whole afternoon!

#4. *Nonna* was a legend on local radio here in Denver. She would join my nephew, sportscaster Vic Lombardi, every Friday morning on KOOL105. She was asked to pick the winners of the upcoming weekend football games, and of course *Nonna* always picked the Broncos. In fact, when the New York Giants and the New England Patriots met for the Super Bowl, we decided to have *Nonna* pick a winner. So Vic asked *Nonna* in a very clear, loud voice — the same voice most people use when they know that someone is a foreigner, as if they were deaf — "*Nonna, Patriots o Giants?*" "*Chi?*" Who? she asked. "Who do you think is going to win, the Patriots *o* Giants?" "Oh I think so Broncos." She always picked the Broncos, even when they were not playing.

#3. Among many other Broncos stories, one was when the Broncos were playing in a game in the early 1980s. It might have been a playoff game. *Nonna* still had not figured out the rules of the game and she probably never did. She cheered when we cheered. But late in the fourth quarter after Broncos punter Mike Horan punted the ball away, *Nonna* turned to us and announced, "*Ne mi piace quel numero 10. Ogne vota che accappa la palla la mena a quell'altra squadra!*" I don't like that number 10. Every time he gets the ball he kicks to the other team!

#2. Whenever *Nonna* went to see Dr. Shpall, our family doctor, she would have a bag, and when the doctor walked in she would hand him the bag. The doctor would peek inside and say thank you, and she would inform him that it was God knows what of whatever she had baked or cooked that week. Of course, the doctor wasn't used to patients always bringing him a variety of food, but in Italy a gift could mean the difference between being diagnosed correctly and not being seen at all by a doctor. It never failed; the appointment was for some specific health issue, but her complaints were for a plethora of pains.

#1. Of course, the all-time number one funny story was when *Nonna* went for her second exam to become a United States citizen and proclaimed, "*Bufalo Bille!*" as the first president of the United States.

Our great matriarch had left us suddenly. She had gone home, and hopefully she was now with her husband, her baby daughter, her parents, and her brothers. And we are left behind, a long, long way from where it all began in the tiny remote village of Pagliarone, Italy. She left us at our new home and the home of our future generations. And even though I miss my little village, I have finally realized that this is home/the home that my parents afforded us as a result of their endless hard work and undying commitment to their family.

My dad and his brother, Umberto, were happy that their sister finally visited us in America. Family celebration at our house, 1993. Top left: Victor Lombardi, Dominic Meloragno, Frances Meloragno, Umberto Lombardi, Lorella Lombardi, Esmeralda Flagiello, Dana Lombardi, Ezio Lombardi, Flavio Carmosino, Leontina Carmosino, Daniella Lombardi, Anthony Lombardi, Adelio Lombardi. Sitting, from left: Maria Lucia Lombardi, Ida Lombardi, Terry Lombardi, Angela Lombardi, Mario Lombardi, Bambina Lombardi, Jackie Lombardi, Dominic Lombardi.

Mamma, her last birthday, 2008

Chapter LI

EPILOGO · EPILOGUE

I suppose we all ask the question, "What if...?" What would my life have been like if we had stayed in Italy, or if we moved back to Italy? Would a chance at a professional soccer career have been there or was that just a dream, a dream that every kid in Italy has? Or, would my life have been filled with a lot of daily prayers and reflection as a Franciscan friar? No matter how much we wonder, what we have is what we were meant to have. You can't change *il destino*, destiny, as my mom would say, for better or for worse. Of course, most of us would say that we would not trade our lives with anyone, not the richest or most famous person on earth, as it should be.

It wasn't so noticeable when I went back to the village in 1975 for our honeymoon. Cows still outnumbered cars, and fields were still green and cultivated. But on subsequent trips I started to see the change. It actually began when the many families left during the emigration of the 1960s. There were house doors with no keys in them, a sign that that house was locked and empty. Before the exodus of the 60s, the population of Villa San Michele was on the verge of breaking its apex of 1,000 residents. In 2014 the voting population of Villa San Michele was just over 100. The wheat fields were now weed fields. The trains that moved the populace from town to town were now nonexistent, as the government closed the rail line that reached the village due to the dwindling passengers.

As my wife, Jackie, and I strolled up and down the cobblestone streets of the village on a September afternoon of 2012, the elderly residents sitting in front of their houses were almost nonexistent. My numerous

Pagliarone in ruins, 2014

aunts and uncles were also gone, with only one aunt remaining, *Zia* Leontina. As we reached the church, we saw a rooster, the only sign of life. The church looked the same on the outside, just as I remembered it. As we walked inside, Don Felice approached and I noticed a graying, shrinking shell of the young, energetic priest with a head of thick black hair, whom I assisted almost fifty years earlier.

"*Pietrantonio!*" Don Felice recognized me. And he was nice enough to move things around on his memorial Mass list to accommodate my request to celebrate Mass that night in honor of my parents. When we returned that evening at 6:00, a handful of women and one older man were reciting the rosary, led by Carolina, my friend Pasqualino's widow. I was very grateful that Don Felice allowed Don Camillo, the retiring ninety-year-old priest from Luigi, to celebrate Mass, his last one. He, the cousin whom my father grew up with in Luigi, was celebrating this last Mass in honor of my father and my mother.

Two years later we were back in our village, this time with my brother and sister and their spouses. We talked about all of us going back and walking the same paths that we walked together almost fifty years ago. On a warm afternoon in August of 2014, Jackie and I, along with my brother, Ezio, and his wife, Bambina, my sister, Maria, and her husband,

Don Felice Fangio, Anthony Lombardi, fifty years later in front of our church, 2014

Vittorio, their daughter, Lorella, and our elderly aunt, *Zia* Leontina —
with objections from her daughter, Adelia — made the walk from Villa
San Michele to Luigi. Adelia worried that the walk might be too much
for her eighty-five-year-old mom, but *Zia* Leontina insisted. It had been
a few years since she had seen the place where she was born and grew up.
The slow, leisurely stroll took about one hour, stopping and reminiscing
at various spots about what and whose houses used to be there.

Finally we were all standing on the disappearing courtyard, in front of
the house in which my brother, sister, my aunt, and I were born. The
house was a mere skeleton of what it was so long ago. The stairs that we
had walked up and down innumerable times were now covered by tall,
thorny weeds and were impassible. The area where our animals roamed

was now overtaken by weeds and wildflowers. The bustling, noisy, small enclave of Luigi was now deserted and eerily quiet. The only sound was the distant barking of truffle hunting dogs in a nearby fenced-in barnyard. We all stood there staring at the abandoned structure, our eyes filled with tears, my aunt crying, as memories of that house flashed in front of our eyes.

Our house in Luigi being overtaken by weeds, 2014

Standing amongst the weeds in front of our birth house. Bambina Lombardi, Ezio Lombardi, Maria Ienco, Anthony Lombardi, Vittorio Ienco, 2014

I envisioned the thin, frail image of my mom feeding our pigs and our chickens, and my dad preoccupied with pulling our donkey, my brother eagerly following our cows. I could see my sister on our balcony, walking down with me in my uniform behind her, school bag in hand, ready to walk to school. My siblings verbalized various frames of our window that was our life in Luigi.

My wife and niece were busy taking pictures of the crumbling houses and barns. We heard a person's voice. Suddenly a small woman appeared; frail, wrinkled, and dressed in black. For an instant it was my mom, or any of the town's women long gone. It was Donetta, a relative. *"Ehh, song armasa sola ee,"* she was the only one left, the only one who came down to that crumbling, abandoned, deserted place.

With cousin Donetta Lombardi in Luigi, 2014

I tried in vain to find a way to walk up the stairs of our house, but the overgrowth of weeds made it impossible. As I tried kicking the thorny bushes, my sister warned me, *"Attenzione a le serpe,"* The snakes, they had not left. They were the only inhabitants from the past still roaming the deserted, crumbling structures. They were not completely alone, as a brightly colored butterfly floated by. I wondered what other visitors came by, as the sun dropped beyond the western horizon. As we left the ghost hamlet for our sleepy village, we all turned and took one last gaze at the remaining standing walls. I quietly prayed that those stones stay strong, stay up until I could bring my seven grandchildren back to this little speck of our world to see and feel a slice of their legacy.

As I look out my kitchen window, with the Rocky Mountains a short distance to the west, I usually recall the mountains I came from in a small village in Italy, and how I traded them for mountains near a big city in America. As was true for most immigrants, my family and I suffered many adversities, but they only served to make us stronger and more determined to succeed. And as I continually say thanks for all that my family has been blessed with, as do my brother and sister and the rest of those immigrants, my mind eventually swims across the Atlantic Ocean and flies to the mountain range with the small valley below, and in my mind I run up the short incline to our house. I fight back the vision of the fallen walls. I close my eyes and take a deep breath. Eventually, the sight of the bustling little collection of houses comes to me, and as I look down the hill I can see the rest of the village, I can see Pagliarone.

Bronze plaque in the church's piazza honoring the town's immigrants. It says:

Per Gli Immigranti
Che Lasciarono gli Affetti e Beni per Garantire alle loro Famiglie e a se Stessi Un Futuro Migliore

To The Immigrants
Who Left Behind Love and Possessions to Insure a Better Future for their Families and Themselves

Stone sign dedication in front of my house, honoring Pagliarone.

Famiglie Di Luigi
(Frazione Di Pagliarone)
Nel 1950
Families Of Luigi
(Hamlet Of Pagliarone)
In The 1950s

PARENTS NAMES, FOLLOWED BY CHILDREN'S NAMES

Antonio and Lucia Lombardi; Michelina, Lina (Termoli, Italy)

Tullio and Matilda Di Franco (France, but now back in Villa San Michele); Maria, Nicola

Luigi (il guardiano) and Vincenza Lombardi (after Luigi died, Vincenza moved to Buenos Aires, Argentina to be with her daughter); Camillo (pastor of church in Alfedena, Italy)

Nicola and Ida Lombardi (Philadelphia, 1956; Denver, 1969); Luigi (Philadelphia, 1958; Denver, 1969), Domenico (Philadelphia, 1958; Denver, 1969)

Armando and Teresa Lombardi; Vittorio (Termoli, Italy), Margherita (San Pietro Avellana, Italy)

Gino (Ginuccio) and Giulia Lombardi; Antonio (Toronto, Canada, 1980s), Pasquale, Antonietta

Alberico and Gasperina Lombardi

Emilio and Silvia Lombardi; Rina (Corrientes, Argentina, 1970s), Maria

Massimo (Massimino) and Rosa Lombardi (Toronto, Canada, 1970s); Antonio (Termoli, Italy), Sandra (Sandrina) (Toronto, Canada, 1970s), Adelmo (Toronto, Canada, 1970s)

Michele (Michelino) and Assunta Lombardi; Angiolina, Maria

Alduino and Irma Lombardi (Corrientes, Argentina, 1954); Claudino (Corrientes), Tonino and Sandro, born in Corrientes

Umberto and Ida Lombardi (Denver, 1966); Maria (Bari, Italy), Terenzio (Denver 1966)

Vittorio and Maria Lucia Lombardi (Denver, 1966); Ezio (Denver, 1966), Maria (Toronto, 1967), Pietrantonio (Toni, Tonino, Anthony, Tony) (Denver, 1966)

PAROLE DIALETTALI E FRASE
DEL NOSTRO PAESE
COMMON DIALECT WORDS AND
PHRASES OF OUR VILLAGE

Our Italian dialect is, for the most part, similar to the proper Italian, with some words shortened, vowels eliminated, and accents, emphasis, and pronunciation altered. But there are some words that are totally dissimilar from the conventional Italian. Following are just some of many of those dialect words. Our village's dialect is listed first, followed by the proper Italian, and then the English translation:

abbashta, basta, enough

accattà, comprare, to buy

allirteh, in piedi, standing up

allucca, grida, yell

allungh, lontano, far away

ammandá, coprire, to cover

Andò shtà? / Dov'è? / Where is he/she?

anniand, avanti, forward; in front

apposhta, per questo motivo, that's why, on purpose

araeteh, indietro, in the back

arcuaerdeh, ricordi, remember

ariettá, vomitare, to vomit

armnì, ritornare, to return

arpunereh, riporre, put away

arrizzateh, alzati, get up

avuann, quest'anno, this year

bia, solamente, only

biegl, bello, handsome

buoneh, buono (bene), good

capiel, cappello, hat

cappotta, giacca, coat

casheh, formaggio, cheese

carià, portare, to carry

cavetsoon, pantalone, pants

ceppa, rami secchi, dried twigs

cigliuccio, uccello, bird

chicat, ciecato, blind

ciminera, camino, chimney

cing, cinque, five

cininn, piccolo, small

citra (cheetra), bambina, baby girl

citro (cheetr), bambino, baby

coccia, testa, head

comè, perchè, why

cria, niente, nothing

cuamesand, campo santo; cimitero, graveyard; cemetery

cundra, culla, cradle

eglia ee, devo andare, have to go

Eh mò! / E ora! / What now!

Embé! È così / So what!

femmina, donna, woman

frattet, fratello, brother

frusceh, foglie, leaves

ghiangheh, bianco, white

ieeruoss, grande, big

ieess, lui, him, he

iettah, getta, throw away

ingushtiateh, arrabbiato, mad

iuasineh, asino, donkey

iuatt, gatto, cat

iurnuata, giornata, day

Kae cazzeh! / Che cazzo! / slang for "What the hell!"

kambá, campare, live

kareah, porta, carry

keenda, come, what

keereh deh, quelli di, those of

Krishteh, Cristo, Christ

kushtiateh, costola, rib

lapseh, matita, lapis, pencil

lecina, prugna, plum

loke, là, there

lota, fango, mud

lutima, l'ultimo, the last

magna, mangia, eat

mammoccia, bambina; ragazza, girl; kid

mammocceh, bambino; ragazza, boy; kid

mammta, tua mamma, your mother

mammuccia, nonna, grandmother

mang, manco, neanche, not even

massera, stasera, tonight

matt, matto, pazzo, crazy

mbuss, bagnato, wet

minnezza, spazzatura, trash

mni, venire, come

mo, adesso; ora, now

muacc, polenta, polenta

muss, menta, chin

omeh, uomo, man

partialleh, arancia, orange

picca, poco, a little

pizzelle, biscotti, cookies

pureh, pure, anche, as well

puzeh, gomito, elbow

qeereh, quello, that

quishteh, questo, this

reeneh, schiena, back (of body)

reh, il, the

saviciccia, salciccia, sausage

sega, saracco, saw

seggia, sedia, chair

sciur, fiori, flowers

scurdateh, scordato, dimenticato, forgot

sheeneh, sì, yes

shocca, fiocca, nevica, it's snowing

shtatela, bilancia, scale

shtracc, stanco, tired

shtuta, spegnere, turn off

shumeh, fiume, river

tarmat, gelato, frozen

tatuccio, nonno, grandfather

tramiend, guarda, look

tsuezz, socco, sporco, dirty

Và fà a Napl, Và fà a Napoli, Go do it in Naples (a milder version of *Và fà in culo*) *Va-fangur, Và fà in culo,* literally a very vulgar term, used in different ways in daily conversations. One can say it to mean: idiot, go away, I'm done with you, you don't know what you're talking about, get away from me, etc. Usually not intended as the literal meaning, my mom sometimes said the slang!

vaglió, ragazzo, kid

varva, barba, beard

vattiateh, battezzato, baptized

vehssuat, spinto, pushed

viv, bevi, drink

vocca, bocca, mouth

vritt, sporco, dirty

vuasht, guasto, spoiled

vuoie, oggi, today

vuruaccheh, braccio, arm

ziella, zia, aunt

zizì, zio, uncle

There was a man in our village that hailed from Napoli. He married a local woman and they had many children. One of their sons was my age. One night a group of us, probably up to no good, knocked on their door. Thankfully the kid answered and we asked if he could come out and play. The boy was sure that his father would not let him out for any reason. So he told his dad that he needed to go to the bathroom (our bathrooms were normally the great outdoors). His father must have known that we were waiting outside, so he clearly yelled out, *"Caca rienn e puó trashì aforeh!"* Shit inside and then just throw it out the door! When we heard that, we hightailed out of there as fast as possible.

As I was running I thought, "What a shitty, strange language that Neopolitan is." And then I thought again, "Ours is not much different." My all-time favorite local dialect phrase is, *Eh-peh-keh-teh-veh-lee-chedia.* I don't know if there is an Italian or English translation for it. My parents would say that to me if I did something good, if I did something bad, if I said something smart, or if I said something dumb, or funny. They said it to me with a smile on their faces, or at times with a frown. There was always that situation where the phrase seemed to be appropriate. It was used not only towards children, but also by adults to other adults. I never had the nerve to say that to my mom and dad or other adults, but I said it many times to my friends. An attempt at a probable translation of it would be, "Way to go...idiot, way to go...genius, what a bonehead move, what a smart move, great comment, stupid comment, etc." Now I say it just to say it, just so I don't forget it. It's been difficult, but occasionally I try to teach it to my family!

Appendix II

INVENTATE "ITALAMERICANO" PAROLE,
CONCOCTED "ITALAMERICANO" WORDS

When the Italian immigrants arrived in America, not only could they not understand English, but they had a hard time understanding some of their compatriots. The dialects were so different that it was difficult to communicate, even amongst themselves. Centuries of isolation created the many dialects, the many languages throughout Italy. In America they assimilated; they learned a little English, a little of the many dialects, and then created new words, English words with an Italian twist. If you were to ask them how to say a certain word in proper Italian, many would not have any idea how to say it, or at times there might not have been a simple translation, so they created their own.

Listed first is the created word, then the English derivation, and last the Italian translation:

acciargia, charge it, *metti al conto*

allacca la porta, lock the door, *chiudi la porta*

apparcà, park (the car), *parcheggia l'auto*

aranò, I don't know, *non lo so*

arriappa, hurry up, *sbrigati*

artiriat, retired, *pensionato*

baccous, back of house (outdoor toilet), *bagno*

baesee, busy, *occupato*

bassamend, basement, *piano sotto*

birrajoineh, beer joint, *cantina*

cheerioss, cereal (any), *cereali*

coshtumeh, costumer, *cliente*

donneshtesa, downstairs, *sotto*

friziat, frozen, *ghiacciato*

garbegeh, garbage, *immondizie*

humburg, hamburger,
  hamburger *(manzo tritato)*

iaÌ, alley, *vicolo*

jongheria, junk, *robaccia*

la blanketta, the blanket, *la coperta*
la checca, the check, *l'assegno*
la cofitabla, the coffee table, *il tavolino*
la frgidera, the refrigerator,
  il frigorifero
la ghellafrenda, the girlfriend,
  la fidanzata
la hosa, the garden hose, *la canna*
  per annafiare
la iaarda, the yard, *il giardino*
la jobba, the job, *il lavoro*
la kecca, the cake, *la torta*
la lunmor, the lawn mower,
  il tagliaerba

la penda, the paint, *la vernice*

mappina, dish cloth, *la tovaglia*
neh vuorì, don't worry,
  non ti preoccupare

pappa, soda, pop, *bibita*
peshù, for sure, *sicuro*

sevnappa, 7UP; pop, *la gassosa*
shtaecca, steak, *la bistecca*
shtora, store, *il negozio*
Si renditat? / Did you rent it?
  / L'hai affittato?
sonamabetcha, son of a bitch,
  il figlio di puttana
songuich, sandwich, *il tramezzino*

Tanksalot, Thanks a lot, *Molte grazie*
Tanksgiv, Thanksgiving, *la festa*
  del Ringraziamento
targhetta, Target, *il negozio che*
  si chiama Target

upshtaesah, upstairs, *sopra*

Back in the 1970s, when long distance phone calls were expensive, my parents would only make phone calls to Italy for special occasions. My father was usually the one that was long-winded. We would all urge him to stop the small talk and get to the reason for the call. On a particular call to his sister, Leontina, he went on and on... The problem was that my aunt would always say, *"Che?"* What? My father would repeat himself and she again would have a hard time understanding some of what he was saying. My father did not realize that he was using some of the "Italamericano" words, slang. I recall him saying, *"What-u-goneh-do," "Arano,"* etc.!

A friend, Tony Iacovetta, went back to the village during the 80s for a visit. He was born in Italy, but was just a baby when he came to America with his Italian-American father and Italian mother. Growing up in Denver starting in the mid 1940s, most toilets were in back of the house. Italian immigrants called the outdoor bathrooms, *"baccous,"* for 'back of the house.' As toilets made their way to the inside of homes, Italian-Americans kept referring to them as *baccous*. Tony was enjoying an elaborate meal with various relatives at his aunt's house in Villa San Michele. He did not speak much Italian except for a few dialect words. Needing to use the bathroom, he turned to his cousin, Michele, and proudly asked, *"Baccous?"* and his cousin replied *"Che? Non capisco,"* he did not understand what he was saying. Tony repeated the word a couple more times, but neither Michele nor the other Italian relatives understood. Frustrated, he finally said *"Peeshà!"* They yelled, *"Haa! Il bagno!"* Tony assumed that *baccous* was Italian for bathroom, since all Italian-Americans from north Denver referred to them by that name!

Emigranti Da Villa San Michele/ Pagliarone Che Sono Vivi Fino A 2015, Villa San Michele/Pagliarone Living Immigrants in the Denver Area, As Of 2015

Most have died, some moved back to Italy, some moved to other parts of the world. Many are alive and well as of 2015. Following is a list of people that made the long journey to the Denver area from a small, remote village in south central Italy. Apologies if I missed anyone.

Angelo Capobianco
Maria Carmosino, Ralph Carmosino, Joe Carmosino
Tony Carmosino
Alfonsina Carmosino
Giuseppina Carmosino, Robert Carmosino
Albert Carmosino
Mary Carmosino
Sabatino (Sam) Ciotola, Rosa Carmosino
Anthony Iacovetta
Salvatore (Sam) Iacovetta, Teresa (Capobianco) Iacovetta
Anthony (Pietrantonio) Lombardi

Ezio and Bambina Lombardi
Ida Lombardi, Terry Lombardi
Ida Lombardi, Louie Lombardi, Dominic Lombardi
Oreste Lombardi
Gilda Lombardi, Edilia Lombardi, Mary Lombardi
Antonio (di Nicola) Lombardi, Carlo Lombardi
Renato Lombardi, Gilda Carmosino Lombardi
Sandro (Alfredo) Lombardi, George Lombardi
Ninetta Lombardi, Salvatore (Sam) Lombardi, Fernando (Fred)
Lombardi, Elsa Lombardi
Antonio Lombardi, Clelia Lombardi
Giovanni (John) Lombardi
Maria Ianiro Lombardi
Giuseppe (Joe) Lombardi

Emigranti Di Villa San Michele/ Pagliarone Fino A 2015, Immigrants From Villa San Michele/ Pagliarone in the Denver Area, As Of 2015

By the late 1960s, immigration to Denver from our village in Villa San Michele/Pagliarone had reached its peak for families and was winding down. Some families had immigrated here in the late 1800s, some short-term and some for the long haul. Many had already passed away, but I think that in the late 60s/early 70s is when you could find the most immigrants from our village in Italy to Colorado. Listed are some of the immigrants and their families. Some were born in Colorado, some in Italy, some were single, some were married, some divorced, some dead! And many of the female immigrants and their daughters married into other ethnic groups and have non-Italian last names. The approximate year of immigration is also listed, when known.

Also, a sampling of the Denver telephone book listing from 1970 is listed, with the last names of people that originated from my village. Some of the names were changed, not at Ellis Island as usually thought, but usually later while in America. Frequently, names were changed for convenience and ease by Americanizing them. Vowels were either changed or eliminated.

493

Iacovetta became Yacovetta, Melaragno became Melarane, Meloragno or Melarango, and Lombardi became Lombardy or Lombard.

Dominic and Giuseppina Capobianco; Teresa, Angelo

Antonio and Adelina Iacovetta

Joe Iacovetta; Anthony, Maryann

Salvatore and Bambina Iannacito

Tony and Giuseppina Lombardi

Nicola and Elia Carmosino; Rosa, Tony, Alfonsina

Michele (Mike) and Giuseppina (Josephine) Carmosino;
    Robert, Joe, Vince

Gennaro and Beatrice Carmosino

Antonio Carmosino; Gennaro, Bernice

Giovanni and Maria (Lombardi) Carmosino; Ralph,
    Teresa, Joe, Marco (1970)

Pietrantonio Lombardi; Colette (1933)

Antonio and Ninetta lombardi; Clelia, Salvatore, Fernando,
    Elsa (1966)

Nicola and Ida Lombardi; Louis, Dominic (1956, 1958)

Nicola and Gilda Lombardi; Edilia, Maria (1962)

Michele and Lidia Lombardi; Antonio, Giuseppe, Carmine

Renato and Gilda Lombardi; Alfredo (Sandro), Giorgio (1967)

Bill (Olindo) and Violet (Meloragno) Lombardi; Pat, Kathy, Bill, Gary

Ezio and Bambina Lombardi; Vittorio, Adelio, Dana, Mario (1966)

Vittorio and Maria Lucia Lombardi; Ezio, Pietrantonio (1966)

Umberto and Ida Lombardi; Terenzio (1966)

More in the 1970 telephone book listings.

UNO SGUARDO A CHI HANNO SPOSATI
A GLIMPSE OF WHO THEY MARRIED

Colorado Marriages, 1858-1939   12,315

Name	Spouse	Date	County	License No.
Lombardi, Adelina	Damiana, Guy	16 Nov 1930	Denver	116742
Lombardi, Adelina	Tancredo, Gerald	27 Sep 1931	Denver	A60
Lombardi, Angelina	Perri, Racmondo	11 Jun 1933	Denver	2423
Lombardi, Angelina	Perry, Raymond	11 Jun 1933	Denver	2423
Lombardi, Angelina	Adducci, Tony	14 Jul 1929	Denver	113004
Lombardi, Angelina	Monaco, Antonio	24 Jun 1928	Denver	110185
Lombardi, Ann	Ferraro, Joe	21 Sep 1936	Arapahoe	19491
Lombardi, Anna	Lombardi, Fernando	18 Aug 1904	Denver	34244
Lombardi, Anna	Iannacito, Salvatore	27 Jun 1920	Denver	75920
Lombardi, Annie	Patete, Michele	05 Dec 1909	Boulder	3215
Lombardi, Anthony	Denofrio, Maria	06 Nov 1898	Denver	22973
Lombardi, Anthony	Runkey, Jewell M.	18 Jun 1929	Arapahoe	12608
Lombardi, Anthony	Capra, Eva	26 Feb 1933	Denver	A2072
Lombardi, Anthony E.	Rico, Elizabeth	15 Nov 1933	Jefferson	B379
Lombardi, Antonette	DeJiacomo, James	25 Nov 1928	Denver	111554
Lombardi, Antonio	Denofrio, Maria	06 Nov 1898	Denver	22973
Lombardi, Antonio	Piserchia, Teresa	23 Jun 1918	Denver	69650
Lombardi, Benny	Lombardi, Mary	18 Jun 1925	Denver	101733
Lombardi, Carl	DiAndrea, Pasqualina	30 Dec 1916	Denver	65724
Lombardi, Carlino	Dandre, Tomi	22 Mar 1893	Denver	14607
Lombardi, Carlo	Lombardi, Eva	08 Jan 1920	Denver	74427
Lombardi, Carlo	Williamson, Addie	11 Jul 1912	Jefferson	5962
Lombardi, Carmin	DePaollo, Edith	10 Feb 1929	Denver	111899
Lombardi, Carmino	Madaleno, Ruth	27 Nov 1897	Chaffee	1110

Name	Spouse	Date	County	License No.
Lombardi, Carolina	Labati, Giovanni	22 Aug 1905	Denver	36473
Lombardi, Consiglio	LaTorre, Frank	13 May 1912	Denver	54240
Lombardi, Domenico	Calabrese, Maria	22 Jul 1900	Dolores	223
Lombardi, Dominic	Paolino, Hilda	17 May 1936	Fremont	8160
Lombardi, Dominic	Legan, Anna	23 Jan 1933	Fremont	7611
Lombardi, Domonik	Fanganillo, Frances	03 Jul 1919	Denver	72052
Lombardi, Dorothy	Dire, Albert	21 Jul 1938	Weld	17087
Lombardi, Edna Hayes	Oleson, Fred	23 Feb 1930	Eagle	89
Lombardi, Effie	Lombardi, Ernest	25 Nov 1934	Denver	3133
Lombardi, Eleanor	Galterio, Ernest	04 Sep 1938	Denver	14157
Lombardi, Elizabeth	Candeliere, Tony	06 Jun 1924	Jefferson	12837
Lombardi, Elizabeth	Lombardi, Salvatore	26 Dec 1915	Denver	63133
Lombardi, Elvira	Ticca, Franceco	14 Jun 1936	Denver	6884
Lombardi, Ercolino	Morris, Bessie	28 Feb 1920	Denver	74897
Lombardi, Ernest	Lombardi, Effie	25 Nov 1934	Denver	3133
Lombardi, Eva	Lombardi, Carlo	08 Jan 1920	Denver	74427
Lombardi, Eva	Baiamonte, Vincent	24 Nov 1935	Denver	5498
Lombardi, Evelyn	Simeone, Anthony	25 Oct 1936	Denver	8171
Lombardi, Felma	Carlini, Louis A.	26 Dec 1909	Denver	47608
Lombardi, Fernando	Lombardi, Anna	18 Aug 1904	Denver	34244
Lombardi, Filomena	Jacobetta, Giovanni	26 Feb 1900	Denver	24639
Lombardi, Flore	Lumbardozzo, Giovina	27 Feb 1899	Garfield	829
Lombardi, Gaetano N.	Tallarica, Angelina	04 May 1924	Denver	98086
Lombardi, George	Teters, Elizabeth B.	01 Nov 1936	Arapahoe	19585
Lombardi, Giovanni	Briola, Mary	26 May 1917	Arapahoe	3525
Lombardi, Giovina	Lombardi, Tony	07 Dec 1937	Denver	12100
Lombardi, Guy	Baca, Mary	03 Jul 1926	Denver	104728
Lombardi, Guydon	Madrid, Mary	31 Aug 1936	Jefferson	B2481
Lombardi, Harry	Hayes, Edna	06 Mar 1928	Garfield	1225
Lombardi, Helen	Capra, Costance	08 Jun 1930	Denver	115246
Lombardi, Herman	Bell, Louise M.	23 Aug 1935	Arapahoe	18276
Lombardi, Herman N.	Lombardi, Rena B.	27 Feb 1938	Denver	12589
Lombardi, Herman P.	Bell, Mildred L.	16 Nov 1934	Jefferson	B1146
Lombardi, Ida E.	Perri, Blaze M.	08 Nov 1924	Denver	100031
Lombardi, Isabell	Gallo, Gene	09 Aug 1933	Jefferson	B166
Lombardi, J. D.	McCabe, Hellen	17 Jan 1923	Jefferson	11822
Lombardi, Jennie	Ross, Adam	14 Dec 1914	Denver	60880
Lombardi, John	Tallarico, Mary	15 Aug 1920	Denver	76510
Lombardi, John	Perry, Thelma	22 Sep 1934	Arapahoe	107090
Lombardi, John L.	Calabrese, Rose	31 Aug 1938	Arapahoe	21748
Lombardi, John M.	Fsuchino, Margaret	01 Nov 1931	Denver	A159
Lombardi, Joseph	Lallie, Minnie	27 Nov 1915	Denver	63107
Lombardi, Josephine	Marrone, Tony	10 Sep 1928	Denver	111054
Lombardi, Julia	Foley, George Lacell	26 Sep 1939	Denver	17221
Lombardi, Liberto	Fabrizzio, Maria Madelina	22 Jul 1901	Fremont	2033
Lombardi, Lillian	Amato, Carl	10 Jul 1926	Arapahoe	9851
Lombardi, Loretta	Niznik, Frances Gordon	13 Jun 1928	Fremont	6936
Lombardi, Lucio	Bruno, Raffaele	17 Apr 1910	Denver	48399
Lombardi, Lucy	Bruno, Raffaele	17 Apr 1910	Denver	48399
Lombardi, Luira	Iacovetto, Beardine	16 Nov 1899	Denver	25114

Name	Spouse	Date	County	License No.
Lombardi, Madolina	Scardina, Anthony	02 Sep 1928	Jefferson	15969
Lombardi, Margaret	Menzeni, Thomas	08 Nov 1920	Jefferson	10107
Lombardi, Margaret	Bates, Dwight H.	10 Mar 1930	Jefferson	17244
Lombardi, Margie	Gianbroco, Jerry	16 Aug 1934	Jefferson	B924
Lombardi, Maria	Tacovetta, Fin'l Fionndo	01 Mar 1908	Denver	42515
Lombardi, Maria	Cirasualo, Geovanni	28 Dec 1905	Denver	37363
Lombardi, Maria S.	DiFabizio, Mariano	03 Jun 1900	Denver	25534
Lombardi, Marie	Catalino, Peter	30 Jul 1906	Mesa	1679
Lombardi, Mary	DeNuzzi, Andrea	12 Aug 1923	Denver	95845
Lombardi, Mary	Lombardi, Benny	18 Jun 1925	Denver	101733
Lombardi, Mary	Latorra, John	25 Aug 1910	Denver	49607
Lombardi, Mary	Route, Louis	26 Mar 1925	Denver	101035
Lombardi, Mary	DeSalvo, Joe	30 Jul 1928	Jefferson	15981
Lombardi, Mary A.	DiAnnie, Peter	19 Jan 1922	Denver	91096
Lombardi, Michael	Yates, Bernice	05 Nov 1937	Denver	11859
Lombardi, Minnie	Larusso, Santino	03 Mar 1924	Denver	97784
Lombardi, Minnie	Lombardi, Pasquale	07 Apr 1907	Denver	40133
Lombardi, Minnie	Miloragno, Pasquale	25 Jan 1919	Denver	71028
Lombardi, Nellie	Inama, August	23 Jul 1925	Boulder	8761
Lombardi, Pasqual	Starkey, Margaret	10 May 1928	Arapahoe	11488
Lombardi, Pasqual	Ferrone, Josephine	21 Nov 1915	Denver	62873
Lombardi, Pasquale	Lombardi, Minnie	07 Apr 1907	Denver	40133
Lombardi, Pauline	Morrelli, Amico G.	20 Jun 1920	Denver	76017
Lombardi, Peter	Santiago, Mary	18 Apr 1888	Denver	5978
Lombardi, Peter	Crutairgo, Mary	18 Apr 1888	Denver	5978
Lombardi, Prospero	Fallasco, Paolina	11 Oct 1925	Denver	102637
Lombardi, Prospero	Falasco, Paolina	11 Oct 1925	Denver	102637
Lombardi, Rena B.	Lombardi, Herman N.	27 Feb 1938	Denver	12589
Lombardi, Rosa	Francalaccio, Anthony	16 Aug 1933	Denver	A2588
Lombardi, Rosanna	DiPilla, Gaetano	29 Nov 1913	Denver	58386
Lombardi, Rose	Iacovette, Flory	27 Jun 1937	Denver	9833
Lombardi, Ruby	DeCarlo, John	01 Feb 1930	Denver	114513
Lombardi, Salvatore	Carmoscina, Florence	03 Jan 1899	Denver	23290
Lombardi, Salvatore	Lombardi, Elizabeth	26 Dec 1915	Denver	63133
Lombardi, Silvia	Mazzocco, Fiori	02 Sep 1924	Denver	99185
Lombardi, Stella	Yacino, Joseph	14 Jun 1916	Denver	64202
Lombardi, Stella	Ginsti, Guiseppi	25 Nov 1917	Denver	67965
Lombardi, Teresa	Feramisco, Joe	05 Oct 1935	Arapahoe	18316
Lombardi, Thomas C.	Russomanno, Mary C.	10 Mar 1930	Jefferson	17245
Lombardi, Tony	Lombardi, Giovina	07 Dec 1937	Denver	12100
Lombardi, Tony	Garramoni, Angelina	31 Mar 1917	Denver	66227
Lombardi, Victor E.	Smits, Harriet A.	02 May 1933	Jefferson	A747
Lombardi, Virginia G.	Lunnon, George W.	30 Jan 1937	Jefferson	B2794
Iannacito, Antonio Anthony	DeNuzzi, Lucille	07 Jan 1934	Denver	1054
Iannacito, Armadora	Dijacomio, Antonietta	27 Sep 1900	Boulder	747
Iannacito, Castantino	Fisco, Marinccia	24 Mar 1893	Denver	14616
Iannacito, Charles A.	Robinson, Ellen A.	05 Sep 1936	Denver	7796
Iannacito, Dominec	Iannacito, Maria	16 Dec 1908	Denver	44978
Iannacito, Elizabeth	Whitworth, Earl D.	08 Sep 1932	Weld	13644
Iannacito, Flora	Catherino, Frank	11 Apr 1912	Denver	54074

Name	Spouse	Date	County	License No.
Iannacito, John	Lillo, Angelina	31 Jul 1927	Denver	107600
Iannacito, Lucille	Garramone, Clyde	24 Sep 1927	Denver	108073
Iannacito, Luizi	Ross, Antonia	17 Aug 1898	Denver	22597
Iannacito, Maria	Iannacito, Dominec	16 Dec 1908	Denver	44978
Iannacito, Mike	Vercellona, Catherine	19 Feb 1930	Boulder	10454
Iannacito, Salvatore	Lombardi, Anna	27 Jun 1920	Denver	75920
Iannacito, Stella M.	Wall, Carl J.	10 Nov 1934	Jefferson	B1129
Iannacito, Tony	Iacino, Rosa	19 Nov 1916	Denver	65355
Yacovetta, Alberta	Ascuitto, Anna	21 Nov 1926	Denver	105761
Yacovetta, Angelina	Conzone, John	27 Jan 1935	Denver	3553
Yacovetta, Angelina	Conzone, Giovanni	27 Jan 1935	Denver	3553
Yacovetta, Anthony	Elenor, Worley	18 Mar 1933	Jefferson	A694
Yacovetta, Anthony	Worley, Elenor	18 Mar 1933	Jefferson	A694
Yacovetta, Carl	Laguarde, Frances	26 Feb 1921	Denver	78850
Yacovetta, Elena	Longo, Antonio	02 Sep 1928	Denver	110971
Yacovetta, Fiori	Milano, Lucia	20 Apr 1905	Denver	31187
Yacovetta, Fred	DeAndrea, Philomena	16 Nov 1930	Denver	116723
Yacovetta, Helen	Mestes, David	30 Jan 1934	Arapahoe	16390
Yacovetta, Leonard	Meloragno, Theresa	30 Sep 1937	Douglas	2178
Yacovetta, Lucy	Colomo, Basilio	10 Apr 1912	Denver	54063
Yacovetta, Maria 'Mary'	Pauldino, Joseph	19 Sep 1920	Denver	76972
Yacovetta, Oranadino	Romorini, Clementina	21 Aug 1915	Denver	62416
Yacovetta, Orlandino	Romorini, Clementina	21 Aug 1915	Denver	62416

Name	Spouse			
Lombardi, Alfred M.	Lombardi, Lucille	17976	17701-18000	Dec 8,1939-Feb 5,1940
Lombardi, Alreno S.	Lombardi, Virginia	45396	45301-45600	Feb 6, 1946-Feb 20,1946
Lombardi, Ann	Beatty, Harry G.	85614	85501-85800	Apr 10, 1953-May 7, 1953
Lombardi, Anna	Calvaresi, Serafino	21636	21601-21900	June 10, 1941-July 3, 1941
Lombardi, Antonio	Smith, Dorothy	98602	98401-98700	Jan 20, 1956-Feb 23, 1956
Lombardi, Arthur A.	Raso, Vera M.	44449	44401-44700	Dec 21, 1945-Jan 5, 1946
Lombardi, Avalina	Polson, James	115779	115501-115800	Jul 28, 1959-Aug 14, 1959
Lombardi, Beatrice A.	Mayhew, Paul H.	27910	27901-28200	Nov 24, 1942-Dec 14, 1942
Lombardi, Bennie	Scoggin, Shirley M.	56070	55801-56100	Aug 7, 1947-Aug 19, 1947
Lombardi, Bonnie M.	Pratt, Howard A.	31304	31201-31500	Jun 26, 1943-Jul 14, 1943
Lombardi, Carolyn	Long, Wayne H.	22545	22501-22800	Aug 30, 1941-Oct 1, 1941
Lombardi, Christine	Bakarich, John J.	48525	48301-48600	Jul 3, 1946-Jul 19, 1946
Lombardi, Clement A.	Rosser, Betty Lou	48851	48601-48900	Jul 19, 1946-Aug 3, 1946
Lombardi, Daniel L.	Personett, Charlotte H.	60526	60301-60600	May 28, 1948-Jun 3, 1948
Lombardi, Darlene	Peltz, Larry	108252	108001-108300	Jan 3, 1958-Feb 18, 1958
Lombardi, Donald L.	Rhines, Helen L.	112435	112201-112500	Dec 8, 1958-Dec 29,1958
Lombardi, Donald N.	Garramone, Elsie	80490	80401-80700	Mar 26, 1952-Apr 18, 1952
Lombardi, Doris C.	Hankle, Robert	64696	64501-64800	Jan 29, 1949-Feb 23, 1949
Lombardi, Etta	Lyon, Glen C.	121697	121501-121800	Aug 18, 1960-Aug 31, 1960
Lombardi, Etta	Malpiede, Joe A.	85263	85201-85500	Mar 17, 1953-Apr 10, 1953
Lombardi, Eva G.	Wasinger, Anthony A.	85729	85501-85800	Apr 10, 1953-May 7, 1953
Lombardi, Evelyn M.	Lail, Richard W.	71399	71101-71400	Jun 3, 1950-Jun 15, 1950
Lombardi, Frank	Leigh, Etta	19836	19801-20100	Sep 30, 1940-Nov 13, 1940
Lombardi, Frederick	Appugliese, Viola M.	54367	54301-54600	May 29, 1947-Jun 9, 1947
Lombardi, George	Peacock, Irene S.	55665	55501-55800	Jul 22, 1947-Aug 7, 1947

Lombardi, Gloria	Stuckey, Lowell	75994	75901-76200	Apr 9, 1951-May 5, 1951
Lombardi, Helen	Molinari, Robert	18835	18601-18900	May 31, 1940-Jun 26, 1940
Lombardi, Helen E.	Perito, Charles	32237	32101-32400	Aug 21, 1943-Sep 11, 1943
Lombardi, Irma	Capaldo, Aldo	88176	87901-88200	Sep 22, 1953-Oct 16, 1953
Lombardi, James C.	Grosso, Lorraine F.	33938	33901-34200	Dec 22, 1943-Jan 19, 1944
Lombardi, James V.	Koehler, Faye	54757	54601-54900	Jun 9, 1947-Jun 20, 1947
Lombardi, John	Gieck, Charlene	109322	109201-109500	May 22, 1958-Jun 6, 1958
Lombardi, John	Masella, Anna C.	47976	47701-48000	Jun 10, 1946-Jun 20, 1946
Lombardi, John A.	Milano, Patricia J.	117896	117601-117900	Dec 11, 1959-Dec 24, 1959
Lombardi, John E.	Marinaro, Lillian V.	32343	32101-32400	Aug 21, 1943-Sep 11, 1943
Lombardi, John P.	DiAnnie, Josephine	46568	46501-46800	Apr 12, 1946-Apr 29, 1946
Lombardi, Joseph E.	Dittman, Elsie M.	37159	36901-37200	Aug 9, 1944-Sep 1, 1944
Lombardi, Josephine	Sciacca, Laurence J.	43167	42901-43200	Oct 3, 1945-Oct 18, 1945
Lombardi, Julia Ann	Cook, Leo W.	28039	27901-28200	Nov 24, 1942-Dec 14, 1942
Lombardi, Lillian I.	Bertollt, Paul G.	47945	47701-48000	Jun 10, 1946-Jun 20, 1946
Lombardi, Lorraine	Beierle, LeRoy	75682	75601-75900	Mar 15, 1951-Apr 9, 1951
Lombardi, Lucille	Acierno, George H.	36924	36901-37200	Aug 9, 1944-Sep 1, 1944
Lombardi, Lucille	Kirk, John	47082	46801-47100	Apr 29, 1946-May 15, 1946
Lombardi, Lucille	Lombardi, Alfred M.	17976	17701-18000	Dec 8,1939-Feb 5,1940
Lombardi, Marlene	Tricarico, Robert	107985	107701-108000	Dec 24, 1957-Jan 23, 1958
Lombardi, Mary J.	Cross, John W.	112161	111901-112200	Nov 14, 1958-Dec 8, 1958
Lombardi, Myrna	Hock, Robert	112075	111901-112200	Nov 14, 1958-Dec 8, 1958
Lombardi, Ora Jean	Wright, William	76058	75901-76200	Apr 9, 1951-May 5, 1951
Lombardi, Pasquale	Cinea, Italia O.	57048	57001-57300	Sep 27, 1947-Oct 17, 1947
Lombardi, Phyllis J.	Greb, William R.	90246	90001-90300	Apr, 1954
Lombardi, Ralph L.	Ditolla, Helen J.	77593	77401-77700	Jul 26, 1951-Aug 5, 1951
Lombardi, Rose M.	LaGuardia, Robert M.	108125	108001-108300	Jan 3, 1958-Feb 18, 1958
Lombardi, Rosemary	Koller, Larry	111039	111001-111300	Sep 4, 1958-Sep 26, 1958
Lombardi, Rosene G.	Kinard, George P.	27912	27901-28200	Nov 24, 1942-Dec 14, 1942
Lombardi, Salvatore	Gust, Isabel C.	22526	22501-22800	Aug 30, 1941-Oct 1, 1941
Lombardi, Sam	Carabetta, Dolores	106390	106201-106500	Aug 29, 1957-Sep 19, 1957
Lombardi, Samuel S.	Matthews, Lucille M.	43820	43801-44100	Nov 20, 1945-Dec 6, 1945
Lombardi, Tony	Hooper, Clara Y.	19812	19801-20100	Sep 30, 1940-Nov 13, 1940
Lombardi, Virginia	Lombardi, Alreno S.	45396	45301-45600	Feb 6, 1946-Feb 20,1946
Lombardi, Virginia E.	Maes, Jerry M.	30541	30301-30600	May 3, 1943-May 22, 1943
Lombardi, William	Carroll, Violet	54935	54901-55200	Jun 20, 1947-Jul 4 1947
Lombardi, Wm.	Nelson, Evelyn M.	81635	81601-81900	Jun 16, 1952-Jul 2, 1952
Lombardi, Yolanda J.	Martinez, Daniel E.	108778	108601-	Mar 28, 1958-Apr 24, 1958
Iannacito, Angeline	Vigil, Edward A. Jr.	65503	65401-65700	Apr 19, 1949-May 10, 1949
Iannacito, Edward P.	Allegretto, Theresa L.	36286	36001-36300	Jun 7, 1944-Jun 24, 1944
Iannacito, Josephine M.	Musso, Edward R.	99535	99301-99600	Apr 23, 1956-May 18, 1956
Iannacito, Lucille	Wall, Kenneth S.	80099	79801-80100	Jan 30, 1952-Feb 25, 1952
Iannacito, Nicholas	DeCarlo, Dorothy A.	66244	66001-66300	May 31 1949-Jun 13, 1949
Iannacito, Richard S.	Hebert, Patricia J.	67719	67501-67800	Aug 26, 1949-Sep 12, 1949
Iannacito, Salvatore	Iacovetta, Caroline	56441	56401-56700	Aug 29, 1947-Sep 11, 1947
Iannacito, Tony	Madsen, Ellen L.	37216	37201-37500	Sep 1, 1944-Sep 25, 1944
Iannacito. Lucille	Sanzalone, Frank V.	45604	45601-45900	Feb 20, 1946-Mar 7, 1946
Yacovetta, Bernard	Fick, Bertha A.	92623	92401-92700	Sep, 1954-Oct, 1954

Yacovetta, Beverly	Turner, Billy G.	95556	95401-95700	Jun, 1955
Yacovetta, George	Chavez, Kay	82975	82801-83100	Sep 2, 1952-Sep 24, 1952
Yacovetta, John R.	Lewis, Irene Z.	88392	88201-88500	Oct 16, 1953-Nov 16, 1953
Yacovetta, Leonard	Erickson, Betty	55510	55501-55800	Jul 22, 1947-Aug 7, 1947
Yacovetta, Lucille Cecelia	Rush, Ellis	63147	63001-63300	Oct 8, 1948-Nov 1, 1948
Yacovetta, Mildred	Carmosino, Albert A.	124981	124801-125100	Mar 31, 1961-Apr 19, 1961
Yacovetta, Rosemarie	Soto, Florentino J.	78716	786001-78900	Oct 22, 1951-Nov 16, 1951
Yacovetta, Thomas A.	Cahill, Theodosia	18783	18601-18900	May 31, 1940-Jun 26, 1940

Uno Sguardo A Dove Vivevano
A Glimpse At Where They Lived

Lombardi Jas V 3325W36Av----------455-6160
Lombardi John 4051Alcott ----------477-7843
Lombardi John 1240GrantAvLouisvl ---666-6065
Lombardi John 4434Grove -----------455-0328
Lombardi John 7370SherdnBlvd ------429-9365
Lombardi John 2227W37Av --------455-1415
Lombardi John C 5040Eliot----------455-9190
Lombardi John E Jr 4440FedBlvd ----477-3760
Lombardi Jos 1844WinfldDr ----------233-9008
Lombardi Jos 5450W26Av-----------237-8088
Lombardi Jos T 1040SAdams---------722-4257
Lombardi Laura 1314Elizabeth--------355-8895
Lombardi Mary 3270AmmonsCt------237-8610
Lombardi Mary 1941W47Av----------455-9141
Lombardi Michael W & Associates
  1545Hooker -------------------534-4201
  Lombardi Michael W
  7840AppleblossomLn -----------429-6216
Lombardi Mike 4132Zuni------------477-1531
Lombardi Nick 4127Zuni------------477-3978
Lombardi Nick 7375W92Av --------424-6072
Lombardi Nicola 4259Wyndt----------433-0270
Lombardi Oreste 4526Wyndt---------477-6451
Lombardi P 4211GreenCt ----------477-5750
Lombardi P W 401Monaco----------333-1731
Lombardi Pasquale 2115Ames -------233-5545
Lombardi Patricia B 7180Quivas------429-3456
Lombardi Ralph L 2670W40Av ------477-7385

Lombardi Ramona 4571Grove--------477-2401
Lombardi Robert C 1300DeanDr------469-0245
Lombardi S S 5120Swadly------------421-7824
Lombardi Salvatore 4195KnoxCt -----477-5733
Lombardi Salvatore P 4630 Shoshone --433-3781
Lombardi Sam 1934W38Av ---------477-6852
Lombardi Sam Mrs 8260Queen -------421-4839
Lombardi Saml J 6826SBellaireWy ---771-4015
Lombardi Tommy 4448Hooker -------455-0920
Lombardi Tony 3911 Osage ---------477-7047
Lombardi Tony 4128Zuni -----------433-7064
Lombardi Tony ins 4875Nwtn -------433-0814
Lombardi Umberto 2732W40Av-------477-5003
Lombardi Victor 1900W47Av --------477-7720
Lombardi Vincenzo 1749W36Av -----477-3208
Lombardi Virginia P Mrs 1939W47Av--433-4706
Lombardi Vittorio 4520Wyndt--------477-1154
Lombardi Wm 3943Clay -------------455-4660
Lombardi Wm C 3246W54Av --------455-0171

Carmosino Albert A atty 250W14Av---255-5403
Carmosino Anthony 7724W39Av-------423-2676
Carmosino D 840MaxwellAvBldr-------442-6301
Carmosino Jas A 8162WLaPl---------985-5636
Carmosino Jerry 4130Clay-----------477-9267
Carmosino Joseph P 2650Yates-------455-8465
Carmosino Mildred Mrs 6240SIvy-----771-3524
Carmosino Olindo 4594Meade -------477-7929
Carmosino P J 4715Meade ---------477-0248
Carmosino Tony 4105Eliot----------455-3986

LOMBARDI

Lombardi Anthony (Eva E) carmn D&RGW h2482 Meade St
" Antonio (Antona) pkr Samsonite Corp h3928 Zuni St
" Armand (Rene) meat cutter Lombardi Meat Market hBsmt 1941 W 47th Av
" Arnie F (Sandra K) (Cosmopolitan Upholstery Co) h2938 W 42d Av
" Arth M stock wkr Am Furn r2936 W 42d Av
" Bros Meat Packers Inc John Lombardi Pres Saml D Lombardi V- Pres Geo Lombardi Sec-Treas 1926 W Elk Pl
" Carl (Pauline) formn Plat Pkg r7685 Irving St
" Carl C (Patricia) agt Guardian Life Ins Co Of America h1004 S Vine St
" Carmine (Edith C) h4233 Vallejo St
" Carol A nurse St Joseph Hosp r4195 Knox Ct
" Carolyn lndry wkr Luke's Hosp h4750 Decatur St
" Cath S (Wid Joseph T) h1040 S Adams St
" Charlene Mrs recpt h4745 Quivas St
" Charles (Erma M) retd h4470 Federal
" Constance (Backroom Boutique) h1660

" James C (Lorraine F) phys 2045 Franklin St Rm 1103 h335 Leyden
" Janet C emp Mannings Cafeteria h43 Decatur St
" Janet L opr Classic Coiffures r3325 V 36th Av
" John (Janice) sheet mtl wkr Van Genderen Co h5040 Eliot St
" John (Rose) pres Lombardi Bros Mea Packers Inc r7370 Sheridan Blvd
" John (Mary) (Colorado Saw & Supply Co) h4434 Grove St
" John (Helen) retd h1375 Washington Apt 104
" John (Anna) carmn C & S Ry r4051 Alcott St
" John (Thelma) formn City & County Dept Of San h2227 W 37th Av
" John A (Patricia G) prsmn A M Prn r9560 W 52d Av (ARV)
" John E Jr (Lillian V) slsmn Hamilto Funds h4440 Federal Blvd
" John J (Constance) slsmn Rosen- No Auto Agcy h1660 Magnolia St
" John P Jr emp Genl Iron Wks r272 40th Av
" Joseph (Ramona) retd h4571 Grove
" Joseph F (Sharlene) (Duffy's Shamro Bar & Restaurant) r9308 S Clayto Way
" Joseph F (Veta P) pres Cardinal Me Co r1844 Winfield Dr (L)
" Josephine (Wid Tony) (Tony's Place) h2940 W 42d Av

" Kathleen studt r4448 Hooker St
" Kenneth W (Sandra D) (Duffy's Shamrock Bar & Restaurant) h10(Cove Way
" Larry h580 S Tejon St
" Laura nurse U Of Colo Med Center h1314 Elizabeth St Apt 2
" Lewis studt r1343 Ogden St Apt 4
" Louis A studt r4259 Wyandot St
" Mario flymn Denver Post r4526 Wyandot
" Salvatore (Bonina) retd h1934 W 38th Av
" Salvatore P (Dolores A) driver Time D C Truck Lines h4630 Shoshone St
" Saml D v-pres Lombardi Bros Meat Packers Inc r5120 Swadley St
" Sherill ofc clk Peerless Prntg r2670 W 40th Av
" Theresa (Wid Carmen) retd h4051 Alcott St
" Thos (Mary C) retd h3533 Mariposa St
" Tony (Cleda) yardmn BNRY h4128 Zuni St
" Tony (Clara Y) agt Prudential Ins h4875 Newton St
" Tony r840 S Oneida St Apt 101n
" Tony (Jennie) retd h3911 Osage St
" Umberto (Ida) lab Platt Pkg h2732 W 40th Av
" Victor (Evelyn) clk C&S Ry h1900 W 47th Av
" Victor (Mary) jan Rocky Mtn News h4520 Wyandot St
" Victor Mrs h740 Pearl St Apt 204
" Vincent J (Faye) musician h3325 W 36th Av
" Vincenzo J retd h1749 W 36th Av
" Wm (Violet A) meat ctr Lombardi Bros Meat Packers h3943 Clay St
" Wm (Evelyn M) slsmn Denver Whol Meat h3440 Sheridan Blvd
" Wm Jr emp Wards r3943 Clay St

Iannacito Antonio (Ellen L) h1327 W 35th Av
" Danl slsmn Rite-Lite Sup r3535 Raleigh
" Edw P (Theresa L) wldr Coors Porcelain h3530 Raleigh St
" John (Ann J) retd h1579 W Burlington Pl
" Mary L (Wid Domenic A) srtr Elitch Greenhse h5020 W 37th Av
" Pasquale (Mary) retd h3927 Kalamath St
" Pasquale A (Bambina) retd h4218 Irving St
" Pauline T jan Elitch Greenhouses r5020 W 37th Av
" Richd S (Patricia J) pres Sam's Produce Inc r8015 Melrose Dr
" Salvatore (Carolina) retd h2736 W 41st

Nostri Ritratti Della Famiglia
Our Family Portraits

Jackie Lombardi, Avery Grieve, Frank Grieve, Aubry Grieve, Anthony Grieve, Daniella Lombardi Grieve, Michaela Mahan Lombardi, Sofia Lombardi, Dominic (Nico) Lombardi, Dominic Lombardi, Olivia Lombardi, Gianni Lombardi, Anthony Lombardi. 2015

Adelio Lombardi with baby Gianna, Danica lombardi, Terri Lombardi, Dante Lombardi,
Alexis Lombardi, Vic Lombardi, Ezio Lombardi, Bambina Lombardi.
front row: Dana Lombardi Quinto with baby Brianna, Isabella Lombardi, Matteo Quinto. 2015

Sierra Ienco, Lorella Ienco, Gino Giancola, Maria Lombardi Ienco, Victoria Giancola,
Joseph Giancola, Vittorio Ienco, Carmela Ienco Giancola, Noah Ienco,
Mary Mastrangelo Ienco, John Ienco. 2015

**Speriamo che questi bambini si ricorderanno di Pagliarone
quando noi non ci siamo più**

**We hope that these children will remember Pagliarone
when we are all gone**

Il Nostro Albero Genealogico
Our Family Tree

The following pages delineate the Lombardi ancestry. It is broken into lettered sequences (-A-B-C-D-E-) for easier understanding. The oldest family lineage is represented by A-B, and appears on page 509, with continuing generations extending both to the right (page 508) and to the left (pages 510 and 511). For a visual guide, a condensed version of the family tree is shown below.

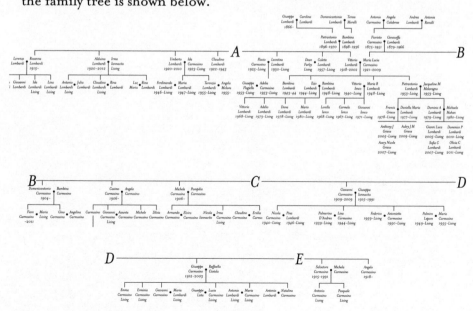

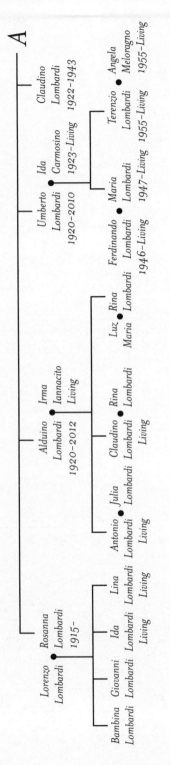

A

Lorenzo Lombardi

Rosanna Lombardi
1915–

Bambina Lombardi
Living

Giovanni Lombardi
Living

Ida Lombardi
Living

Lina Lombardi
Living

Alduino Lombardi
1920–2012

Irma Iannacito
Living

Antonio Lombardi
Living

Julia Lombardi
Living

Claudino Lombardi
Living

Rina Lombardi
Living

Luz Maria

Rina Lombardi

Umberto Lombardi
1920–2010

Ida Carmosino
1923–Living

Claudino Lombardi
1922–1943

Ferdinando Lombardi
1946–Living

Maria Lombardi
1947–Living

Terenzio Lombardi
1955–Living

Angela Melorgno
1955–Living

A

B

Giuseppe
Lombardi
1866–

Carolina
Lombardi

Domenicantonio
Lombardi

Teresa
Morelli

Andrea
Lombardi

Antonia
Ranalli

Antonio
Carmosino

Angela
Calabrese

Fiorinto
Carmosino
1875–1951

Genoveffa
Lombardi
1879–1966

Pietrantonio
Lombardi
1896–1970

Bambina
Lombardi
1898–1936

Vittorio
Lombardi
1918–2002

Maria Lucia
Carmosino
1921–2009

Flavio
Carmosino
1925–Living

Leontina
Lombardi
1930–Living

Dean
Farley
Living

Colette
Lombardi
1957–Living

Ezio
Lombardi
1944–Living

Bambina
Lombardi
1948–Living

Vittorio
Ienco
1940–Living

Maria B
Lombardi
1948–Living

Pietrantonio
Lombardi
1953–Living

Jacqueline M
Melorgno
1953–Living

Giuseppe
Flagiello
1953–Living

Adelia
Carmosino
1953–Living

Bambina
Lombardi
1943–44

Dana
Lombardi
1978–Living

Mario
Lombardi
1980–Living

Lorella
Ienco
1968–Living

Carmela
Ienco
1967–Living

Giovanni
Ienco
1971–Living

Francis
Grieve
1978–Living

Daniella Maria
Lombardi
1977–Living

Dominic A
Lombardi
1979–Living

Michaela
Mahan
1980–Living

Vittorio
Lombardi
1968–Living

Adelio
Lombardi
1973–Living

Anthony J
Grieve
2005–Living

Avery Nicole
Grieve
2007–Living

Aubry J M
Grieve
2009–Living

Gianni Luca
Lombardi
2005–Living

Sofia C
Lombardi
2007–Living

Domenico P
Lombardi
2010–Living

Olivia C
Lombardi
2011–Living

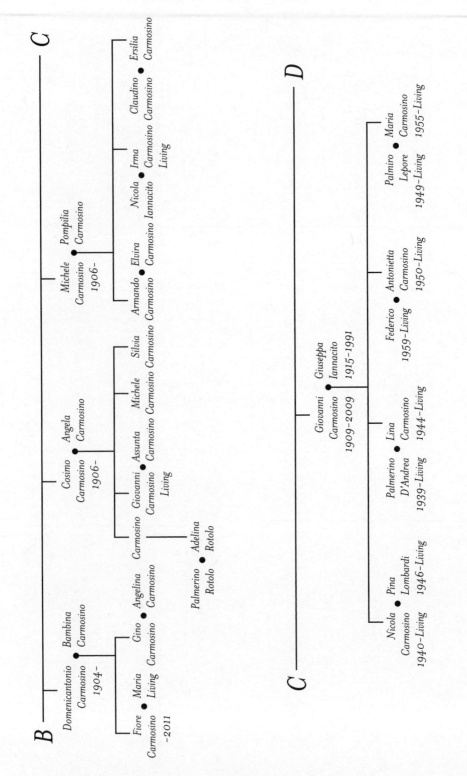

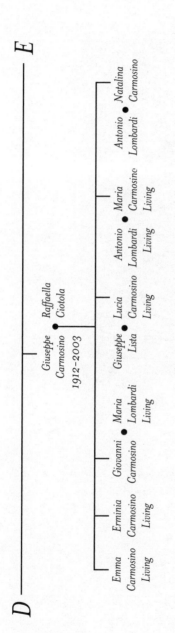

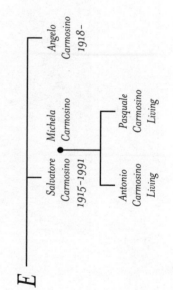

*W*here many writers would begin with a list of their previous literary works, this author confesses to having penned only a few letters to the editor! Pietrantonio lives in Golden, Colorado with his wife Jackie where they love to entertain family and friends, whether with games of bocce on their court, usually accompanied with an array of adult drinks and cheap cigars or in their kitchen with savory meals and lively conversations. On most Saturdays you will find them at a sports complex watching one of their seven grandchildren's playing soccer and on many Sundays Pietrantonio is playing the most popular game with longtime fellow players, young and old. At the age of 64 he still hopes for that call up from his favorite Italian team, Juventus!

Summer days are spent tending to his vegetable garden while keeping an eye on his chickens as they and other critters try to invade his Garden of Eden. For the past ten years Pietrantonio's winter nights have been occupied trying to make sense of his "War and Peace" version of "Nonno, Tell Us A Story".

The author may be contacted at — pietrantonio.lombardi@gmail.com